inheritan

D0592778

MEN IN A DEVELOPING SOCIETY

Geographic and Social Mobility in Monterrey, Mexico

LATIN AMERICAN MONOGRAPHS, NO. 30

Institute of Latin American Studies

THE UNIVERSITY OF TEXAS AT AUSTIN

Men in a Developing Society

Geographic and Social Mobility in Monterrey, Mexico

JORGE BALÁN

HARLEY L. BROWNING

ELIZABETH JELIN

with the assistance of Waltraut Feindt

PUBLISHED FOR THE *Institute of Latin American Studies*
BY THE UNIVERSITY OF TEXAS PRESS, AUSTIN & LONDON

419106

HN
120
.M6B34
1973

Library of Congress Cataloging in Publication Data

Balán, Jorge, 1940–
  Men in a developing society.

  (Latin American monographs, no. 30)
  Bibliography: p.
  1. Social mobility—Monterrey, Mexico.   2. Occupa-
tional mobility.   3. Migration, Internal—Mexico—
Monterrey.   I. Browning, Harley L., joint author.
II. Jelin, Elizabeth, 1941–   , joint author.
III. Texas. University at Austin. Institute of Latin
American Studies.   IV. Title.   V. Series: Latin
American monographs (Austin, Tex.) no. 30.
HN120.M6B34   301.44′044′09721   72-6282
ISBN 0-292-75004-8

Manufactured in the United States of America
Composition by G&S Typesetters, Austin
Presswork by Capital Printing Company, Austin
Binding by Universal Bookbindery, Inc., San Antonio

CONTENTS

FIGURES

MAP

TABLES

PREFACE

The central problem addressed in this book, how and why men move geographically and occupationally within the context of a developing society, has been an area of concern of social scientists for a long time. Since at least Karl Marx and Max Weber, the emergence of capitalism and industry have been linked to the emergence of formally free labor and its sectoral and geographic redistribution. For Marx, capital and wage labor conditioned each other, with each bringing the other into existence. For Weber, legally free labor, composed of a mass of people who were economically compelled to sell their labor on the market without restrictions, was the essence of a capitalist society. In contemporary social science, the discussion has moved from the conditions attending the emergence of capitalism to the question of rates, forms, and consequences of social and geographical mobility under various structural conditions. In this monograph we take a somewhat different direction, focusing on the intersection of history and biography: we study the unfolding of migratory and occupational experiences during the lifetime of men who live in a changing society.

Since this book is intended as the culmination of the Monterrey Mobility Project, some observations about the project are in order here. Like many others, we cannot claim to have followed the general guidelines on survey analysis advanced in most methodology textbooks. We had no master plan whereby we first established our theoretical framework, determined our research goals, and then set about a systematic search for the community that best met the prior criteria. The project came into being because of fortuitous circumstances whereby people with like concerns happened to get together, finding they had the time, money, and, therefore, the opportunity to do the study. Our institutional affiliations when we began the project, and the matching of

Browning's interest in geographic mobility with that of Balán and Jelin in social mobility, explain why a mobility study of Monterrey came into being. However fortuitous the choice of that rapidly growing manufacturing metropolis of northern Mexico, we hope in the following pages to convince the reader that it was a sound one.

During the six years between our field work in Monterrey and the completion of this book, research on migration and mobility has been very active. Also, conceptions of development have changed considerably. Our work cannot fail to reflect some of these innovations. A research project follows a dialectical process, which is not always recognized: both from within our body of data and from new trends in the area new hypotheses and interpretations are constantly emerging. Only the most obvious inconsistencies derived from this dialectical process have been erased. Although we stop here, we hope this is not the final word to be said about the Monterrey Mobility Project. Other people with different interests and perspectives now have access to our data through the International Data Library of the Survey Research Center at Berkeley, and we hope they will make use of them.

In these six years a number of publications based upon the Monterrey data have appeared, and a full listing of them is given in Appendix C. However, our intention in writing this book was never one of simply gathering a number of articles between hard covers. We wanted to write a broadly interpretative book that would eschew, save for a couple of chapters, a technical presentation of our data, and therefore would be of interest to persons concerned with the processes of development beyond our own academic specialties of sociology and demography. Thus, much of the material presented here has not appeared in print before, and the presentation itself differs considerably from the more technical one prevailing in our articles and other publications.

The style of the book reflects the fact that four people have written it. We have not attempted to eliminate the somewhat different perspectives that each of us brings to the task. However, all of us had a hand in all chapters, so the book is a genuine collaborative effort; thus, we do not attempt to indicate who has had primary responsibility for which chapters of the book, and our names on the title page are listed alphabetically. Since problems and perspectives vary throughout the book, real and apparent incongruences remain. A good example is the definition of migrant, which is not the same throughout, depending on the problem at hand.

Sample surveys conducted in Monterrey in 1965 and in a smaller town, Cedral, in 1967 provide the main source of data for our project. Two caveats regarding the Monterrey survey are in order. Our sample included 1,640 men aged 21–60 chosen through a two-stage stratified cluster design in which older men and those living in areas with higher incomes were overrepresented. Most tables in the book are based on the actual sample, but occasionally a "representative" sample is used (and it is always identified as such at the foot of the table). It is constructed by weighting the strata according to their sampling ratios.

No tests of significance are provided in this book. Recently a lively literature of pros and cons has grown up around this problem (most readily available in the recent reader by Denton E. Morrison and Ramon E. Henkel, *The Significance Test Controversy*). Our own position is that significance tests are not helpful in this study for several reasons. First, our sampling procedures do not meet the assumptions appropriate to such tests. Second, our sample size is large enough so that in most cases the differences we are interested in easily meet the requirements for significance at the .05 level. More important, we have tried not to make our argument dependent upon small differences. In many situations we base our conclusions on a succession of tables demonstrating the same patterns. Therefore, reporting of tests of significance would be of only "symbolic" value.

ACKNOWLEDGMENTS

In the six years of its existence the Monterrey Mobility Study has accumulated many obligations that we are now happy to acknowledge. Tradition dictates a strict protocol in listing one's debts—sponsors, colleagues, assistants, secretaries, and, finally, spouses—that we will not ignore.

The project was jointly sponsored by the Centro de Investigaciones Económicas of the Facultad de Economía, Universidad de Nuevo León, and the Population Research Center of the Department of Sociology at The University of Texas at Austin. At the time of the survey, Jorge Balán and Elizabeth Jelin were visiting professors at the Universidad de Nuevo León, while Harley Browning was director of the Population Research Center. Each institution contributed much in facilities and personnel. At both institutions the research was greatly facilitated by independent grants from the Ford Foundation. This fact may be used to document the "monopolio" role of the Ford Foundation in sociological research in Latin America. We must state that at neither institution was there any attempt by Ford personnel to influence either the form of the investigation or the subsequent reporting of results. We were free to go our own way throughout the course of this investigation.

A large number of colleagues have helped the project along in various ways, but two merit special recognition. In Monterrey, Lic. Eduardo L. Suárez, who at the time of the survey was director of the Centro de Investigaciones, demonstrated from the beginning a keen understanding and sympathetic interest in the project. His vigorous and unconditional espousal of the enterprise was particularly important, especially during the critical period immediately preceding and during the actual field work. In Austin, John P. Harrison, then director of the Institute of Latin American Studies, contributed greatly. He arranged the initial contacts between Monterrey and Austin and was instrumental in obtaining the Ford grant for the Population Research Center. Equally important was his enthusiastic interest in the project, an interest going far beyond any administrative obligation. To both men our deep gratitude for their moral and material support. At a later stage in the project, when a draft of this manuscript was circulated, we received encouragement and helpful critical comment from Joseph Kahl, Bryan Roberts, and Alan Simmons.

The Monterrey Mobility Study has benefited from a succession of research associates and assistants. Alejandro Martínez was an effective field director of the Monterrey survey, and two years later Arturo Avendaño displayed initiative and judgment as the field director of the Cedral project. Both in Monterrey and in Cedral the interviewers were male students from the Facultad de Economía of the Universidad de Nuevo León. Our thanks go to them for a superior performance, often carried out under trying circumstances. In Austin, where much of the processing and analysis was done, we relied on the skill and imagination of a succession of programmers, particularly Lee Litzler, Keith Fuller, and Bill Dissley. Lee had the responsibility of originating most of the programs that permitted the building of life histories within the computer. Richard Rockwell was a cooperative advisor on various statistical and programming problems. For several years Tom Bogel, Cathy Litzler, John Houghton, and Ed Fonner did the many "handicraft" jobs such a project requires.

This is an appropriate point to acknowledge the stimulation and pleasant association we derived from those colleagues and associates who drew upon the Monterrey and Cedral data for work that appears under their own names. In Monterrey they were Arturo Avendaño and Alejandro Martínez, and in Austin, David Alvirez, Kenneth Land, Adolfo Mir-Araujo, Richard Rockwell, Denton Vaughan, and Alvan Zarate.

A succession of secretaries helped us over the years. Carmen Sullivan, Jan Cloud, Linda Thompson, Barbara Taylor, Janice Davison, Maribeth Fonner, and Marianne Riegg not only have typed thousands of pages of manuscript willingly without complaint, but they also have contributed to author morale far more than they themselves realize.

We have now arrived at the last stage of acknowledgment protocol, where it is customary to cap the edifice of praise and gratitude with extravagant tributes to the writers' spouses. Surely the combination of abnegation, cooperativeness, and cheerfulness so often extolled makes them seem a breed apart, closer to human perfectability than has been thought possible. But here is where we must deviate from tradition. Although the title page lists four surnames, two couples are represented. Our spouses have participated fully in this project at all stages, experiencing all the excitement and the tedium of such an enterprise. They too must fully share the responsibility for what is contained in this book. The project has been a pleasurable and rewarding experience for us, and in part it is due to the lack of spouse role segregation.

PART ONE
SETTING THE SCENE

1. Introduction

      This book is about migration, occupational mobility, and the process of stratification as experienced by men in the context of an industrializing society. More specifically, ours is a case study of Monterrey, Mexico, a successful example of development from the point of view of the growth of industrial product. It is based mainly on a sample survey of 1,640 men interviewed in that city in 1965.

      One of our goals in this book is to provide a detailed description of the three areas of the men's lives mentioned above. Since immigration has been very low in Mexico, we will focus on internal migration, taking up in order the areal origins of the migrants, their selectivity in terms of origin population, the process of migration to Monterrey, and the occupational integration and adaptation of the migrants in the city. Also, migratory status, the distinction between migrants to and natives of the city, is closely examined for its effects upon occupational mobility. In its own right, occupational mobility is dealt with in both its vertical dimension (status mobility) and its nonvertical dimension (situs mobility). Such topics as entrance into the labor force, paths of upward mobility, and the relationship between situs and status mobility are considered in detail within the complete work lives of the men. Our third area of major concern, the process of stratification, is defined here as the ways by which men come to occupy a succession of positions in the social hierarchy. The main elements in this sequence include social ori-

gins (family and community), educational attainment, and occupational status as it changes throughout the work life. Thus, occupational
positions and their changes are included in our studies of occupational
mobility and of the process of stratification, but in the latter we are concerned only with the vertical dimension of status and its connection
with the prior and subsequent positions that the men occupy.

Our concentration on these three areas goes beyond the descriptive
level. We will also indicate the causal connections between events and
statuses in the lives of these men. We are concerned with such questions as why some men achieve higher educational levels than others,
what determines the age and the type of job a man has upon entering
the labor force, and under what conditions it is more likely that migration to the city will result in upward mobility. We will not attempt to
separate clearly the descriptive and explanatory features of the analysis
of the various features of the men's lives and their interrelationships.

Our concern with migration, occupational mobility, and the process
of stratification derives from the links they have with the basic structural transformations in a society undergoing the process of industrialization. Thus, internal migration clearly is linked to urbanization, the
proportional shift of the population to urban areas. Occupational mobility results partially from transformations in the occupational structure—sectoral relocation, upgrading of skill levels, bureaucratization.
The process of stratification is related to the system of social strata,
and transformations in the structure and shape of the latter (i.e.,
growth of new strata, changes in the criteria for placement) affect the
process of stratification. Because of this concern with structural transformation and industrialization, our second goal in this book—the first
being the description and analysis of processes at the individual level—
is to explore, for the case of Monterrey, the relationship between structural change and these three processes. In other words, in analyzing occupational mobility, migration, and the process of stratification, some
explanatory statements will take as independent or explanatory variables the structural aspects of society and their transformation. For instance, declining migrant selectivity will be partially explained by
changes in the level of regional urbanization, while the decreasing parental influence on educational attainment will be attributed in part to
the transformation of the stratification system. Moreover, some of our
interpretations will take the reverse causal direction, as for example in
the last chapter when we use our information on individual mobility

(geographic and occupational) to arrive at conclusions about the extent of group and class conflict in Mexican communities.

We need to make it as clear as possible at this point that we are painfully aware of the many problems involved in moving from the level of aggregates of individuals, as represented by survey data, to the structural transformation of societies or communities.[1] We in no way pretend in this book to provide a theory of economic development or industrialization, either in general terms or for Mexico in particular. Nor will we attempt an explanation of how or why industrialization, urbanization, or changes in the stratification system have taken place in Mexico. Our purposes are much more modest: to describe and analyze the lives of our men in three key areas and to explore the two-way links between these processes and societal change.

Occupational Mobility, the Process of Stratification, and Industrialization

Under the more familiar heading of "social mobility," sociologists have shown a persistent interest in the relationship between industrialization and occupational mobility and the process of stratification. Since the pioneering work of Sorokin, *Social Mobility*, or the even earlier comments by the classic writers of the discipline, there has been a great deal of speculation, theoretical discussion, and, in recent decades, empirical research on this topic.[2] This seems to be an area, however, where the old dictum about the cumulative aspect of the scientific enterprise can be seriously challenged (unless, of course, one prefers to challenge the scientific status of sociology itself). In spite of some progress, faulty methodology and unwarranted assertions continue much in use, even after subjection to devastating critiques. It is not our purpose to review in depth the field here, but we do want to provide a brief overview, if only to help the reader in locating our own study.

It can be argued that much of the impulse in studying social mobility derives from the conception of industrial society as an "open" so-

---

[1] The "levels of analysis" problem has not yet been satisfactorily resolved. For a statement of some of the difficulties see Johan Galtung, *Theory and Methods of Social Research.*

[2] The most recent review of the literature on the relationship between industrialization and social mobility is that by Donald J. Treiman in "Industrialization and Social Stratification," in *Social Stratification*, ed. E. Laumann.

ciety.[3] It therefore follows that, given the link between industrialization and rates of social mobility, historically and structurally an
increase in industrialization will bring about higher rates of social mobility. Yet only a few years ago Otis D. Duncan introduced his discussion, "Methodological Issues in the Analysis of Social Mobility,"
with the following assertion: "The juxtaposition of themes—social mobility and economic development—may invite acceptance of an unwarranted assumption. In point of fact there is and can be no fixed and
determinate general relationship between measures of economic growth
and indexes of social mobility, either over time in one country or between countries at a point in time."[4] More recently, Donald J. Treiman
reviewed the field of industrialization and social stratification. He generated seven propositions relating industrialization with the process of
stratification, that is, the more industrialized a society, then the smaller
the effect of father's on son's occupation, the greater the effect of education, the smaller the effect of father's occupation on son's education,
and the higher the rate of "exchange" mobility. But, as he acknowl-
edged, "evidence regarding the seven propositions we have specified
here is extremely sparse," both from the standpoint of comparative
studies of various societies and from longitudinal analyses of one society. None of the propositions in this area, Treiman concluded, "can
be taken as established; all require empirical verification."[5]

The inconclusiveness of our knowledge in this area is all the more
frustrating because there have been so many empirical studies of social
mobility carried out mainly during the last two decades. With the possible exception of demographic studies, no area of sociology has produced so many empirical investigations in so many different countries.
These studies have been based on both national and city samples and
have been carried out in developed countries (England, Denmark,
Sweden, and the United States, among others) and in developing countries.[6] In Latin America, important studies include the Bertram Hutch-

[3] This is, for example, the approach of Seymour M. Lipset and Reinhard
Bendix in *Social Mobility in Industrial Society.*

[4] Otis D. Duncan, "Methodological Issues in the Analysis of Social Mobility," in *Social Structure and Mobility in Economic Development,* ed. Neil J. Smelser and Seymour M. Lipset, p. 51.

[5] Treiman, "Industrialization and Social Stratification," pp. 220–221.

[6] A dated but still valuable review of the field, with a comprehensive analysis of empirical studies, is by S. M. Miller, "Comparative Social Mobility: A
Trend Report and Bibliography," *Current Sociology* 9, no. 1 (1960): 8–39.

inson study of São Paulo, the cooperative four-city project of Rio de Janeiro, Montevideo, Buenos Aires, and Santiago, and a number of others.[7] There also have been a number of attempts at comparative analysis (Lipset and Zetterberg, Miller and Bryce), as well as the use of social mobility rates culled from a variety of studies for other purposes (Cutright).[8]

It is not our intention to belittle the importance or the contribution of all these studies, but one should ask why they throw so little light on the relationship between industrialization and social mobility. It is not easy to answer this question, because there are so many technical and methodological aspects involved.[9] The previously cited article by Duncan and, more importantly, the book he wrote with Peter M. Blau, *The American Occupational Structure*, discuss many methodological issues in the study of social mobility and its relationship with industrialization. We need not here recapitulate their critique, which we largely accept. However, we do want to suggest that, in dealing with industrialization and its effects on social mobility, a very important source of difficulties has been the "global" approach to these two phenomena taken in most empirical studies. Social mobility tends to be conceived as *one* attribute of a *total* society, while industrialization in most cases

[7] A review of Latin American studies of social mobility, including the four-cities project, is found in Sugiyama Iutaka, "Social Stratification Research in Latin America," *Latin American Research Review* 1, no. 1 (Fall 1965): 7–34.

[8] Seymour M. Lipset and Hans L. Zetterberg, "A Theory of Social Mobility," in *Class, Status, and Power,* ed. Seymour M. Lipset, and Reinhard Bendix; S. M. Miller and Herrington Bryce, "Social Mobility and Economic Growth and Structure," in *Comparative Perspectives on Industrial Society,* ed. William A. Faunce and William H. Form; and Phillips Cutright, "Occupational Inheritance: A Cross-National Analysis," *American Journal of Sociology* 73, no. 4 (January 1968): 400–416.

[9] Methodological discussions of social mobility are plentiful. On the one hand, there have been a large number of attempts to improve the measurement of mobility. A sample of these include Saburo Yasuda, "A Methodological Inquiry into Social Mobility," *American Sociological Review* 29, no. 1 (February 1964): 16–23; and Leo A. Goodman, "On the Statistical Analysis of Mobility Tables," *American Journal of Sociology* 70 (March 1965): 564–585, and the references cited in this article. On the other hand, there have been critiques of standard approaches to the study of mobility. See, for example, O. D. Duncan, "Methodological Issues in the Analysis of Social Mobility," and Harold L. Wilensky, "Measures and Effects of Social Mobility," in *Social Structure and Mobility in Economic Development,* ed. Neil J. Smelser and Seymour M. Lipset. Wilensky calls for more emphasis on intragenerational mobility as an explanatory variable.

is left unanalyzed, the assumption being that most people know it has something to do with growth in per capita income, technological progress, increase in the division of labor, and similar factors.

The global approach to mobility implies an emphasis on the development of indexes of vertical or status mobility. Typically, the discussion centers around the "mobility table," or the cross classification of respondents according to status of origin (father's occupation, generally) and status of destination (respondent's present occupation). The goal seems to be the measurement of the degree to which origin and destination are associated, taking as the standards of comparison the theoretical maximum of mobility (which depends on the number of strata and the proportional distribution of the population in the strata) and the theoretical minimum, determined by the differences between marginal distributions at origin and destination (if some strata shrink and others grow, people must move). In other words, the main research questions become: How much mobility has occurred within the maximum possible, given the distribution of positions? And, how much of the mobility can be attributed to two different factors: "structural" versus "exchange" mobility? The former originates in the transformation of the shape of the stratification system between two points of comparison (father and son), while the latter is centered in the exchange of people between strata.[10]

We believe that this global approach is at the same time too ambitious and too simplistic. It is too ambitious because through the study of a cross section of a population it attempts to grasp the "openness" of the stratification system of a society—and the structural changes within it. It is too simplistic for three reasons. First, it neglects the fact that mobility is a process that takes place over time. The customary practice of taking but two statuses within this period and then assuming that any difference, or lack of it, adequately captures the changes that take place within the time period is at best debatable. Second, the global approach tends to ignore all forms of nonvertical mobility, even when it is explicitly recognized that within-strata mobility might be as important as mobility between strata. And third, it does not pay enough attention to the differences in mobility experienced by various

---

[10] See Joseph Kahl, *The American Class Structure*; and David V. Glass, ed., *Social Mobility in Britain*. A thorough methodological critique of this approach is found in O. D. Duncan, "Methodological Issues in the Analysis of Social Mobility."

segments and strata of the population, since the mobility rate applies only to the total population.[11]

We will be less ambitious in our goal. For reasons well argued by Duncan, we find the measurement of structural and exchange mobility faulty. And, because we do not believe that social mobility can be apprehended or conceptualized in a general way for the total population, we will not use any existing index or develop a new one. At the same time, we will recognize the complexity of the phenomenon in several ways: by considering several forms of mobility, and not only that involving the vertical dimension; by considering complete work histories, thus dealing in detail with intragenerational mobility and not just intergenerational mobility; and by looking at the occupational mobility, *and* stability as the case may be, experienced by the men during different periods of their lives. In analyzing change through time, while recognizing the difficulties involved when the source of data is a cross section of a population, we will use cohort analysis. In studying the mobility experienced by men in a given cohort a life-cycle approach will be used. These concepts (cohorts, life cycle, and generation as reflected in the respondent's position when compared to his father and his son) are discussed in detail later in this chapter.

In dealing with the status dimension of mobility, we have found Blau and Duncan's recasting of the problem very useful.[12] We conceive, as they do, the problem as one of attainment of status throughout a period of time. By decomposing the phenomenon of status mobility into its component parts (origin, destination, and intervening points), a causal model is built to include the set of influences that explain the final status. Therefore, rather than referring to social mobility, we will make reference to the process of stratification (or, perhaps better put, the process of status attainment).

Industrialization, at least as it has been approached with respect to social mobility, is seen in gross, undifferentiated terms. Typically, the

[11] S. M. Miller, in a recent statement ("A Comment: The Future of Social Mobility Studies," *American Journal of Sociology* 77, no. 1 [July 1971]: 62–65), takes a view consistent with ours regarding the state of social mobility studies. Among other comments, he refers to the lack of consideration of age as a variable, the lack of concern for change over time, and the lack of consideration of the mobility of particular groups of a society.

[12] Peter M. Blau and Otis D. Duncan, *The American Occupational Structure*, Chap. 4.

process is seen as conforming to the logic of a unitary scale.[13] Some societies have more of it than others, and those that today are more industrialized were in the past much like the less industrialized countries of today. Furthermore, although it is conceded that industrialization has many dimensions, it is assumed that they tend to cluster in such a way that we can speak of industrialization as a unitary phenomenon. As a consequence, it is taken for granted that cross-societal comparisons can effectively replace longitudinal studies and that societies of similar degrees of industrialization are quite homogeneous.

Ours is a case study, and only occasionally will we introduce comparisons with other societies. We believe it is necessary that the particular historical circumstances attending industrialization in Mexico and Monterrey be explicitly considered, in order to link it to occupational mobility. Later in this chapter we will discuss the more general and distinctive features of industrialization in Latin America. Chapter 2, devoted to the historical and contemporary process of industrialization in Monterrey, will benefit from the earlier discussion that clarifies those aspects in which Monterrey is or is not a typical case within a general model. Subsequently, when discussing the effects of industrialization for occupational mobility and the process of stratification, specific aspects of the former will be considered as having effects on particular forms of the latter two.

Urbanization, Migration, and Occupational Mobility

Migration is a vital part of the industrialization process, for it is necessary that large numbers of people leave their place of birth in rural areas and move to urban centers.[14] This transfer of population results in a rise in the level of urbanization of a country (the proportion of the total population living in urban areas).[15] In turn, urbanization is

[13] The above-mentioned studies of Lipset and Zetterberg, Miller and Bryce, and Cutright, in varying degrees conceive of industrialization in this way.

[14] For a clear statement on this point, see Simon Kuznets, "Introduction: Population Redistribution, Migration, and Economic Growth," in *Population Redistribution and Economic Growth, United States 1870–1950*, ed. Hope T. Eldridge and Dorothy Swaine Thomas.

[15] A good survey of the various facets of the urbanization process is provided by Philip M. Hauser and Leo F. Schnore, eds., *The Study of Urbanization.* See also Kingsley Davis, "The Urbanization of the Human Population," *Scientific American* 213 (September 1965): 41–53; and the United Nations, *Growth of the World's Urban and Rural Population, 1920–2000.*

related to industrialization, for there is no known case of large-scale industrialization taking place without being accompanied by an increase in urbanization.

Stated in this manner, the fundamental structural processes of migration, urbanization, and industrialization seem to be interrelated in an unproblematic fashion. But, as the burgeoning literature on this subject testifies, the interrelationships among the three are complex and, once beyond the generalities, as in the above paragraph, are still not well understood. In particular, with reference to the developing countries of today, the question is how much urbanization can go ahead of industrialization, meaning by the latter an increase in manufacturing. This point is particularly important for Latin America, since its pattern differs from the now industrialized countries. In the main the initial thrust of urbanization preceded industrialization, being a response in part to the development of the export economy. As a result, Latin American countries of today on the average have a considerably higher level of urbanization than is to be found in other developing regions.[16]

Because Latin America has a rather high level of urbanization in relation to its level of industrialization, its urban development has been subjected to considerable criticism, with such terms as *overurbanization, hyperurbanization,* and *pathological urbanization* frequent in the literature. (This is not the place to enter into an extended discussion of the merits of such criticism, except to say that there has been relatively little evidence brought to bear upon the issue, one way or the other.)[17] The debate on the consequences of rapid urbanization in Latin America

[16] Recent surveys of Latin American urbanization can be found in Glenn H. Beyer, ed., *The Urban Explosion in Latin America*; Richard M. Morse, "Recent Research on Latin American Urbanization: A Selective Survey with Commentary," *Latin American Research Review* 1, no. 1 (Fall 1965): 35–74, and his latest statement, "Trends and Issues in Latin American Research, 1965–1970," *Latin American Research Review* 6, no. 1 (Spring 1971): 3–52, and 6, no. 2 (Summer 1971): 19–75; and Francine F. Rabinovitz and Felicity M. Trueblood, eds., *Latin American Urban Research,* Vol. I. Denton R. Vaughan has compiled 1697 references, most of them recent, in *Urbanization in Twentieth Century Latin America: A Working Bibliography.*

[17] For developing countries in general, N. V. Sovani has provided an incisive critique in "The Analysis of Overurbanization," *Economic Development and Cultural Change* 12, no. 2 (1964): 113–122. John Friedmann and Tomás Lackington put matters in historical and political perspective in "Hyperurbanization and National Development in Chile," *Urban Affairs Quarterly* 2, no. 4 (1967): 3–29.

has been paralleled, as could be expected, by a similar debate on the migration to cities.[18] Some analysts and policy makers see it quite negatively and therefore recommend that it be discouraged. Others, while not denying negative features of such migration, see it as a way of speeding up the process of economic development. There are predispositions to view the process either favorably or unfavorably according to the intellectual heritage of one's discipline, although there is considerable variation within each discipline.

For example, on the whole, economists are more likely to see migration in favorable terms because they take for granted that labor mobility is necessary for the effective development of an expanding economy. Sociologists, on the other hand, with their heritage of ideal-typical dichotomies (e.g., Gemeinschaft-Gesellschaft, folk-urban, traditional-modern), are inclined to see migration negatively because the city is defined as what the small, traditional community is not: heterogeneous, unstable, impersonal. This reasoning leads easily to the mainly deductive statements about personal and social disorganization that can be found in the literature on developing countries.

Whatever intellectual heritage an analyst brings to this problem, the first step ought to be an examination of the evidence. The debate about migration too often has assumed migrants to be an undifferentiated mass. (As we will document for the case of Monterrey, there is a considerable heterogeneity of migrants with respect to their areal, communal, and social origins.) The important question is not so much *how many* people migrate as *who* migrates and, in terms of return migration, who stays.

What we are talking about is migrant selectivity. Whether there are differences between migrants and their populations of origin, and whether there are differences between those who stay in the community of destination as compared with those who return to their community of origin, has a great bearing on how well migrants fare in competition with natives and, beyond this, an evaluation of the macrolevel problem of the costs and benefits of cityward migration in developing countries.

This is a highly complex matter, particularly since for migrant selectivity there are few if any invariant relationships holding across space

[18] The following paragraphs are based in part on Harley L. Browning, "Migrant Selectivity and the Growth of Large Cities in Developing Societies," in *Rapid Population Growth*, ed. National Academy of Sciences.

and time. The degree of migrant selectivity, both in terms of populations of origin and of destination, inevitably is affected by the changing rural-urban balance, the tempo of urbanization, and the nature and vigor of the industrialization process, to mention some of the most important factors and without introducing regional variation.

A key area linking industrialization, urbanization, and migration is the absorption of migrants into the labor force of cities. The parallel to this macroprocess is the microlevel question, How is the placement of a man in the urban occupational structure related to his migratory status? This is a major concern of our investigation.

Studies of geographic mobility share some of the characteristics and problems that have been alluded to in the study of social mobility. In both instances the recent rapid growth of empirical studies has not led to a theoretically cumulative body of knowledge. More specifically, little research has been designed expressly to examine closely the relationship between migratory status and occupational mobility. In investigations of social mobility a question or two on migratory status is included (generally, place of birth), while migration studies have, at best, a few questions on occupation at one or more ages. The problem in the subsequent analysis of such data is their inadequacy to establish the temporal relationship between the two kinds of mobility. In evaluating a man's occupational mobility, it is not enough to know that he is a migrant, meaning only that he was not born in his place of present residence. Where the man grew up, the age at which he left his community of birth, his age at arrival in the community of destination (in our case to Monterrey), the number of migrations and the kinds of places lived in, and whether there was return migration—all these facets of a man's residential history may have considerable influence on the kinds of jobs he has had, the sequence in which they were held, and, consequently, his occupational mobility. The residential and work sections of the Monterrey life histories provide us with the opportunity to closely relate changes in the one with changes in the other.

In the context of developing countries, rural-urban migration, in our case rural-metropolitan migration, is of special significance, not only because of its numerical importance but also because of its crucial role in effecting the transition from an agrarian to an industrial society. To what degree, if at all, is a rural background a handicap in mounting the occupational ladder in the city? And independent to, but related with, occupational mobility, is the matter of the adaptation of migrants to the city, to its tempo, and to its environment. Again, the rural-origin migrant is of special interest because migrants coming from urban areas presumably will have fewer difficulties in accommodating themselves to a large-city environment than will rural-origin migrants.

The Nature of the Process of Industrialization in Latin America

We earlier referred to the changes in occupational structure, population distribution, and system of stratification that occur with industrialization. Although in this book we will be concerned with these structural changes only as they affect migration and occupational mobility, it is not possible to assume that the meaning of these concepts is unequivocal, that industrialization signifies the same thing in all historical and geographical contexts, and that it always brings similar consequences. On the contrary, it is today a commonplace, mainly among social scientists interested in Latin America, to emphasize the variations and the uniqueness of each historical experience in this regard.[19]

For Latin America, the sociologist Glaucio Dillon Soares has written about the "new industrialization," in order to contrast the experience of currently developing countries with that of the older industrial ones.[20] Richard Adams, an anthropologist, distinguishes between "primary" and "secondary" development, in order to differentiate between the processes of incorporation of technological innovations in societies that originated them and in those that are now importing them.[21] In a similar vein the economist Albert Hirschman refers to the "early" industrialization of England, the "late" experience of Germany, Russia, or Japan, and the "late, late" industrialization of Latin America.[22] Clearly, it is not just the timing of industrialization that concerns these authors, but rather the important structural differences that result from the particular historical experience.[23]

[19] No one has been more influential, in this respect, than Celso Furtado. See his *Economic Development of Latin America.*

[20] Glaucio A. D. Soares spells out these conditions in "The New Industrialization and the Brazilian Political System," in *Latin America: Reform or Revolution?* ed. James Petras and Maurice Zeitlin.

[21] See Richard N. Adams, *The Second Sowing: Power and Secondary Development in Latin America.*

[22] Albert O. Hirschman, "The Political Economy of Import—Substituting Industrialization in Latin America," *Quarterly Journal of Economics* 82 (February 1968): 2–32.

[23] A significant contribution stressing the specific historical conditions of

Underdevelopment, as Celso Furtado rightly has indicated, is not a "natural" stage through which all societies must go, but rather a particular historical reality resulting from the expansion of capitalism into backward, precapitalist, and preindustrial countries. The nature of development in these societies is much conditioned by their colonial and neocolonial relationship to the more developed industrial countries.[24] Politically, nearly all Latin American countries are ex-colonies, and independence, even coming as it did in the early nineteeth century, has been accompanied by various kinds of political control as exercised by more powerful countries. Culturally, Latin American countries have been exposed to a whole range of influences from the industrial countries, ranging from ideologies of development to leisure-time consumption patterns. Economically, as is well known, Latin American nations first became integrated into the world economy as producers of primary products. In recent decades, when many began to industrialize through import substitution, new forms of dependency upon the industrial countries have developed.[25]

To the extent to which the major Latin American countries were exposed to similar relations with the developed countries during important stages in their histories, they developed key similarities. Thus, in the last several decades, as industrialization really got started, they faced many common problems deriving from similar structural conditions.

From our perspective, the import of technology and of organizational patterns, within the general context of economic and political dependence, is the more relevant characteristic needed to understand industrialization in the major Latin American countries, as contrasted with the experience of countries who had gone through this process at an earlier time. How did this "new" industrialization affect occupational structure, population distribution, and the stratification system?

We find it useful to begin with a consideration of labor supply and demand. In the earlier patterns of industrialization we can distinguish

---

change in Latin America is Fernando H. Cardoso and Enzo Faletto, *Dependencia y desarrollo en América Latina*. See also CEPAL, *El cambio social y la política de desarrollo social en América Latina*.

[24] See Tulio Halperin Donghi's recent *Historia contemporánea de América Latina*. In this important book the author treats the independent period of Latin American history as "neocolonial."

[25] See Cardoso and Faletto, *Dependencia y desarrollo en América Latina*.

two sources of labor for industry. First, there is the labor freed by the breakdown of subsistence agriculture and traditional crafts. Second, there is the labor generated by population growth. In England, the "classic" example of early industrialization, the enclosure legislation that drove the peasants off the land and the destruction of home industries in competition with the factory system were the primary processes generating labor for industry.[26] In most Latin American countries, agricultural production was to a considerable extent oriented to commercial markets long before industrialization began, and in most cases it was the stagnation rather than the commercialization of agriculture that drove agricultural workers off the land and into urban occupations. Domestic industry, on the other hand, never was of great importance, since the existing urban markets traditionally were supplied with imported manufactured goods, since at least the nineteenth century.

In comparing now industrialized countries with those in Latin America, more important than the different conditions attending the flow of labor out of the traditional sector is the considerably higher rate of population growth of the Latin American countries, which has to be absorbed into the labor force. Under the impact of new medical and public health technology, these countries have been able to reduce their death rates substantially within a very short period of time, while birth rates have continued at high levels. Thus, rates of growth up to three times those prevalent in the industrializing countries of the nineteeth century (excepting the United States) have become common in Latin America during recent decades.

In terms of labor supply, then, the characteristic feature of Latin American countries is the greater flow of labor into the nonagricultural economy, determined basically by rapid population growth and stagnation of the agricultural economy. At the same time there is no breakdown of the agricultural economy and society, or of the traditional crafts, comparable to the earlier models of industrialization. Looking at the side of labor demand, the differences also are striking. The early industrialization model, as Hobsbawn has shown, functioned under technological conditions that required large numbers of unskilled labor

---

[26] E. J. Hobsbawn makes a comparison of the labor supply during European and Latin American industrialization in "La marginalidad social en la historia de la industrialización europea," *Revista Latinoamericana de Sociología* 5, no. 2 (July 1969): 237–248. See also his *Industry and Empire.*

to operate what today would be considered unsophisticated machinery. Cheap labor, including that of women and children, was a condition for the growth of such industries as textiles and coal mining. Latin American countries now enjoy the advantages *and* disadvantages of being able to copy the technology generated during many decades of industrial growth in the more advanced countries. Petroleum, rather than coal, has become an important source of energy, and few men are needed to produce it. Nylon, a synthetic replacement for cotton, involves a quite different industrial process, one that again is basically capital rather than labor intensive. These examples could be multiplied, but we need not belabor the issue. The fact is that the more dynamic sectors of Latin American industry operate under a relatively capital-intensive technology that was created in the advanced countries for situations of labor scarcity rather than abundance.[27]

Beyond the purely quantitative differences in labor demand, there are also qualitative aspects to be considered. The new industrialization creates a greater demand for skilled workers, technicians, and other occupations requiring relatively high levels of training. In the larger and more efficient enterprises that constitute the dynamic centers of growth, the demand for trained personnel grows proportionally faster than that for unskilled workers. There is, furthermore, a rapid bureaucratization of industry, following to some extent the patterns of the more advanced countries. These trends necessarily result in an emphasis upon formal criteria for employment, generally those based upon education. Given a choice provided by an abundant supply of labor, and influenced by the pervading value placed upon education in the modern world, modern enterprises in Latin America often set educational requirements (credentials) of some sort for all positions, even though the actual performance of tasks may require little formal education.

The shift out of the agricultural sector in most Latin American countries is taking place as a reaction to population growth and agricultural stagnation rather than as a response to mechanization and greater productivity. (Even so, the proportional decline in agriculture is quite often accompanied by an increase in absolute numbers.) The tertiary

[27] Empirical case studies of the urban labor force in Latin America include Guillermo Briones and José Majía Valera, *El obrero industrial;* Bertram Hutchinson, et al., *Mobilidade e trabalho: Um estudo na cidade de São Paulo;* and David Chaplin, *The Peruvian Industrial Labor Force.*

sector, more so than the secondary sector, gains from this shift. As Fernando H. Cardoso and José L. Reyna put it, ". . . the formation of extensive tertiary sectors, which was a later effect of industrialization in Western Europe and the United States, becomes manifest from the beginning of industrialization in Latin America."[28] The increase in tertiary activities reflects the growth of services like health and education, the increasing importance of the state, and the greater complexity of the economy. It is partially to be explained by an international demonstration effect: Latin American countries cannot delay so long as did England, between the start of industrialization and the spread of medical and educational services, the inauguration of social security systems, and the development of unions. They can no more delay these changes than they can delay universal enfranchisement for men and women or the formal abolition of child labor. Furthermore, economic activities classified under the tertiary sector in these countries include a considerable proportion of disguised unemployment, consisting of men and women who are unable to find occupations in other, more productive, activities. Thus, the growth of the tertiary sector reflects many things: the needs generated by the industrialization process and the growth in per capita income, the demonstration effect of advanced countries that creates needs more "proper" at a later stage of development, and the greater elasticity of the service sector in absorbing labor not required in the technologically more advanced secondary sector.[29]

Another difference between the older industrial countries and Latin America is in the area of bureaucratization. Wilbert E. Moore and other authors have indicated an increase in wage and salaried workers, a decrease in self-employment, and the growth of large-scale economic

[28] Fernando H. Cardoso and José Luis Reyna, "Industrialization, Occupational Structure, and Social Stratification in Latin America," in *Constructive Change in Latin America*, ed. Cole S. Blasier, p. 32.

[29] For Latin America as a whole, the tertiary sector is considered within the larger sectoral context by ECLA, "Structural Changes in Employment within the Context of Latin America's Economic Development," *Economic Bulletin for Latin America* 10, no. 2 (October 1965): 163–187. See also the same agency's earlier statement, "Changes in Employment Structure in Latin America, 1945–1955," *Economic Bulletin for Latin America* 2, no. 1 (February 1957): 15–42. Paul I. Singer, in *Fôrca de tralbalho e emprêgo no Brasil: 1920–1969*, uses a subclassification of the tertiary sector that allows him to unmask its heterogeneity. He distinguishes "production services," "individual consumption services," and "collective consumption services."

units as consequences of industrialization.[30] In the Latin American case, self-employed people typical of the disguised unemployment situation are not necessarily driven out of business, since they live in a situation largely marginal to the modern economy and have few other choices of employment. The growth of large enterprises, however, is proceeding quite rapidly in Latin America, and the gap in productivity between them and the smaller and less efficient enterprises is enormous. This contrast between the modern economic sector of the urban economy and the smaller enterprises (including the self-employed) has led to numerous discussions in the literature. Those employed in unstable, low-paying jobs in inefficient enterprises, the self-employed, and the chronically unemployed, are all considered to be "marginal" to the process of industrialization.[31] Capital-intensive industrialization that absorbs only a small proportion of the labor force but generates a large share of the growth in product will, under conditions of abundant supply of labor, generate marginality in urban areas side by side with the marginality that exists in the agricultural sector.

In the process of Latin American industrialization there occurs in the leading sectors, as in the later stages of industrialization in the advanced countries, an upgrading of the labor force. Skilled workers, technicians, and white-collar employees increase at a faster rate than unskilled workers. But the tertiary sector, representing a larger proportion of the labor force, does not show the proportion of nonmanual positions that it does in Western Europe or the United States. Thus, an overall expansion of occupations at the middle level of the hierarchy, as happened in the industrial countries, is slow or does not take place at all.

[30] Wilbert E. Moore, "Changes in Occupational Structures," in *Social Structure and Mobility in Economic Development*, ed. Neil J. Smelser and Seymour M. Lipset.

[31] Marginality, in its cultural, ecological, and class dimensions, has become one of the key concepts developed by Latin American social scientists. For the class dimension, the one more relevant to our discussion, see the special issue on "La marginalidad en América Latina" in the *Revista Latinoamericana de Sociología* 5, no. 2 (July 1969), especially the article by José Nun, "Superpoblación relativa, ejército industrial de reserva y masa marginal," pp. 178–236 (reviewed critically by Fernando H. Cardoso in "Comētário sobre os conceitos de superpopulação relativa e marginalidade," in *Sôbre teoria e método en sociologia*). Also see Aníbal Quijano, *Notas sobre el concepto de marginalidad social*; and Roger Vekemans and Jorge Giusti, "Marginality and Ideology in Latin American Development," *Studies in Comparative International Development* 5, no. 11 (1969–1970): 221–234.

In Latin America industrialization has rapidly produced great differentiation within the lower strata. The overall shape of the stratification pyramid does not change drastically, but there is a considerable gap between workers integrated into and workers marginal to modern industry. Independent of this feature is the fact that industrialization has not led to as much of a redistribution of income in Latin America as is now the case in advanced countries. This contributes to the marked inequality between strata, weakens the middle strata, and maintains the pyramidal shape of the system. Finally, the role of education in screening out illiterate or semiliterate men from positions in modern industry serves to perpetuate the stratification system.[32]

In summary, the slow absorption of manpower in modern industry, the striking differences in productivity between various sectors of the economy, the high value placed upon education while overall attainment is still low, and the weakness of the traditional middle strata both in agriculture and outside agriculture—all these elements help to explain why industrialization in Latin America does not necessarily bring greater equality and a more profound change in social stratification. Actually, the most prominent characteristic of social stratification in many Latin American countries, the extreme inequality in income and wealth, may have increased with industrialization.

The pattern of urbanization that has developed in Latin America differs from that of the now developing areas in Africa and Asia and also that of the now industrialized countries. Although Latin America is classified as a developing area, it has a strikingly higher level of urbanization than other developing areas. According to the 1970 estimates made by Kingsley Davis, the urban proportion of the total population of Latin America was over one-half, 55 percent. In contrast, for both Africa as a whole and Asia, excluding Japan, the comparative figure was only 22 percent.[33] A combination of Ibero colonization practices that favored cities, substantial immigration to several countries,

[32] Changes in social stratification are analyzed by Gino Germani in "Grados de desarrollo, tipos de estratificación y movilidad social en América Latina," in *Política y sociedad en una época de transición*; and by Glaucio A. D. Soares in "Desenvolvimento economico e estructura de classe," *Dados*, no. 6 (1969), pp. 91–128. See also the Introduction by Claudio Véliz in *Obstacles to Change in Latin America*; and Torcuato di Tella, *Teoría del primer impacto de la industrialización*.

[33] Kingsley Davis, *World Urbanization 1950–1970*. Volume 1. *Basic Data for Cities, Countries, and Regions*.

and, most of all, the relative lack of constraints on rural-urban migration in recent decades all helped to make Latin America more "urban" than the level of economic development would lead one to expect.

Latin America differs from the now industrialized countries in that the thrust of its urbanization preceded industrialization. Leaving aside the somewhat muddled issue of overurbanization, this sequence had its consequences for the "system of cities" that has evolved in Latin America. The development of the export economy in the nineteenth century and the first three decades of the twentieth century fostered a pattern in which urban centers, and the services they provide, were not evenly or widely distributed throughout the country. The "extractive" character of the export economy, whether it was minerals or crops, had an "enclave" nature that seldom required the existence of middle-size cities and a well-developed communication system that could tie together different regions of the country. The main urban beneficiary of the export economy was the largest, or primary, city. Whereas exports could be sent out from numerous small ports, most of the imports were channeled to and through the first city, and it was often the only place in the entire country that could offer much in the way of urban services and amenities.[34]

Thus, while the export economy did not create the pattern of high primacy—a situation whereby the first city is many times larger than other cities and is economically, politically, and culturally dominant— it intensified the pattern. Nor did the import-substitution phase of industrial development change things, at least in the first decades. Since it was initially limited to assembly-type operations that supplied consumer goods to replace the "finished" products traditionally imported, accessibility to consumer markets took precedence in deciding where to locate plants. The primary city, with by far the largest market for manufactured goods in the country, naturally was the overwhelming choice. As the cases of São Paulo, Medellín, and of course Monterrey indicate, it was possible for cities other than the primary capital city to develop industrially, but the generalization still holds that within Latin America the spatial development of industry has been very uneven, and this has had its effect upon the spatial and size distribution of cities.

---

[34] Harley L. Browning, "Primacy Variation in Latin America during the Twentieth Century," paper delivered at XXXIX Congreso Internacional de Americanistas, Lima, Peru, August 2–9, 1970.

Mexico and Monterrey as the Context of the Investigation

The previous discussion of industrialization in Latin America necessarily was couched in very general terms, and it did not attempt to do justice to the enormous differences among Latin American countries. It is obvious that even the major and more industrialized countries (Brazil, Mexico, Argentina) show considerable differences in economic structure, political institutions, and urbanization. We have chosen to study Mexico, and within it a city characterized by heavy and rapid industrialization. To what extent can Mexico and Monterrey be taken as typical within the Latin American context?

The reader will be best prepared to address this question at the end of this book, when all the findings will have been set forth. At this point, nonetheless, it can be said that the patterns of development outlined in the previous section have in general been experienced by Mexico. At the same time, the rapidity of change in Mexico and the heavily industrial character of Monterrey together make for a somewhat atypical situation within the broader context of Latin America, and this point should be borne in mind in evaluating what is to follow. Some brief comments about Mexican development in general, and particularly during the past several decades, are in order, with the account of the growth of Monterrey to be deferred until the following chapter.

Mexico's course of development in the twentieth century was greatly influenced by the violent and prolonged revolution that began in 1910. While it did not bring about as profound a transformation as was to occur in subsequent revolutions in Russia, China, or Cuba, the Mexican revolution did permanently alter the social and economic structure of the country. As Barrington Moore, Jr., rightly indicates, the nature of agrarian societies and the particular circumstances of the breakdown of the old order and the changeover to commercialized agriculture are relevant, indeed crucial, for an understanding of the choices open to a society undergoing modernization.[35] Thus, the extreme exploitative nature of Mexican agrarian society in the first decade of the twentieth century, and the no less extreme economic and political concentration that characterized it, together with the permanent change brought about by the revolution give Mexico an early distinction within the Latin American scene.

[35] Barrington Moore, Jr., *Social Origins of Dictatorship and Democracy.*

If the partial and erratic redistribution of land that followed the revolution did not greatly ameliorate the living conditions and life chances of the great majority of peasants, it did bring the shattering of the old agrarian landowning class. Furthermore, the political developments, in the form of a one-party system that has now endured into its fifth decade and in which a variety of interests and groups find accommodation and allow for the peaceful transmission of power with at least formal regard for democratic procedure, must be considered in part as a consequence of the revolution. Both the orderly circulation of governing elites and the continuity of the political order during the last crucial decades stand out as atypical in the Latin American context, where one and quite often both features have been absent.[36]

The decades of the twenties and thirties do not show up in statistical indicators as a period of important change, but beneath the surface the institutional restructuring of the Mexican society was proceeding, especially during the presidential term of Lázaro Cárdenas (1934–1940). The period of rapid economic growth was set off by World War II, and in the last three decades industrialization, urbanization, population growth, and redistribution have proceeded at a rapid pace. In many ways these structural changes, and the stimuli that fostered them, are little different from those experienced by the other major countries of Latin America. In most respects, however, Mexico seems to have had "more of it," and in the important index of growth of gross national product it has been among the most rapidly growing countries not only within Latin America but throughout the world as well.[37]

The rapidity of change in Mexico can be appreciated from a glance at Table 1-1, where seven common indices of development are given for the period 1921–1980, the 1980 figure being an extrapolation of recent trends. Within the lifetime of the older men in our sample there has been more structural change of Mexican society than for any comparable

[36] For an analysis of the social and political structure of Mexico in the post-revolutionary period see Pablo González Casanova, *Democracy in Mexico.*

[37] Mexico's economic development since the revolution is well covered by a number of recent works. See Leopoldo Solís, *La realidad económica mexicana: Retrovisión y perspectivas*; Clark W. Reynolds, *The Mexican Economy: Twentieth-Century Structure and Growth*; and Raymond Vernon, *The Dilemma of Mexico's Development.* See also a number of articles in Vols. I and II of the collective work, *El perfil de México en 1980*, especially David Ibarra, "Mercados, desarrollo y política económica: Perspectivas de la economía de México" (Vol. I); and Víctor L. Urquidi, "La economía y la población" (Vol. I).

TABLE 1-1. Indices of Mexican Development, 1921–1980

Year	Population (millions)	Percent in Places 10,000 +	Percent in Places 100,000 +	Percent Male Labor Force in Nonagriculture	Percent Males 6+ Literate	Male Li⸱ Expectan⸱
1921	15	17	6	26	25	32E
1940	20	22	11	32	40	40
1960	35	38	24	47	64	58
1980E	67	52	38	62	80	65

NOTE: For 1921–1960, all figures are derived from census reports, except male life expectancy, which is taken from Centro de Estudios Económicos y Demográficos, *Dinámica de la población de México*, Chap. 1. The 1980 estimates are extrapolations from the 1970 census and other data.

time span in the country's history. In 1921 (and there had been little change in any of the indices, even that of population, since the revolution of 1910) Mexico had all the characteristic features we identify with underdeveloped countries: a labor force dominated by subsistence agriculture, a low level of urbanization, a short life expectancy, a high degree of illiteracy, and a very low per capita income.

It will be observed that the more rapid tempo of change took place after 1940, when the process of industrialization gained momentum. In the face of very high rates of population growth and a massive movement of people toward the cities,[38] and more recently the shift to more capital-intensive forms of industrialization, problems of labor absorption became critical, in spite of the impressive growth in industrial product. The relative success of development in the Mexican case, therefore, does not mean that it has been free of the difficulties of Latin America outlined in the previous section.

In this respect, one should be cautioned that the figures given in Table 1-1 by no means tell the whole story. For example, regional differences, always important in Mexico, have widened rather than narrowed in recent decades. Thus, some regions are now highly urbanized,

[38] An account of Mexican population changes in the twentieth century is found in the study of the Centro de Estudios Económicos y Demográficos, *Dinámica de la población de México*. For urbanization see Luis Unikel, "El proceso de urbanización en México: Distribución y crecimiento de la población urbana," *Demografía y Economía* 2, no. 2 (1968): 139–182.

while others have remained quite rural. Similar wide variations are to be found in agricultural employment and in illiteracy. A fundamental and persistent problem that Mexico has not solved is the continuing large mass of impoverished peasants. Although agricultural output has increased substantially, this increase has resulted mainly from heavy investments in commercial agriculture in restricted areas that make up only a small part of the rural population. Consequently, the great majority of the peasants have derived little benefit from either industrialization or agricultural development. They combine with the "marginal" urban working-class sector, whose members have not found employment in the modern industries, to form a bloc that represents more than one-half of the population.

With the above in mind, it should come as no surprise to find that Mexico, among the large countries of the world, has one of the most extreme concentrations of income.[39] In a calculation made for 1963, the lowest 40 percent of the Mexican population received only 11 percent of the total income, while at the other end the top 10 percent took in nearly 50 percent. What is equally important, as is demonstrated by Ifigenia de Navarrete in her recent review of the evidence, incomplete though it may be, is that the already great concentration of income has, if anything, become more extreme in recent decades, the very time of the Mexican economic "miracle." During the 1940–1950 period, for example, average wages in both agricultural and nonagricultural sectors declined in real terms, but, since wages in the latter sector are on the average considerably higher, the sectoral transfer out of agricultural employment meant an increase in mean wage for the country's labor force as a whole. Doubtless the large supply of unskilled and semiskilled labor was at least partially responsible for the unfavorable situation of most peasants and workers during a period of rapid industrialization. In very recent years there is some indication that the top 5 to 10 percent in income distribution have had some relative loss. But this redistribution did not go to the lower sectors but benefitted the middle-income groups, including some white-collar employees and the labor aristocracy of organized skilled workers.

These inequalities in the process of economic growth need to be stressed, because Monterrey, being heavily industrial and with large,

[39] See Ifigenia M. de Navarrete, "La distribución del ingreso en México: Tendencias y perspectivas," Vol. I of *El perfil de México en 1980*; and also Solís, *La realidad económica mexicana*, Chap. 7.

modern factories, is not to be taken as representative of Mexico as a whole, or even metropolitan Mexico. We certainly do not wish to suggest that the experience of Monterrey and the Monterrey men can be readily extended to the rest of Mexico or to Latin America as a whole. But if Monterrey is an extreme case, it is not so deviant that it falls outside the pattern we have outlined for Latin America, that is to say, a capitalistic development, but with an important economic role played by the state and a pattern of industrialization much influenced by trends in the now developed countries. Monterrey also shares with other Latin American communities a rapid population growth that is fueled both by high rates of natural increase and by net in-migration, with many of the migrants originating in rural areas. There is also plenty of evidence of the "marginality" of a substantial part of the labor force. Monterrey's extreme position results from its more "successful" performance, as judged by growth in gross and per capita product. In this sense, we are examining a case study of industrialization under conditions more optimal than those generally found in Latin America.

Life Cycle, Cohorts, and Generations: A Conceptual Note

In this study we want to show, as concretely as possible, how a large number of men *experience* a period of rapid economic development, particularly in the areas of migration, occupational mobility, and status attainment. Our basic framework for describing and interpreting the events and processes in these areas and for showing how they are related to other areas, such as family formation, or the various interrelationships among the three areas is the concept of the life cycle.[40] But we want also to relate their life histories to the larger context of Mexican economic development and modernization, and for this purpose we have found cohort analysis to be a useful tool in understanding the changes in men's lives brought about by the structural transformation of society.[41] Furthermore, from either of these two perspectives—that

[40] A good general survey of the use of this concept is found in Leonard D. Cain, Jr., "Life Course and Social Structure," in *Handbook of Modern Sociology*, ed. Robert L. Faris.

[41] The use of cohorts in the study of social change is set forth by Gosta Carlsson and Katrina Carlsson, "Age, Cohorts, and the Generation of Generations," *American Sociological Review* 35, no. 4 (August 1970): 710–718; and Norman Ryder, "The Cohort as a Concept in the Study of Social Change," *American Sociological Review* 30, no. 6 (December 1965): 843–861.

centered in the men's lives and that relating them to societal change—it soon becomes obvious that the men's lives cannot be isolated from those of their parents and their offspring. For this reason, the idea of generational analysis is helpful in integrating the lives of the men within a longer time span. Although the concepts of life cycle, cohorts, and generation are familiar within sociology, it is necessary to spend a little time in discussing how we propose to use them.

Cohorts may be defined as groups of people who are exposed to the same general environment at the same time. Most often cohorts are identified by time of birth, but other bases are possible, as for example our construction of cohorts by time of arrival in Monterrey. We define age cohorts as groups of men who were born within a given period of time, generally five- or ten-year intervals. Being contemporaries, their lives are affected by at least some events that are common to all. The society in which they live and its changes provide the broader framework of their lives. Of course, nobody lives in society in the abstract, but rather within particular groups (family, friends, neighborhood, work). Society, in other words, affects the lives of men in an indirect way, its influence being filtered by a series of groups and organizations. But the fact that these groups and institutions belong to a given society and that there is some coordination between the various societal elements, as well as the fact that some societal events (i.e., revolution, depression, or war) affect all men, makes birth cohorts a useful tool of analysis.

Other events that similarly affect the men belonging to a given cohort are related to the life cycle. The life cycle refers to the temporal ordering or organization of men's lives that emerges from biological, cultural, and social determinants: biological aging or maturation, cultural definitions of age statuses, and the social roles that men are encouraged to play in given institutional spheres according to their age status. Since life cycles are both biological and social, there are important variations between different groups. Some, for instance, may define adulthood earlier than do others, even within the same society. However, some patterning of the life cycles of men belonging to a specific cohort is to be expected. The age when children are supposed to start schooling or work, the time to get married and begin a family, or the age restrictions attached to various jobs all affect men of similar biological age.

In rapidly changing societies, succeeding cohorts will be confronted with different conditions. In the United States, to take several examples, we could identify cohorts by their differential exposure to Dr. Spock's book on infant and child care, to television, or to the Vietnam war. All three should produce discernible differences in behavior between successive cohorts, the earliest of whom were not exposed to these influences. Intercohort differences can be used to test hypotheses concerned with societal change. Even the life cycle itself may be altered from one cohort to the next, as with a war that decimates the male population of a certain age, thus affecting the female's life cycle in marriage, family, and work. Throughout this book, consequently, we will introduce intercohort differences wherever they appear to be relevant to indicate social change.

The concept of generation does not have a uniform meaning in the sociological literature. Here we will use it to refer to the relationship between parents and children. Its importance for the present study lies in the fact that the family of orientation provides the first social identity for every individual, while his family of procreation operates similarly for his children. In studying the men's lives, we will want to investigate the extent to which the previous generation, that of their parents, serves both objectively as a determinant of the men's life chances and subjectively as an important frame of reference used by the men to evaluate their success or failure. The family context is useful to understand both continuities and discontinuities through time, and the concept of generation is used to provide cutting points in the time sequence. In other words, in studying the men's lives and how they are affected by societal change, we will link them with both those of their parents and those of their children.

Perhaps our approach can be appreciated by reference to Table 1-2. Mean scores of occupational status are presented in the table for the Monterrey men, classified in four birth cohorts, at different times in their lives. Comparable scores are presented also for their fathers. The occupational scores of the four cohorts at the present (1965) are underlined, and we may begin with them. The differences are quite small, and if one were to look only at the underlined figures it might be concluded that age makes little difference for occupational attainment. This would be in error, for it does make a difference. On the one hand, there is an increase in mean scores as the men grow older. In all cohorts, the older the men the higher the average score. The two older cohorts, however, show a considerable increase up to age 35, after which it levels off. On the other hand, each succeeding cohort has, at a similar stage in the life cycle, a higher average score than the previous cohort. The differences in starting points, for instance, are striking. By age 25 the men in the youngest cohort had already surpassed, on the average, a level that the older men had achieved only near the end of their work lives.

What clues about occupational achievement in a developing society does this table provide? Approximately forty years have elapsed since the oldest cohort started working, and also forty years separate the older and the younger men in the sample. The upward movement that we find for the older cohorts can be interpreted as combining the effect of historical time (or economic development) with personal time (or life cycle) in proportions that we cannot disentangle. But the difference between the oldest and the youngest cohorts at the same age has to be attributed at least partially to changes in historical time. We must say partially, because most men in the youngest cohort at age 15 lived in Monterrey, while most men in the oldest cohort at the same age lived in rural communities, and occupational positions differ greatly between rural and urban areas. But this indicates considerable rural-urban migration, so the intercohort differences also reflect social change in Mexico.

TABLE 1-2. Occupational Scores of Fathers and Respondents at Various Ages, by Birth Cohort, Monterrey, 1965

Birth Cohort of Respondent	Mean Occupational Score					
	Father	Respondent				
		Age 15	Age 25	Age 35	Age 45	Age 55
1905–1914	2.45	1.67	2.22	2.55	2.71	2.81
1915–1924	2.60	1.76	2.40	2.77	2.96	
1925–1934	2.60	2.03	2.60	2.95		
1935–1944	2.74	2.26	2.85			

NOTES: Occupational scores are based upon a five-point scale, from 1 (lowest) to 5 (highest).

Age 15: occupation at that age or, if respondent is not yet in the labor force, first occupation; age 25: for men ages 21–30, last occupation; age 35: for men ages 31–40, last occupation; age 45: for men ages 41–50, last occupation; age 55: for men ages 51–60, last occupation.

Father's occupational score is taken at his age when respondent was born.

Finally, the scores for the fathers are useful in evaluating at what age, on the average, do the sons' achievements exceed those of their fathers. For the older men their score never greatly surpasses that of their fathers. But the young men quite early in their lives achieve a higher score. It should be emphasized that our analysis uses aggregate data—we speak about average scores—but this result could also be confirmed by calculating the percent of respondents whose occupations are of a higher status than those of their fathers.

During the preliminary stages of this research we were impressed by the large gap that existed between two approaches to the study of men's lives in the areas of work, migration, and family formation. One of them, best represented by the work of anthropologists like Oscar Lewis, consisted in qualitative studies in depth of a handful of cases, based upon life histories as complete as possible.[42] The end result of this approach is a rich but impressionistic picture of the men chosen for the study, one in which the literary merits are difficult to separate from the scientific ones. The reader may or may not be impressed by the content, but there is an inevitable gap between the actual description and any kind of theoretical statements that may antecede, or follow, it. The other approach, more common among sociologists, has generally consisted in the segmenting of men's lives, a kind of dissection. Only one or two areas are chosen for analysis, and generally the various aspects of the men's lives are not related to each other, except for the most superficial connections. More important, only a few points in time rather than the whole sequence of events are considered, either because the data were gathered in this manner or because the analyst had the data but chose to ignore the sequential aspects of the men's lives. But, unlike the case studies in depth, questions of the representativeness of men chosen for the study and the quantification of occupational mobility are given proper attention. Generally speaking, this approach has been used in sample surveys with relatively large numbers of cases.

This appraisal of the field led us to consider innovations that could help in bridging the gap between these two approaches. We wanted to be able to consider complete behavioral sequences and to relate them to various aspects of the men's lives. At the same time, we could not ac-

[42] The best known of Lewis's works are *The Children of Sánchez: Autobiography of a Mexican Family* and *La Vida: A Puerto Rican Family in the Culture of Poverty—San Juan and New York.*

cept the strategy of relying only upon the relatively complete biographies of a few men, selected with little or no regard to sampling theory. We therefore worked within the usual framework of sample surveys, using a two-stage stratified cluster design. The sample of 1,640 men aged 21–60 is large enough to permit inferences about the universe and to allow for multivariate analysis. (See Appendix A for a full account of the design and execution of the survey.)

In addition, however, we developed a technique that would enable us to collect partial life histories in key areas of the men's experience. (Appendix B provides a description of the technique for collecting life histories.) The core of our interview schedule consisted of a form designed to obtain selected information, year by year, about the respondent's residence, education, family of procreation, health, and work. The information was collected sequentially, for predefined areas, and the instructions given to the interviewers included both a set of definitions of what was relevant for the study and how to obtain it. The latter instructions were rather simple: we told them to help the interviewee remember the events of his life by encouraging him to relate one area to the other, and to use age and year as abstract contextual elements in which the event should finally be placed. Along with the life-history form were many other questions of the type one usually finds in surveys. A few questions were inserted as a check on the information in the life history.

Organization of the Book

This book is divided into three parts. The first is devoted to setting the scene, within which the men's life histories will be examined. Besides the Introduction, there are two chapters dealing with the community level. Chapter 2 describes the historical development of Monterrey as a manufacturing center and the industrial and occupational composition of the labor force at the time of the survey in 1965. The third chapter takes up the kinds of regions and communities, ranging from rural to metropolitan, from which migrants to Monterrey originate. Monterrey provided us with a community that was rapidly growing, both economically and in population. We also wanted to know more about the communities providing Monterrey with migrants, particularly rural-origin migrants, so in 1967 we conducted a smaller survey (380 men) in Cedral, San Luis Potosí, an agriculturally oriented community 250 miles south of Monterrey, located in an arid, economically depressed region that long has been an important source of migrants to Monterrey.

Part Two forms the bulk of the book. Its six chapters are ordered chronologically, as well as could be managed, to follow the life cycles of the Monterrey men. The structure of the book and the most important variables and their relations to one another are best comprehended by an inspection of Figure 1-1. This figure also will be helpful for Chapter 10, where there is a statistical analysis of the process of stratification, but at this point our concern is only in showing the sequence to be followed.

Chapter 4 takes up a variety of factors that are antecedent to a man's first job. Of central importance is his educational attainment because of its impact upon his subsequent occupational achievement. The variables representing family and community origins are considered individually and then subjected to a multivariate analysis to determine their relative importance. Chapter 5 takes up the questions, How do boys and young men in Mexico become fully incorporated into the labor force? What kind of work do they get? and What is the relationship of their education to their first job? The analysis then follows the men through the crucial first ten years (a "shopping around" period) of their work lives, with particular attention devoted to a comparison of those who began work in Monterrey with those who began in rural communities or small towns.

In Chapter 6 attention shifts from work histories to the men who migrated to Monterrey. Are migrants positively or negatively selective when compared to comparable populations in their communities of origin? The social and economic context of the last move to Monterrey is examined in detail, beginning with reasons for terminating last employment, moving through the kinship composition of the migratory group and forms of assistance to migrants, and ending with the initial adjustment of migrants in Monterrey. The purpose of this sequence is to ascertain the myth and reality of migration to large cities like Monterrey. The following chapter (7) considers aspects of the family in Mexican society and how it is incorporated into the life cycle. Age at first marriage and its influence on occupational mobility is examined, along with the early stages of family formation.

After the diversions of migration and marriage, Chapters 8 and 9 return to a consideration of the men's work histories. The concern of Chapter 8 is not only to measure the amount of occupational mobility

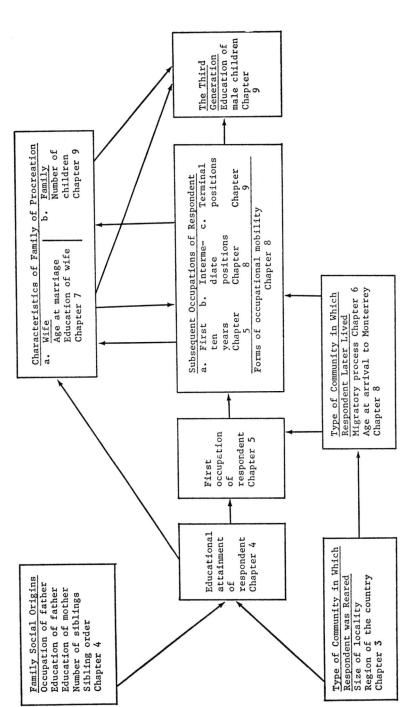

Figure 1-1. Basic Model for Life Cycle and Process of Stratification

experienced by the men during the middle years of their work lives, ages 25 to 45, but also to explore the forms of nonvertical mobility the men take. The relationship of migratory status to occupational mobility, first taken up in Chapter 5, is again considered for this age interval. In addition, careers, stable work histories, self-employment, and downward mobility are individually dealt with. The main point to be stressed is the fluidity of the occupational structure. Chapter 9 takes the older men, aged 45 and over, and looks back at their life histories from the vantage point of their terminal or near-terminal positions; something that cannot be done for any other birth cohort. In this chapter we also take up the third generation (sons of the older men) and look at their educational attainment in comparison with that of their fathers.

Part Three is made of two distinct chapters. Chapter 10 provides a statistically oriented overview, principally by the use of path analysis, of the process of stratification across three generations (the respondent's fathers, the respondents, and their sons). The object is to analyze the determinants of occupational and educational achievement. Chapter 11 leaves the microlevel of interpretation that had been used in following the men through their life histories and moves to the macrolevel. Instead of a concern with the placement of men in the stratification system, we will address the question of class relations and, particularly, class conflict. The question here is, What are the conditions in Monterrey that foster or mitigate class conflict? This in turn leads to a consideration of group conflicts and its relationship to migration, both for communities of origin (Cedral) and for communities of destination (Monterrey). Another problem dealt with in this chapter is the relationship of migration and social disorganization. Finally, the question is raised concerning the future of the Monterrey men and whether the mechanisms that have worked to the advantage of the community during a period of rapid social change will continue to do so in the intermediate future.

2. The Development of Monterrey as an Industrial Center

Monterrey, as the undisputed capital of northeast Mexico, is a part of the Mexican North, a region that since colonial times has had characteristics that differentiate it from the rest of the country.[1] In the words of Howard F. Cline, "Many adjectives can be used to describe the North. It is large, thirsty, active, new, and above all, unique."[2] It is a huge still mostly empty area, much of it desertic or semidesertic. The population was and is very unevenly dispersed, generally clustering in those few areas with sufficient water. Unlike the central region, where scarcity of land has been a factor since colonial days and where that pressure has increased with the recent rapid demographic growth, water, not land, has been the main determinant of

---

[1] The historical development of Monterrey (and the state of Nuevo León) has received some attention, but a comprehensive and systematic work on the subject remains to be written. There are a number of "anecdotal" histories, e.g., Virgilio Garza, Jr., "Brief Sketch of the Industrial Development of Monterrey," in *Basic Industries in Texas and Northern Mexico*; and Santiago Roel, *Nuevo León: Apuntes históricos*. The most serious studies are Frederic Mauro, "Le développement économique de Monterrey, 1890–1960," *Caravelle*, no. 2 (1964), pp. 35–126; and Isidro Vizcaya Canales, *Los orígenes de la industrialización de Monterrey 1867–1920*. See also Mary Catherine Megee, *Monterrey, Mexico: Internal Patterns and External Relations*.

[2] Howard F. Cline, *The United States and Mexico*, p. 106.

wealth in the North. The haciendas of the North were even larger than those of the central region, but they were sparsely populated, isolated from markets, and of little economic value to themselves. The Indians, or rather the lack of them, were another distinguishing feature of the region. Not only were they much fewer in numbers, but they also were with few exceptions warlike and nomadic. They never provided the Spaniards with the large and docile labor supply they had become accustomed to in central Mexico.

The capital of Spain's richest colony was Mexico City, its administrative and cultural center. Within its hinterland developed the peculiar combination of Spanish and Indian practices that has formed the Mexican cultural heritage. The North never was fully integrated into this heritage; indeed, in its far reaches at least, it was never really firmly within the hands of the central colonial government. Cattle rather than maize was the main product with wheat and cotton exported to other regions of the colony. Mining in the "old" North of San Luis Potosí, Zacatecas, and Durango was early important, but for a number of border states it did not assume significance until the nineteenth century.

Following independence (1810–1821) the Mexican government tried at various times to speed up colonization, to improve the poor communications with the rest of the country, and to maintain a more effective rule over that part of Mexico. Such efforts were ineffective, since the central government itself was weak and highly unstable. The loss of almost one-half of the Mexican territory to the United States in the war of 1846–1847 was in part a consequence of the relative isolation and low population density of the region.

Thus, for a long time the North felt itself on the periphery in terms of the polity as well as geographically. Forced by the geography to be self-reliant, made more egalitarian by frontier conditions and the lack of a servile native poulation, the men of the North developed their own special character. This character was formed mainly by the changes that have taken place in the last hundred years, but it is clearly traceable to colonial times.

The Industrial Development of Monterrey

Monterrey is thoroughly within the spirit of the North. Not all cities develop a mystique of their own, but there is no doubt of the mystique of Monterrey in the Mexican context: it is hard work and industriousness, seasoned with stinginess. Like the *antioqueños* in Colombia and the *paulistas* in Brazil, the *regiomontanos*, or inhabitants of Monterrey, stereotypically are perceived as an industrious people. Their reputation for being stingy, which may be simply a willingness to save some of their disposable income, is famed throughout Mexico. Oscar Lewis reported that even in Tepoztlán, a small and somewhat isolated town some 650 miles south of Monterrey, the school children knew that the "regiomontanos son codos" (the people of Monterrey are stingy).[3] And the characters used by Carlos Fuentes in his novel, *La muerte de Artemio Cruz*, to depict the industrial tycoons of Mexico naturally had to be from Monterrey.

Whatever the origin of this mystique and its stereotype, the *regiomontanos* themselves not only accept the designation, but they are also proud of it. Every so often one finds in the local newspapers an article or a commentary about the miracle of Monterrey's industrial development. These sources argue that the early inhabitants of Monterrey became so industrious precisely because of the difficult conditions (arid lands and warlike Indians) they encountered, unlike the settlers of richer lands in central Mexico or in the tropical southern area, who had only to reach out their arms to collect the fruits of nature.

Our task, however, is not to trace the development of this mystique but to account for the industrial growth of Monterrey. Until the second half of the nineteenth century Monterrey was not a very important provincial town, probably not exceeding ten thousand in population. No matter how doughty its inhabitants, it is unlikely that any observer of the time would have predicted that Monterrey would become the leading city in northeastern Mexico, let alone the third largest in the country and second in industrial output. Probably a city other than Monterrey would have been selected as the regional capital. Saltillo, little more than 75 kilometers from Monterrey, seemed the better candidate. It was larger and appeared to have a superior geographic situation. Yet time after time Monterrey bested its rival in competition for regional supremacy.

The city certainly had few natural or man-made advantages working for it. There was no rich and densely settled agricultural hinterland surrounding Monterrey, and no important mineral resources were close at

[3] Oscar Lewis, *Life in a Mexican Village: Tepoztlán Restudied.*

hand. Raw materials for manufacturing were lacking. And it hardly seemed possible that Monterrey could be transformed into an important commercial center, considering the lack of population and the very poor communications with both Mexico City and the United States. Yet a series of external events provided the *regiomontanos* with the opportunities they needed to transform Monterrey into the capital of the frontier.

The first of these was the loss of Texas and other northern territories to the United States in the war of 1846–1847, an event that moved the Mexican-American border south to within 150 miles of Monterrey via Laredo, Texas. Of course, this did not constitute an advantage until border commerce increased and better transportation facilities became available. The next event to have a lasting effect on the commercial development of Monterrey was the American Civil War. The blockade of the coasts of the Confederacy was so effective that the export of cotton from the South was seriously hindered. During the war years some of it was routed through northern Mexico and the port of Matamoros. Monterrey managed the shipping of cotton abroad and the import of goods destined for the American South, a lucrative business.

Thus the American Civil War, and to a lesser extent the French intervention in Mexico, fostered the formation of commercial capital in Monterrey. However, even by the 1870's the state of Nuevo León, whose capital was Monterrey, as well as the other states in northeastern Mexico, had little weight in the Mexican economy. The lack of good communications with the rest of the country continued to be the major barrier to internal development. Construction of the railroad network during the last two decades of the century helped to overcome this obstacle. In 1880 the railroad from Mexico City to Laredo (passing through Monterrey) was begun, with completion eight years later. Since then most of the Mexican trade with the United States has taken this route, first by railway and later by the Pan American highway—the first hard-surface road to penetrate deeply into the Mexican interior. The United States early became what it has continued to be: the dominant purchaser of Mexican exports and the main supplier of her imports. Other railway lines were completed during the 1880's and 1890's that connected Monterrey with Torreón to the west and with Tampico to the east. As Samuel Dicken puts it, "With the completion of these railroads Monterrey found itself in the most strategic position in northern Mexico. Then, and not until then, the superiority of its situation became effective."[4]

The development of the railroad system was an important accomplishment of the government of Porfirio Díaz (1876–1910). A second major economic feature of his regime was the substantial increase in foreign investment—encouraged directly by favorable governmental policies and indirectly by the political stability introduced by the dictatorship. Most of the investment went into the export sector of the economy. At that time the main Mexican exports were mining products, and Monterrey became an important center for their shipment to the United States. Moreover, the McKinley Tariff in the United States had favored the refining of minerals in Mexico since 1890.

Also important was the forceful intervention of Bernardo Reyes, the governor of Nuevo León and a major political figure of the Díaz regime, who fostered the industrialization of Monterrey, among other ways, by enacting a state law in 1888 giving tax exemptions to industries established in Nuevo León.[5] The first steel mill in Mexico, in fact the first in all of Latin America, was founded in Monterrey in 1900. (Characteristically, it was first planned to be located in Saltillo, but, partly as the result of the manipulations of the energetic governor of Nuevo León, it was moved to Monterrey.)

Briefly described, these were the origins of the commercial and industrial development of Monterrey up to the time of the revolution in 1910. The entrepreneurs of that city were always quick to capitalize upon the opportunities that came their way. American capital was by no means absent, especially during the Díaz regime, but it should be stressed that from the very beginning Monterrey's industrial destiny to a large extent was in local hands. The capital accumulation may have been of commercial origin, but what distinguishes the economic history of Monterrey from many other cities of Latin America is that the business leaders, instead of contenting themselves with commercial dominance of northeastern Mexico, progressively extended their operations to a manufacturing basis, and much of it was destined for export to

---

[4] Samuel Dicken, "Monterrey and Northeastern Mexico," *Annals of the Association of American Geographers* 29, no. 2 (June 1939): 139.

[5] The influential role of governor Bernardo Reyes in Monterrey's development has been described by Eberhardt Victor Niemeyer, Jr., "The Public Career of General Bernardo Reyes," Ph.D. Dissertation, University of Texas, 1958.

other parts of Mexico and abroad. By this time the two great family groupings that have dominated Monterrey had emerged. The brewery group, owners of Cervecería Cuauhtemoc (founded in 1891), and the iron-and-steel group, controllers of Cía. Fundidora de Fierro y Acero de Monterrey, had laid the foundations for the family capitalism that still is so characteristic of the city.

Since its inception the industrial development of Monterrey has been influenced by its position as a frontier city. The lack of a large local market made it necessary for the city to become an export center both to other parts of Mexico and abroad. To meet competitive standards at the international level, its industries had to be efficient and technologically modern. Furthermore, the very nature of the leading sectors of the city's industries—iron and steel, smelting of minerals, brewery serving national markets, and glass products—were inconceivable without relatively high capital investment. Other more traditional industries producing for the national market could develop in smaller economic units and with a labor-intensive technology, but this was not the case of the leading sectors of the Monterrey economy. And the capital was largely self-generated, for even the most severe critics of Monterrey's family capitalists do not deny that they have continually reinvested a large part of the profits from their operations. The combination of wealth and ostentatious display so frequently found in Latin America is not characteristic of the "stingy" *regiomontanos.*

Thus, the three or four decades prior to 1910 were ones of prosperity and development, and this advancement is reflected in the population growth. In 1880 the city had an estimated 30,000 inhabitants. The number had increased to 79,000 in 1910, according to the national census (see Table 2-1). In the scale of urbanization of that era, a city of nearly 80,000 was a sizeable one; Mexico City had not yet reached the half-million mark. There were only twenty-nine cities over 20,000, and eight out of ten Mexicans lived in localities of less than 5,000 inhabitants. Of the largest Mexican cities, only Monterrey could be called an industrial city in the modern meaning of the term.[6]

The revolution of 1910 not only brought an end to *pax porfiriana,* but it also permanently altered the course of Mexican history. Since our task here is to account for the industrial development of Monterrey,

---

[6] The data on cities and urban populations in this chapter are taken from Harley L. Browning, "Urbanization in Mexico," Ph.D. Dissertation, University of California at Berkeley, 1962; Chap. 2.

TABLE 2-1. Growth of Metropolitan Areas of Monterrey and Mexico City, 1900–1965
(Population in Thousands)

Year	Monterrey	Percent Change	Mexico City	Percent Change
1900	62		345	
1910	79	27	471	36
1921	88	11	713	51
1930	134	52	1,029	44
1940	186	39	1,530	49
1950	356	91	2,830	85
1960	695	95	4,806	70
1965	950E			

SOURCE: Mexican census reports, 1900–1960. The 1965 estimate for Monterrey is by Romeo Madrigal, Centro de Investigaciones Económicas, Universidad de Nuevo León.

we cannot give a balanced account of the causes and consequences of this upheaval. Monterrey was not in the center of the military or political action, but the city naturally was seriously affected by the violent years that came after 1910. Steel production fell off dramatically and the railway, a prime target for military forces, was often times immobilized for long periods, creating havoc with the delivery of raw materials and the shipment of finished goods. Public order was disrupted, and the city was occupied several times by revolutionary troops. Despite these dislocations, the process of development launched in previous decades was not obliterated or reversed, but it was much slowed. The population of Monterrey even grew by 11 percent between 1910 and 1921, a time when the country's population, at least according to the admittedly incomplete census of 1921, declined by 6 percent. In the interval 1921–1930, a time when Mexico as a whole still was trying to recover from the effects of the previous decade, and the government was occupied with putting down various uprisings by military *caudillos,* Monterrey recorded an increase in population of 52 percent. It will be recalled that the city's economy was, to an extent unusual in Mexico, tied to developments abroad. Thus, during the 1920's exports increased under the stimulus of a boom in the American economy; with the result that, despite the continuation of internal political problems, there was relative prosperity.

The Great Depression hit Monterrey hard and demonstrated how dependent it was on the American and world economy. But in the last half of the thirties some recovery took place. During the presidential term of Lázaro Cárdenas (1934–1940) there was a good deal of government-stimulated demand, and, as Monterrey was the main national producer of steel, it provided for many national enterprises, such as the railroad system.

Although it can be argued that the political and economic changes that took place in Mexico during the twenties and thirties laid the groundwork for what was to follow, the real turning point of Mexican industrialization came only with the Second World War. It brought about, for one thing, effective protection for national manufacturers, because countries that traditionally exported manufactured goods to the Mexican market could no longer do so. Instead, some of them became customers for Mexican exports. Existing facilities were put to full use and, wherever possible, were enlarged. Exports to the United States were greatly increased. Furthermore, in 1944 the government introduced a system of direct import controls, thus protecting national manufacturing from foreign competition.

Mexico, particularly the metropolitan centers of Mexico City and Monterrey, was ready to take full advantage of war conditions and the new governmental policies. The value of manufacturing production tripled between 1939 and 1947, a formidable growth even allowing for the depreciation of the peso. One of the leading sectors was iron-and-steel production based in Monterrey. The United States could not produce iron in quantities large enough to satisfy its needs; instead of exporting iron to Mexico, the United States reversed its role and became an importer. Only since World War II has the metallurgical industry become the leading sector of Monterrey's economy.

The war-induced Mexican boom was assumed by many economists and others to be a temporary phenomenon. Somewhat to the surprise of everyone, the process of rapid industrialization launched during the war years has continued until the present day. The course of national development for this period was sketched in the preceding chapter.[7] Monterrey shared fully in the government-sponsored drive toward the industrialization of the country. The greatest impetus was provided during the presidential term of Alemán (1946–1952), but every subsequent president has put industrialization first among national goals. As

[7] See footnote 37 of Chapter 1 for references.

in so many countries, the iron-and-steel industry came to symbolize the goal of industrialization, and the Monterrey firms received direct and indirect help from the national government. The extensive highway construction program throughout the period helped to bring Monterrey into closer contact with the rest of the country.

Monterrey's role as a frontier city did not disappear in postwar times. On the contrary, there was an intensification of contacts with the United States. Trade between the two countries, originally stimulated by the war, has continued strong. Monterrey's position on the Laredo–Mexico City route, the main overland trade corridor between the two countries, was, of course, a gain. In the 1950's cotton became the single most important dollar-earning export, and a good deal of this production originated in northeastern Mexico. Monterrey's industrialization was much facilitated by the import of gas from the south Texas fields. And American investment increased in the Monterrey region, although proportionally not as much as in the Valley of Mexico. The postwar period has seen the emergence of tourism as a major feature of the economy. Monterrey is a convenient stop on the Pan American highway for those traveling to the heart of Mexico, and the city also has become a favorite destination, especially of Texans who want to go beyond the border towns but not to the center of Mexico. The bracero program was another form of Mexican–United States exchange that provided a net benefit for Monterrey.

One result of the contacts with the United States as well as internal development was that Nuevo León, like the other northern border states, was able to increase its population at a much faster rate than that of the country as a whole throughout the 1945–1965 period. This growth principally resulted from net in-migration to the state; most of it originating from states to the south.

The experiences of the country and of Monterrey have another parallel. The impressive expansion of the Monterrey economy evidently has not led to a more even distribution of income. In Chapter 1 the work of Ifigenia de Navarrete was cited to show that for the country as a whole there was an increase in the concentration of income between 1950 and 1963, the Gini coefficient of concentration rising from .50 to .55. In a 1965 survey carried out in Monterrey and sponsored by the Centro de Investigaciones Económicas of the University of Nuevo León, Jesús Puente Leyva found income to be highly concentrated, with the top 20 percent of Monterrey families receiving 56 percent of all income.[8] The Gini coefficient is .49, which is lower than that for Mexico as a whole, but the latter includes a large bloc of subsistence farmers who do much to raise the index of concentration. (Evidence from other large cities in Mexico suggests that Mexico City has a somewhat higher degree of concentration than Monterrey, but Guadalajara is substantially lower in this respect.) Puente Leyva believes that the degree of income concentration in Monterrey probably has not changed greatly in recent decades, and whatever change has occurred has been toward an even greater concentration. Certainly the small group of top family capitalists in Monterrey has enormous income. No one knows their exact net worth, but they control enterprises whose assets are in the hundreds of millions of dollars.

Monterrey and Mexican Regional Differences

A prominent feature of Mexico's economic development during the past generation has been its regional unevenness. This trend is not unusual, for, in most countries experiencing development, change has tended to be concentrated in a few rather than all regions. The result is that the gap between the leading and the lagging regions within a country widens rather than diminishes during the early stages of development.[9]

One way of demonstrating this regional inequality and how it has changed over time is to examine the level of urbanization. While not a direct measure of economic development, urbanization is clearly related to the process. In Table 2-2 the percent of the population living in places twenty thousand and over (an unequivocal designation of "urban" in Mexico) is presented for the country as a whole, for the North region (made up of ten states), and the South region (three states). In 1900 both the North and the South were below the national average. By 1940 the North had drawn slightly ahead of the country, while the South had actually declined from its already extremely low level of urbanization at the beginning of the century. In 1960 the North had pulled well ahead of the country and had reached a level of urbanization comparable to that of most developed countries. The South,

---

[8] Jesús Puente Leyva, *Distribución del ingreso en un área urbana: El caso de Monterrey, Mexico.*

[9] An insightful discussion of regional disparities in Mexican development, including comments on the factors affecting the relative success of Monterrey and Saltillo, is to be found in Paul Lamartine Yates, *El desarrollo regional de México.*

TABLE 2-2. Urbanization in Mexico and Two Regions (Percent of Population Living in Places 20,000+)

Year	Country	North [a]	South [b]
1900	9	7	3
1910	11	9	3
1921	13	13	3
1930	16	17	2
1940	18	19	2
1950	26	30	5
1960	33	42	8
Percent of change, 1900–1960	267	500	167

SOURCE: Mexican census reports, 1900–1960.
[a] States of Baja California Norte, Baja California Sur, Chihuahua, Coahuila, Durango, Nayarit, Nuevo León, Sinaloa, Sonora, and Tamaulipas.
[b] States of Chiapas, Colima, Guerrero, and Oaxaca.

if we were to look only at the percent gain from its 1940 base, had a most impressive quadrupling of its proportion in places twenty thousand and above, much better than the North, which scarcely more than doubled. But of course this is highly deceptive, being an artifact of the extremely low origin base of the South. During the twenty years the North added 23 percentage points, the South only 6. Put another way, the percentage point difference between the South and the North in 1940 was 17; in 1960 it was 35. Regionally then, the gap has continued to widen, despite the continued overall national growth.

Paul Lamartine Yates has demonstrated this disparity conclusively, using a variety of data. For example, the total accumulated investment per capita (industrial, commercial, and infrastructural) for the period 1946–1955 averaged 4,920 pesos for the three states of the Northeast (Coahuila, Nuevo León, and Tamaulipas), while the South (Chiapas, Guerrero, and Oaxaca) averaged only 636 pesos. These regional differences are pervasive, ranging from educational attainment to productivity per worker to consumption indices. Doubtless, among major countries of the world, Mexico now ranks high in extent of regional differences. It is, therefore, indispensable for an understanding of our study of Monterrey to be aware that it is located within a region that is among the most advanced in all of Mexico. Yet, even within the most advanced regions and states there is considerable diversity, as will be demonstrated in the following chapter.

There is another aspect of Mexican development that bears not only on regionalism and economic growth but also more directly upon the place of Monterrey in the national structure, specifically in the Mexican urban hierarchy. Mexico, in common with nearly all the other countries of Latin America, is a centralized country, and this centralization is readily observable in the prominence of the first city. An examination of the urban hierarchy of Mexico shows that Mexico City is much larger than any of the other major cities of the country; in the past fifty years it has ranged from five to seven times the population of the second city, Guadalajara. This demographic dominance reflects Mexico City's political, economic, and cultural dominance within the country. This condition, one that has been termed "high primacy" by Kingsley Davis,[10] has been a characteristic feature of Mexico since before the conquest. It has also been a cumulative process, with the capital city gathering to it a large variety of activities under the varying conditions of the colonial, independence, and postrevolutionary periods. The Valley of Mexico is not endowed with natural resources so as to encourage the development of manufacturing, but because of its commanding position (not the least of which is by far the country's greatest concentration of consumers) it has been so successful in attracting industry that it accounts for over 50 percent of the value added for Mexico as a whole—an astonishing concentration for a country as large in population and area and as advanced in development as Mexico.

This is not the place to detail the ways in which Mexico City is dominant, nor to describe the mechanisms by which this dominance was attained.[11] For us, what is important is to indicate Monterrey's place vis-à-vis Mexico City. Compared with a number of other important cities of Mexico, Monterrey has escaped some, if by no means all, the negative consequences of Mexico City's dominance. Several factors help to explain this situation, some of which have already been introduced. One is simply the distance separating the two places. While Monterrey's peripheral position to the bulk of the population of Mexico was and still is a handicap in many ways, the one thousand kilometers that separate it from the capital city have made it impossible for the latter

10 Kingsley Davis, *Las causas y efectos del fenómeno de primacía urbana con referencia especial a América Latina.*
11 See Browning, "Urbanization in Mexico," Chaps. 6 and 7.

to include Monterrey within its own hinterland, a fate that some other cities, such as Puebla and Querétaro, did not escape. Second, Monterrey essentially is a "new" city postdating the colonial era, and it is not encumbered by some of the institutional impediments to rapid growth that have continued to hold back some of the cities of the central plateau. Third, being on the frontier has encouraged a spirit of independence and a willingness to go it alone instead of looking to the federal government in Mexico City for help and guidance. In this respect Monterrey bears a family resemblance to Medellín in Colombia and São Paulo in Brazil, two other instances where impressive economic growth has been pushed forward in a provincial center in spite of, or perhaps even because of, the fact that it was not the capital city.[12] Fourth, the ability to compete implied in the last point is in part due to Monterrey's continuous orientation to external markets, both within and without the country. Fifth, Monterrey has been able to generate internally, by and large, the capital needed to fuel her industrial expansion and has not been dependent upon the great financial institutions in Mexico City. Indeed, at the present time Monterrey is in a position to export capital to other growing areas of Mexico, even to Guadalajara. In short, for a variety of reasons Monterrey has achieved a measure of economic autonomy that is still relatively rare in Mexico.

The Economic Structure of Monterrey

Having sketched some of the historical and regional factors affecting Monterrey's development, we are now ready for a more detailed account of the economic structure of the city at or about the time of the study in 1965. Monterrey's reputation as an industrial center is reflected in its labor force statistics: in a 1966 survey 44 percent of the economically active male population was employed in manufacturing. Besides its importance as the main source of employment in Monterrey, the manufacturing sector also is the most productive one in the city. As a matter of fact, manufacturing productivity per worker is probably the highest in the country. Data are not available on a city basis, but for 1960 the census of industry figures of value added in pesos per worker in mining and manufacturing by states was as shown in Table 2-3. It should be noted that, while productivity per worker in large enterprises

---

[12] Albert O. Hirschman comments on this phenomenon in *The Strategy of Economic Development,* p. 186.

TABLE 2-3. Productivity per Worker in Mining and Manufacturing

Area	All Enterprises	Enterprises with up to Six Workers	Enterprises with Six Workers or More
Nuevo León (Monterrey)	84,598	35,405	87,512
Distrito Federal (Mexico City)	64,770	52,211	65,784
Mexico (country)	62,579	40,398	64,711

SOURCE: Dirección General de Estadistica, *VII Censo industrial 1961: Resumen general* (Mexico City, 1965), Table 2.

is substantially greater in Monterrey than in Mexico City, the reverse is true for the smaller enterprises.

Almost 40 percent of the employed males in manufacturing in our representative sample work in metallurgical or metallurgy-related industries. Some 10 percent work in iron foundries, steel mills, and metal-refining industries. Cía. Fundidora alone employs some six thousand workers. A second steel factory was created more recently. Although its product is also important, it employs considerably fewer workers because it is more automated. In any case, the type of production and marketing conditions prevalent in the industry make it necessary for Monterrey's steel companies to be technologically sophisticated and to maintain production at sufficiently high levels to ensure an adequate return on the high capital investment.

Since basic metallurgical industries have important backward and forward linkages, many industries that use steel and steel products as a major input have established their plants in Monterrey. Presently these enterprises produce machinery, household appliances, and transportation equipment, and they employ more people than does basic metallurgy. The largest part of the production of these industries is not consumed locally but is exported to other regions of the country and abroad. These enterprises can compete effectively with those in the capital city in part because of their proximity to their main input, steel and steel products. They are all relatively large and modern for the same reasons given above for basic metallurgy.

Another important manufacturing activity, accounting for 14 percent of the employment in this sector, is the production of nonmetallic mineral products—glass, concrete, ceramics, and clay products—principally for industrial and construction use. The development of the glass industry was an offshoot of the brewery business and was favored by access to cheap natural gas from Texas fields, available since the thirties. As a rule, these factories also operate under scale economies and are large and modern. Although the particular historic and economic determinants of the location of other major plants in Monterrey vary considerably (brewery, chemicals, cigarettes), they too are technologically modern.

In summary, because of historical reasons, proximity to sources of energy and raw materials, and linkage effects, the manufacturing sector of the Monterrey economy has a proportionately large number of very big and modern enterprises with high capital inputs and supplying markets mainly outside the city.[13] By contrast, the establishment of industries in Mexico City, whether by native or foreign capital, was primarily a response to a large and rapidly growing local market. With a population in excess of eight million inhabitants, Mexico City proportionately has far more than its share of the purchasing power of the nation. Monterrey has only somewhat over one million inhabitants and nowhere near the wealth that is concentrated in the capital. Consequently, it is understandable why Monterrey mainly is a center for the production of capital goods, while Mexico City is a center for the production of consumption goods. Save for the prominent exceptions of the brewery, a cigarette factory, and a cookie company, consumption goods industries only recently have begun to develop in Monterrey, and many are branches of national or international companies.

But not all manufacturing establishments in Monterrey are large and modern. Recall that, while Monterrey was above the national average in worker productivity for enterprises with six or more workers, it was below the average for establishments with fewer than six workers. Side by side with large factories producing for national and international markets are a large number of small and inefficient producers. In this sense we can speak of Monterrey as having a bimodal manufacturing structure. Thus, the "dual" aspect of the economies of cities

[13] An analysis of some of the entrepreneurial decision-making processes that lead to technological innovation and high capitalization in Monterrey and other cities is found in Paul Strassman, *Technological Change and Economic Development: The Manufacturing Experience of Mexico and Puerto Rico.*

in developing areas is also present in Monterrey, although that city is exceptional in the importance of its modern manufacturing sector. Characteristic of the small light manufacturers are those units in food processing and garment manufacture that in effect have replaced household activities. Tortillas are not made any more within the home. The housewife has the alternative of buying tortillas from a *tortillería*, or getting the corn ground into *masa* by mills, *molinos de nixtamal*. These establishments are densely scattered through the working-class neighborhoods of the city. They supply their local clientele with the help of unsophisticated machines operated by a few unskilled workers. Similar arrangements can be found in the small establishments turning out clothing that formerly was made at home. In aggregate, such industries are not insignificant in their employment, but the size of the establishment and the technology employed are uniformly low.

When we turn to the other sectors of the economy we do not find to nearly the same degree the modern technology characteristic in the main of the manufacturing sector. The most striking contrast is with the construction industry, the employer of 10 percent of the adult economically active males. This sector has generally low capital inputs and the highest proportion of unskilled labor. The main reason to explain this fact, by no means peculiar to Monterrey but common throughout the country, is that construction technologically is a flexible sector, where various combinations of capital and labor are feasible. Since capital traditionally has been scarce and labor abundant, especially low-skilled labor, it is often cheaper to use fewer mechanical devices and more "hands." And architecturally modern buildings can be erected with rather primitive construction techniques. Furthermore, economic fluctuations affect the construction industry quite drastically, and it always has been easier to lay off workers (who with few exceptions are not unionized) than to keep expensive machinery idle. It is no surprise, therefore, that among the nonagricultural sectors of the Mexican economy construction has experienced the lowest gains in productivity over the past several decades.[14] Work on construction projects constitutes a main source of jobs for workers with no previous industrial experience and with low educational levels—a description

[14] A. J. Jaffe, *People, Jobs, and Economic Development*. For conditions in the construction industry in Latin America as a whole, see ECLA, "Structural Changes in Employment within the Context of Latin America's Economic Development," *Economic Bulletin for Latin America* 10, no. 2 (October 1965): 163–187.

fitting most men of farm background recently arrived in the city. They must take what they can get, with the result that wages, job stability, and career advancement are much poorer in construction than they are in manufacturing.

Commerce is an important source of employment (16 percent of male labor force) and is an interesting contrast to manufacturing. Whereas the latter is characterized by large and modern enterprises, the commerce sector, if we exempt financial activities whose important firms are either affiliated with the large industrial complexes of Monterrey or are branches of organizations whose main offices are located in Mexico City, is nearly synonymous with "petty commerce." There are only two or three large department stores, one of them a local branch of the American Sears chain, whose main offices are in Mexico City. Stores catering to middle- and upper-class clients are almost entirely lacking. Probably most of the middle-size and relatively elegant stores in Monterrey depend mainly upon the tourist trade. This leaves the large number of small *tiendas de abarrotes* (grocery stores) and *misceláneas* (stores selling a little of everything: fruits, household supplies, and what not) catering to the working-class market. They tend to be one-man or at least one-family enterprises.

One consequence of the weak development of commerce, as well as the corresponding lack of specialized services, is that visitors sometimes are surprised to learn that Monterrey has arrived at the "million" category. Certainly the core of the city, the downtown area, seems unimpressive for a city of that size. But a lack of tall and impressive downtown buildings is not the heart of the matter, nor can we simply attribute it to the fact that Monterrey has a great many low-income people among its population—so does Mexico City or, more appropriately, Guadalajara.

Why does Monterrey sometimes give the impression of being a big little city? The answer lies, in part, in the fact that it is an industrial center, and there is still a suggestion of the factory town about it, although this is fading rapidly. More important is the fact that, while Monterrey is the undisputed regional capital of northeastern Mexico, one of the most developed regions of Mexico, the "central place" advantages accruing to it are less than would be expected. For one thing, there simply isn't a large hinterland population needing Monterrey's goods and services. But even the population that does exist is largely lost to Monterrey's merchants because of the United States border. The same border that was instrumental in the commercial and industrial development of Monterrey now has handicapped, to the point of almost crippling, its commercial development. Not only do retailers in south Texas draw away those customers in northeastern Mexico who otherwise might have been attracted to Monterrey, but there also is precious little consumer loyalty in that city itself. Most of middle- and upper-class Monterrey citizens do a major part of their shopping for items other than food in the towns across the border. Prices, quality, and, perhaps, prestige account for the strong preference for American rather than Mexican goods. Continuing efforts on the part of the local chamber of commerce and even of the national government to change these habits have had little success. The poverty in both the number and the variety of retail outlets in Monterrey is a consequence of this situation. Monterrey by virtue of its size merits the designation "metropolitan," but it clearly is not as metropolitan in the range of goods and services provided as would be expected when based upon size alone.

The service sector is the remaining sector to be considered. It employs about one-fourth of the economically active population of Monterrey. However, it employs 48 percent of all employed females but only 17 percent of all males in the labor force. This distinction is quite important, since many females in this sector are employed in domestic service, the lowest paid and least prestigeful of female urban employment. Many men in this sector also are to be found in low-paying and low-status jobs.

Public bureaucracy, an important source of middle-income jobs in Mexico City, is not so important in Monterrey, for the state and municipal bureaucracies are relatively small. Local and state revenues in Mexico are much smaller than federal revenues, and local and state governments simply have a very small weight in the economy. Professional and educational services, although numerically of some importance in Monterrey (there are two universities), are proportionally smaller than in Mexico City.

This account of the major sectors of the Monterrey economy has shown that some men are in technologically advanced environments while others are not. The size of the enterprise where they work may be taken as an indicator of "modern" versus "traditional" components of the labor force. Size is a good if not infallible indicator of bureaucratization and level of technological efficiency. Large enterprises will have, on the average, a more intricate and sophisticated division of labor, higher capital inputs, and higher productivity per worker. Table 2-4 shows the distribution of the representative sample of men ages 21 to 60 by size of enterprise. One-third of the men are employed in enterprises with over two hundred persons, undoubtedly the highest percentage one could find in any large Mexican city. At the other extreme 11 percent are self-employed. Roughly speaking, a third of our men are employed in very small enterprises (five persons or less), and another third are in quite large ones. Consequently, the designation of Monterrey as characterized by large-scale and technologically advanced industry, while true, should not be used to describe the conditions of work of the entire male labor force.

The Occupational Structure of Monterrey

So far our account has taken metropolitan Monterrey as the unit of analysis. We have followed its efforts to grow and become a large city and to improve its position vis-à-vis such competitors as Saltillo and Mexico City. We have examined the main sectors of its economy in terms of such considerations as technology and size of enterprise. Turning to the occupational structure, we still are concerned with typifying the city, but we are now closer to the subject matter that will occupy us throughout the remainder of the book: men and their jobs.

Before entering into a description of the detailed components of the occupational structure, it is worthwhile to consider a more general feature, namely, the relatively low degree of bureaucratization in terms of the number of white-collar occupations in Monterrey. As noted, large and modern enterprises prevail in the manufacturing sector. Generally speaking, the more modern the technology, the higher the ratio

TABLE 2-4. Distribution of Men, by Size of Enterprise

Number in Enterprise	Percent of Respondents
1	11
2–5	19
6–20	14
21–200	23
201+	33
Total	100
	(1,454) a

a Excluded are 186 cases with no information.

of white-collar to blue-collar workers. Fully automated factories, for example, employ few manual workers and many technicians, clerical workers, and sales people. However, Dale B. Truett has shown for selected industries that, although productivity per worker is higher in Monterrey than in Mexico City, the ratio of white-collar to blue-collar workers tends to be smaller. He suggests two reasons for this unexpected finding: "First, large companies which have plants both in the Center (Mexico City) and in Nuevo León (Monterrey) will tend to concentrate their administrative and executive personnel in Mexico City for obvious reasons. Second, economic and industrial life is simply more complex in the larger of the two areas. For example, coordination in the field of transport and distribution must require more administrative (not necessarily technical) personnel in the Center than in Nuevo León."[15] We may add to his second reason that complexity is greater when the product is sold to a relatively large number of smaller clients (Mexico City) than when it is exported to a few large purchasers abroad or to other regions of the country (Monterrey).

These two sources of underrepresentation of white-collar workers and technicians in manufacturing may, with some modifications, be extended to other activities. Banks and department stores, for example, tend to be branches of national companies whose main offices are located in Mexico City.

The service sector traditionally supplies a substantial number of white-collar occupations. But here again the situation of Monterrey is rather exceptional among cities of its size class. Both public and private bureaucracies are relatively underdeveloped, providing relatively fewer positions for clerks and professionals when compared to service laborers. In both cases this is in part a result of Monterrey being a provincial city in a country with a long tradition of political and administrative concentration in the capital city.

Another reason for expecting a relatively small proportion of white-collar workers in Monterrey lies in the peculiar situation of commerce already described. Store owners and salesmen generally contribute greatly to the white-collar population. However, most "owners" in Monterrey have one-man stores, and the salesmen, especially in food, are quite close to street vendors, an occupational category that Melvin M.

---

[15] Dale B. Truett, "Productivity Differences in Like Industries in Mexico's Major Areas of Industrial Concentration," unpublished manuscript, 1964.

Tumin and Arnold S. Feldman rightly have called "blue-collar sales-men."[16] In other words, the economic organization of commerce in Monterrey until now has not favored the emergence of a proportionally important middle-class sector.

The occupational distribution of the representative sample of males ages 21 to 60 working in the Monterrey Metropolitan Area in 1965 is given in Table 2-5. For each occupational group two other items of information are presented to help in evaluating the characteristics of these occupations. For some time the Mexican government has attempted to set a minimum legal wage.[17] Since no sanctions are applied to those who pay below this rate, it serves only as a standard for what should be the lowest payment for a full-time work week among manual workers. There are regional differences reflecting cost-of-living differences throughout Mexico, and the figures periodically are reviewed and revised upward. In 1965 the minimum legal wage established by the government for the Monterrey Metropolitan Area was 145 pesos a week. (The conversion rate is 12.50 pesos per U.S. dollar.) Because of coding procedures, in the second column of Table 2-5 we use a somewhat higher figure of 163 pesos (13 dollars). Roughly speaking, the percentages in the column indicate the proportion of men in each occupational category earning the recommended legal minimum wage or less. As such, it is an indicator of the concentration of the economically marginal men in the major occupational groups. Finally, the third column presents the proportion of men in each occupational group whose community of origin (defined as the place where they lived most of the time between the ages of 5 and 15) was rural.

This table includes information about a select part of the total economically active population. Females, who on the average have much lower positions than males in the occupational hierarchy, are excluded. A survey carried out in Monterrey in 1964 showed that 52 percent of working females earned less than 150 pesos a week.[18] Also excluded from our sample are the very young and the very old, both characteristically underemployed and earning low incomes. According to the

16 Melvin M. Tumin and Arnold S. Feldman, *Social Class and Social Change in Puerto Rico.*
17 This is done on a yearly basis by the Comisión Nacional de los Salarios Mínimos.
18 See Jesús Puente Leyva, "Estructura de la ocupación y el nivel de los salarios en el área metropolitana de Monterrey," in *El salario mínimo en Monterrey.*

TABLE 2-5. Distribution of Males, by Occupational Groups and Selected
Characteristics, Monterrey Metropolitan Area

Occupational Groups	Percent Distribution	Percent Earning Minimum Legal Wage or Less	Percent Rural Community of Origin
Nonmanual			
Professionals	4	1	10
Technicians	3	15	7
Managers and proprietors	5	0	17
Office workers	4	11	19
Sales agents, salesmen	4	0	17
Retail salesmen, food	3	20	54
Supervisors	4	2	26
Upper manual			
Vehicle operators	7	25	28
Operatives and craftsmen, manufacturing	23	18	24
Operatives and craftsmen, construction	3	7	31
Lower manual			
Unskilled production workers	9	63	30
Construction laborers	6	86	54
Service workers	9	44	30
Janitors, watchmen, stevedores	8	53	52
Street vendors	4	64	58
Others	2	53	35
Total	100 (1,623)[a]	30 (1,623)[a]	30 (1,623)[a]

SOURCE: Representative sample.
[a] Excluded are 17 cases who were not in the labor force.

same source, 71 percent of the workers between ages 14 and 20 earned less than 150 pesos. Among those aged 21 to 49, the corresponding percentage was 33, and it was 59 percent for workers 50 years and over. (In all cases figures are for both sexes.)

The first five occupational groups in the table undoubtedly are white collar. They comprise about one-fifth of the total. (The proportion of white-collar workers among the entire economically active population, including females and young and old workers, is smaller.) Two categories—office workers and salesmen—are quite small, given the overall level of economic development of the city. As explained in the previous section, there are several reasons to account for this fact.

The various "sales" categories require some comment. Even disregarding street vendors, there are almost as many salesmen in food (3 percent) as all other salesmen (retail nonfood and wholesaling) taken together. This comparison shows quite clearly the meager development of commercial activities in Monterrey.

Probably the most impressive feature of Table 2-5 is the large proportion of all men working as operatives and craftsmen in manufacturing, 23 percent. The ratio of skilled workers in manufacturing to unskilled production workers is quite high: 2.7 to 1. Compare this, however, with the situation in construction. For each operative or craftsman in construction there are two laborers. This ratio confirms what has already been noted: the manufacturing sector is much more mechanized and relies heavily upon workers with some training, while the construction industry relies more on large numbers of unskilled men using their physical strength.

A considerable number of men are employed in occupations that demand almost no skills and that are unrelated to the process of production in manufacturing and construction: janitors and stevedores, service workers, and street vendors. The men in these categories, plus construction laborers, constitute the bottom of the male occupational hierarchy in Monterrey. They constitute more than a quarter (28 percent) of the sample. They have jobs that pay poorly and have low security of employment. In all these categories, save service workers, a substantial majority earn less than 163 pesos a week. It may appear that unskilled production workers should also be added to this bottom grouping, since nearly two-thirds of them earn less than 163 pesos a week. However, as will be shown in a subsequent chapter, many unskilled production workers are relatively young and with time will considerably improve their earnings. Their chances for occupational advancement are much better than for those men working as street vendors, construction laborers, and the like. The low salaries of unskilled production workers reflect their recent entry into the labor force rather than the low productivity of their jobs.

Overall, 30 percent of all men earn close to or below the minimum wage. With the exception of unskilled production workers, one may consider that all occupational categories where a substantial proportion of men earn such low wages constitute sectors marginal to the modern economic structure of Monterrey. One is tempted to predict that as this process continues these sectors will become smaller, although never eliminated. Whether this is to happen, however, will depend not only upon the economic opportunities within the city but also upon the volume of migrants to Monterrey, particularly those with limited education and skills. Their presence in Monterrey affects the total economy, since they tend to push down wages. These men are eager to take any sort of job, since most positions open to them are highly unstable and represent endemic underemployment.

A look at the third column of Table 2-5 shows that many of the marginal occupational categories have a high proportion of men from rural backgrounds. None of the occupational categories is completely closed to men of farm background. Ten percent of the professionals have this origin. Salesmen in food retailing, an occupational group not very low in the hierarchy, at least in the percent with low earnings, has one of the highest proportions of migrants from rural areas. This is one of the activities most transferable from the rural to the urban environment, and it is traditional in this sense. The pattern of food retailing may be "marginal" in the sense of not being part of the modern industrial structure, but it is fully integrated in the sense that the main market of these food merchants (the working classes) is a product of that industrial structure. And, of course, this category is upgraded by the exclusion of street vendors. In any event the expansion of supermarkets into working-class areas and an increase in the purchasing power of that class eventually will drive many of these small food proprietors out of business.

The Historical Context of the Monterrey Men

The lives of our Monterrey men encompass a momentous period in Mexican history. A few were born before the beginning of the Mexican revolution, and a larger number will live to see the arrival of the twenty-first century. Throughout the twentieth century the country will have been transformed from a classic type of undeveloped country to one that by the year 2000 should be found within the ranks of industrial nations.

In Table 2-6, for each of the four birth cohorts used in this study, some salient features of the economy and society are given at birth and also twenty years later, when nearly all the men have entered the labor force. The last three cohorts arrived to manhood under the economically favorable conditions of the late Cárdenas era and World War II and beyond. Only the earliest cohort was much affected by the disruptions following the revolution and the Great Depression. In other words, the work experience of the Monterrey men predominantly took place within the national context of an expanding economy.

The national context is important, but it need not reflect the life circumstances of the men themselves. We know that the context of those who were born and grew up in Monterrey was one of intense economic growth. Only in Mexico City has there been a comparable development of industry. But, of course, not all the men grew up and spent their entire work lives in Monterrey. What were the conditions of those who did not? It is to this question that we turn in the following chapter.

TABLE 2-6. Schematic Depiction of National and Local Conditions at Time of Birth and Twenty Years Later for Each of Four Birth Cohorts

Birth Cohort	Conditions at Birth	Conditions at Age 20
1905–1914	Last years of *porfiriato*; first period of revolution	Establishment of more stable government; Great Depression
1915–1924	Last years of fighting; period of reconstruction	The Cárdenas era; World War II and economic boom
1925–1934	Establishment of more stable government; Great Depression	Industrialization and development of national infrastructure
1935–1944	The Cárdenas era; World War II and economic boom	Korean War boom; foreign investment; tourism

3. Characteristics of Communities
of Origin of Migrants to Monterrey

If Monterrey were a city whose population growth came very predominantly from within, that is, by natural increase (births minus deaths), then the discussion of Monterrey's historical development and economic structure would suffice to set the stage for the analysis in the rest of the book. But of course Monterrey is not self-contained in its demographic growth. Far from it. Any urban center that has grown as rapidly as Monterrey in the course of the last generation—springing from 186,000 in 1940 to an estimated 950,000 at the time of the survey in 1965—cannot have done it by natural increase alone.

The growth was fed from three sources: areal expansion, natural increase, and net in-migration. First, we are dealing with the metropolitan area of Monterrey. In 1940 it included only the *municipio* of Monterrey (an areal unit whose closest approximation in the United States is the county). But by 1965 the expansion of the built-up area of the agglomeration had overflowed the limits of the Monterrey *municipio* to include four adjacent ones: Santa Catarina, Garza García, San Nicolás, and Guadalupe. The physical expansion of Monterrey has made a contribution independent of natural increase and net in-migration, but compared to them it has been comparatively minor. Luis

Unikel has analyzed the contribution of natural increase and net in-migration for the *municipio* of Monterrey alone (it contains over 80 percent of the total 1965 metropolitan population) between 1940 and 1960.[1] He estimates that, of the 5.9 per annum growth rate between 1940 and 1950, 3.6 was due to net in-migration or 61 percent of the total. The corresponding figures for the 1950–1960 decade were 6.3, 3.3, and 52 percent. Extrapolating the trend to the 1960–1965 period, we can assume that net in-migration dipped somewhat below 50 percent. Therefore, excluding the effect of the geographic expansion of the Monterrey Metropolitan Area, we can conclude that for the entire twenty-five–year period net in-migration accounted for roughly half the growth of population.

For our sample—men aged 21–60—migration is much more important. Only 30 percent of the representative sample was born in Monterrey.[2] The difference between the figures for the sample of men aged 21–60 and for the total population is to be accounted for by the fact that the young age group (under 21) represents more than one-half the total population of Monterrey, and the great majority of this group were born in Monterrey. Most of the migrants have children after their arrival to the city, and they contribute importantly to the natural increase component.

We will be preoccupied throughout this book with differences between natives and migrants. Place of birth is the most common criterion used to separate natives and migrants in many studies, particularly those based upon census data. Therefore, it appears that 70 percent of our men fall into the migrant category. But we are not satisfied to rely upon the "accident" of birth to make this extremely important, for our purposes, distinction. A man born a few weeks before his parents mi-

[1] See Luis Unikel, "El proceso de urbanización en México: Distribución y crecimiento de la población urbana," *Demografía y Economía* 2, no. 2 (1968): 139–182. For other Latin American cities see Eduardo E. Arriaga, "Components of City Growth in Selected Latin American Countries," *Milbank Memorial Fund Quarterly* 46, no. 2, pt. 1 (January 1968): 237–252.

[2] A high proportion of adult inhabitants born outside the city is apparently typical of fast-growing cities in Latin America. Alan B. Simmons reports that 72 percent of the population aged 15–59 of Bogotá, Colombia, was born elsewhere. See his *The Emergence of Planning Orientations in a Modernizing Community: Migration, Adaptation, and Family Planning in Highland Colombia*. Juan C. Elizaga provides a detailed examination of Santiago, Chile, in *Migraciones a las áreas metropolitanas de América Latina*.

grated with him to Monterrey would be classed as migrant, although all his sentient experience took place in that metropolitan center. We believe that a sociologically more relevant distinction is required. It has already been introduced in the last chapter, but we have not commented extensively on it: community of origin—where the individual spent the largest part of his formative years, taken here as the period between the ages five and fifteen.[3] It is during this age interval that individuals acquire their basic orientation to the world outside the family circle as well as the fundamentals of their formal education. In the representative sample, 16 percent of the men were born outside Monterrey but grew up in that place. We choose to call this group natives by adoption. Using as a criterion community of origin, 54 percent of our representative sample are to be considered migrants. The question immediately arises, "Where do these migrants to Monterrey come from?"

Source of Migrants

Let us begin with a classification by community size class. In Table 3-1 the distribution of migrants to Monterrey is given for four size classes plus "foreign" (mainly from the United States), which is not classified by size. (For purposes of comparison, the distributions for community of birth and community of last residence before migrating to Monterrey also are given, but they will not be commented upon at this point.) Several features of the classification require comment. We choose to make the break between rural and urban at the 5,000 point. What should numerically constitute the break between rural and urban in Mexico has been the subject of debate for some time. The Mexican census criterion is 2,500, a figure that probably was borrowed from that used by the U.S. Bureau of the Census. Most authorities are in agreement that the figure is not appropriate for the Mexican milieu, it being too low. Rural Mexico is largely composed of village settlements. Many of these villages in recent decades have grown much beyond the 2,500 figure while retaining their agrarian character. To call them

3 Other investigators have defined community of origin somewhat differently than we have here. Seymour M. Lipset and Reinhard Bendix, in their Oakland mobility study (*Social Mobility in Industrial Society*), asked respondents where they lived most of the time between ages 13 and 19. Peter M. Blau and Otis D. Duncan in *The American Occupational Structure* take the community their men were living in at age 16.

urban makes little sense. It has been suggested that "urban" in Mexico should be at the 10,000, 15,000, or even 20,000 mark.[4] Any of these is clearly preferable to 2,500. We have chosen to use the figure of 5,000 because of our focus on northern Mexico rather than the country as a whole. In the arid North, large villages common to most of the rest of Mexico are not frequently found. The great bulk of settlements with a population of 5,000 or over display urban characteristics.

One more feature of the community size classification needs to be explained. When it was coded for each respondent, the population was not entered as of one particular date—the census year of 1960. The respondent's community of birth, of origin, and any other places he may have lived in are classified according to the population at the census year nearest to the time the respondent lived there.

TABLE 3-1. Distribution of Monterrey Men According to Community of Birth, Community of Origin, and last Community Resided in Prior to Migrating to Monterrey, by Size Class of Community (In Percent)

Community Size Class	Community of Birth	Community of Origin	Last Residence before Monterrey
Rural (up to 5,000)	44	30	26
Small urban (5,000–19,999)	14	11	10
Medium urban (20,000–99,999)	10	9	12
Large urban (100,000 and over)	2	2	9
Foreign (size unspecified)	1	1	4
Monterrey	30	46	40[a]
Total	101 (1,635)[b]	99 (1,634)[b]	101 (1,632)[b]

SOURCE: Representative sample.

[a] Monterrey is community of origin, no subsequent migration.

[b] Excluded are 5, 6, and 8 cases, respectively, with no information.

[4] Unikel believes that fifteen thousand is the best single cutting point for Mexico as a whole ("Ensayo sobre una nueva clasificación de población rural y urbana en México," *Demografía y Economía* 2 [1968]: 1–18).

Table 3-1 leaves no doubt that the majority of migrants to Monterrey have their origins in small communities, with well over one-half coming from rural ones. A mere 4 percent originated in metropolitan centers of 100,000 or more. This ought not surprise us, for Mexico has been an agrarian country, and very predominantly so, until the last few decades. Although the North, as we saw in the previous chapter, is more urbanized that the country as a whole, it too has been mainly rural until the last decade. When we think of migrants to Monterrey, therefore, we will have rural-to-urban ones mainly in mind, although an important proportion of them do have urban backgrounds.

An important and unexpected feature of place of origin by size class is not given in Table 3-1. When we divide the migrants into groups by time of first arrival to Monterrey, the percent with rural community of origin is shown in Table 3-2. Among the most recent cohorts, there is a higher proportion of rural migrants; but during the same period Mexico urbanized rapidly, and the rural sector declined. Between 1940 and 1960 the proportion in rural places in the country dropped from 72 to 56 percent, and the North has had a greater proportionate drop. Why do migrants to Monterrey show an opposing trend? It is partially due to the decreasing selectivity of migrants to Monterrey, a subject to be fully explored in Chapter 6.

What about the geographic origins of the migrants? Four states abut on Nuevo León: Coahuila to the west, Tamaulipas to the east, San Luis Potosí to the south, and Zacatecas to the southwest. Including Nuevo León, these five states account for over four-fifths (81.4 percent) of all migrants to Monterrey. Thus, proximity is related to migration. But the states are large in area and the distance from Monterrey to the outer limits of most of them exceeds five hundred kilometers.

The five states providing the great bulk of migrants to Monterrey differ considerably in their levels of social and economic development.

TABLE 3-2. Time of First Arrival of Men with Rural Community of Origin

Time-of-First-Arrival Cohort	Percent Rural Community of Origin
Before 1941	54
1941–1950	51
1951–1960	59
1961–1965	60

Using the "well being" index developed by Yates (made up of an
unweighted average of ten indicators, including such diverse items as
mortality, teacher-student ratio, social security coverage, and per capita consumption of sugar and gasoline),[5] the states rank among the
thirty-two states and territories of the republic in 1960 as shown in
Table 3-3. By ranking on the well-being index and in level of urbanization, there is a clear separation of the three border states (Nuevo
León, Coahuila, and Tamaulipas) and the two states of the Old North
(San Luis Potosí, and Zacatecas), which have not shared to any extent
the industrial boom since World War II. The first three are close to the
top of the hierarchy and the last two are near the bottom.

We know, however, that states are heterogeneous in the socioeconomic characteristics of their subareas. We can base our analysis of these
characteristics on the work done by the Comisión Nacional de los Salarios Mínimos.[6] It grouped the country's thousands of *municipios* into 111
relatively homogeneous socioeconomic groupings called *zonas*. Claudio
Stern then ranked all of the *zonas* according to three 1960 census indicators of economic development: percent urban (places 2,500+); percent of the labor force in secondary and tertiary activities; and per
capita worker income.[7] For the purposes of the Monterrey study the
111 *zonas* were reduced to 77, mainly by combining *zonas* in parts of
the country remote from Monterrey.

TABLE 3-3. Characteristics of States Contributing Most Migrants to Monterrey

State	Rank on Well-Being Index	Percent in Places 10,000+	Percent of All Migrants to Monterrey
Nuevo León	3	64	22
Coahuila	7	55	23
Tamaulipas	8	52	8
San Luis Potosí	24	22	20
Zacatecas	29	11	8

SOURCE: Columns 1 and 2: México, Dirección General de Estadística, *VII Censo
general de población, 1960. Resumen general*; column 3: representative sample.

[5] Paul Lamartine Yates, *El desarrollo regional de México.*
[6] Comisión Nacional de los Salarios Mínimos, "Salarios mínimos por zonas y mu-
nicípios," in *Memoria de los Trabajos de 1963.*
[7] Claudio Stern, "Un análisis regional de México," *Demografía y Economía* 1
(1967): 92–117. For a comprehensive review of various attempts to divide Mexico
into regions, see Claude Bataillon, *Las regiones geográficas en México.*

The results indicate beyond any doubt that most Mexican states are internally heterogeneous. It happens that Nuevo León is itself the best demonstration of this point. Within the state boundaries are five *zonas*. Their ranking on the list of 77 *zonas* is as follows: Monterrey (metropolitan area), 2; Sabinas Hidalgo, 22; Montemorelos, 46; Nuevo León, Norte, 54; and Nuevo León, Sur, 77. In just this one state we have practically the entire range of development represented. Nuevo León is unusual in the breadth of its distribution but not so in representing the diversity to be found within most state borders. If we were looking at the state level, Nuevo León would place very high in socioeconomic ranking, since metropolitan Monterrey, with over 60 percent of the total population, dominates the overall state figure and masks the existence of quite backward areas.

We now return to the question of whether Monterrey draws migrants mainly from high or low socioeconomic areas, but this time working with *zonas* rather than states. Using the representative sample, we took all the migrants to Monterrey and their *zona* of community of origin. They were then allocated to three categories, from high to low socioeconomic ranking. These categories are shown in Table 3-4 by time-of-first-arrival cohorts. An examination of the "All Arrivals" column leads us to conclude that Monterrey draws migrants almost equally from high- and low-ranking *zonas*, since both the higher and lower socioeconomic ranks individually contribute roughly 40 percent of all migrants. This is an important finding and the question arises as to whether Monterrey is distinctive in this respect among large Mexican cities. Comparable data are lacking, but we suspect that it is not. Both

TABLE 3–4. Socioeconomic *Zonas* of Community of Origin, Classified in Three Categories by Time of First Arrival to Monterrey (In Percent)

Socioeconomic Category	Time of First Arrival				All Arrivals
	Before 1941	1941–1950	1951–1960	1961–1965	
Category I	38	38	40	41	39
Category II	18	18	20	25	20
Category III	45	44	40	34	41
Total	101	100	100	100	100
	(200)	(250)	(304)	(127)	(881)[a]

SOURCE: Representative sample.
[a] Excluded are 26 cases with community of origin in a foreign country.

Mexico City and Guadalajara, for example, are situated in areas containing the full range of socioeconomic *zonas.*

The reader still has not been provided with any description of the kinds of areas from which migrants are drawn, other than their rural-urban and socioeconomically high-low distribution. It is, of course, impossible to portray all the sorts of communities from which the migrants originate. Our solution to this problem is to take the twelve *zonas* that individually contribute at least 3 percent or more of all migrants to Monterrey as indicated in the Map. Together they account for 77 percent of all migrants. They are considered in three groups, in conformity with their classification by socioeconomic category in Table 3-5.

TABLE 3-5. Principal *Zonas* Contributing Migrants to Monterrey

Zona	Percent of All Migrants
I *Highest socioeconomic status*	
Coahuila, Saltillo (4)[a]	7
San Luis Potosí, Sur (7)	6
Comarca Lagunera (8)	5
Distrito Federal,	
area metropolitana (10)	3
Coahuila, Piedras Negras/	
Acuña–Sabinas (11)	3
Subtotal	24
II *Intermediate socioeconomic status*	
Nuevo León, Montemorelos (3)	8
Coahuila, Sur (6)	6
Tamaulipas, Centro (9)	3
Subtotal	17
III *Lowest socioeconomic status*	
San Luis Potosí, Norte (1)	15
Nuevo León, Norte (2)	11
Zacatecas, rest of state (5)	7
Nuevo León, Sur (12)	3
Subtotal	36
Grand Total	77
	(881)[b]

[a] Numbers in parentheses refer to identification on map.
[b] Excluded are 26 cases with community of origin in a foreign country.

68

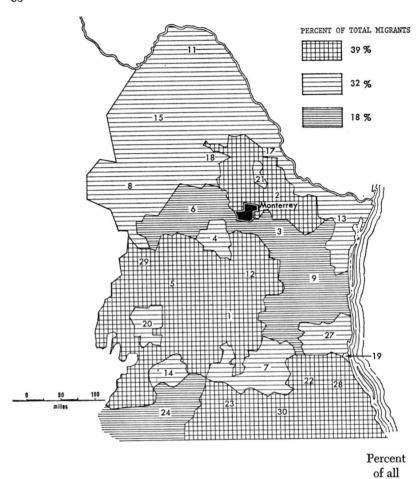

PERCENT OF TOTAL MIGRANTS

	39 %
	32 %
	18 %

No.	Zona	Percent of all Migrants to Monterrey
1.	San Luis Potosí, Norte	15
2.	Nuevo León, Norte	11
3.	Nuevo León, Montemorelos	8
4.	Coahuila, Saltillo	7
5.	Zacatecas, Resto del Estado	7
6.	Coahuila, Sur	6
7.	San Luis Potosí, Sur	6

8. Comarca Lagunera	5
9. Tamaulipas, Centro	3
10. Distrito Federal, area metropolitana[1]	3
11. Coahuila, Piedras Negras // Coahuila, Acuña–Sabinas	3
12. Nuevo León, Sur	3
13. Tamaulipas, Matamoros	2
14. Aguascalientes	2
15. Coahuila, Centro	2
16. Guanajuato, Bajio[1]	2
17. Laredo–Anahuac	1
18. Coahuila, Monclova	1
19. Tamaulipas, Tampico–Cd. Madero	1
20. Zacatecas, Centro	1
21. Nuevo León, Sabinas Hidalgo	1
22. San Luis Potosí and Hidalgo Huasteca	1
23. Guanajuato, Norte	1
24. Jalisco, La Costa–Valle de Autlán // Jalisco, Centro // Jalisco, Bolanos–Los Altos // Nayarit	1
25. Durango, Centro[1]	1
26. Durango, Norte-Oeste-Sur[1]	1
27. Tamaulipas, Altamira	*
28. Veracruz, Huasteca	*
29. Durango, Este	*
30. Querétaro, Norte	*
Total	98

[1] *Zonas* not shown on map
* Less than one-half percent

The first group is composed of five *zonas*. They are geographically dispersed and the one thing they have in common is the inclusion of important urban concentrations. Of course, even within this group there is a sizable rural component (especially in the Comarca Lagunera and San Luis Potosí *zonas*); it is not intended to give the impression that all migrants within this group come from metropolitan or even urban environments. But only from these *zonas* does Monterrey receive migrants from large cities. Furthermore, a description of the cities in this group can help to explain why the rural migrants coming from these rich *zonas* chose Monterrey instead of the nearby city.

Saltillo, the most important as a source of migrants, is only eighty-five kilometers from Monterrey, and proximity in itself helps to account for the migratory flow. But there is more to it than that. As we noted in the last chapter, a century ago Saltillo was Monterrey's main competitor in northeastern Mexico, but for a variety of reasons it has fallen well behind. Yates calls it an "unlucky" city. It lost out to Monterrey in the founding of the first steel mill. Much later, when the government-sponsored Altos Hornos steel mill was in the project stage, Saltillo once again was considered as the logical place for the installation. Nonetheless, the mill ended up in Monclova. Still later, it was considered but rejected as a site for a factory to make railway cars, and in 1960 it was investigated, again without success, by at least two important motor car firms. Saltillo by no means is an economically moribund city—it has a number of substantial manufacturing firms—but its development economically and demographically has been notably inferior to that of Monterrey.

San Luis Potosí, the capital city of the state of that name and dominant within the *zona* of San Luis Potosí, Sur, is another example of a city that for much of Mexico's history was far more important than Monterrey but within the twentieth century has receded within the latter's shadow. As late as 1910, San Luis Potosí ranked fifth among Mexican cities, and with 68,000 it was not much smaller than Monterrey (79,000) in fourth place. But San Luis Potosí was overly dependent upon a soon-to-decline mining industry, and its hinterland was economically stagnant. A "traditional" city, it appears not to have produced entrepreneurs to lead it in new directions. As a result, by 1960 it had fallen to eleventh in rank and within fifty years had little more than doubled in population. Monterrey's impressive industrial expansion, therefore, has been an enticement to Potosinos hard to resist.

The Comarca Lagunera is another example of a metropolitan area unable to hold its own people, but the reasons are quite different from the case of Saltillo or of San Luis Potosí. Comarca Lagunera is the name given to an area on the border of Coahuila and Durango that during the time of the *porfiriato*, prior to the revolution, had been developed into one of the most important centers of commercialized agriculture in all Mexico, based on an extensive system of irrigation. Torreón in Coahuila and Gómez Palacio a few miles away in Durango grew as "central places" for this rich agricultural area. The disruptions occasioned by the revolution and subsequent agrarian reform measures, in combination with a severe problem of salination of the irrigation system, brought a period of hardship to the Comarca Lagunera. It reached a height during the nineteen forties. In a time of economic boom for most other large urban Mexican centers, Torreón–Gómez Palacio grew at a rate less than the national average. In recent years something of a recovery has been made and the urban complex has begun to attract some manufacturing activities. Incidentally, the area, some 360 kilometers from Monterrey, may be said to mark the western limit of Monterrey's attraction for migrants. The western cities of Ciudad Juárez, Chihuahua, and Hermosillo are themselves booming, and the flow of migration in this region has a pronounced south-north, rather than west-east, direction. This trend holds for such depressed areas as those found in the state of Durango.

The last two *zonas* in this grouping don't have the problems of the first three. The Mexico City Metropolitan Area is the one distant *zona*, 959 kilometers from Monterrey, that provides a sizable number of migrants. Mexico City, with its great demographic mass—its population of about 4.8 million inhabitants in 1960 was nearly as large as the total population of the five states supplying most of Monterrey's inmigration—sends out migrants to many parts of the republic. Given the dynamism inherent in the development of a primary city like Mexico City, one may ask why it should send out any migrants at all. But then, why are there substantial migratory flows between Los Angeles and Houston, two fast-growing metropolitan centers in the United States? A good deal of the migration from Mexico City to Monterrey may be subsumed under career migration—specialists sent out to man branch establishments—and others attracted by what they believe to be opportunities for economic advancement. This is white-collar and skilled blue-collar migration.

The last of the *zonas* is in northern Coahuila and contains two border towns: Piedras Negras and Ciudad Acuña. The border cities of Coahuila and Tamaulipas are not important sources of migrants to Monterrey, although Nuevo Laredo, Matamoros, and Reynosa are closer to that city than is San Luis Potosí and the cities of the Comarca Lagunera. The border cities, particularly since 1940, have been characterized by remarkably rapid growth. The dozen places throughout the entire length of the Mexico-U.S. border with a population of at least 15,000 in 1960 grew 163 percent between 1940 and 1950 and 115 percent in the period 1950–1960.[8] For Piedras Negras, however, the comparable figures were an almost sedate 76 and 55 percent. They may indicate why Monterrey was able to draw migrants from this border *zona.*

The second grouping is made up of three *zonas,* all belonging to the intermediate category, and originating 17 percent of all migrants. It has an east-west orientation, being on a plane somewhat to the south of Monterrey. There are some important cities (Ciudad Victoria, Ciudad Mante, and Parras), but they are not industrialized, providing only central-place functions for their agricultural hinterlands. Indeed, what most distinguishes this grouping of *zonas* from the one that will be discussed last is its well-developed commercial agriculture. Citrus fruits, sugar, cotton, and winter vegetables are important crops. (Coahuila, Sur, is a good deal more arid than the other two *zonas.*) Good soils, relatively abundant water, and advanced farming and marketing practices have been basic to the development of this commercial agriculture.

Although essentially an agricultural region, it never has been an area isolated from urban life, at least in recent times. In the towns, and to a somewhat lesser extent in the rural areas, one is impressed with the provision of goods and services, with the high level of literacy, and with the modern way of life, in contrast to some of the desertic areas not very distant from Monterrey. In spite of the relatively rich agricultural economy, the *municipios* in this area consistently have lost migrants to Monterrey. The latter attracts men because urban wages are higher and urban jobs are more stable than rural employment. Because of the moderately high level of living, there are rather good school facilities, but they are mainly limited to the primary level. The towns provide secondary-level schooling, but, if the students wish to continue beyond this level, migration to Monterrey is required. Once educated they tend to stay there, for suitable occupational positions at home in what is basically an agricultural economy are scarce. In short, this region sends migrants to Monterrey, but not because conditions are necessarily bleak and unfavorable at home. A rather prosperous agriculture has failed to retain much of the population increase precisely due to its relative efficiency—the predominance of private farms rather than ejidos and a tendency to mechanize some procedures (like

[8] Harley L. Browning, "Urbanization in Mexico," Ph.D. Dissertation, University of California at Berkeley, 1962, pp. 134–143.

packing and some processing) have resulted in high rates of seasonal unemployment. This and the superior opportunities offered in the metropolitan environment of Monterrey explain the heavy flows of migrants from this region.

Finally, we have arrived to the third grouping of *zonas* and the most important one in providing migrants to Monterrey, since it contributes 36 percent of the total. It is a large area that sweeps down from north of the city (Nuevo León, Norte), is briefly interrupted by the east-west grouping just discussed, and then continues south (Nuevo León, Sur, and San Luis Potosí, Norte) to terminate in the southwest (Zacatecas, rest of state). It is among the most backward regions of the entire country. It is almost entirely desertic or semidesertic, but, in spite of the unpropitious conditions of insufficient and erratic moisture and thin soils, nearly four-fifths of the labor force is engaged in agriculture and other primary activities. The rurality of the region is indicated by the fact that the only urban center of any size within the entire region is Matehuala, with a 1960 population of 19,927. Subsistence crops of maize and beans are grown everywhere, but yields are so low and harvests so uncertain that many people must supplement farming by "gathering" activities, particularly the collection of the desert plant, lechuguilla, from which is then extracted the tough fiber, ixtle.

Historically, mining was a mainstay of the money economy of the region, and it was the major incentive for the original colonization of the region. The most important urban centers bordering on the southern part of the region, San Luis Potosí and Zacatecas, were dependent to a large extent upon this activity. But for many decades, dating as far back as the revolution of 1910, mining in the region has been in decline, resulting from a combination of the exhaustion of long-worked ore bodies and unsatisfactory prices on the world market. Some smaller centers even became ghost towns.

Although the area we are describing is rural and very poor, it should not be dumped into the same category as equally backward areas in southern and central Mexico, for two important reasons. First, an Indian culture never has been significant in this northern area, and for many decades there have been almost no Indians. Unlike the cultural duality we find in most of Chiapas and Oaxaca, all of the population speaks Spanish, and the people have no cultural identity other than being Mexican. Second, population density is very low. Unlike other parts of Mexico, where land is in short supply, land here is plentiful but of poor quality. Water is the scarce resource, and the settlement pattern is closely associated with availability of water.[9]

In view of unrewarding agriculture and depressed mining conditions, it is understandable that there has been substantial out-migration from this region for decades, not only in the form of seasonal migration to other parts of Mexico and to the United States as agricultural laborers but also as permanent migration, mainly to cities of the north including, of course, Monterrey. In recent decades this process has received a further impetus deriving from the rapid population growth based upon natural increase. In common with other parts of Mexico, the death rate has fallen markedly since World War II. In contrast to the meager and unreliable yield of the land, the fertility of the Mexican men and women of the area has been highly dependable and bountiful—for those in stable unions the average number of children ever born has been in the neighborhood of eight. Under the conditions of low mortality and high fertility, population growth due to natural increase has exceeded 4 percent per annum in recent years, an unusually high figure.

Cedral: A Case Study of a Community with Substantial and Sustained Out-Migration

In the summer of 1967, two years after the Monterrey survey, we went back into the field to conduct a study of a community with heavy out-migration, much of it directed to Monterrey. Having obtained information on migrants to Monterrey, we wanted to shed light on the migratory process by looking at the other side of the story, that of a community of origin. Cedral, a *municipio* in northern San Luis Potosí,

---

[9] The conditions of life in rural areas of Mexico are vividly portrayed by Moisés T. de la Peña, *El pueblo y su tierra: Mito y realidad de la reforma agraria en México*. Stavenhagen has dealt extensively with the social structure of rural Mexico, introducing explicitly in his analyses the differentiation between Indian and Ladino. See especially Rodolfo Stavenhagen, *Las clases sociales en las sociedades agrarias*; "Classes, Colonialism and Acculturation," in *Comparative Perspective on Stratification*, ed. Joseph A. Kahl; and "Social Aspects of Agrarian Structure in Mexico," in the book he has edited, *Agrarian Problems and Peasant Movements in Latin America*. The latter book also includes an analysis of the ejidos in the Laguna region by Shlomo Eckstein, "Collective Farming in Mexico," and a number of articles about the rural situation in other Latin American countries. See also, Pablo González Casanova, Internal Colonialism and National Development," *Studies in Comparative Internal Development* 1, no. 4 (1965): 27–37.

was selected for several reasons. First, the *zona* in which it is located, San Luis Potosí, Norte, was the single most important source of migrants to Monterrey, providing 15 percent of the total. Second, all our statistical indicators told us that the area is one of the poorest and most rural in Mexico, and we were particularly interested in rural-urban migration originating in depressed areas. Since the *municipio* also had an urban place, it provided us an opportunity to examine rural-urban contacts within the *municipio*. (Cedral town, with 4,221 in 1960, is below the 5,000 figure we have used to differentiate urban and rural, but, as will become apparent in subsequent discussion, it is urban in function and ambience.) Finally, Cedral is far enough from Monterrey (about 370 kilometers) so as to make the decision to migrate a significant one. However, communications between the two places are good—a railroad and more recently a major highway—so distance would not greatly inhibit out-migration. In addition to gathering information about the *municipio* itself, we interviewed 380 men aged 15–64: 312 from the town of Cedral and 68 from two rural ejidos in the *municipio*. More details about the study design and its execution will be found in Appendix A.

Cedral merits a more extended discussion than we have given to other communities of origin. For one thing, we have more information that permits us to provide a more complete and rounded picture of the community. We will still emphasize the economic basis of life, but for the first time we can introduce a discussion of intergroup relationships, particularly those involving class. The description of Cedral should also be useful to the reader because, from time to time in the rest of the book, additional information from the Cedral survey will be introduced. The following sketch of the community should help the reader to "place" these facts. We do not maintain that Cedral is completely representative of all communities to be found in *zonas* of category III, but we do believe that its history and present socioeconomic structure typify the environmental background of a substantial share of rural migrants to Monterrey.

Cedral suffered considerably from the breakdown of the mining economy brought about by the revolution of 1910. At that time it was a center for the processing of ores obtained from the important mine in neighboring Real de Catorce, as well as serving as a commercial and service center for the latter's population. The mine closed in Real de Catorce and within a few years it was transformed into a ghost town, declining from some 7,000 to a few hundred inhabitants. Cedral town, which had a population of 4,469 in 1910, lost 1,000 inhabitants in the following decade. Its increase since then has been so slow that in 1960 the population of 4,221 was still below that of 1910, and it has grown even slower than the rural part of the *municipio*. The rural population in 1960 was 8,909.

Following the collapse of the mining economy, the population of the *municipio* has been almost entirely dependent upon agricultural and related activities. Of course, in the town there are nonagricultural activities. About one-half of the men interviewed did not make their living primarily as farmers or farm workers; they were small shopkeepers, artisans, government employees, truck and taxi drivers, construction workers, and so on. There is no manufacturing worthy of the name in Cedral, but there is a variety of shops and personal services. The town has a commercial area and a grid layout of streets. But its reason for existence is agriculture and one-half of the town population is engaged in farming, going out daily to the fields.

Besides the existence of a nonagricultural sector and an urban ambience, the main difference between the town and the rest of the *municipio* consists in the fact that the former has access to underground water, while the latter depends entirely upon seasonal rainfall. As early as the twenties some rather primitive wells were dug, but it was not until the introduction of gasoline pumps that the cultivation of commercial crops was made possible. Tomatoes, onions, and other market crops are grown in irrigated plots. Lacking this source of water, the farmers in the rest of the *municipio* are restricted to the traditional maize and beans. Since in most years these crops are inadequate for even their minimal subsistence needs, most of them also work in the extraction of ixtle.

Families outside the town live in scattered settlements, all of them with fewer than five hundred inhabitants.[10] Generally they are clusters of houses inhabited by families with some kinship relationship. In most cases they form collective ejidos, that is, land distributed by the government as communal property, in accord with the agrarian reform program. Although the *ejidatarios* do not directly own the land, this is of no great importance, since the land itself is almost worthless. (Par-

10 The description of rural conditions in the Cedral area draws upon Eloisa Alemán A., "Investigación socioeconomica directa de los ejidos de San Luis Potosí," M.A. Thesis, Universidad Nacional Autónoma de México.

enthetically, many migrants to Monterrey from such areas simply abandon their privately owned land and dwellings when they leave, there being no market for the property.)

The agrarian "question," specifically the relative merits of ejidal versus private property systems, that has so long been a matter of national debate, is reflected in the microcosm of Cedral. In this particular case, however, there can be little doubt as to who has the best of it. Unlike the farmers in the rest of the *municipio*, the town farmers work under the private property system. The best lands, those with underground water available, were not subjected to expropriation and ejidal distribution; this distinction explains in part why commercial crops, irrigation, and private property go together in the town and are absent elsewhere. The other reason is that irrigated agriculture requires a substantial capital investment, and the ejidos have been unable to obtain credits to buy pumps, seeds, and the other elements needed for commercial crops. Private owners have relatively better access to credit sources, limited as they are, a condition prevalent in virtually all of Mexico. Up to the present no ejido has irrigation. One had underground water and a pump, but it was being utilized by a governmental agency to provide water for urban consumption.

In Cedral town we find a considerable division of labor and elaboration of the local system of stratification. In its agricultural sector, there is a small number of owners of medium-sized farms who use some capital, employ a considerable number of day laborers during the crop season, and are pretty much aware of the market conditions for their products. Although they are not exactly the prototype of the modern farmer oriented to innovation and mechanization, they clearly live in a market economy. There is a money market, where they must go for credit; a produce market, which determines how much they will get for their crops; and a labor market, where they contact men to work their fields. A part of the town land also is worked by sharecroppers, who do not have the land or the financial resources to irrigate their own land. They make arrangements with richer farmers or shopkeepers for the credit to finance their sharecropping operations. Other than their weaker position in the money market, their activities are very similar to the farmers who own and work their own irrigated land.

There is in the town no modern-day equivalent of the old *hacendado,* a landowner who dominates the life of the community. Only three or four families have sufficient financial resources to acquire additional irrigated lands. Consequently, no one man or a few men monopolize the agrarian wage-labor market. On the contrary, the large number of day laborers living in the town often change employers. Of necessity they change types of jobs as well because for six months of the year the local farms provide very little work. The men then take whatever work may be available in the town, or they migrate to other rural areas needing temporary labor, or they may go to the cities, often to Monterrey. One of every three men in our urban sample has been, for at least one time, a short-term migrant (six months or less), and a similar proportion has been a long-term migrant (more than six months). There is, as might be expected, a considerable overlapping of the two categories.

The system of stratification in the town agricultural sector is mainly determined by property: land and other forms of capital. In the non-agricultural sector we also find considerable differentiation along the same lines. Some few shop owners who have acquired sufficient capital operate as money lenders as much as merchants, providing loans at high interest rates, principally to farmers in need of quick cash. Most shop owners, however, operate on a very modest, and usually marginal, scale. They run retail operations, such as food stores, cantinas, and a variety of repair shops (bicycles, radios, etc.). Some governmental employees, such as teachers and low-level bureaucrats in municipal, state, and federal agencies, form a limited group of white-collar, salaried people. They aren't paid much, but the low cost of living in Cedral (especially for housing and services) enables them to enjoy a fairly high relative standard of living. The rest of the nonfarm population of the town is quite heterogeneous: all sorts of self-employed artisans, workers on the railroad, street vendors, and a "floating" labor supply who will do anything they can for a living (including farm work when demand is high), changing and alternating jobs as various opportunities arise.

In contrast to the town situation, we find in the rest of the *municipio* practically no division of labor between economic units, and within each unit the only basis for the division of labor is based upon sex and age. Understandably, we do not find important differences in social stratification. The large majority of the population is composed of *ejidatarios*, who have almost worthless ejidal lands. They grow subsistence crops and supplement this meagre living with the gathering of

ixtle and occasional work as day laborers. As subsistence farmers, raising maize and beans, the *ejidatarios* work in a closed economy; they
rarely sell any of their crops, they do not hire any laborers, and they
do not use any capital. All farming activities are carried out by the
family group, with little or no cooperation between families. Variations
among families, due to the amount or quality of land they have, are
minimal. The collection of ixtle is carried out by the fathers and their
older children. They make short trips to the hills to select and cut the
leaves from two plants that grow naturally in the desert. They bring
them back home where, by a laborious manual technique, the hard
fiber is extracted. This fiber is then sold at a fixed price to a government agency. In effect, the latter subsidizes the *ixtleros*, for the market demand for the fiber is small. Sometimes the *ixtleros* sell to some
shops that function as intermediaries. In any case, their income from
this source is small, though indispensable, and sometimes they are paid
in goods rather than cash.

The work activities, level of living, and problems of most *ejidatarios*
are practically the same. In our study we interviewed sixty-eight families in two ejidos, but we could have relied upon fewer cases, since the
answers to our questions showed little variability. We are dealing with
unusually poor and homogeneous communities, but it would be a mistake to consider them as completely closed ones. One type of contact,
however limited, with the external world has been mentioned: the
monopsonic one provided by the government for ixtle. More important are the temporary jobs taken in town and the seasonal migrations. Actually, a considerably larger percentage of the out-of-town
men have been short-term migrants than have the town men (59 and
36 percent respectively), but fewer of the former have been long-term
migrants (28 compared to 35 percent). It is our impression that the
very limited experience occasioned by migration to other communities,
generally to work as agricultural laborers, contributes little to the
widening of the men's life perspectives, except in those cases where
it has led to permanent out-migration from rural Cedral. These men,
of course, were not encountered in our Cedral sample.

Given the differences in economic organization that we have set
forth, it is no surprise to find other differences in the ways of life, attitudes, and fund of information of the town when compared to the out-
of-town dwellers. Only 25 percent of the rural men could read or
write, while 56 percent of the town men were literate. Radio owner-

ship, newspapers, and other means of information were available, even if somewhat limited, in the town. A larger percent of the town people had relatives in cities and either visited them or received visits every so often. During the yearly festivities for the local saint, Cedral receives thousands of visitors, many of them Cedraleños presently living in other communities. The yearly festival provides the pretext for many return migrations, as well as the opportunity for many youngsters desirous of leaving Cedral to make arrangements with relatives to take them back to whatever place the relatives reside in. Very importantly, these yearly contacts add considerably to the fund of local information about what is going on outside Cedral: the existence of job opportunities, exposure to and opportunity to appraise other ways of living, and undoubtedly some "demonstration effects" on the part of the visitors eager to show off to the home folk their rise in standard of living. Very little of this sort of contact is available to the dwellers of the ejidos.

Communities in Flux

The object of this chapter has been to describe briefly the kinds of communities of origin of those men who did not grow up in Monterrey. It turned out that this group was more than one-half of the total representative sample of men aged 21–60 living in Monterrey in 1965. As in the preceding chapter dealing with the growth of Monterrey, our main concern has been with the economic basis of life in such communities. This is in accord with the principal goal of this study, the interpretation of geographic and occupational mobility, both of which are much influenced by economic factors.

We found that well over one-half of our migrants to Monterrey grew up in rural communities of origin. The remainder came from urban areas, but predominantly from smaller places that serve as trading and service centers for the surrounding rural population. The rural-urban distinction still has great force in Mexico, but we hope that our prior discussion of the three groupings of *zonas* has made evident the considerable variation in economic conditions and prospects of places classified as either urban or rural. Not all large urban places are booming, and not all rural areas are poor and backward. Even a place like Cedral, whose anatomy we examined in more detail, turned out to be a community with more differentiation than we had anticipated. Selected because it was in the most backward of areas providing migrants to Monterrey, we anticipated a community based entirely upon subsistence agriculture. It came as a surprise to find the existence of irrigated commercial agriculture, which had a considerable impact upon the economic and social structure of the *municipio*.

Cedral, as we warned, is not to be equated with all the small communities in Mexico. If nothing else, its historical association with mining gives it a special, if not unique, background. But Cedral does share, especially within the last generation, some features that are also to be found in many other communities of Mexico and not just within the North. In common with them, the local economy is stagnating, with little if any expansion of occupational opportunities. At the same time, Cedral and these communities are becoming less isolated and increasingly integrated into the national society.

National integration has been an explicit goal of the Mexican government since the revolution, but for several decades both it and the economy were so weak that little could be accomplished. In the last three decades, however, this situation has changed. The heavy governmental emphasis on industrialization required the development of the national infrastructure. Although the rural population has not shared in the direct benefits of the economic growth of the country, the expansion of some services and facilities—such as electricity, roads, mass communications, and to some extent education—has changed the life of the otherwise stagnant communities. Luis González gives an account of this process for a community in Michoacán on the central plateau in his delightful book, *Pueblo en vilo: Microhistoria de San José de Gracia*. Like Cedral, San José is a *mestizo* community, with the urban center of the *municipio* being almost the same size as that of Cedral. San José, too, is dependent upon the primary sector, but in this case cattle and dairying are the mainstay of the economy. But, as is the situation with Cedral, the agriculturally based economy has not been able to grow and keep pace with the demands that have been placed upon it. The comparatively weak development of the local economy of both communities has been exacerbated by another significant change in the last several decades: the remarkable rise in population growth due to natural increase. As González puts it, "The demographic explosion is already there: the economic miracle is not so apparent." He is particularly effective in describing how the community and its way of life have been changed in the last generation by the introduction of objects and ideas from the outside, ranging from paved roads to television sets.

The combination of the above factors—the relative stagnation of the local economy, the striking upsurge in the natural increase of the population, and the breakdown of isolation and the penetration of the outside world—has had unsettling effects on San José, as it has had on Cedral. It is in these terms that González describes San José, from the perspective of his four-hundred-year review of the history of the place, as a community now "in suspense, insecure, unstable." The judgment fits Cedral, and it also applies to Oscar Lewis's Tepotzlán[11] and George Foster's Tzintzuntzan[12] and doubtless thousands of other agrarian-centered communities in Mexico. For all of them, substantial net out-migration is one response. The major flow from San José, Tzintzuntzan, and Tepotzlán has been to Mexico City and from Cedral it has been to Monterrey, but the conditions provoking out-migration and the reasons for departure are much the same.

[11] Oscar Lewis, *Life in a Mexican Village: Tepoztlán Restudied.*
[12] George M. Foster, *Tzintzuntzan: Mexican Peasants in a Changing World.*

PART TWO
THE LIFE HISTORIES

4. Community, Family of Origin, and Educational Attainment

Education is an appropriate subject with which to begin a discussion of the life cycle of Monterrey men. Whether or not education is the key to economic development, and the expansion of a public school system the central aspect of the modernization of any country, there is little doubt that at both the societal and the individual levels modernity and education necessarily are linked. This is no less the case in Mexico or Brazil than it is in England, Japan, or China. One of the reasons for the centrality of education is that industrialization is linked to an occupational structure where an increasing proportion of positions demand levels of skill for which formal education is a requirement. The occupational prospects of a majority of men in industrial or industrializing societies depend on formal education. Furthermore, in societies where life styles and life chances are greatly dependent on occupational status, education becomes even more crucial.

In the following chapters we will have an opportunity to explore in detail the role of education in this regard. Here, our main objective is to discuss the educational attainments of the Monterrey men, exploring the links between attainment and background factors, such as parental socioeconomic status, community origins, and family context. A more statistically oriented treatment of these links is found in Chapter 10, where we will evaluate the determinants of educational attainment in the broader context of the men's work lives and their sons' attainment.

We will begin this chapter with a brief account of the educational attainment of the Mexican population as a whole, in order to establish a context for the Monterrey men. This will require a description of the organization of the Mexican educational system. The regional variation that is so prominent in Mexico also holds for education; and in line with this, we shall want to discuss variations in the communities of origin of the respondents to the extent they affect educational attainment. Then we shall turn to a consideration of the way in which the man's family of origin affects the amount of education he receives. The chapter will conclude with the results of a multivariate analysis of family and community determinants of educational attainment.

The National and Community Context of Educational Attainment

Education in contemporary Mexico is of great importance because it is still rather scarce. Unlike in developed societies, where nearly everyone is exposed to at least eight to ten years of schooling and where illiteracy is almost unknown, not even a minimal educational attainment is widely distributed in Mexico. In a way this lack is unexpected, for one of the battle cries of the revolution, besides land redistribution and effective suffrage, was universal education. The Díaz regime had been frankly elitist in its educational policies, and in 1910 more than three-quarters of the population were illiterate. The Constitution of 1917 proclaimed education to be free, universal, and compulsory. While none of the postrevolutionary governments have denied the importance of education or the necessity of reducing illiteracy, the results have been disappointing.[1]

In 1960, fifty years after the revolution began, 38 percent of the population six years and over reported themselves illiterate, certainly an improvement since 1910, the last year of the *porfiriato*, when 77 percent of the population did so. However, these literacy rates, based on self-reported ability to read and write, overestimate the progress made. Doubtless today there are a great many more people who have attended one or two grades of primary school, or who were taught in one of the government's mass literacy programs, and these men and women will certainly tend to report themselves as literate. But it is very likely that their schooling has been insufficient, and functional literacy has

---

[1] A general evaluation of the Mexican educational system can be found in Charles N. Myers, *Education and National Development in Mexico.* An earlier study, using 1940 census data, is José E. Iturriaga, *La estructura social y cultural de México.*

not been attained or, if attained, it has been lost because the opportunities to use daily the written word are limited, especially in many rural areas. A more realistic picture is obtained by defining, as we prefer to do, as functionally illiterate those persons having less than four years of schooling. If we take the Mexican population fifteen years old and over in 1960, almost seven out of ten persons old enough to have completed their primary training are unable to handle their language adequately in written form.

A brief description of the formal structure of the educational system in Mexico is appropriate at this point, since it differs substantially from the American system. The educational system in Mexico is separated into three levels: primary, middle, and high. *Primaria* school has six grades, and at its completion students are expected to be able to read and write, to perform basic arithmetical functions, and to have a cursory knowledge of history, geography, and natural sciences. Although rural schools previously differed substantially from urban ones, today their programs are very similar, and, whether federal, state, or privately supported, their structures do not vary substantially. Middle-level schools, to which students graduating from *primaria* may go, can be divided into two cycles: secondary, or basic, and postsecondary. Within each of these cycles several alternative paths are open. The one leading to higher education at the universities, where academic training is stressed, includes *secundaria* school of three years followed by *preparatoria* school of two or three years. Vocational, technical, and teacher training schools represent the other type of middle-level schools. None of the vocational and technical schools lead to higher education. Graduates from teachers' schools can continue further studies at the *normal superior* to obtain licenses for teaching at the *secundaria* schools.

At the higher level we find mainly universities, where students quite early must choose a professional career. That is, by their thirteenth year of schooling (six of *primaria*, three of *secundaria*, and two or three of *preparatoria*), and often before; since the *preparatorias* are specialized, students must make up their minds about what kind of university degree, if any, they are going to strive for. The traditional schools, law and medicine, still attract the largest number of students, although in an industrial environment like Monterrey, sciences, engineering, and business administration have more recently attracted a large proportion of students. Most of these schools or *facultades* have five-year curricula.

Forty or fifty years ago, when the older respondents in our sample were of school age, the majority of the school-age population in the country did not have an opportunity even to enter school. Educational facilities were clearly insufficient, and they were mostly absent in rural areas, where three of every four Mexicans lived. *Primaria* schools were by and large geared to a minority of urban children, and middle and higher institutions were limited to Mexico City and a few provincial capitals. However, after the revolution, important changes took place. Ostensibly, the goal was to extend educational opportunities to the masses of people so as to achieve universal literacy, and this necessarily meant programs directed toward the large numbers of peasants and their children. Rural education and *primaria* schooling in general at first were favored by revolutionary governments. But the obstacles were overwhelming and the results quite meager. If low educational levels are a condition of underdevelopment, underdevelopment makes it difficult to raise educational standards.[2] The poverty and isolation of rural areas, lack of modern means of communication, scarcity of teaching personnel, difficulties in allocating a larger proportion of the governmental budget for educational purposes when alternative needs were urgent, linguistic and cultural barriers imposed by the high proportion of Indian population in many regions—all these taken together help to explain why the revolutionary goals were so difficult to achieve.

Rural educational programs have for all practical purposes been abandoned since the 1940's. The shift to policies fostering industrialization was accompanied by an increasing emphasis on the training of the human resources most needed for industrial development. Thus, middle and higher education were strengthened, but partly at the expense of primary education, since there was no overall increase in the proportion of the federal expenditure devoted to educational purposes. These policies resulted in even greater inequalities between regions and between rural and urban areas in terms of the educational levels of the population. Of course, variations in literacy and schooling always had been present, but the concentration of developmental efforts in Mexico City, other urban centers, and the northern states made the differences more striking than before. Although general educational levels in Mexico kept increasing, the increase was due in part to the improve-

<hr>

[2] The various attempts and failures to develop rural education programs for Mexico are analyzed in Ramón E. Ruíz, *Mexico: The Challenge of Poverty and Illiteracy.*

ment experienced by those areas that, because of their rapid growth, represented a larger proportion of the total population.[3] The disparity in educational attainment is brought out in Table 4-1, which permits a comparison of the country as a whole, two of its leading urban areas, Mexico City (Distrito Federal) and Monterrey, and the rest of the country. At all levels, but particularly for higher education, the differences are striking.

It is understandable why universities and institutions of higher learning have been concentrated in just a few urban centers in Mexico. In part, it is a matter of "external economies," for only in the largest urban centers can universities count on the many inputs necessary for their

TABLE 4-1. Some Indicators of Educational Attainment, Mexico, 1960 (In Percent)

Group	Total Country	Distrito Federal	Monterrey	Rest of Country
Population 6 years and over that is illiterate	38	17	15	42
has not completed one year of schooling	44	22	20	48
Population 12 years and over that has finished *primaria*	19	45	45	14
Population 15 years and over that has completed the first educational cycle[a]	5	17	15	3
Population 18 years and over that has completed second educational cycle[a]	2	8	6	1
Population 23 years and over that has completed higher education[a]	1	3	2	—[b]

SOURCE: Adapted from Table IV-4, Víctor L. Urquidi and Adrian Lajous Vargas, *Educación superior, ciencia y tecnología en el desarollo económico de méxico.*
[a] The 1960 Mexican census gives only years of education completed, not by the educational cycle. Here it is assumed that 6 years are required to complete *primaria*, 9 years to complete the first cycle, 12 years for the second cycle, and 16 years for the higher (university) cycle.
[b] Less than one percent.

[3] An analysis of regional differences in education that we have relied upon in this chapter is Adolfo Mir-Araujo, "Ecological Inequalities in Educational Attainment in Mexico," Ph.D. Dissertation, University of Texas, 1970. For a more general discussion of regional differences in Mexico, see Paul Lamartine Yates, *El desarrollo regional de México*; and Claudio Stern, "Un análisis regional de México," *Demografía y Economía* 1 (1967): 92–117.

existence. The great majority of university teachers are part-time, supporting themselves mainly by their work as doctors, lawyers, or engineers. Students too are very rarely provided with fellowships, so they must depend upon part-time employment and living with their families while attending school. When they graduate, their main employment opportunities are to be found in these same large cities. To some extent similar arguments can be used to explain the concentration of facilities for middle education in urban centers, although in this case they are to be found also in middle-sized cities. In any case, historically, the result has been a pronounced regional inequality in educational facilities, favoring the more developed states and Mexico City. Just as an indication, consider the fact that even as late as 1959, 69 percent of the total Mexican enrollment in higher education was concentrated in the Distrito Federal.[4]

Primaria education remains a crucial problem in Mexico today because a large number of children still are unable to complete the six years of *primaria*. The certificate that is awarded for completion of this cycle is fast becoming a requisite for even the lowest types of jobs in modern enterprises. The excellent study by Adolfo Mir-Araujo of ecological inequalities in educational attainment will serve as a basis for this discussion.[5] Consider first the data in Table 4-2 regarding self-reported illiteracy rates for the country as a whole, the state of Nuevo León (where Monterrey is located), and two other states, the poorest among those providing a sizable migration to Monterrey, by urban and rural residence. The variations between states, and within them between rural and urban areas, are impressive and are a result of the uneven process of development experienced by the country. In 1960, only 63 percent of the school-age population (ages 6 to 14) was attending *primaria*. Although this is a crude measure, since many of those not attending school may be graduates, may attend later, or may be attending *secundaria*, it reflects the situation in the country as a whole. Variations between regions are large. In Nuevo León (a high-ranking state in terms of economic development as well as educational levels) 75 percent was attending school; in Zacatecas and San Luis Potosí only 51 and 62 percent went to school.

[4] The data for higher education are taken from Víctor L. Urquidi and Adrian Lajous Vargas, *Educación superior, ciencia y tecnología en el desarrollo económico de México.*

[5] Mir, *Ecological Inequalities.*

TABLE 4-2. Percent of Population Six Years and Over Who Are Illiterate (1960)

Area	Country	Nuevo León	Zacatecas	San Luis Potosí
Urban	24	16	29	29
Rural	52	28	40	56
Total	38	19	37	47

SOURCE: México, Dirección General de Estadística, *VII Censo general de población, 1960. Resumen general*, Table 19.

Even when a relatively high percentage of children are enrolled in school, few of them progress to graduation. This shows up in the lack of enrollment balance between various school grades: in 1960 about 30 percent of the students in all urban schools of the country was enrolled in first grade, while only 9 percent was enrolled in the sixth grade. The imbalance in rural schools was much more marked. Comparing again Nuevo León with the less developed states, we find that in Nuevo León the first grade constituted 25 percent of those enrolled in urban schools, while in San Luis Potosí and Zacatecas the figures, respectively, were 30 and 38 percent. More revealing is an analysis of the retention rates in *primaria* schools. Mir has calculated the rates shown in Table 4-3 for the cohort first enrolled in 1955 in urban schools. Only four out of every ten students in the country enrolled in *primaria* progressed up to the sixth grade, and somewhat fewer graduated. In a poor state like Zacatecas, where a majority of the population is rural, only one out of five of those enrolled in first grade got to the sixth grade. Thus, in poorer states not only does the educational system provide services for a considerably smaller proportion of the population, but also even those who do begin school generally remain only for a few years and then drop out long before the more concrete rewards (in terms of functional literacy and, beyond that, a *primaria* certificate) are achieved. Mir also estimates the cost per student of *primaria* in Nuevo León to be about three times higher than it is in Zacatecas. However, since many more students graduate in the former state, the cost per graduate of *primaria* is about the same. He goes on to suggest that a student completing *primaria* in Nuevo León or other high-ranking states gets a higher quality education than a student who finishes the same level in Zacatecas or other low-ranking states.

The abysmal differences in educational levels between leading and

TABLE 4-3. Retention Rates in Mexican Urban *Primaria* Schools
for Country and States (In Percent)

Area	Grade					
	1	2	3	4	5	6
Country	100	68	61	53	46	40
Nuevo León	100	78	74	67	59	52
San Luis Potosí	100	71	62	53	45	39
Zacatecas	100	51	41	31	25	21

SOURCE: Adapted from Table 4.8 of Adolfo Mir-Araujo, "Ecological Inequalities in Educational Attainment in Mexico," Ph.D. Dissertation, University of Texas, 1970.

lagging states and between rural and urban areas are partially explained by the variations in quantity and quality of educational facilities. In Mexico the largest share of educational costs is assumed by the federal and state governments, mainly at the *primaria* school level. Thus, governmental educational policies are directly relevant for an understanding of variations in educational services available to different sectors of the Mexican population. Those policies cannot neglect the variation in costs and resources; other things being equal, to provide education for children in rural and poor areas is more expensive and resources more difficult to mobilize than in prosperous cities like Monterrey. Also, there is a clear question of perceived priorities in terms of national development, as well as of relative power of groups and organizations interested in the distribution of the national and state budgets.[6]

Besides the pronounced variation in the distribution of educational facilities, there is also the matter of how formal education relates to the needs and expectations of people in various types of communities. Consider a rural *municipio* like Cedral, San Luis Potosí, where we carried out our 1967 survey. Over two-thirds of its population lives in rural settlements with poor communications with the outside world. The local economy is largely based upon subsistence agriculture and exploitation of desertic plants to obtain ixtle. The settlements are homogeneous communities, with little if any division of labor beyond that determined by age and sex and almost no internal stratification.

[6] For an economic analysis of education in Mexico see Víctor Gallo Martínez, *Estructura económica de la educación mexicana.*

The large majority of the families live close to subsistence levels and depend on economic activities that are carried out almost in isolation. It is clear that, in these communities, formal training or written instructions have little place in the social and economic activities of the people. Because of limited contact with the outside world, most of it in an oral form (the transistor radio being a recent means of mass communication), the chances of obtaining information and becoming aware in a realistic way of other ways of life—where formal education plays a greater role—are very restricted. The situation in the only urban place in the *municipio* is somewhat different. Nonagricultural occupations exist, agriculture is market oriented, considerable variation in style and levels of living are present, and although formal education does not play a key role in the internal stratification system it certainly can be perceived as being related to the occupational hierarchy. Equally important is the greater degree of communication with the cities: people travel more often to and from cities, newspapers are available.

These community characteristics (isolation, extent of the occupational division of labor, heterogeneity) affect the way education is perceived and the type of socialization experienced by the children. For them the availability of a variety of economic roles that can be picked up as models and the relationship between these roles and formal education, as well as parental encouragement, are crucial in determining their approach to the educational institution. The contrast of both the isolated villages and the town in Cedral, on the one hand, and the social environment in the cities, on the other, is manifold and sharp. For the urban poor, with whom the situation can be compared more fairly, the city offers a far greater range of institutional and personal contacts, many of which involve written forms of communication. More important, such contacts can be crucial in shaping attitudes and expectations regarding future occupational roles. The job his father holds is but one of the occupational roles that may serve as a model for the city boy. His father may work in a setting where many occupations are visible to him and indirectly to his son. Outside the work situation, the adult male kinship network is often one of considerable social heterogeneity. Additionally, in Mexican cities there is not a very rigid socioeconomic zoning, so neighborhoods frequently include families from different social strata. Thus work, family, and neighborhood allow father and son contacts, sometimes rather intimate, across strata that can stimulate expectations and encourage further schooling. The boys themselves generally are quite free to circulate throughout the city, spending a good deal of their waking hours in the streets. In this way they come in contact with other social strata and social situations sharply different from their own.

Finally, in the school itself children come in contact with boys of somewhat different family backgrounds who may stimulate their ambitions. The teachers have training superior to rural teachers, and they can do a better job of teaching and awakening interest in academic matters. In summary, the range of social interactions and stimulations is much wider in large cities than in rural localities and small towns.

The sharp contrast between the educational attainment of the Cedral and Monterrey samples, presented in Table 4-4, is a clear reflection of how the factors we have just described have affected their educational opportunities. Indeed, the Cedral sample was largely obtained in the town (80 percent of the interviewees, while the town contains only 25 percent of the *municipio* population), and yet two-thirds of the men did not stay long enough in school to guarantee themselves functional literacy. The corresponding proportion in Monterrey is only one-third. Almost no Cedraleño went beyond *primaria*, while 27 percent of the Monterrey men did. Of course, if more Cedraleños stayed longer in school (during the few years when a secondary school was open in Cedral or by traveling to the nearest larger town, Matehuala) they

TABLE 4-4. Men's Educational Attainment in Monterrey and Cedral (In Percent)

Educational Level Attained	Monterrey[a]	Cedral[b]
None	11	23
Primaria: 1–3 years	22	44
Primaria: 4–5 years	17	15
Primaria complete: 6 years	23	12
Middle education, first cycle: 7–9 years	15	6
Middle education, second cycle: 10–11 years	4	0
University incomplete: 12–15 years	3	0
University complete: 16 years and over	5	0
Total	101	100
	(1,640)	(380)
Mean years of schooling	6.0	2.8

[a] Men, aged 21–60, representative sample.
[b] Men, aged 15–64, actual sample.

probably left Cedral in order to find jobs commensurate with their education.

As we have indicated in previous chapters, only a minority of the Monterrey men actually were born and raised in the city. The relevant fact for their education is not where they live now, but their community of origin. Our discussion leads us to expect that size of community of origin and the socioeconomic rank of the region in which it is located are important in explaining the educational attainment of the men currently living in Monterrey. The mean number of years in school for the Monterrey men, classified by these two variables, is given in Table 4-5. The men raised in Monterrey or other large cities have twice as many years of schooling, on the average, as those who grew up in rural places. Small urban is separated from the rural category by one and one-half years of education. Men coming from Mexican cities of 100,000 or more and from abroad have better educational levels than those raised in Monterrey, suggesting that the former are a select group of migrants, since it is unlikely that other large cities in Mexico have an overall educational level much above that of Monterrey. A pattern similar to community size is found for the classification according to socioeconomic rank of the region. The men from the lowest category have an even lower mean score than all men from rural origin, suggesting that the former is a more homogeneous category. Actually, category V in the ranking includes mainly rural communities in economically depressed regions. The average is very similar to that found in Cedral, a *municipio* that belongs to that category.

TABLE 4-5. Schooling of Men, by Size and Socioeconomic Category of Community of Origin

Schooling	Rural	Small Urban	Medium Urban	Large Urban Monterrey	Other	Foreign
Mean years	3.8 (495)	5.3 (190)	6.2 (165)	7.5 (711)	8.9 (45)	8.7 (28)

	V (poorest)	IV	III	II	I (richest)
Mean years	2.7 (92)	4.0 (265)	4.6 (166)	5.2 (192)	7.3 (925)

Family Background

If the communities are so important for educational attainment, how can the family environment influence it? Although the community has a bearing upon education by means of the educational facilities it has to offer, the family provides the most immediate context within which the children's ambitions are generated, and it provides the concrete means to attain educational goals.[7] Considerable attention, in the industrial countries in particular, has been devoted recently to the impact of the family of orientation on educational expectations and achievement because it has come to be recognized as the key for an understanding of the way social inequality is transmitted from one generation to the next. Because education looms so large as the main avenue for occupational achievement—about which we will have more to say in subsequent chapters—the differential ability of families to provide their children with an education becomes the main avenue by which the family's relative position in society is transmitted to the new generation.[8]

In what specific ways does the family of orientation have an effect upon the son's educational achievement? There are two important mechanisms: the family's ability to pay for the various costs of their children's education, and the value placed on education by the parents and their success in implanting in their sons the motivation to enter

[7] To date relatively little has been done on a systematic basis to study the effects of family background on educational attainment in Latin America. See Sugiyama Iutaka, "Estratificación social y oportunidades educacionales en tres metrópolis latinoamericanas," *América Latina* 5, no. 4 (October 1962): 53–71. In the United States considerable attention has been given to the topic. For example, see the study by Beverly Duncan based upon a 1962 national sample, "Education and Social Background," *American Journal of Sociology* 72, no. 4 (January 1967): 363–372. The effects of income on education are studied by Patricia C. Sexton, *Education and Income*. Perhaps the most ambitious—and controversial—study of determinants of education in the United States, or elsewhere, is James S. Coleman, et al., *Equality of Educational Opportunity*.

[8] For a discussion of various family-related determinants of educational aspiration (and achievement) see Richard A. Rehberg and David L. Westby, "Parental Encouragement, Occupation, Education, and Family Size: Artifactual or Independent Determinants of Adolescent Educational Expectations?" *Social Forces* 45 (March 1967): 362–374. William H. Sewell has summarized the findings of the longitudinal Wisconsin study in "Inequality of Opportunity for Higher Education," *American Sociological Review* 36 (October 1971): 793–809.

school and to continue in it. The costs of education are direct and in-direct, and the economic status of the family obviously affects its ability to absorb these costs. Although in Mexico there are free, or virtually free, educational institutions at all levels—primary, middle, and university—there are still direct costs for the parents. Suitable clothes, school supplies, and the like, often represent a considerable burden in relative terms for low-income families with many children. Middle-class parents often send their children to private schools and this practice can add up to a considerable sum. The costs of education rise as the number of years of schooling increases.

There are also the indirect costs. If adolescent boys continue studies beyond the primary level, their entrance into the labor force, at least as full-time workers, is delayed. Parents who keep their sons in school must give up the possibility of receiving additional income from a working son's wages, or lose their assistance as unpaid family workers on the farm or in the business. In rural areas, during the crop season or at any other time of the year when there is a labor shortage, adolescents, and even young children, may be almost as useful as adults, given the low mechanization of agriculture in Mexico. In the cities, in spite of legal restrictions on the employment of children, boys still can make a significant contribution to family income by taking all sorts of odd jobs (as described in the following chapter) or by helping in the family store, artisan's *taller*, or repair shop. It is not unusual, for example, for construction workers to take their sons to the work site as helpers, whether or not they are paid a wage. Furthermore, in most apprentice-ship positions, whether it is as a carpenter's helper or as bus driver's assistant, the boy is gaining work experience that in time will permit him to assume full status as a worker. The short-term gains from such an arrangement often exceed those deriving from a year or two more in school.

The direct and indirect costs of education place a greater burden on low- rather than high-income families, since they represent a greater proportion of total family income for the former. Income inequality between families is reflected in inequality of educational opportunity. But when a system of public education is built up to service all social strata, and the costs of education are assumed largely by the state, it can certainly work as a mechanism for income redistribution in favor of the lower strata by giving their children educational opportunities on a more egalitarian basis.

Retrospectively, what the father did for a living is the best single indicator of the family's economic status when the men were school-age boys. That was, in most cases, the main source of income. Although it would be impossible to estimate average income for a variety of occupations in the past, their relative statuses are not difficult to determine, since it can be safely assumed that they are not greatly different from today's. Thus, we have used father's occupation as an indicator of economic status and have classified the fathers in four broad categories, lower and upper manual and lower and upper nonmanual. Since these labels are not very illuminating, a cursory description is in order. In the lower-manual category the largest group is made up of farm laborers and subsistence farmers (either semiindependent like sharecroppers and *ejidatarios,* or independent farmers). Our argument is that the levels of living of these two groups of men were very similar, as they are today, and that property rights on very poor land with no investments do not make any appreciable difference in income. The situation is different for farmers raising mainly cash crops, hiring wage labor, and using irrigation, all of whom were placed at a higher level. Besides the agriculturalists, many men with nonfarm occupations also are found in the lowest stratum: unskilled laborers of all kinds, street vendors, and unskilled service workers. Forty-six percent of the respondent's fathers belonged to this almost undifferentiated lowest stratum. Among the upper manuals we find mainly skilled workers, self-employed workers who did not hire wage laborers and had little capitalization, and market-oriented small farmers, all making up about one-third (31 percent) of the men's fathers. The nonmanual groups are small indeed: in the lower-nonmanual group (13 percent) are mainly small shop owners and clerical workers, while in the upper nonmanual (5 percent) we find mainly managers, professional workers, and owners of large enterprises.

The number of years in school spent by the men are heavily dependent on father's occupation (see Table 4-6). About ten years of

TABLE 4-6. Men's Schooling, by Father's Occupational Level

Schooling	Lower Manual	Upper Manual	Lower Nonmanual	Upper Nonmanual	No Information
Mean years	3.7	6.8	10.5	13.5	4.4
	(748)	(516)	(206)	(76)	(94)

schooling separate, on the average, the lowest and highest groups, a far wider range than is found among categories of community of origin. Very few of the men raised in poor families had any education beyond *primaria,* while nearly all the children of richer families did. Parenthetically, it should be noted that the average for the men who failed to provide information on father's occupation (6 percent) is similar to that of the sons of men in the lowest stratum. The majority of the men in the "no information" category did not know their fathers, either because they died early in the man's life or because the fathers abandoned their families, both possibilities being closely associated with a low economic status.

The second important way by which the family influences the education of the sons, above and beyond the economic mechanism involved in the determination of educational opportunities, is through the values and attitudes the parents have toward education and their willingness and ability to inculcate in their offspring a positive and an active orientation toward getting an education. These parental attitudes are not independent of economic status, but one should not expect to find so high a correlation between them that attitudes could not in themselves make any difference. Later in this chapter and in Chapter 10 we will attempt to separate their effects upon the men's educational attainment. Here we will assume that such a family climate toward education exists and, although we cannot measure it retrospectively in a direct form, father's and mother's educational levels will serve as an approximation. Better educated parents will have higher ambitions for their children than those with lower education. They are more open to the modern world, where formal training plays a tremendously important role for occupational opportunities. They may have wider social relations that cut across class boundaries, and therefore they can assimilate values and norms characteristic of people placed above them in the stratification system. Educated parents understand better the school assignments of their children, can implant and reinforce in them the belief in the functional value of education, and can be in closer contact with the educational institution. Thus we can expect parents' education to be related to the level of expectations and the ability to implement those expectations.

The educational distribution of fathers and mothers of the Monterrey respondents, as given in Table 4-7, presents the form of a broadly based pyramid, with the great bulk found at the lowest educational levels (62

TABLE 4-7. Parental Educational Attainment (In Percent)

Educational Level Attained	Fathers	Mothers
None	25	31
Primaria incomplete: 1–5 years	37	36
Primaria complete: 6 years	20	21
Middle education: 7–11 years	6	5
University education: 12 years plus	2	1
No information	10	6
Total	100	100
	(1,640)	(1,640)

SOURCE: Representative sample.

percent of the fathers and 67 percent of the mothers not having completed *primaria*). These percentages are even higher if we assume that "no information" means by and large low levels of schooling, as we did in considering father's occupation. Probably about 60 percent of both fathers and mothers were functionally illiterate.

The effects of parental levels of education on the men's schooling can be observed in Table 4-8. The range of average number of years of schooling is similar to that found between categories of father's occupation. The "no information" category has an average only slightly better than that presented by the sons of fathers and mothers with no formal education.

TABLE 4-8. Men's Schooling, by Parents' Educational Attainment

Schooling	None	Father's Education *Primaria* Incomplete	*Primaria* Complete	Middle or University	No Information
Mean years	2.9	5.7	8.0	12.3	3.8
	(387)	(562)	(351)	(167)	(173)

	None	Mother's Education *Primaria* Incomplete	*Primaria* Complete	Middle or University	No Information
Mean years	3.0	5.9	8.9	11.4	4.2
	(499)	(518)	(397)	(118)	(108)

Another aspect of the family merits attention because of its possible effect upon educational attainment: family size. A large number of siblings could be an important handicap for education, especially for the children of low-income families, where very scarce resources must be shared. As a rule, the men were born into large families. The mean number of siblings is six, and adding the respondent makes seven children, a figure that reflects the high fertility levels of Mexico. Eleven percent of the men were born into families with twelve or more children, while only 2 percent had no siblings. The mean number of years of schooling of respondents by number of siblings is given in Table 4-9. Less than one school year separates the lowest from the highest category. The lack of relationship of number of siblings with education is at odds with the importance we assigned to the various direct and indirect costs that families must assume in the education of their children. Surely such costs, however calculated, must have a sizable differential effect according to size of family. Larger families do have greater expenses, and the resources allocated for the education of each particular child are less than in smaller families. To illustrate, a family with ten children surviving through the six years of *primaria* would have to provide for sixty school years, while a family of three would have only eighteen years to support.

This lack of relationship is difficult to explain. Probably our respondents' parents would have been less surprised than we are, since most Mexicans (mainly in the older generation) tend to dismiss the cost involved in having many children, and they definitely do not believe that a large family is either an economic burden or a handicap for their children's future. Quite often they point out that, the larger the number of children and the greater the economic need, the greater the pressure upon the father to work hard, with the end result being a similar amount of resources available per child in large as in small families (of course, within the same social class).

For some of our readers this lack of relationship may be puzzling on

TABLE 4-9. Men's Schooling, by Their Number of Siblings

| Schooling | Number of Siblings | | | | |
	9 or More	7–8	5–6	3–4	0–2
Mean years	5.7	5.5	5.8	5.9	6.1
	(368)	(297)	(370)	(347)	(242)

another count, since the number of siblings could be related to educational attainment as a consequence of differential fertility. Better educated parents, or those with higher levels of living, or those living in urban as opposed to rural areas can provide a better education for their children, and they also tend to have a smaller number of children. However, the latter was not the case among our respondents' parents. There was practically no differential fertility according to any of those variables. Actually, we may argue that among the parents the number of children was seldom a matter of choice, very few families practicing any sort of family planning. Therefore, fertility can hardly reflect the motivational environment that would also be conducive for higher educational attainment among the offspring. Thus, the lack of fertility differentials and the absence of choice in completed fertility help to explain the lack of relationship between number of siblings and educational attainment among the Monterrey men. Still, the explanation is incomplete because it does not account for the possible effects of the costs in raising a large family upon the children's opportunities.

Finally, we investigated the relationship between education and two other family-related variables: respondent's birth order, taking only brothers, and respondent's age at the death of the father. Birth order can be relevant for education, since in Mexico it still is the norm that in the case of the absence of the father, by death or other causes, the oldest son takes the father's role in economic and disciplinary respects. This responsibility can affect the educational chances of the boy, particularly if he is the oldest in a large family. Death of the father during the early years of the respondent's life should make for a considerable handicap in the boy's chances for educational advancement, both in matters of economic support and in guidance and discipline. The mean number of years of schooling of respondents classified by these two variables is given in Table 4-10.

The respondent's birth order with respect to that of his brothers shows practically no relationship with education, excepting "only male," which is only 8 percent of the cases. On the basis of this evidence, we must conclude that birth order is not relevant for educational attainment. The disruption of the family occasioned by the death of the father while the son was young confirms our expectations: those men who lost their fathers while they were very young do show a lower average education than the others, mainly when compared with those

TABLE 4-10. Men's Schooling, by Family Characteristics

| Schooling | Birth Order of Brothers | | | |
	Oldest	Youngest	Middle	Only Male
Mean years	6.0	6.1	5.9	6.8
	(469)	(380)	(636)	(136)

| | Death of Father | | | |
	Respondent 5 or Less	Respondent 6–10	Respondent 11–20	Respondent 21+ or Father Living
Mean years	4.2	4.5	5.5	6.8
	(137)	(108)	(185)	(1,164)

whose fathers died after they were of school age (or whose fathers are currently alive).

Multivariate Analysis

We have thus far taken each determinant of educational attainment individually, looking at the bivariate relationships between family and community background variables and the number of years of schooling completed. It is obvious that these background variables are interrelated, so that we should consider them in combination to determine their joint and individual effects upon educational attainment. One would like to answer questions as to the relative importance of each of the variables discussed in the previous section, as well as to the way these variables combine their effects. Also, a measure indicating how much of the men's educational attainment can be accounted for by their background is useful in evaluating the extent to which "ascription" and "achievement" count for their adult statuses. The answers to these questions can be sought with the help of such statistical techniques as multiple linear regression analysis. The reader who wishes to pursue a more technical treatment of these questions may do so in the first part of Chapter 10. At this point, however, some of the findings obtained with regression analysis and their implications, as well as other results based upon analysis of variance, will be presented.

In Table 4-11 the Monterrey sample is divided into seven groups, each formed by a particular combination of background variables. These combinations were arrived at with the use of the Automatic In-

Table 4-11. Education of Monterrey Men, by Selected Background Characteristics

Characteristics of Respondent	Mean Years of Schooling	Standard Deviation
Father nonmanual, university education	14.3	3.7
Father nonmanual, middle-level education	12.1	4.1
Father nonmanual, *primaria* education or less	8.1	4.0
Father manual, mother some education, father *primaria* completed or more	7.7	4.0
Father manual, mother some education, father did not complete *primaria*	5.2	3.4
Father manual, mother no education, respondent raised in urban community	3.6	3.0
Father manual, mother no education, respondent raised in rural community	1.9	2.1
Total	6.0 (1,640)	4.6

teraction Detector (AID),[9] a statistical technique based upon the analysis of variance that selects, out of a series of possible predictors, those whose combination best explains the variance in a dependent variable—in this case, education. For each of the groups the mean number of years of school completed as well as the standard deviation are given.

The men belonging to the top group are in most cases sons of professionals and top managers or entrepreneurs, indicated by the fact that their fathers had nonmanual occupations and at least some university education. This is clearly an elite background, considering how few in Mexico had these characteristics several decades ago. Within our sample, the sons of these men, whose families had the money and expectations that were useful in providing them with the best educational chances, represent only 3 percent of the total. A majority of them had attained some university education, as indicated by an average of over fourteen years of schooling. The men belonging to the following two groups also had nonmanual fathers, but with only a *primaria* or *secundaria* education. The latter group—father nonmanual with *pri-*

---

[9] A full discussion of AID is given by John A. Sonquist and James N. Morgan in *The Detection of Interaction Effects.*

maria education—comes quite close in mean number of years of schooling to the top manual group.

The next four groups all have manual fathers. The top one among them includes men whose fathers had at least completed *primaria* and whose mothers had some education. Between the fourth and fifth groups the distinction between fathers who completed and those who did not complete *primaria* is associated with a difference of two and one-half years of schooling. The two bottom groups are composed of men whose fathers were manual workers and whose mothers had no education, that is, men whose families of orientation were in the lowest socioeconomic stratum. Within that stratum, however, whether the man was raised in a rural or an urban community results in an important difference in terms of years of school completed: the rural men have on the average almost two years less of schooling. The majority of these men are sons of farm laborers or *ejidatarios* whose mothers had no schooling. On the average, they attended school less than two years and most of them cannot presently read and write. The educational gap between this group and the one at the top is very large, with a difference of twelve years of schooling.

The characteristics of the families of orientation (father's occupation and education, mother's education) stand out as most relevant for educational attainment, although to what degree they are important we will discuss below. None of the variables related to family context (birth order, number of siblings, age at father's death) were chosen as a predictor by the AID program. Size class of community of origin was used once, but socioeconomic ranking of the communities was not selected.

One interesting finding is that the influence of the mother's education is most strongly felt among the lower economic strata, that is, among men whose fathers had manual occupations. This finding may reflect the greater importance of the mother in the socialization of lower-class children or, perhaps better stated, the weaker influence of the father in these families as compared to middle- and upper-class families. For various reasons, the father in lower-class families is more often absent, either physically or psychologically. In these cases, the mother necessarily must assume a more important role. Consequently, in such families the mother's educational level makes a considerable difference with regard to educational aspirations and plans for the children. Where resources are scarce, the decision to delay the earnings produced by the boy's entrance into the labor force and the willingness to maintain him in school may rest more often on the mother than on the father. It should also be noted that size class of the community of origin has a clear-cut effect only upon the very lowest socioeconomic group. Why should this be so? In the first place, there is a great homogeneity of community origins among the upper groups: the nonmanual, better-educated population of Mexico lives in urban areas. In addition, an urban rather than a rural location is crucial for poor families and their children's education because of two reasons. First, schooling does not have to compete so much with economic activities, such as agriculture. Poor boys can hold part-time jobs and still go to school. Second, in an urban setting the school is closer to home, and the distance factor may be a determinant when the motivation is not very high.

We have yet to give a clear-cut answer to the question of the relative weight of the various background characteristics in determining our respondents' education. The results of the multiple linear regression analysis are of relevance. Taking seven independent variables—father's occupation, father's education, mother's education, size class of community of origin, socioeconomic region, number of siblings, and age at father's death—and using a technique that measures only the linear and additive effects of these variables, we find that the first three have an effect considerably greater than the others. Their relative weight, moreover, is very similar. Size class of the community of origin and the socioeconomic region make significant contributions, but since both are highly intercorrelated indicators of the community context, little is gained by taking both.

Almost one-half of the variance in number of years of schooling is explained statistically by these background variables. The three family-of-orientation variables alone account for 45 percent of the variance. This last result may be looked at from at least two different perspectives. One would emphasize the amount of variance left unexplained, implying that a considerable "freedom" to attain an education is still present, since more than one-half of the variation in educational achievement of the men seems not to be related to the social class of the families of orientation (as measured by occupation and education).

The second perspective in evaluating the effects of parental socioeconomic background upon education is a comparative one. In this regard, Treiman, as well as other authors, has hypothesized that "the more industrialized a society, the smaller the influence of parental status on educational attainment." The arguments adduced to support this hypothesis are based on two concommitants of industrialization: the expansion of a public system of education that plays down the importance of financial capability of the family to send the children to school and the process of urbanization, since urban children from all strata have educational facilities more readily available and are under less pressure to leave school early to enter the labor force. These arguments have already been discussed in this chapter, and we find them correct. However, the concrete evidence to substantiate the correlation between industrialization and degree of inequality of educational opportunities—both by comparing societies of various degrees of industrialization and by considering changes in a particular society undergoing industrialization—is almost nil. Compared to the situation in the United States, as reported by Otis D. Duncan and R. W. Hodge and by Beverly Duncan, the Monterrey results do indicate that in the more industrialized society (the United States) the effects of parental status are somewhat lower.[10] Beverly Duncan, however, does not detect any change over time in the United States by using intercohort comparisons in her national sample. Our own data, limited as they are to a city sample, indicate such an intercohort decrease in the effects of family origins on education, thus giving some support to the historical relationship between industrialization and inequality of educational opportunities.

The Temporal Dimension of Educational Attainment

So far our discussion has been centered on our men's educational attainment when related to social background factors, and we have given little attention to the temporal dimension, so important in Mexico, a society experiencing rapid social change. Forty years separate the oldest from the youngest of our men, and in this time male life expectancy has doubled, the population of the country has much more than doubled, and the proportion of the total population living in cities has risen substantially. How have the Monterrey men been affected in terms of their educational attainment?

The men have been affected a great deal, as may be seen by a glance

---

[10] Otis D. Duncan and Robert W. Hodge, "Education and Occupational Mobility: A Regression Analysis," *American Journal of Sociology* 68, no. 5 (May 1963): 629–644; and Beverly Duncan, "Education and Social Background."

at the four ten-year birth cohorts given in Table 4-12. The contrast between the oldest (1905–1914) and youngest (1935–1944) cohorts is
especially striking. Nearly a quarter of the older men had no schooling,
but this figure had been reduced to 5 percent for the youngest cohort.
At the other end of the educational spectrum the contrast is equally
marked. Less than 2 percent of the oldest cohort had any university exposure. Among the youngest men, 12 percent had this exposure. For all
men, one-half had finished *primaria* or had gone beyond it. Among the
older men, hardly more than a third had done so, while within the
youngest cohort nearly two-thirds at least had completed the first phase
of the Mexican educational system.

In Monterrey it is to be expected that the younger men would do
better. In the first place, a larger proportion of them spent their formative years in an urban environment. Monterrey is the community of
origin for 59 percent of the youngest cohort, in contrast to 32 percent
of the oldest one. The comparable figures for rural communities of
origin are 21 and 39 percent. Second, the economic circumstances of
the family, as reflected in father's occupation, also show an intercohort
difference, though not in so striking a fashion. The percent of fathers

TABLE 4-12. Levels of Education of Monterrey Men, by Birth Cohorts (In Percent)

Education	Birth Cohorts			
	1905–1914	1915–1924	1925–1934	1935–1944
None	24	15	11	5
Primaria: 1–3 years	23	27	26	16
Primaria: 4–5 years	17	15	19	16
Primaria complete: 6 years	20	22	23	25
Middle education, first cycle: 7–9 years	11	13	11	20
Middle education, second cycle: 10–11 years	2	2	3	7
University incomplete: 12–15 years	1	1	2	6
University complete: 16 years and over	2	5	6	6
Total	100	100	101	101
	(378)	(436)	(365)	(451)

SOURCE: Representative sample.

in the lowest economic stratum (farm workers and unskilled manual workers) declined from 55 to 44 percent from the oldest to the youngest cohort (or 60 to 50 percent if the "don't knows" are allocated to the lowest stratum). The rather mild upgrading that we find for the fathers says nothing about the possibility that within-stratum incomes might have risen substantially. We lack direct information on this point, but it is generally agreed that the economic lot of the lowest stratum has not improved greatly during the last few decades. The other strata probably experienced an appreciable betterment of income, so the relative position of the lowest groups might have actually deteriorated.

Third, parents' education shows a rather similar pattern. The proportion of fathers with no schooling declines from 31 to 20 percent from the oldest to the youngest cohort, with the mothers experiencing a greater decline, from 44 to 21 percent. Parents who completed *primaria* or more showed much less of a change: fathers and mothers having the same figures, a rise from 25 to 28 percent. Among the other variables we have discussed, there is comparatively little variation. What all of this means is that the characteristics of the parents do change somewhat, but the change is not as pronounced as what has happened to their children's education.

Younger people have higher levels of education even after we control for the effects of other relevant variables. Men whose families of orientation were similar and who were brought up in communities of the same size class, but separated by four decades in time, show on the average almost two and one-half years of schooling difference in favor of the younger ones. The "net" effect of birth cohort indicates the growth of educational opportunities for everyone; not as impressive as it might be, but still a significant change.

A different question is whether the effects of the other variables, mainly those related to family of orientation, remain the same among the younger as among the older men. (A statistical answer to this question is found in Chapter 10.) We found that for the youngest birth cohort the economic status of the family of orientation is much less relevant for their educational attainment than for the oldest cohort, the other two cohorts being intermediate. Educational differences between categories of father's occupation, other things being equal, were twice as large among the oldest men than among the youngest. Inversely, mother's education had a greater effect among the younger men. Father's education has a similar effect in all cohorts. The overall importance of the three family-of-orientation characteristics has decreased considerably over time. Most interesting, perhaps, is the fact that, while the economic status of the families (as measured by father's occupation) lost much of its impact, mother's education grew in importance.

As previously discussed, the decline in the impact of economic status upon education can be interpreted as the result of increasing public expenditures in education related to industrialization. Thus, it is possible for children coming from various backgrounds to take advantage of similar facilities. The fact that free or almost free education is made available to increasingly larger proportions of the Mexican population, and for longer time periods, has a definite impact in diminishing the importance of economic differentials. We interpret the increasing effect of mother's education to be a consequence of two different trends. In the first place, when the economic status of the family loses some of its salience, other factors in the family environment may gain importance. If schools are few and far away, and the cost of educating children and postponing their participation in the labor force is large in relation to family income, there is less opportunity for parents motivated to educate their children to actually put them through school. Although these motivations and expectations are related to the economic status of the family, the former will have a greater effect when the latter is less important.

The second explanation for the growing importance of mother's education is based on our impression of the strengthening of the role of the woman in Mexican society, and more specifically within the context of the family. Traditionally, women have had only a secondary role in the making of decisions within the family. The trend for an increasing importance of women in family decision-making, in our opinion, is related to two observable changes. First, the educational gap between males and females has narrowed. Several decades ago there was a substantial difference in illiteracy by sex. By 1960 the difference for the youngest cohorts by sex was practically eliminated. Second, there has been an increase in the participation of females in the labor force (other than domestic service). Thus, a weakening of educational differences between sexes and the opening of new areas of activity outside the home, at least for the younger women, probably are making for a more egalitarian relationship between husband and wife in the family context and a greater initiative on the part of mothers to push their children's education. In short, the declining salience of family's economic status makes room for other influences to operate, while the enhancing of the mother's status in the family environment makes her education more relevant in the formulation of the children's educational plans.

What about Cedral? Do we also find there important educational differences between cohorts? As can be seen in Table 4-13, there is a sharp decrease in the percentage of men who never attended school, dropping from over one-half of the older men to less than 10 percent among the younger men. There is a corresponding increase in the proportion of men completing four or more years of schooling. The reader should be reminded that our sample was heavily drawn from the urban center of the *municipio*. But, at least for that locality, we can certainly see a change, with almost all boys having at least a minimum contact with school. Probably at the present time one-third of the town boys finish the first six grades of schooling.

In Cedral, unlike Monterrey, we cannot attribute the higher levels of education to any radical change in community origin or family background: the large majority, young or old, were raised in Cedral and are sons of farm laborers or farmers whose levels of living have not, on the average, increased greatly. We found almost no differences in father's or mother's literacy according to respondent's birth cohort. Thus, in Cedral we have to attribute the improvement not to a change in family background but to changes in the community.

The variation in schooling among the Cedral cohorts reflects not only the better educational facilities now available. There have been other changes (mainly operating in the *municipio* center) that have

TABLE 4-13. Educational Levels of Cedral Men, by Age (In Percent)

Education	15–24	25–34	Age Groups 35–44	45–54	55–64
None	9	17	18	34	54
Primaria incomplete: 1–3 years	36	51	52	37	37
Primaria incomplete: 4–5 years	28	13	10	19	5
Primaria complete: 6 years	22	13	12	6	2
Post-*primaria*: 7 plus	5	6	8	5	2
Total	100	100	100	101	100
	(75)	(109)	(88)	(65)	(43)

worked to stimulate interest in schooling and to make manifest the rewards it can bring. The town youngsters have a better chance today to learn about the kinds of jobs available in cities like Monterrey through the mass media, trips to the cities, and visits of relatives back to Cedral. Improved communications (highways, radios, newspapers) explain the breakdown of cultural isolation, which has happened in spite of the lack of any real development of the local economy. Even if there has been no great elaboration of the local division of labor, the youngsters can identify with urban occupations that serve as role models, and thereby they become aware of the built-in educational requirements that these occupations have. If in Monterrey we can consider the improvement in educational levels largely as a reflection of industrialization and development of the city, in Cedral widespread literacy is largely a consequence of development of the nation rather than of the community. This in part explains why many parents still look with some suspicion or at best with neutrality on their children's schooling. On the one hand, they may think that they are being exposed to "bad" (nontraditional) influences. On the other hand, they fear that if the child is educated he will want to leave the community, while they may want to use his labor in the family enterprise, farm and nonfarm. Outside the town, in the ejidos, these parental attitudes are even stronger and are not so effectively counterbalanced by external stimuli that create educational motivations among the children. In a traditional and an economically stagnant community, the rise of educational levels is a disruptive factor. The disruption is exogenous, resulting from national development. We will argue later in this book that, at least partially, the disruptive element (the better educated, younger men) finds an external solution: out-migration.

5. Entry into the Labor Force and Early Work Experience

       This is the first of three chapters that focus on the occupational histories of the Monterrey men. Here we are concerned with two aspects of their work lives, namely, entrance into the labor force and work experience up to age 25. We first address ourselves to the question of when and where the men enter the labor force, and what are the determinants of variations in timing and location. Then we analyze the crucial initial period of work up to age 25, emphasizing upward vertical mobility and the role of migration. In Chapter 8 we will follow the men through the middle years (25–45) of their work lives. Besides a continuation of interest in the vertical dimension of mobility and the relation of migration to this mobility, this chapter stresses the non-vertical aspects of occupational mobility. Chapter 9 takes the older men, 45 and over, and tries to account for how they arrived at the positions they occupy. It should be kept in mind that the division of work histories into the age intervals (up to 25, 25–45, 45–60) is quite arbitrary, and it was done only to facilitate exposition and analysis. Chapters 6 and 7, on migration and marriage and family, interrupt the work-history sequence. They are so ordered to conform to the life-cycle approach. Some readers may prefer, after reading Chapter 5, to go directly to Chapters 8 and 9, to have the work histories in one uninterrupted sequence, and then go back to pick up Chapters 6 and 7. In any case, we will keep to a minimum cross references between the three chapters centered on the men's occupational histories.

The Blurry Beginnings of Occupational Life

The transition from education to work usually is seen as the major point dividing two stages of the life cycle: adolescence and adulthood.[1] But this transition is not always clear-cut, depending on how formalized are the definitions of roles in the society. In some societies, where education is not carried out as a segregated activity by a specialized institution and the separation of home and work is not made, there is no such transition from education to work. Usually there are other ways to symbolize the entrance into an adult status, especially through *rites de passage*. In contrast, in modern industrial societies the entrance to various institutional spheres and the assumption of full status in each of them mark the various stages of the life cycle. Indeed, the assumption of new statuses in industrialized countries is hedged by legal restrictions, for example, age when schooling may be terminated, full-time assumption of occupational role, and entry into marital union. Entrance into and full participation in the labor force result in the adoption of adult responsibilities.

In a rapidly changing and developing society like Mexico's, for those men participating in the technologically more advanced sectors of the economy where roles are more clearly defined, the transition from education to work is clear. But this is not the case in other sectors of the economy where it is often difficult to establish a clear-cut moment when the man may be said to enter the labor force.

There mainly are two situations where the boundary between work and nonwork status is difficult to draw. One is involvement in any type of family enterprise, whether rural or urban, where members of the family group contribute their labor without receiving any income ("unpaid family workers" is the way they are described in censuses). The other situation is paid work, but of an unstable and occasional nature.[2]

---

[1] A summary of various schemes for dividing the life cycle into stages can be found in Leonard D. Cain, Jr., "Life Course and Social Structure," in *Handbook of Modern Sociology*, ed. Robert L. Faris. This article includes a comprehensive bibliography on the subject.

[2] Some of the difficulties in distinguishing between work and nonwork, especially in agriculture, are discussed in the United Nations publication, *Handbook of Population Census Methods*, Vol. II. *Economic Characteristics of the Population*. It rec-

Both are particularly important for the Monterrey study, since, as we shall see, a large proportion of the men began their occupational lives in these positions.

In a society where agriculture is carried out primarily at a subsistence level, there is little distinction between household duties and farm activities. In such a situation, "work" and household duties are mixed and cannot be separated. Oscar Lewis, in his study of a "traditional" village in central Mexico, describes the work cycle of young Tepoztecas as follows:

Children learn to work slowly and, with few exceptions, the belief that heavy labor will weaken a growing child governs the amount of work parents expect from their offspring . . . At about the time they enter school, about age five, both boys and girls begin to do simple tasks in the house. As they get a little older they are generally glad to run errands near by, carry a small can of water or corn dough, or chase the chickens from the garden.

At the age of six, many children are sent alone to the corn mill or to the plaza to buy small articles . . . At about age six, boys occasionally accompany their fathers to the fields. They look forward to this, and the first trip is an important occasion in their lives. Small boys are not expected to work in the fields but may help in weeding, watching the animals and tools, gathering wood for the fire, and in running errands. From about eight years of age, many boys regularly carry the noon meal to their father in the fields and are required to help with the weeding and cultivation.

As boys get older, their principal work is to pasture the animals and to guard them from being lost or stolen . . . the boys are required to rise early, take the animals to pasture before school, and bring them home after school. Boys are frequently kept out of school to watch the animals or do some other work. From about ten years of age, boys join their fathers and brothers in the field daily to learn the work of a farmer. By the time a boy is fifteen he generally can drive a plow and go through the necessary steps in planting and harvesting . . . At home, boys of fifteen or so usually haul water, water the plants, take care of large animals, provide firewood, pick fruit, and help shell corn.[3]

---

ommends some arbitrary but uniform criteria for this distinction in census taking, applicable to cross-sectional data. Most studies on the employment of youth are based on cross-sectional data using age-specific participation rates rather than retrospective longitudinal information. See Eleanor H. Bernert, *America's Children*; and John Korbel, "Labor Force Entry and Attachment of Young People," *Journal of the American Statistical Association* 61, no. 313 (1966): 117–127.

[3] Oscar Lewis, *Life in a Mexican Village: Tepoztlán Restudied*, pp. 99–100.

On the basis of this description one very well can ask, When does the worklife of a typical Tepoztecan boy begin? Social scientists analyzing the case are bound to disagree, and any decision would have to be arbitrary, for there is no single moment when the boy changes drastically his activities and enters a well-defined and clear-cut role. Many of our Monterrey men were brought up and began working in communities similar, in this respect, to Lewis's Tepoztlán.

In the cities working-class boys have a wider range of alternatives in beginning their occupational lives. Many start by helping their fathers. This is almost invariably the case when the father is self-employed—be it as the owner of a small grocery store, a repair shop, or some artisan activity. From early childhood the sons are expected and required to help in minor tasks and in general to make themselves useful. Fathers working in construction jobs also may use their sons as helpers, even when they are not self-employed. Children also are expected to help at home and the boys, in particular, are often sent on errands for their mothers. In carrying out these assignments, the boys may help out neighbors by running some of their errands. Generally, no money is given for this help, but it may develop into a "service" to households of the neighborhood—bringing water from the neighborhood tap, taking lunch boxes to the men's work site, and so on—and, becoming regularized, it may develop into a job.

Working-class boys early may begin selling a variety of goods in the city streets: newspapers, *chicles*, toys. They also may offer a variety of services, ranging from "taking care of cars" (a way of asking for a tip without doing anything, but at least giving assurance to the owner that the boy will not damage the car during his absence) to shining shoes. Somewhat older boys can pick up more stable work in delivery services: tortillas, drug store products, and the like. Modernization has created a new service: the carrying of grocery bags of shoppers in supermarkets.

Life for most working-class boys is much more centered in the streets than in the home. The extremely restricted quarters and the risk of incurring parental ire by being underfoot do not make their homes attractive places in which to spend time. By contrast, being a shoeshine boy means getting away from home, interacting with other boys, and having adventures in the city streets. These features are often more important to the boy than the little, if any, money that he can make on his "job." For him work is a casual and an unstable activity, governed by factors other than economic calculus. It's not an unpleasant way of occupying himself, and, if he is fortunate enough to pick up some money, so much the better. Thus, his participation depends more upon his mood than demand-supply conditions of the market.

From an economic point of view, all these activities are of very low productivity, but they may be of considerable importance for the boys and their families. First, the activities expose the boys to many aspects of work, so they serve a socialization function. Not only may the boys learn specific skills, but also the jobs give them some sense of importance, and the experience strengthens their independence and makes them better able to fend for themselves. Furthermore, although whatever income earned may be very little and highly irregular, it can be of some relative importance for a very low income family. At the very least it may permit the boys to provide their own food while they are away from home (mothers do not try to control their son's diet and regularity of meals among this socioeconomic stratum). In some cases the experience gained in these kinds of work is directly applicable to the kind of employment the boys will have when they are older. The employment structure of many developing countries includes a substantial proportion of underemployed persons, not only among young persons just entering the labor force, but also among adults. The men spend long hours at their jobs, but as they are inherently unproductive they do not earn much. A boy may be destined to remain his entire work life in the job he began with, as street vendor or shoeshine boy. This is simply a hard fact of underemployment, rather than any flaw in defining what is or is not work.

In summary, the transition from not working to working is for many men a blurred one. Work and nonwork are not opposite and contradictory terms. This is especially so in the underdeveloped countries, where the social definition of the position and roles of a young boy is not as clearly established as in highly developed societies. In the United States, for instance, many youngsters work, and are encouraged to do so by their parents, at various jobs—newspaper boys, baby sitters—during the school year. But it is quite clear that these are activities subordinate to the main job of going to school, and the "work" itself is not thought of as being linked in any way to subsequent occupational position. Besides the differences in the definition of the roles of youngsters, the actual contribution to the family income in the two types of countries differs. The difference in earnings between a boy and an adult in

Mexico is considerably smaller than in the United States. Furthermore, as jobs, job titles, and the rights and duties inherent in occupational positions become more formalized and subject to legal rules (and this happens during the process of economic development), work separates itself more clearly from other activities and becomes a distinct and identifiable area in the lives of people.

The blurriness of the transition in Mexico undoubtedly has some effect on the reliability of information collected in the Monterrey survey, for different men use different sets of implicit criteria in their responses. Agricultural employment is especially troublesome, for there is wide variation in the age the men report as the beginning of their work lives. Consider some concrete cases. One man reported that he began working at age 5, helping his father on the family farm. His responsibility until the age of 16 was caring for the two hundred goats his father owned. But between the ages of 10 and 16 he also worked occasionally as a hired laborer on other farms. Another respondent, also brought up in a rural area near Monterrey, whose father was a farmer producing mainly maize, beans, and squash, reports that he began working at age 22. He started by going to the forest to cut wood and then transporting it to town for sale. He was self-employed, with a young boy helping him. No job is reported before age 22, but it is very doubtful that he did not help in the family plot during several years. This probably means that for him "work" is gainful employment with a money income, so he did not report his previous activities. Between these two extreme cases there is a considerable variation in reported ages, doubtless reflecting the moment when each man believed he began making a significant contribution—a quantitative rather than a qualitative change in his activities. We believe, however, that extreme cases such as we have reported tend to balance one another out, without greatly altering the general pattern of reported age at entry into the labor force.

Variations in age at entry into the labor force can be accounted for by both contextual and individual variables. That is, on the one hand, we can look for characteristics of the environment, such as the economic organization of production, and, on the other hand, for characteristics of the men (i.e., their levels of education) to explain at what age they will enter the labor force. Among the former, what interests us is the age requirements for participation in economic activities under various types of economic organization. The most evident variation is that between agricultural and nonagricultural production: in rural areas where small family farms predominate and a complex technology is not used, very young boys are economically productive.[4] There are no formal requirements for employment there, since, even if the employer is not the family, legal rules are nonexistent or not enforced. Furthermore, the actual ability of a young boy to participate productively in nonmechanized activities is almost as great as that of an adult. In urban areas, where nonagricultural activities predominate, a more complex technology and formalized rules inhibit or restrict the participation of youths in many economic activities.[5] The extreme case is exemplified by large enterprises that do not employ anybody under a given age, generally 16, in part because of laws restricting child labor (that other enterprises can ignore more safely) and in part because they can make little use of it.

The age requirements for participation in economic activities have changed during recent decades. In part this has been only a consequence of the proportional shift from agricultural to nonagricultural activities in the Mexican economy. Furthermore, formal age requirements in the nonagricultural sector have increased as a consequence of technological development as well as for humanitarian reasons that underlie laws against child labor (generally accompanied by laws requiring parents to send their children to school up to a given age).

It can be expected that, among the men of Monterrey, the size of the community of residence when they entered the labor force, as well as birth cohort, would affect the age at beginning work. The former reflects the relative predominance of agricultural and nonagricultural activities, while the latter indicates changes that have taken place during recent decades. The most relevant individual characteristic, educational attainment, is clearly correlated with place of residence and birth cohort, since rural residents and those born earlier have lower levels of education. But above and beyond this correlation, we can expect that the more years the men stayed in school the later they entered the labor

[4] Several authors have stressed the importance of children's contribution in Mexican agriculture. See Moisés T. de la Peña, *El pueblo y su tierra: Mito y realidad de la reforma agraria en México*; and Nathan L. Whetten, *Rural Mexico*.
[5] Paul T. David, in a study published in 1942 (*Barriers to Youth Employment*), provides a systematic analysis of the institutional obstacles to employment of youth in the United States. Although the institutional arrangements are now different, many of his findings still hold.

force. Therefore, in explaining variations in age at entry into the labor
force, we will deal with three interrelated variables, two of which can
be considered as contextual, or "background," variables and the third
as an individual, or intervening, one. In Table 5-1 we present the
average age at entry into the labor force by birth cohort, size of place

TABLE 5-1. Average Age at First Job for Birth Cohorts, by Place of Residence and Education
at Time of Beginning Work

Birth Cohort	No Education	1–3	4–5	6	7–9	10 or More	All Educational Levels
			Years of School Completed[a]				
Born 1905–1914							
Rural	10.6	12.0	13.4	13.7	—[b]	0.0	11.7
Urban	12.0	11.4	12.8	13.6	—[b]	—[b]	12.7
Metropolitan	10.9	13.0	13.8	14.0	15.9	20.0	14.7
Subtotal	11.0	12.2	13.5	13.8	15.7	19.8	13.3
Born 1915–1924							
Rural	11.0	11.9	12.8	15.0	—[b]	—[b]	12.5
Urban	11.2	11.3	—[b]	14.3	—[b]	—[b]	13.3
Metropolitan	10.1	11.5	13.3	14.5	15.5	19.8	15.0
Subtotal	10.9	11.6	13.1	14.5	15.5	20.0	13.9
Born 1925–1934							
Rural	10.5	11.1	12.4	13.6	—[b]	—[b]	12.0
Urban	9.4	11.0	13.4	14.0	—[b]	—[b]	12.4
Metropolitan	12.8	11.7	13.4	14.0	15.9	20.4	15.4
Subtotal	10.6	11.3	13.1	13.9	15.9	20.3	14.0
Born 1935–1944							
Rural	9.6	11.4	11.7	13.4	—[b]	0.0	11.7
Urban	—[b]	11.6	12.0	14.4	—[b]	—[b]	13.0
Metropolitan	10.6	11.3	13.1	14.0	15.6	18.8	15.2
Subtotal	9.9	11.4	12.6	14.0	15.6	18.8	14.5
All cohorts							
Rural	10.6	11.6	12.6	13.9	15.6	—[b]	12.0
Urban	11.1	12.2	13.0	14.0	15.6	19.2	12.9
Metropolitan	10.8	11.8	13.4	14.1	15.7	19.5	15.1
Grand total	10.8	11.6	13.1	14.1	15.7	19.5	13.9

[a] Six years of schooling is completed *primaria* education; 7–9 years correspond to high
school, 10 or more to *preparatoria* or university education.

[b] Cell number is less than 10.

of residence, and years of school completed. For all men, the average age at beginning work is almost 14, with the range being from 4 to 30. The variation between means, although not that wide, is also quite impressive, being more than ten years. The greatest variation is present between educational categories, the means for the totals ranging from 10.8 for those with no schooling to 19.5 for those with ten or more years of schooling. Between birth cohorts and residence categories they are much more modest: from 13.3 for the oldest to 14.5 to the youngest birth cohorts, and from 12.0 for rural to 15.1 for metropolitan men. It seems clear that the greatest variations in age at first job are between educational categories, while within them some minor differences are accounted for by birth cohort and residence.

Entry into the Labor Force and First Occupation

The occupations available to a young man entering the labor force depend upon the economic organization of production in the place where he lives. The main economic activities and the productive organizations vary according to the size of the localities and the degree of industrialization. The occupational alternatives open to young men living in these various localities therefore will vary greatly. Here we will analyze the occupations held by men entering the labor force in rural (up to 5,000), urban (5,000 to 100,000), and metropolitan (100,-000 and more, including Monterrey) areas.

There is little variety in the job alternatives open to a man living in a rural area in Mexico. Agriculture dominates the occupational world, and few employment opportunities exist outside it. Within agriculture the positions available will depend partly upon the prevailing system of property relations. The predominant system of rural landholding in those Mexican areas where most migrants to Monterrey originate is the small family plot, either directly owned or occupied as *ejidatarios*, tenants or sharecroppers. Thus the majority of men in rural areas entered the labor force in agriculture (Table 5-2), and most of them as family helpers rather than as laborers. Almost all nonagricultural men in rural areas entered unskilled manual positions and in a variety of occupations: miners, helpers in small grocery stores, street vendors.

In comparison to the rural labor market, the metropolitan one is very complex. The division of labor is much greater, and there is a large variety of jobs available to young men just entering the labor force. No single occupational category dominates the distribution. The men are

TABLE 5-2. Occupational Category of First Job, by Place of Residence and 1965 Distribution
(In Percent)

Occupational Category	Rural (up to 5,000)	Urban (5,000– 100,000)	Metropolitan (over 100,000)	Total	1965 Distri- bution
Professional and technical	0	1	10	6	9
Managers	0	0	1	0	9
Office workers	1	5	12	8	7
Agents and salesmen	0	1	3	2	4
Semiskilled and skilled workers	0	1	3	2	29
Blue-collar salesmen	0	2	2	2	5
Unskilled production workers	4	20	22	17	8
Unskilled service workers	13	28	30	25	17
Farm workers and farmers	76	27	5	27	1
Other unskilled occupations	6	15	12	11	12
Total	100 (416)	100 (281)	100 (916)	100 (1,613)	101 (1,548)

concentrated in those kinds of occupations requiring no special training or experience, but a number of these exist. Most of the men (69 percent) enter unskilled manual occupations. Some of these occupations have been described above, being invariably those of lowest productivity and greatest instability. Included are helpers in grocery stores, shoeshine boys, street vendors, stevedores, delivery boys, and similar occupations. These jobs tend to be concentrated in the service sector and in commerce, and in very few cases do they involve any learning of a specific skill or trade that will be useful for future mobility. In Table 5-2 they are grouped under the heading "unskilled service workers."

Other unskilled manual occupations offer a learning experience that will be helpful in future occupational changes. They include especially jobs as helpers and apprentices to skilled workers. A formal apprenticeship system is not common in Mexico. The learning of a skill or a trade is done informally by watching and helping a skilled worker. Many boys start out their work experience by helping a garage mechanic or a bricklayer, to cite just two examples. The job usually involves only very simple tasks; it means being always on call to provide the *maestro* with needed tools or materials ("tener la herramienta a mano"). Though no formal teaching of the skill is involved, simply by being around and watching and, more rarely, asking questions, the boys learn enough so that at a later time many of them can enter the ranks of skilled work-ers. These occupations exist more often in the manufacturing and repair sectors and are grouped in the table under the heading "unskilled pro-duction workers." It should be mentioned, however, that the classifica-tion is not based on the type of industry—manufacturing under produc-tion workers, services under service workers—but on the specific occu-pation a boy has. For instance, a helper of a mechanic in the mainte-nance crew of a large department store falls in the category of produc-tion workers, although the enterprise is a commercial one. That is, the difference between these two basic categories of unskilled workers lies in whether or not the man is involved in the process of transformation or repair of a product or raw material (production workers).

White-collar positions are important occupational alternatives for young men in metropolitan areas. Twenty-six percent fell into this category. These men are the most highly educated and they enter the labor force at older ages than unskilled workers. Within the white-col-lar world, some occupations are more suited for young men without previous experience than others. Young entrants tend to occupy clerical and office positions or technical and professional ones. Very few enter the labor force as managers or salesmen.

The last column in Table 5-2 permits a comparison of the metropol-itan category (nearly all the men entering the labor force in these areas did so in Monterrey) with the occupational distribution of all Monte-rrey men at the time of the survey. The differences between the two columns reflect the varying entry requirements of occupations and changes in time in the occupational structure. Thus, while 29 percent of the men in 1965 held positions as skilled and semiskilled workers, only 3 percent entered the labor force in them. Among the white-collar occupations, 9 percent of the men were managers in 1965, but less than 1 percent entered the labor force as managers. The requirements for entry into the skilled manual categories and the managerial ranks ex-plain these differences. Men need work experience, maturity, and (in some cases) capital to enter these positions. Many of the men entering the labor force as unskilled workers move to the skilled category during their lifetime, and, in a parallel way, office workers become managers.[6]

Urban areas fall in between the rural and metropolitan areas in terms

[6] For entry occupations in the United States, see Otis D. Duncan, "Occupational Trends and Patterns of Net Mobility in the United States," *Demography* 3, no. 1 (1966): 1–18.

TABLE 5-3. Occupational Categories of First Jobs, by Birth Cohort and Place of Residence (In Percent)

Birth Cohort

Occupational Category	1905–1914				1915–1924			
	Rural	Urban	Metr.	Total	Rural	Urban	Metr.	Total
White collar	2	8	18	11	1	8	23	14
Skilled and blue-collar sales	0	3	5	3	0	2	4	2
Unskilled production workers	2	27	24	17	4	16	16	12
Unskilled service workers	12	27	39	27	20	29	35	29
Farm workers and farmers	75	23	5	32	72	31	8	32
Other unskilled occupations	9	11	9	10	3	14	14	11
Total	100 (127)	99 (88)	100 (170)	100 (385)	100 (130)	100 (88)	100 (217)	100 (435)

Occupational Category	1925–1934				1935–1944			
	Rural	Urban	Metr.	Total	Rural	Urban	Metr.	Total
White collar	1	3	30	18	0	10	28	22
Skilled and blue-collar sales	2	2	5	4	0	7	7	6
Unskilled production workers	5	21	25	19	5	14	24	20
Unskilled service workers	11	25	27	23	5	29	23	21
Farm workers and farmers	74	25	5	27	89	31	3	19
Other unskilled occupations	7	24	7	10	1	9	15	12
Total	100 (93)	100 (63)	99 (205)	101 (361)	100 (66)	100 (42)	100 (324)	100 (432)

of the occupational alternatives they offer. Of special interest is the fact that even in these urban places more than a quarter of those entering the labor force did so as farm workers. Proportions similar to the metropolitan distributions are to be found for the various unskilled categories. It is in the white-collar occupations that the urban places are much inferior to the metropolitan areas.

As can be seen in Table 5-3, there are almost no intercohort differences in the first occupations held by the men who entered the labor force in rural areas. While the evidence is indirect, we may conclude that, at least for the areas that provide migrants to Monterrey, there has been relatively little change in the rural occupational structure over a forty-year period. Among the metropolitan residents, however, some interesting and consistent intercohort changes show up. First, the proportion of men holding unskilled positions as their first job declined from 77 to 65 percent from the oldest cohort (born 1905–1914) to the youngest (born 1935–1944). This decline took place primarily in the low-productivity and unstable unskilled occupations, the service occupations, such as delivery boys and shoeshine boys. The decline indicates the gradual—and it is no more than this—decrease of some occupations characterized by low productivity and low specialization, that is, occupations that lack clearly determined and formally prescribed tasks assigned to them.

Complementary to this intercohort change is the increase in the proportion of men entering white-collar occupations, up from 18 to 28 percent. This increase is consistent with the general upgrading of the labor force in metropolitan areas affected by the process of industrialization. The occupational category showing the greatest increase is office workers.

The Life Cycle, Education, and Entry into the Labor Force

The time in the life cycle when a man enters the labor force and the occupation he holds at that time are related to what happened to him in the previous stage of his life, that is, his education. Educational credentials are an entry requirement for many occupations, both in the form of specific degrees for specialized occupations and as a general requirement of a certain level of education (without specification of the type of education) for others.[7] Thus, a professional university degree is

[7] Few studies focus on the relationship between education and first jobs. Roger Girod and Firouz Tofigh ("Family Background and Income, School Career and

required for entering the professions; a *primaria* school diploma is required in many large enterprises for any type of job. In our sample we find that almost no man entering a white-collar position had less than completed *primaria*. But not all men who went beyond *primaria* entered the labor force in white-collar positions. One-fifth of those entering as unskilled production workers, for instance, had gone beyond *primaria*.

These findings contain few surprises. What constitutes a more interesting issue to discuss here is how the intercohort increase in educational levels, as analyzed in Chapter 4, affects the levels of education of men entering the various occupations. This increase in educational levels can have two different consequences. First, it may affect the distribution of entry occupations, so that there is an increase in the proportion of men entering occupations that always required a higher level of education. Second, it may produce an increase in the average education of the men entering some occupations.

Table 5-4 presents the data on the average years of schooling attained by men entering the labor force in selected occupations by birth cohort. In the case of the white-collar occupations, there has been no change in the average education of the men entering these positions, while at the same time there has been an increase in the proportion of men entering these occupations, already discussed above. This is a

TABLE 5-4. Average Years of Schooling of Men Entering Labor Force in Selected Occupations, by Birth Cohort

Occupational Category	Birth Cohort			
	1905–1914	1915–1924	1925–1934	1935–1944
Professional and technical	14.3	14.3	14.0	14.5
Office workers and salesmen	9.4	10.4	9.9	10.2
Unskilled production workers	4.7	5.8	5.1	6.2
Unskilled service workers	4.0	4.7	4.5	4.7
Farm workers and farmers	1.6	2.0	2.6	3.1

Social Mobility of Young Males of Working-Class Origin—A Geneva Survey," *Acta Sociologica* 9 [1965]: 94–109) show the importance of success or failure in the early stages of schooling for the occupational positions held when entering the labor force. Michael Carter's *Into Work* deals with the entry into the labor force of graduates of "secondary modern" British schools.

clear case of a distributional change, an increase in the number of positions, without alterations in their nature and the requirements built into them. No intercohort difference in average education exists among men entering unskilled service positions. In this case, the overall increase in the level of education of the men is accompanied by a slight decline in the proportion entering these occupations. On the other hand, unskilled production workers show some intercohort increase in education, and, as seen before, there is also an increase in the proportion of men entering the labor force in these positions. The only case where there is a clear and consistent increase in the average education is among farm workers. This unexpected finding will be taken up in detail when we discuss the temporal sequence between education and work.

A different but related aspect of the link between education and entering the labor force is the temporal sequence between the two events. The "normative" temporal sequence for the life cycle includes, after the period of early socialization within the family context, a fairly lengthy educational stage, requiring attendance at officially sanctioned schools antedating full participation in the labor force.[8] But this temporal sequence—first study, then work—is not always strictly followed. Let us now analyze the principal deviations from this normative sequence in terms of the three main occupational categories in which the men began their work lives: farm workers, unskilled workers, and white-collar employees.

The kinds of skills required of farm workers in Mexico demand little if any formal education, especially among the family helpers in subsistence agriculture who predominate in our sample. Farm work is the occupational category with the lowest level of education and with the highest proportion of men who never went to school and who therefore cannot follow the normative life-cycle pattern. The improvement in Mexican education has touched even the rural areas and is reflected in the increase in the average education of farm workers (Table 5-4) and the decline in the number of men who never went to school (see Table

[8] S. N. Eisenstadt (*From Generation to Generation: Age Groups and Social Structure*) stresses the preparatory nature of childhood and adolescence in modern societies. For a provocative view of the "future" society, where the normative sequence stressed by Eisenstadt will not hold, because of rapid technological obsolescence, and where much retraining and education during the work life will be necessary, see Wilbert E. Moore, "Aging and the Social System," in *Aging and Social Policy*, ed. John C. McKinney and Frank T. DeVyverx.

5-5). One-half of the farm workers in the oldest cohort never attended school, and this proportion drops to 21 percent among the farm workers in the youngest cohort. In many rural areas there have been few structural changes and farm labor continues to be the main occupation available. Under such conditions, the increase in educational opportunities can have two effects: an out-migration of the better-educated men to areas where there are superior occupational opportunities, and

TABLE 5.5. Temporal Sequences between Education and Work Followed by Men Entering Labor Force in Various Occupational Categories, by Birth Cohort (In Percent)

| Sequence | Birth Cohort | | | | |
	1905–1914	1915–1924	1925–1934	1935–1944	Total
Farm workers					
Normative[a]	30	36	59	59	44
Part time[b]	5	4	7	9	6
Idle[c]	15	21	11	11	15
No schooling	50	39	23	21	35
Total	100	100	100	100	100
	(125)	(137)	(95)	(81)	(438)
Unskilled workers					
Normative[a]	48	59	60	57	56
Part time[b]	12	9	9	17	12
Idle[c]	26	27	25	22	25
No schooling	14	5	6	4	7
Total	100	100	100	100	100
	(209)	(227)	(187)	(228)	(851)
White-collar workers					
Normative[a]	63	68	52	57	59
Part time[b]	18	18	31	40	30
Idle[c]	18	13	17	3	11
No schooling	0	0	0	0	0
Total	99	99	100	100	100
	(38)	(60)	(64)	(97)	(259)

[a] Includes men who began working the last year of their schooling or the first or second year after finishing their education.
[b] Includes men who began working at least two years before finishing their education.
[c] Includes men who were idle for at least two years after finishing school and before beginning work.

the increase in education of the farm workers. Even when the boys have gone a few years to school, they have little choice but to enter farm work, where their schooling, that is, the acquisition of functional literacy, will not in most cases affect their performance or their rewards as farm workers.

Among unskilled workers the educational attainment is considerably higher. More than one-half entering the labor force in such positions had finished *primaria*, and only a few had never attended school. In general, the men who entered the labor force as unskilled production workers have higher levels of education than the men entering other unskilled occupations, and their educational level has increased somewhat from the oldest to the youngest birth cohort (see Table 5-4). With the growth of large industry in Monterrey, the opportunities for unskilled production work in large plants have increased in the last fifteen to twenty years. (They are also the enterprises where entry requirements in general have become more formal and rigid.) Since the men who entered the labor force as unskilled workers have in general relatively low levels of education (82 percent had six years of schooling or less), we could expect that they would enter the labor force at young ages. Yet about one-fourth of the men who entered the labor force as unskilled workers were idle for a period of two or more years between the time they finished school and when they entered the labor force. Actually, they were idle on the average for almost four years.

How is it possible for so many young men to be idle for such a long time? Are they simply lazy? The men were not asked their reasons for leaving school, but several factors could be involved. Whatever the reason for leaving school, the economic structure of the country is not prepared to absorb all the boys who leave school early—and for reasons independent of the population explosion that has greatly increased the numbers in recent cohorts. In an industrial city like Monterrey, large enterprises (accounting for about half of the labor force), in conjunction with organized labor, place barriers to the entry of very young men into their organizations. The lower age limit has been put at 16 or thereabouts. Large industry is governed by relatively modern criteria, and the situation of Monterrey is not unique. Industry imports not only advanced technology—which in itself leaves little room for early adolescent participation—but also norms and organizational features applicable to the labor force. These last imports are not always consistent with the economic and social reality of the receiving countries, and this creates "lags," asynchronic change. In Mexico the gap occurs between the educational reality, which means the early departure from school, and the formal restrictions on age at entry into the labor force. The large enterprises require only the completion of six years of *primaria*, which normally occurs about age 13, but they hire only at age 16 or older.

Large industry is, of course, not the only source of employment in a city like Monterrey, and it is not an employment alternative in most rural and urban places. Why is it that we also find men in these areas remaining idle for several years? The answer will be found in the lack of employment opportunities in general, especially of jobs that do not fall under the heading of "disguised unemployment." The men remain idle rather than getting into already overcrowded and unproductive occupations. Of course, there are men going into other entry occupations who also remain idle for a time between schooling and work, but they exist in much smaller proportions than among unskilled manual workers.

The last of our three entry situations is the case of white-collar workers. A number of these occupations have very specific educational requirements. All professions, and most of the technical positions, require a specific degree and licensing for entry. Other white-collar occupations, such as sales and office positions, do not have these fixed requirements, but they may require some specialized training. Because of the longer period of education required for white-collar positions, the "gap" problem between leaving school and beginning work is not as pronounced as it is for other occupations. What distinguishes this group is the increase in the proportion of men entering these occupations while still attending school; that is, as part-time workers. In the oldest cohort 18 percent entered the labor force in this manner, while 40 percent of the youngest cohort did so. Why this trend? Only a few decades ago higher education largely was restricted to a small elite. Only rich people could afford it, and men did not have to work in order to support themselves, since their families could assume the burden. The increase in educational opportunities described in Chapter 4 has by no means made of higher education the mass phenomenon that it has become in the United States, but it has permitted many working-class men to go on with their education. This can be done, however, only with considerable economic strain, and it is mainly these poorer men who must find some part-time job in order to support themselves while studying. In some cases the jobs they get provide training and experience in the occupational field they will pursue upon finishing their education. Thus, we find accounting students working in banks, law students working as court clerks, architecture students in construction firms, and so on. But these arrangements are not always possible, and it is sometimes necessary to find jobs that are not related to their future occupation, for example, medical students as school teachers.

Early Work Experience

The first ten years of work experience are quite crucial in the lives of men. In the first stages they can explore alternatives by trying out different jobs before they decide what line of work to remain in for much of their lives.[9] Of course, many men show little evidence of such rational searching during their occupational lifetimes. Some continually change their work but without any discernible improvement in their condition. Some literally have no promising alternatives to explore; they take any job they can get.

The consideration of the first ten years introduces certain problems of comparability. For our analysis, age 15 will be taken as the lower age limit, so we will be considering only the ten years between ages 15 and 25. Actually, there is very little difference in the distribution of occupations at first job and at age 15, and the analysis will be much simplified because age controls will not have to be introduced. In a few cases, where advanced education in preparation for technical and professional positions is required, the men will have had little full-time work experience before age 25. We will restrict ourselves to the men who were 25 or older in 1965. The youngest men in our sample, those who were 21 to 24 in 1965, are omitted from the following analysis. We must also take into account the place of residence and the migratory history of the men. Many began their work lives outside Monterrey, and some moved there during the ten-year interval. Because residence makes a considerable difference in occupational attainment, we will first take up the men whose early work experience was in Monterrey

[9] An empirical study that deals with the pattern of job changes and that stresses the pattern of shifting jobs rather frequently in the first years of work experience is reported in Delbert C. Miller and William H. Form, "Measuring Patterns of Occupational Security," *Sociometry* 10 (1947): 362–375; and in William H. Form and Delbert C. Miller, "Occupational Career Pattern as a Sociological Instrument," *American Journal of Sociology* 54, no. 4 (1949): 317–329.

(natives to the city plus the migrants arriving before age 15) and then address ourselves to those men whose early work experience was all or partly outside Monterrey.

Much of our analysis in the next pages, as well as in Chapter 8, will be based on a hierarchical classification of occupations in four levels: unskilled and skilled manual, lower and upper nonmanual. (A selection of occupations included in each of the four levels is presented below.) This classification is needed to order and simplify the handling of the mass of data available. Furthermore, we need a hierarchical ordering of occupations to discuss vertical and horizontal mobility in their various forms.

Upper nonmanual: professionals, managers, entrepreneurs, technicians.

Lower nonmanual: office workers, salesmen (other than in food stores), supervisors and foremen.

Upper manual: operatives and craftsmen (either self-employed or employees), salesmen in food stores, small commercial farmers.

Lower manual: unskilled workers, farm laborers, *ejidatarios*, sharecroppers, subsistence farmers.

Early Work Experience in Monterrey

The first years in the labor force are ones for learning skills, "shopping around," exploring alternatives, and in some cases already settling down into the job that will be kept for most of the work life. The metropolitan environment of Monterrey offers many opportunities for jobchanging and exploratory behavior. Very few men in the city held at age 25 the same job they had ten years earlier. This early exploratory behavior doubtless is increasing along with the growing industrialization and division of labor. The proportion of men holding the same job between ages 15 and 25 declines from 17 percent in the oldest cohort (men 51–60) to 7 percent in the youngest (men 21–30).

We have already seen that more than 60 percent of the men entering the labor force in metropolitan areas—and in effect this means Monterrey, for it is 95 percent of the total—did so in unskilled manual positions. What can unskilled entrants achieve in ten years of work experience? What are their chances of moving to other occupational positions, and, if they do so, to which ones will they move? Analyzing the jobs held during the ten-year span by the men who started their work lives in Monterrey, we find that 37 percent moved to skilled manual positions, 9 percent moved to nonmanual positions, 8 percent had irregular histories with movements up and down across the occupational levels, and the remaining 46 percent stayed in unskilled positions. Most of these latter men, however, changed jobs within the unskilled ranks. Considering the trend over time, there has been some increase in the proportion of men experiencing some mobility: from 48 percent in the oldest cohort to 59 percent in the youngest one (see Table 5-6).

Some unskilled occupations are more conducive to upward mobility than others. Occupations of a preparatory nature, where a man can learn the skills or get the training necessary to enter more skilled positions, provide the best opportunities for advancement. The preparatory occupational category par excellence in an industrial city like Monterrey is unskilled production work. Of all moves out of unskilled jobs in these ten years, 46 percent were from a production position. To state it differently, this occupational category shows the highest probability of upward movement. Of all moves out of unskilled production work, 56 percent were to occupations of a higher level, while 44 percent were to other unskilled occupations. In the other unskilled occupations, about 30 percent of the moves were upward and 70 percent were horizontal. Some of the men who experienced the upward move from unskilled production positions had that kind of job since they entered the labor force until the moment they moved to the better occupation. Others entered the labor force in other unskilled occupations, made a

TABLE 5-6. Vertical Mobility between Ages 15 and 25 of Men Who Started Their Work Lives in Monterrey in Lower Manual Positions, by Birth Cohort (In Percent)

| Position Moved to | Birth Cohort | | | | |
	1905–1914	1915–1924	1925–1934	1935–1944	Total
Lower manual	52	52	39	41	46
Upper manual	35	30	41	43	37
Lower nonmanual	5	10	6	2	6
Upper nonmanual	2	3	4	3	3
Up and down	6	5	10	11	8
Total	100	100	100	100	100
	(112)	(143)	(126)	(95)	(476)

horizontal move to production work, and from there made the upward move. For this second group of men, production work represents the bridge by which the upward move is made.[10]

Attributing the higher chances of upward mobility from production work to its preparatory nature implies that the men move to occupations functionally related and hierarchically superior to the ones they hold. The training they acquire while working in the unskilled production positions is necessary to accomplish the move. We will use the concept of *career* to refer to a set of ordered occupations functionally and hierarchically related, so that experience in one of them is a necessary requirement for entering the next one.[11] What we are suggesting, therefore, is that production work is frequently part of a career line, and that it offers more chances of career-oriented moves than the other unskilled occupations.

A number of unskilled occupations do not generally permit their occupants to gain the experience or skill necessary to move up to another occupation. They are not part of a career line. Janitors, stevedores, street vendors, and shoeshine boys are such positions. Besides the production-related occupations, others that are likely to be part of a career are office boys who may become clerks, construction laborers who can turn into skilled bricklayers, and some service workers who can change, for instance, from being delivery boy in a store to a sales position. In the case of production workers, however, the career lines are more clear. This is due in part to the fact that they are more often found in large enterprises, where there is a higher degree of formalization of positions and of the requirements for entry into each of them. Thus, it is easy to find in the large enterprises of Monterrey a gradation of blue-collar occupations that goes from third-class helper up through three classes of operatives to first-class craftsman.

Of all moves made from unskilled to higher positions between ages 15 and 25, 38 percent were career-oriented moves. (The definition of a career-oriented move refers to a move to a higher and related occupa-

[10] The concept of bridging occupations is introduced by Leonard Broom and J. H. Smith in "Bridging Occupations," *British Journal of Sociology* 14, no. 4 (December 1963): 321–334.

[11] On this rather restricted definition of career, see Harold L. Wilensky, "Orderly Careers and Social Participation," *American Sociological Review* 26, no. 4 (1961): 521–539, and "Work, Careers, and Social Integration," *International Social Science Journal* 12, no. 4 (1960): 534–560.

tion within the same enterprise. For a more detailed description of the operational definition, see Chapter 8. It should be clear that this figure is based on the number of upward *moves*, and not on the number of *men*. It cannot be taken, therefore, as evidence of the prevalence of career lines in Monterrey.) As could be expected from the discussion presented above, production work offers more opportunities to move according to career lines than other unskilled occupations. Six out of every ten upward moves from the former are career oriented, while only two out of ten from all other unskilled categories are. Holding an unskilled production job offers a double advantage: the probabilities of experiencing an upward move are higher than for other unskilled occupations, and the probabilities of experiencing that move in an orderly manner, as part of a career line, are also higher.

Let us now look at the changes over time in the opportunities of upward mobility offered by the various occupations. Intercohort comparisons indicate that, besides the increase in mobility discussed above, there has been a change in the relative standing of occupations with respect to the prospects they offer. Upward movements out of production positions represented 42 percent of all upward moves in the oldest cohort and 53 percent in the youngest. This trend of increasing concentration of the channels for mobility in the production jobs is accompanied by a decline in the opportunities offered by the service jobs. Forty-three percent of all upward moves were from service positions in the oldest cohort, with 24 percent in the youngest. This change is in part a reflection of the fact that there has been a general decline in the proportion of men holding service jobs, but it goes beyond what can be explained by that decline. If we take the probability that a move out of a service job will be upward, there has been a decline from .36 to .29 between the oldest and the youngest cohorts.

We encounter here a case of a change in the relative position of a group of occupations due to the process of industrialization. Unskilled service occupations accounted for a substantial proportion of the entry positions thirty or forty years ago; 35 percent of the men in the oldest cohort held such positions when large-scale industry was not as dominant as it is today. At that time, moreover, the gap between industry and the commerce and service sectors was not as clear-cut as it is today, for big differences in productivity did not exist between the sectors. Service and commerce positions at that time offered only slightly lower opportunities for advancement when compared to the production ones.

The increasing preponderance of manufacturing in the economy of Monterrey has caused a decline in the proportion of young men entering the labor force in service positions. At the same time the gap between the two sectors representing high and low productivity has widened, causing the discrepancy in the opportunities offered by production and service occupations.

Up to now we have not considered the destination occupations of the upwardly mobile unskilled workers. The great majority of them moved to skilled manual positions, including a few to blue-collar sales positions. Less than 10 percent moved to nonmanual occupations. Among the latter are many who entered the labor force as part-time workers in unskilled occupations and as soon as they finished their schooling moved to nonmanual positions related to their educational training. One respondent, for instance, reported being employed as a helper of a mechanic in a garage while attending commerce school, and as soon as he graduated he was hired as a clerk in a bank. One-fourth of the moves from unskilled to nonmanual occupations were reported by men employed as office boys who advanced later to clerical positions within bureaucratic career settings.

The work experience before age 25 is not so important for men who entered the labor force in nonmanual occupations, for most of them had only a few years of work experience up to that age. One-fourth of them entered the labor force after age 22, and one-half of those who entered before that age were part-time workers in their first jobs. Most of these men began working in clerical positions, later moving to technical and professional occupations when they received their educational degrees. Other than this education-related pattern of mobility, some nonmanual workers were able to advance within the bureaucratic organizations in which they were employed, from clerical positions to department heads, managers, and the like. Of course, quite often it takes many years to move up the bureaucratic ladder, and this longer-term movement will be examined in Chapter 8.

Early Work Experience outside Monterrey

The occupational experience of the men who started their work lives in nonfarm positions outside Monterrey does not differ greatly from that described in the previous section for the men who entered the labor force in Monterrey. The experience of those in farm occupations merits a closer inspection, since organization of production and division of labor are basically different in agricultural production. The occupational alternatives open to these men are much more limited. However, for them, too, the first ten years of work experience are of crucial importance, since at this time many change residence as they look for better occupational opportunities. Migration is age selective, since it is mainly young adults looking for jobs in the cities who move out of rural areas. Thus, it can be expected that many men who started in farm occupations moved into nonfarm positions during the age interval 15 to 25, while simultaneously moving out of rural areas.

One-half of the men who began working outside Monterrey did so in farm occupations, mainly as family helpers and farm laborers. Family-operated units, either in subsistence agriculture or in commercial agriculture, predominate in the areas where most migrants to Monterrey come from. Youngsters typically help their parents on the farm, while in many cases taking jobs as farm laborers during the crop season. In this respect they do not differ from other youngsters whose parents do not own or share land, or are not recipients of ejido land—most wage work in the region is seasonal and limited to four to six months of the year. Furthermore, for youngsters in many areas, wage work as farm laborers implies seasonal migration to the areas where commercial crops are raised: the wheat and cotton regions of the North and the farm areas in Texas and California. Seasonal employment is basic for the rural population, since unemployment is high and cash income throughout the year is very low. Mainly young adults, but not only them, have found in legal and illegal entrance to the United States an important source of income.[12] In Cedral, the agriculturally oriented community described in detail in Chapter 3, we found that 40 percent of the men had had at least one short-term migration for agricultural work outside the region, either to northern Mexico or to the United States.

Many long-term migrations actually started as seasonal migration for farm work. Monterrey, as well as other cities, has operated as a recruiting center for farm laborers who want to work in the United States. Many do not obtain the permit or change their minds and de-

---

[12] The recent volume by Leo Grebler, Joan W. Moore, and Ralph C. Guzman, *The Mexican-American People*, discusses the movement across the border, especially in Chapter 4. An extensive bibliography is provided.

cide to stay rather than going back home. Others take residence in the city on their way back from the United States. But a considerably greater number of men moved to Monterrey (or other cities) with no intention of picking up seasonal farm work. Their decisions, considering them from the present, were to take up "permanent" residence in the city, but actually many might have started with the hope of making some money and going back home. What is important is that most moves out of predominantly agricultural regions into Monterrey and other cities, either seasonal or permanent, are closely linked to the lack of occupational opportunities in the communities of origin and more concretely to the high incidence of seasonal unemployment.

Of all men who started working in farm occupations, 45 percent were still there by age 25. In a good number of cases, 30 percent of those remaining on the farm, there was a move from family helper or farm laborer to independent farmer. These men assumed control of the family farm as a consequence of death or retirement of their fathers, or received ejido land as part of the land-distribution program in Mexico. In either case, as we will see in Chapter 7, becoming independent is closely associated with marriage and the start of family formation. However, in practically all cases we are dealing with men who had responsibility for very small plots of poor land, largely devoted to subsistence agriculture, so that, although independence entails a change in status in the community, it hardly means any betterment in level of living. On the contrary, the men will be less prone to move to a city at a young age when their chances of obtaining relatively well paid jobs are better and, thus, their chances of upward mobility later on when they come to the city might actually decrease. Those who start work in farm jobs and then move to urban areas take jobs at the bottom of the occupational hierarchy, since they lack formal education and experience in nonfarm jobs. Construction work, street peddling, and irregular service occupations like washing cars and similar jobs are the typical occupations taken by young men moving from farm to nonfarm jobs. But many are able to find more stable kinds of employment, and their youth is an important factor in moving up during their first years in the city.

Residence, Migration, and Early Occupational Mobility

We have analyzed thus far the early work experiences of the men who started their work lives in Monterrey and elsewhere, distinguishing among the latter between those who started in farm and nonfarm occupations, as well as between those who moved to Monterrey during the ages 15 to 25 and those who did not arrive until later. We now may ask: What are the effects of these distinctions upon the vertical occupational mobility experienced during these ten crucial years? What are the differences for those who started in Monterrey compared with those who arrived from other places? To what extent does a farm background constitute a handicap for occupational mobility in the city?

Since the men began their occupational histories in different statuses, with natives to the city having on the average higher occupational levels upon entering the labor force than migrants, we control for this by considering in Table 5-7 only those men who began working in the lowest occupational status, unskilled and farm workers. Actually, as indicated above, these two categories include a majority of the men at this early period in their work lives. Consider first the three categories of unskilled workers at age 15: those who began working in Monterrey (Table 5-7, column 1) show a similar occupational distribution at age 25 as those who arrived in the city during this period, while those who remained outside Monterrey show a smaller proportion moving up to upper manual and nonmanual occupations. In other words, Monterrey seems to allow for greater upward mobility than other places—as indicated by the lower upward mobility experienced by the men who arrived after age 25 (columns 4 and 5). The main point of the comparison, however, is the similar achievements of those who started in Mon-

TABLE 5-7. Occupational Level at Age 25 of Men Who Were in Lower Manual Positions at Age 15, by Migratory Status and Farm-Nonfarm Background (In Percent)

Occupational Level at Age 25	Entered Labor Force in Monterrey	Migrants to Monterrey			
		Age 16–25		After Age 25	
		Unskilled	Farm Workers	Unskilled	Farm Workers
	(1)	(2)	(3)	(4)	(5)
Lower manual farm	—	—	—	—	71
Lower manual nonfarm	52	53	75	62	25
Upper manual	38	34	20	24	4
Nonmanual	10	13	4	14	—
Total	100	100	99	100	100
	(459)	(130)	(122)	(153)	(215)

terrey (column 1) and those who migrated during this period and were in nonfarm jobs (column 2). In both cases almost one-half of the men were able to climb the occupational ladder during these ten early years of occupational life, although few of them moved a great distance into nonmanual jobs. Migrating to the city at a young age, when opportunities to move are in general quite high, does not imply any disadvantage as compared with those who were already there.

We have purposely chosen to compare men who started in unskilled nonfarm occupations. What are the effects of a farm background? It seems to be an important variable in determining vertical mobility during ages 15 to 25. Men who were farm workers at age 15 and moved to the city before age 25 (column 3) tend to occupy lower positions than those who were unskilled workers when both groups are compared at age 25. For various reasons—lower educational levels, lack of nonfarm occupational experience—starting work on a farm constitutes a handicap. But this conclusion should be interpreted in the light of two other considerations.

First, the change in situs from farm to nonfarm, although it generally does not entail a change in status, might be experienced by the men as upward mobility.[13] There are differences in income, even when the cost of living is considered, between unskilled urban workers and farm workers, in favor of the former. Furthermore, the great differences in facilities and public services between rural and urban areas make the move to Monterrey an advantageous one in non-work-related areas: recreational, medical, and educational facilities, for instance. There are, of course, other items, like housing, where the city offers a negative picture when compared with rural areas. In any case, we suggest that a change in situs in itself many times entails some upward mobility, both in work and nonwork areas.

Second, a comparison between farm workers who moved to Monterrey and those who did not move during the ten-year period shows again the relative advantages of the city's environment. Even discounting the move from the lowest farm to the lowest nonfarm occupations as upwardly, one-fourth of the men who came to the city during

---

[13] The issue of whether a change in situs from farm to nonfarm employment with no change in status does or does not involve upward mobility is analyzed by Arnold H. Feldman in "Economic Development and Social Mobility," *Economic Development and Cultural Change* 8 (1960): 311–320.

this period (column 3) achieved higher statuses, while only 4 percent of those who did not arrive moved up (column 5). The typical way of advancement in the farm, from family help or farm laborer to operator of a subsistence farm, as we argued before, cannot be considered as an upward move.

6. The Social and Economic Context of Migration to Monterrey

The difficulty in keeping key life-cycle events neatly in chronological order now presents itself. We are ready to tackle the problem of accounting for how migrants to Monterrey got to that place, but this will mean backtracking a bit in the lives of most of our men. At the end of the last chapter we had left them at age 25, ten years or so after entering the labor force, but the majority of migrants began their move well before this age. The fact is that early work experience and migration often coincide, and the same may be said of marriage and early family formation. If for the sake of exposition we must separate them, this should not be construed as an admission that they are separated in actuality. This is precisely one of the more difficult problems of life-cycle analysis: the fact that many of the key events are packed within a few years of the late teens and early twenties, and thus it is difficult to disentangle the independent effect of any one of them.

In this chapter we will examine various features of the migratory process, beginning with the question of whether migrants are different from nonmigrants in the community of origin, a crucial question for any subsequent discussion of native-migrant differences. Next we want to provide a rather detailed account of the actual migration to Monterrey and the social and economic context in which it occurs. We will also want to explore the role of return migration for both Monterrey and Cedral. Finally, we will make some more general comments about the migratory process, but deferring until the last chapter any discussion of the consequences of migration upon both a community of origin (Cedral) and a community of destination (Monterrey).[1]

Migrant Selectivity

Back in Chapter 2 we discussed in some detail the socioeconomic characteristics of the areas from which the migrants to Monterrey were drawn. It was demonstrated that migrants came in about equal proportions from high- and low-ranking *zonas*. We said nothing at that point, however, about the selectivity of the migrants themselves, but confined discussion to the areas from which they originated. Migrant selectivity always has been a persistent problem in the analysis of migration. Are migrants positively or negatively selective, or do they show no differences when compared to those in their communities of origin?[2] In Chapter 4 we saw that community of origin had an effect upon educational attainment. But here our interest has shifted to trying to find out whether those who migrate to Monterrey are better educated than those of comparable age and status who remained behind. If they

[1] There is a burgeoning literature on internal migration in Latin America, based in part on analyses of census data and upon the much increased use of sample surveys. The most up-to-date survey of these studies is two reports given at the 1970 Conferencia Regional Latinoamericana de Población. They are available in English as Juan C. Elizaga, "Internal Migration: An Overview," *International Migration Review* (Spring 1972); and John J. Macisco, Jr., "Some Directions for Further Research on Internal Migration in Latin America," idem. The monograph by Elizaga, *Migraciones a las áreas metropolitanas de América Latina*, is especially recommended for its extensive report on migration to Santiago, Chile. See also Richard M. Morse, "Internal Migrants and the Urban Ethos in Latin America," paper delivered at the Seventh World Congress of Sociology, Varna, Bulgaria, September, 1970. The phenomenon of migration to two barrios in Guatemala is analyzed in Bryan Roberts, *Organizing Strangers: Poor Families in Guatemala City*. For an illuminating analysis of a different context of rural-urban migration see John D. Caldwell, *African Rural-Urban Migration*. This work is particularly valuable for its discussion of return migration.

[2] Our understanding of migrant selectivity is handicapped by the paucity of studies on this subject. See Elizaga, *Migraciones a las áreas metropolitanas*; and Alan B. Simmons and Ramiro Cardona G., "La selectividad de la migración en una perspectiva histórica: El caso de Bogotá (Colombia) 1929–1968," paper presented at the Conferencia Regional Latinoamericana de Población, Mexico City, August, 1970. A general review is Harley L. Browning, "Migrant Selectivity and the Growth of Large Cities in Developing Societies," in *Rapid Population Growth*, ed. National Academy of Sciences.

are, then they are positively selective. If they are less well educated, they are negatively selective. There are, of course, other factors, such as occupational position and even a psychological one like propensity to assume risk, that can be addressed in terms of selectivity.

The difficulty in answering the question of selectivity arises from the fact that nearly all studies of migrants are limited to one locale, the community of destination. The Monterrey study, it is true, is supplemented by that of Cedral, but it is only one community and is clearly inadequate to be the basis for generalizing about all the communities of origin of migrants to Monterrey.

Obviously it is an impossible task to gather for the populations of all the communities of origin of the migrants to Monterrey the same kind of survey information that we were able to do for Monterrey. The Mexican decennial census, however, can be called upon to help provide a partial, if not completely satisfactory, resolution of this problem. At least for 1940 and 1960, there are data on education and occupation for the male population that can be made comparable to the survey results. We will ask two principal questions of these data. First, is there migrant selectivity? Specifically, what differences in educational attainment and occupational position exist between migrants to Monterrey and the comparable populations from which they originate? Second, assuming there is migrant selectivity, has it changed over time? In other words, are the most recent migrants to Monterrey more or less selective than those who arrived at an earlier time?

Educational and Occupational Selectivity

The results of the educational and occupational comparisons are presented in Table 6-1. Here the *zonas* are grouped in five categories, using the criteria explained in Chapter 3. This grouping enables us to examine variations in migrant selectivity by socioeconomic areas of origin. In general, we can say that there is positive selectivity both in education and in occupation; a greater proportion of migrants than the census population (with the exception of Category I) have six or more years of schooling and were employed in nonagricultural activities. A glance at columns 6 and 7 indicates that most differences are positive, that is, in favor of the migrants, and are quite substantial in some cases.

The general statement that migrants are positively selective, however, masks the important variations present among the five socioeconomic categories and the change that has occurred between 1940 and 1960.

TABLE 6-1. Percentages of Male Migrants to Monterrey Who Have Six Years or More Schooling and Were Employed in Nonagricultural Activity in Year before First Arrival, by Socioeconomic Category of *Zona* of Community of Origin and Time of First Arrival with Corresponding Percentages for All Males Aged 15 and Over in Category of *Zonas*

Item and *Zonas* Contributing at Least 2 Percent of Migrants, by Category in Terms of Socioeconomic Ranking	Time of First Arrival			Census		Selectivity Indicators	
	Before 1941 (1)	1941–1950 (2)	1951–1960 (3)	1940 (4)	1960 (5)	(1–4) (6)	(3–5) (7)
Six years schooling							
Category I (highest)	39	51	62	48	51	−9	+11
Category II	31	44	46	14	23	+17	+23
Category III	50	31	25	8	15	+42	+10
Category IV	51	32	27	5	8	+46	+19
Category V (lowest)	34	10	13	3	6	+31	+7
Mexico, total country	—	—	—	12	21	—	—
	(166)	(206)	(242)				
Nonagricultural activity[a]							
Category I (highest)	76	74	82	89	95	−13	−13
Category II	74	76	61	36	41	+38	+20
Category III	68	36	44	19	15	+49	+29
Category IV	61	46	42	20	18	+41	+24
Category V (lowest)	—[b]	68	24	15	13	—[b]	+11
Mexico, total country	—	—	—	31	41	—	—
	(101)	(161)	(205)				

[a] Percent based on migrants who were employed in year before first arrival.
[b] Not calculated; statistic based on fewer than 10 sample cases.

Between these two census dates there has been in the country as a whole an increase in educational levels; the percent with six or more years of schooling grew from 12 to 21, and an increase in the proportion of the population engaged in nonagricultural activities from 31 to 41 percent. However, among migrants to Monterrey the trend has been exactly the opposite. Reading the totals for all categories, we find that between the early and late times of arrival those with six or more years of schooling decreased from 43 to 34 percent, and those with nonagricultural employment from 71 to 50 percent. Thus, migrant selectivity as measured by these two indicators has decreased. Furthermore, this trend seems to be different for the various categories of origin.

Among migrants coming from the zonas of lower socioeconomic standing—categories III, IV, and V—we find a consistent decline in selectivity. Those with six or more years of schooling, for instance, represented 50 percent of all migrants from category III coming before 1941, but only 25 percent of those coming between 1951 and 1960. A better way of looking at this trend is by considering the selectivity indicators calculated in columns 6 and 7. For these categories of origin the indicators are positive (excepting those for Category I), but the comparison in 1940 (column 6) yields considerably greater differences between migrants and the census population than those in 1960 (column 7). The decrease in selectivity is observable for both education and occupation. In Category III, for instance, the indicator for education declines from +42 to +10, and that for occupation from +49 to +29.

The picture is somewhat different when we consider the other two categories of zonas, I and II. Category I shows puzzling results, including what seems to be negative selectivity in both variables for 1940. Both categories also show increasing rather than decreasing selectivity in education (while this is not present in the occupational measure). We believe that the deviant case of Category I can be accounted for by the different composition of the migrant-versus-census populations. The Distrito Federal (Mexico City) completely dominates the census-based figures with over 90 percent of the population of Category I for both 1940 and 1960. Within that category, migrants from the Distrito Federal, however, represented only 6 percent of the earliest arrival cohort, while Saltillo accounted for two-thirds of them. In the 1951–1960 period, Saltillo contributed only 43 percent of the migrants and the Distrito Federal 39 percent. Of course, migrants from the Distrito Federal tend to have a considerably higher educational background than those from Saltillo. One-third of the early migrants from Saltillo have six or more years of schooling, while at a later date this has risen to 56 percent. In other words, change in the proportion of migrants coming from the various *zonas* comprising this category and real changes in the direction of increasing selectivity account for the deviance of Category I, and probably also of Category II.

The Context of Declining Selectivity

While we can say that migrants are positively selective of the populations from which they originate, the most surprising finding, and the one meriting a somewhat extended explanation, is that migrants have become increasingly less selective over time,[3] with the more rural and backward *zonas* (Categories III–V) accounting for this decline. What were the conditions in earlier periods and what has been behind the more recent undifferentiated migration from the backward areas?

The migrants who arrived to Monterrey before 1941 came at the close of a period representing a long and painful adjustment to the effects of the revolution of 1910. As we noted in Chapter 2, both the government and the economy were relatively weak for much of this period. Migration itself had to be much more of a "pioneer" experience than for subsequent generations.[4] The few men in rural and urban areas of northeastern Mexico who had acquired by one means or another a relatively good education were much more likely to be aware of the opportunities in large cities like Monterrey and also to be motivated to go there. Getting there was not as easy prior to 1941 as it is now. Paved roads were a rarity, and the railroad was limited in its routes. Newspapers and radios were uncommon outside the larger cities. In short, migration during this era required considerable initiative and as such was selective of those best prepared and most determined to improve their lot.

In contrast, the more recent arrivals in Monterrey have found the move less of an adventure. The economic boom that first developed as a consequence of World War II and has largely continued since then generated jobs in cities, including many in construction and other work requiring little skill. The great road-building program and the dense

---

[3] Simmons and Cardona, it may be noted, do not find evidence of a change in migrant selectivity for Bogotá.

[4] A discussion of "pioneer" and "mass" migration, along with other types, is found in William Petersen, *Population*, Chap. 20.

network of bus routes that it brought into being made the journey to Monterrey from hundreds of places easier and relatively cheaper. The greater dissemination of the mass media, in part due to the widespread extension of electrification, brought the outside world into formerly isolated communities and thereby kindled first an interest in and then a desire to migrate to the cities. The bracero program made long-distance movements rather commonplace in countless Mexican villages.

Along with the above factors, there is another one not yet mentioned that has been quite important in accounting for the decreasing selectivity of recent years. Monterrey's growth in recent decades has been very rapid, going from 134,000 in 1930 to an estimated 950,000 in 1965. The intercensal increase for the three decades beginning in 1930 was, respectively, 54,000, 170,000, and 324,000. Assuming, for the purposes of argument, that net migration accounted for one-half of the growth for each decade, there was a sixfold increase, from 27,000 to 162,000, in the number of migrants between the first and the last decade. Inevitably, the demands placed on the "reservoir" of potential migrants living in the areas that have supplied Monterrey with most of her migrants have steadily increased. Remember that Monterrey never has had a monopoly of access to this reservoir, for a number of other cities in northeastern Mexico, especially those on the border, have had considerable success in attracting migrants. Fifty-six percent of the migrants to Monterrey in our sample came from rural areas. Yet, this rural population has expanded quite slowly since 1930. Taking the three states (Nuevo León, Coahuila, and San Luis Potosí) representing the birthplace of 74 percent of all migrants, the total rural population (5,000 and over) was 956,000 in 1930, 1,169,000 in 1940, 1,343,000 in 1950, and 1,463,000 in 1960. The increase of 53 percent in thirty years is much less than the "demands" placed upon it by Monterrey's far more rapid rate of growth. Increasingly, therefore, all parts of the reservoir population are affected, not just the small minority of those with a comparatively good education.

The Social and Economic Context of Migration to Monterrey

Having established that migration to Monterrey is selective, we now must consider how the migrant gets there. Adequate accounts of what actually takes place in the course of migration from one place to another are uncommon, whether in developed or in developing countries. Censuses, by their very nature, are ill-suited to obtain such information, and until recently the sample survey had not been used for this purpose. One of the major objectives of the Monterrey study was to obtain detailed information on the chronology of the migratory process from its beginnings in the community of departure to last arrival in Monterrey. A battery of questions was addressed to the circumstances attending the last move to Monterrey (it was not feasible to get this information for all moves) and to the initial accommodation in that place.

We believe such a descriptive and chronological account of the migratory process is necessary because the bulk of the writing on this subject has been speculative in nature—a series of deductions about migratory behavior originating from certain theoretical orientations. The most important of these can be termed "The Great Dichotomy," a powerful theme that has recurred continually in the history of sociology. Its lineage is long and impressive, dating at least as far back as the mid-nineteenth century with Maine's "status and contract"; recurring in Tönnies's "Gemeinschaft and Gesellschaft," Spencer's "military and industrial," Durkheim's "mechanical and organic," Redfield's "folk and urban"; and finally descending to contemporary variations on "traditional and modern."[5] Whatever illumination "The Great Dichotomy" may have cast on other aspects of social life, its application to the migration process led to a conception that was generally unfettered by evidence. The community of origin, the village in the rural-urban migration sequence, was said to be characterized by close, intense, and emotionally gratifying familial and communal interpersonal relations. By definition, therefore, at the other end of the dichotomy, the city as the community of destination must display opposite characteristics of distant, cold, and impersonal social relations. In such a perspective the migrant is seen as being wrenched from the community of origin, of which he was an organic part, and embarking alone upon the journey to the great city. There, unshielded by any sort of social protection provided by the family or other "primary" social groups, he is confronted by the full force of an impersonal, even hostile, urban environment. Is it any wonder that rural-urban migration viewed in this theoretical framework could be anything but a traumatic experience whereby individuals are torn from the deep social roots of their community of

[5] Henry S. J. Maine, *Ancient Law*; F. Tönnies, *Fundamental Concepts of Sociology*; Herbert Spencer, *Principles of Sociology*; Émile Durkheim, *The Division of Labor in Society*; and Robert Redfield, *The Folk Culture of Yucatan*.

origin and then exposed in vulnerable isolation to all the forms of disorganization and anomie endemic in the urban environment. How closely does this conception correspond with reality? Beyond our chronological account of migration to Monterrey will lie this question and the appropriateness of the above model of the migratory process. In particular, we will want to examine the role of family and kinship relationships at all stages of the migratory process.

Let us begin with the departure from the man's community of origin. One of the most important actions in a migrant's life is when he first leaves home—the environment that has fashioned his outlook on the world. It can be argued that the earlier this occurs the greater the chances of successful adaptation to a new environment. In contrast, the older the age at which migration occurs, the more difficult it will be to sever social relations in the community and the more difficult it will be to change engrained modes of behavior.

The great majority of migrants leave their community of origin at a relatively early age. About a third left prior to their sixteenth year, with nearly all of them making the trip with their family of origin. Nearly two-thirds had left before age 21. These findings are consistent with many other studies reporting migration to be most common among late adolescents and young adults.[6]

While we have established the fact that migrants tend to leave their community of origin at an early age, we do not know how long an interval passed between their departure and their first arrival in Monterrey. Conceivably, migrants might spend a considerable amount of time in other, most often smaller, communities that would serve as anticipatory socialization for life in Monterrey. This is not often the case, for 63 percent of all migrants moved directly from their community of origin to Monterrey, 17 percent took up to ten years, and the remaining 20 percent more than ten years until first arrival. It is worthy of note, when size of community of origin is considered, that 59 percent of those of rural origin came directly to Monterrey. Thus, for the majority of these kinds of migrants, there is no possibility of advance socialization to metropolitan Monterrey by way of residence in some smaller urban place.

[6] For Latin America see Juan C. Elizaga, "Internal Migrations in Latin America," in "Components of Population Change in Latin America," ed. Clyde V. Kiser, *Milbank Memorial Fund Quarterly* 43, no. 4, pt. 2 (October 1965): 144–161.

This finding, incidentally, is contrary to the expectations of the well-known stage (sometimes known as step) migration model. This venerable "law" (as originally formulated by E. G. Ravenstein in 1885) maintains that migration will be by "steps" from smaller to successively larger places.[7] This model seems to provide a fairly good fit for a number of countries, including the United States. It carries a most important implication concerning the adjustment of migrants, for the model should make more tolerable the urbanization process, since it means that migrants are not required to change their environment radically. Socialization to urban environments is carried out in progressive stages, with the movement from rural areas to metropolitan centers sometimes taking two generations or more.

The fit of the model to Monterrey is a poor one for a number of reasons. The stage-migration model assumes a population distribution pattern whereby all parts of a given territory are equally habitable, with a geometric arrangement of different size communities such that any person randomly selected within the territory (excluding the perimeter areas) would be located the same distance from communities of different sizes as any other person. But in Mexico, and particularly in areas providing the bulk of migrants to Monterrey, the population distribution is very uneven because of geographical and historical factors, and the urban hierarchy itself has many "holes," that is communities of the expected size are lacking. Consequently, for some migrants the proper community is difficult to "find." The model also presumes a well-developed transportation system linking all communities of the size hierarchy. It further assumes that urban places are not greatly different in their economic attractiveness to prospective migrants. But, of course, many small and medium-size places are bypassed for the very good reason that there are few jobs available to migrants. Finally, the model entirely ignores the social context of migration, especially the fact that most people migrate to places where they have relatives or friends awaiting them.

As could be anticipated, there is a relationship between age at arrival and the amount of time required to get to Monterrey. Nearly all migrants (97 percent) who came between ages 11 and 15 came directly

[7] The original formulation of the stage-migration model is found in E. G. Ravenstein, "The Laws of Migration," *Journal of the Royal Statistical Society* 48, pt. 2 (June 1885): 167–235.

from their community of origin. By contrast, of those who were between ages 41 and 60 at first arrival in Monterrey, only about one-half came directly, while more than a third took at least twenty years to make the transition. The latter might be called "wanderers," but only about 10 percent of them had ten moves or more, the others simply stayed longer in the intervening communities.

Having established the early departure from community of origin and a direct movement to Monterrey for the majority of the migrants, let us now consider the social and economic context of the last move to Monterrey (first and last move are the same in 81 percent of the cases). When we ask, Why do men migrate? or more directly, Why do our respondents decide to migrate to Monterrey? we are faced with a complex and difficult matter that cannot be given a simple answer. Many factors impinge upon the decision to migrate, ranging from those more remote in a person's past (e.g., level of educational attainment) to those of an intermediate nature (e.g., drought conditions over a period of years), down to the immediate percipitant of the move (e.g., loss of job, solicitation of relatives, a sudden impulse to change environments).[8] Aside from the problem of recall in asking persons to re-create the circumstances of their move, most people are themselves scarcely aware of all the considerations that entered into their decision. (Actually, questions in this area were asked only of those who were adults when they migrated and already had work experience before coming to Monterrey.)

However difficult it may be to account for all the factors bearing upon migration, one point has been reasonably well established in many studies. When men are asked to explain why they migrated, invariably economic reasons related to their work are selected as most important. We first asked the men the open question, "What influenced your decision to move?" and then we asked them to select the most important of the reasons they volunteered. Two-thirds (68 percent) gave work as the most important factor influencing their decision to move. It is probably not accidental that this figure is quite similar to the 65 percent reporting work in response to a similar question asked in a national survey conducted by the U.S. Bureau of the Census for the year

[8] A brief survey of the literature on decision to move is given by Henry Shryock, "Survey Statistics on Reasons for Moving," paper presented at the Meetings of the International Union for the Scientific Study of Population, London, September, 1969.

beginning in March of 1962, and the 62 percent reported by Juan Elizaga for males migrating to Santiago, Chile.[9]

Next in importance are family reasons. The 17 percent for Monterrey compares with 14 percent reported for the U.S. sample and 8 percent for the Santiago one. But family reasons are difficult to interpret because of the diversity of situations subsumed under this label. For example, one young man may come to Monterrey under the sponsorship of relatives who assist him in getting an education and then a good job, while another young man may be drawn to Monterrey in response to a call to assist aging or ailing parents, a move that may be to his economic detriment.

Interestingly enough, education is far more important for older men than for the other groups; one of every seven of these men migrated primarily for that reason. Obviously, the education is not for themselves but for their children. In Mexico, as we have seen, the lack of educational facilities in rural areas and small towns makes it obligatory for the advanced student to go to a larger urban center. Overall, Monterrey probably has the best facilities for higher education outside Mexico City. The older man, while perhaps not regarding migration as a means of directly improving his own lot, sees it as an opportunity for materially improving the chances of his children.

Only 3 percent of the migrant men select community as the principal reason for migrating. They must respond to some degree to Monterrey as a place to live and work, but it is quite clear that this factor considered in itself only rarely is decisive in bringing about migration.

If work is so important in influencing the decision to migrate, it is incumbent to consider the work situation of the migrants prior to the move. Agricultural employment is important (40 percent of the total migrants were so employed). As was noted in the section on selectivity, the lowest percent is to be found among those who arrived before 1941 (37 percent), and then it builds up to a high of 52 percent in the 1951–1960 period. The selectivity of the earlier migrants accounts for this trend, which is contrary to the national decline in importance of agriculture.

It might be assumed that it was the men's dissatisfaction with the conditions of their work that set off the whole migratory process.

[9] U.S. Bureau of the Census, "Reasons for Moving: March 1962 to March 1963," in *Current Population Reports*, Series P-20, no. 154, August 22, 1966; and Elizaga, *Migraciones a las áreas metropolitanas.*

Rather surprising, in an answer to the question "Were you satisfied with your last job before coming to Monterrey?" over half (56 percent) reported themselves satisfied and only 30 percent unequivocably expressed dissatisfaction with their job. Why then did they quit? When they were asked this question, 28 percent clearly indicated expulsive reasons connected with work (terminated, or "went badly"), while 44 percent mentioned work in the context of getting a better position and a higher income. The remaining men were about equally divided into those reporting family and "other" reasons. Generally speaking, the more precarious or uncertain the job, the higher the proportion reporting expulsive reasons. Nearly four of every ten men in agriculture were "forced" off the land, and only mining approached this figure, doubtless reflecting the decline of mining in northeastern Mexico.

Once the migrant has made a decision to terminate his employment or has had this decision made for him by others or by natural factors, the question arises as to how long an interval exists between leaving work and the move to Monterrey. Six of every seven made the journey within one month. Evidently, men do not "hang around" after leaving their work, and it is likely that the decision to move began to form in their minds well in advance of actually leaving the job.

Only 11 percent said that they considered some other destination before making their choice to come to Monterrey. This does not lend much support to a conception of "migrant man" who carefully balances the advantages and disadvantages of remaining in a place. When the scales tip toward the unfavorable end, he then systematically considers opportunities in a number of alternative destinations, choosing that one offering the best prospects for one of his background.

The decision to move to Monterrey doubtless was influenced to some extent by direct acquaintance with the city. Nearly two-thirds of the migrants had been to Monterrey for some reason prior to the final migration. This figure rises from 52 percent of the men arriving before 1940 to 75 percent for the latest arrivals (1961–1965). Clearly, for most migrants the move to Monterrey was no perilous voyage into uncharted seas.

Not all the men considered the move to Monterrey to be a permanent change of residence at the time it was made. Two-thirds reported that they had come to Monterrey with definite expectations of staying. Twenty percent were more tentative, arriving with the idea of seeing what would happen. If things went well, they planned to remain. As could be expected, the figure is a good deal higher for those arriving after 1960 (25 percent) than for the earlier arrivals. The percentage declines to a low of 9 for those coming before 1941, because those for whom the trial did not work out had already left Monterrey by the time of the survey. The rest (16 percent) came with the idea of staying only for a time and then returning to their place of origin.

The majority of men arrived in Monterrey with nothing more tangible than the hope of finding a satisfactory job. Only 23 percent arrived either with a signed contract or with a definite job promised to them. A mere 10 percent of the men who worked in agriculture before coming to Monterrey had either a contract or a specific job lined up. In contrast, 27 percent coming from jobs in manufacturing and 41 percent from services (including armed forces) had such an arrangement. Obviously, these differences are linked to the marketable skills that the migrants bring to the metropolitan environment.

At the end of the series of questions dealing with reasons for leaving their jobs and coming to Monterrey, we asked the question "Finally, are you satisfied with having come to Monterrey?" Overwhelmingly (92 percent), the men reported themselves satisfied. Only 3 percent gave an unqualified "no" answer.[10] Of course, the fact that nine of every ten men said they were satisfied must be put in proper context. It is well known that some people will report themselves satisfied with their present situation, no matter what it is. And many of the migrants to Monterrey who were dissatisfied had left, so our sample is selective of those who were most successful.

Nonetheless, even if we discount a part of the 92 percent figure, it is undeniable that the great majority of migrants were satisfied with their decision to migrate to Monterrey. When asked why they were satisfied, the answers varied, depending in part on the background of the respondent. For example, 18 percent reported satisfaction simply because they were able to satisfy the minimal conditions for livelihood ("I have work," "I'm not hungry"). Of those employed in agriculture, mining, and construction before migrating, about a third responded in this manner. This background involves risky and undependable work,

[10] Similar results are reported by Ramiro Cardona Gutierrez in a study of squatter settlements in Bogotá. In response to the question "Do you consider that you're the same, better, or worse than before migrating?" 87 percent said they were better off and only 3 percent said they were worse off ("Migración, urbanización y marginalidad," in *Seminario nacional sobre urbanización y marginalidad*, p. 63).

and it is likely that the migrants, lacking skills having a high value in the urban environment, simply do not have high aspirations. Although most of the men reported they migrated because of work-related reasons, only 19 percent mentioned their job specifically. One-fourth mentioned the higher standard of living ("earn more," "live better") in Monterrey. Another 15 percent mentioned a variety of family reasons, and 10 percent mentioned the community, the latter reason being more common among the higher-status migrants.

Since there are only a few cases of expressed dissatisfaction with the decision to migrate to Monterrey, they cannot be analyzed in detail. The men mainly were disappointed with their income and level of living or with the community. Only 16 percent mentioned dissatisfaction with their jobs as such.

The Composition of the Migrant Group

Thus far, we have discussed the context of last migration to Monterrey only from the point of view of the man himself. We have not taken into account the social and particularly the familial context in which the migration takes place. To do so, we will first identify the marital status of the men upon arrival in Monterrey, and then we will examine the migration itself in terms of the persons involved.

For our purposes we classify migrants into three groups, taking into account that marital status is closely linked to age at migration: Young Bachelors (aged 16–25, who were unmarried at last arrival to Monterrey), Young Family Men (aged 26–35, who were married with children upon last arrival), and Older Family Men (married men with children who were age 36 or over upon last arrival).

While marital status restricts the possible combinations of the migratory act, it does not permit us to predict who will migrate with whom. For example, a young bachelor cannot migrate with his family of procreation, but he can make the trip alone with his family of origin or with other relatives or friends. A married man with children may also include his parents, making it a three-generational group. But who moves with whom at what time may vary. The father may come alone, then send for his wife and children, and after a time call for his parents. The migration of groups permits a rather large number of possible combinations.

Turning now to the actual migration and linking it to marital and

TABLE 6-2. Composition of Migratory Group, by Family Life Cycle (In Percent)

Migratory Group	All Migrants	Young Bachelors	Young Family Men	Older Family Men
Family of origin	34	66	2	1
Respondent alone	19	31	8	9
Family of procreation	39	0	72	83
Family of origin and procreation	6	0	15	5
Other combinations	2	3	3	1
Total	100	100	100	99
	(891)a	(274)	(184)	(208)

a Excluding 13 cases with no information.

family status, we find the combination shown in Table 6-2. Less than one-fifth of the migrants come alone, and even among the young bachelors it is less than a third. There are no significant changes in the above pattern by time-of-arrival cohorts.

The dimension of migration not yet touched upon is the sequence and timing of movement when persons other than the respondent are involved. Logically we may identify (1) *solitary migration*, when the man comes alone and no one precedes or follows him; (2) *simultaneous migration*, when everybody in the migratory group, however constituted, comes at the same time; and (3) *split migration*, when members of the migratory group come at different times. Of course, the allocation of men to these categories must be in terms of their situation at the time of the survey. A man classified as a solitary or a simultaneous migrant may at some subsequent time become a split migrant by the arrival of some relative.

Table 6-3 presents the distribution of the three types of migratory groups by position in family life cycle and by the farm-nonfarm background of the migrants. More than half of the family men experienced a simultaneous migration. Typically, the family comes as a unit to the city. In contrast, the young bachelors come as part of a split group or alone.

Table 6-3 also makes it clear that men of farm background are more likely to engage in the "bridging" process characteristic of split migrations. This trend can be linked to the greater risk confronting migrants

TABLE 6-3. Type of Migration, by Family Life Cycle and Farm-Nonfarm Background (In Percent)

Type of Migration	All Migrants	Young Bachelors (A)			Young Family Men (B)			Older Family Men (C)		
		Farm	Nonfarm	Total Group A	Farm	Nonfarm	Total Group B	Farm	Nonfarm	Total Group C
Solitary	20	24	34	31	15	4	8	10	9	9
Simultaneous	38	15	20	18	44	73	62	50	53	52
Split	42	61	46	51	41	23	30	40	38	39
Total	100 (884)[a]	100 (88)[b]	100 (146)[b]	100 (274)	100 (71)[b]	100 (112)[b]	100 (183)	100 (91)[b]	100 (110)[b]	100 (205)

[a] Excluded are 20 cases with no information. Included are men who arrived before age 16 and who did not fall into the three life-cycle categories.
[b] Based only on migrants who worked before coming to Monterrey.

from farm backgrounds, who are uncertain whether they will find suitable employment in the metropolis.

Finally, there is the time interval between the first and the last arrival in the split-migration pattern. It sometimes takes a considerable period to reunite the family group. Even among the young family men, almost one-half (44 percent) require more than a year to bring the family together, and over 40 percent of all young bachelors are involved in a sequence that takes more than three years to work itself out. The temporal aspect of split migration bears upon an aspect of migration that is sometimes overlooked in the literature. Migration, in the perspective of familial units, is best seen as a continuous process not limited to the number of days an individual, with or without companions, needs to make the journey to another place. A sizable part of the migration to Monterrey involves family groups that take months and years to complete the transfer. It is a relatively stable pattern, for there are no great differences when the migrants are examined by time-of-arrival cohorts. This fact implies that for any specific time we can confidently predict for Monterrey, or other places with substantial in-migration, a fair volume of subsequent migration, simply as a consequence of the split-migration pattern. In other words, migration to Monterrey generates its own momentum and becomes, even if to a limited extent, somewhat independent of economic opportunity.

Migration to Monterrey and Forms of Assistance

We have established the fact that most migrants were acquainted with the city prior to last arrival. But did they know anyone there, and if so, did this mean that they had an easier adjustment to the city? If assistance is made available to the migrants, in what form is it?

A very large proportion (84 percent) of the migrants to Monterrey had relatives or friends there at the time of last migration.[11] Because of the heavy flow of migrants into that place in recent decades, the probability of having someone there should be greatest for the more recent arrivals. This assumption is confirmed by the figures, which rise from

[11] Browning, on the basis of evidence from various parts of the world, advances the proposition that "a substantial majority (in most cases at least two-thirds) of migrants to large cities in developing areas have relatives or friends living there" (Browning, "Migrant Selectivity and the Growth of Large Cities in Developing Societies," p. 298).

77 percent of the earliest cohort to 86 percent for the most recent one. But the difference over this time period is rather small. Apparently, the familial and friendship networks of Monterrey were established well before the migratory flow reached its greatest intensity after 1941.

But the presence of relatives or friends in itself does not mean that help will be forthcoming. Two-thirds of those with someone in Monterrey received help in some form. We don't know, however, how many who did not receive assistance asked for but were denied help. Probably only a small fraction. The most common form of assistance (70 percent of all aid) is the providing of food and shelter, something the families are best equipped to offer. Our data suggest that the kinship network is rather effective in taking care of the basic needs of the migrants when they first arrive in the metropolis. (This form of assistance is quite stable by time of arrival.) All other forms of assistance (finding jobs, finding housing, and direct financial contributions) are not common, with money transfers being rare (7 percent). Cash for this purpose is undoubtedly in short supply.

The migrants cannot expect much help from those "back home." Only about one in eight received any kind of help, and most of it took the form of a one-way bus ticket, predominantly to young, single migrants. But the lack of assistance is only to be expected, since the poor economic prospects and scarce cash resources are instrumental in bringing about the migration of many men in the first place.

Here is where the phenomenon of split migration becomes relevant. In this kind of migration help can flow in two directions: from those in Monterrey to the other members of the group and vice versa. To illustrate, a family may send a son to school in Monterrey. After he has finished schooling and has obtained a job, he may help the rest of his family come to Monterrey, or he may pay for the Monterrey education of one or more of his younger brothers or sisters. In those cases of split migration where there was six months or more time between first and last arrivals, 47 percent of the first arrivals sent back money to those remaining, while in the other direction only 19 percent forwarded money to the avant garde in Monterrey. The latter helped in various ways when they did not send money. It may be puzzling that only 10 percent of all nonmonetary aid is help in finding work until we remember that the latecomers often are wives and children who normally would not be in the labor force.

Living Arrangements upon Arrival

Migrants who first live with relatives or friends are in a position to be introduced to the city by guides they know and trust, and this assistance presumably eases their accommodation to the Monterrey environment. More than one-half (58 percent) of the migrants first lived with relatives or friends already established in Monterrey. The range for the family life-cycle groups was narrow. Migrants from farm backgrounds are much more likely than those with nonfarm backgrounds to receive lodging from relatives and friends—72 percent for the former and 51 percent for the latter. Thus, those presumably most in need of primary group contacts in the new environment are most likely to have them. An interesting sidelight reflecting the pattern of male dominance of the Mexican family structure is the fact that, of the married migrants who lived with relatives, 71 percent resided with relatives of the husband, while only 21 percent lived with relatives of the wife. It is unlikely that these percentages reflect a much lower incidence of the wife's relatives in Monterrey. It is more reasonable to assume that the husband generally will try to avoid dependence upon his wife's relatives for fear that it will weaken his authority within his own family.

But what about those migrants who lived independently of established relatives or friends upon their arrival to Monterrey? Did they live separately because they didn't know anyone? This pattern is true for only four of every ten migrants who lived independently. About a third knew somebody, but they received no help. The rest received assistance in finding housing, either from relatives or from the company they worked for. There are significant differences among the family life-cycle groups who lived independently in terms of knowing anyone in Monterrey: 53 percent of the young bachelors did not know anybody, compared with 25 percent of the young family men. Most of the young family men living independently evidently did so because of their own choosing; 43 percent of them were aided in finding housing by relatives or friends or the company.

The young bachelors should be the group most closely conforming to the stereotyped image of the migrant alone in the big city. But only 38 percent of them lived independently; the rest resided with parents or with their employers (masters of apprentices, shopkeepers, military). Most of the young bachelors living independently were to be found in *pensiones* or similar arrangements. A Mexican *pensión* is a far cry from an impersonal hotel; it is usually run by a *señora* who provides meals, and the young lodgers more often than not share rooms.

Besides living with relatives, other forms of contact with kin upon arrival in the city are possible. The extent of kinship contacts of the migrants can be summarized as in Table 6-4, in which the migrants are grouped in five categories according to the amount of kin interaction. Migrants in Category 1 are most deeply involved in a network of family relations in Monterrey. Not only do they live with relatives, but they also are in close contact with other relatives who live in the same neighborhood. When asked how often they visited these relatives during the first year in Monterrey, 60 percent answered "more than once a week," 26 percent "once a week or every 15 days," 10 percent "once a month or less," and only 4 percent "never visited." Migrants in Category 3 visit to a similar extent. We ranked migrants in Category 2 above those in Category 3 because living with relatives means closer interaction than visiting, however frequent. We can say, however, that all migrants in the first three categories (69 percent of all migrants) are members of close-knit kinship networks. We cannot maintain that the migrants in Category 4 do not interact with kin, since we have no information on contacts with relatives in Monterrey who live outside the neighborhood, but we can certainly assume that greater spatial separation reduces the frequency of contacts. The migrants in Category 5 (one of every seven

TABLE 6-4. Kinship Interaction of Migrants

Category	Percent	Number
1. Lived with relatives, had additional relatives in neighborhood	20	(171)
2. Lived with relatives, had no additional relatives in neighborhood	38	(337)
3. Lived independently, had relatives in neighborhood	11	(100)
4. Lived independently, no relatives in neighborhood but elsewhere in the city	17	(145)
5. Lived independently, no relatives in neighborhood or in the rest of the city	14	(124)
Total	100	(877)[a]

[a] Excluded are 27 cases with no information on one or more of the three questions used to make up the index.

men) are the ones who had to make their start in the city without the presumed benefit of family relations.

We say "presumed" benefit, for it is not warranted to conclude that those migrants without extensive kinship contacts in Monterrey necessarily are worse off than those who have them. The benefit to be derived will depend upon the background of the migrants. For those originating in rural or small urban places, the kinship network may provide a buffer between the migrant and his new environment. But those coming to Monterrey from medium and large urban places (especially career migrants) are much less in need of kinship networks to ease the transition from one environment to another. The relationship of "background" variables to kinship networks is indicated in Table 6-5 in terms of the percent participating in kinship networks (Categories 1, 2, and 3). The relationship is consistent for all three variables: the more agrarian the background, the more likely the migrant will be a member of kinship networks. Thus, the people who supposedly need more help from their kin are the ones who are more likely to get it.

To close this account of the chronology of the move to Monterrey, there remains the question of ties and contacts maintained by the migrants in communities they have lived in before. Some 88 percent still have relatives and friends there, the figure rising from 77 percent in the earliest arrival cohort to 93 percent in the latest one. And those who have people back home tend to maintain contacts of some kind. Four of every five keep up their ties by visits or writing. It is for us not accidental that the 88 percent with relatives and friends in other places is quite similar in magnitude to the 84 percent of the migrants to Monterrey who had relatives there prior to time of last migration.

TABLE 6-5. Migrants' Participation in Kinship Networks by Background Characteristics

Size Class of Community of Origin	Percent Partici- pating	Education	Percent Partici- pating	Last Employment before Arrival in Monterrey	Percent Partici- pating
Rural	73	*Primaria* or less	73	Farm	82
Small urban	70	Beyond *primaria*	55	Nonfarm	62
Medium urban	62				
Large urban	56				

This is the reason why we place such emphasis on migration as a process.

Return Migration to Monterrey and Cedral

Some people not only write or visit but they also return to live in a community of previous residence, more often than not to their community of origin. In a few instances this takes the form of retirement to the community of origin, but this form of return migration is not nearly so common as it is in some African contexts.[12] Return migration in Mexico seems to be much more frequent at younger ages. It always has been one of the more shadowy features of the migration process, principally because of the difficulty in obtaining satisfactory data for this phenomenon. The nets cast out in national censuses to obtain data on migration allow return migration to slip through. Fortunately, our life-history approach enables us to know exactly how many migrations were made to any previous residence. Our first assignment then is to establish the incidence of return migration.

For the representative sample of Monterrey, 17 percent are return migrants to Monterrey, that is, they left the city only to come back later. An additional 6 percent experienced a return migration to some other place. (In this section we will not be concerned with this group.) In Cedral 29 percent of the men had return migration to Cedral. Due to the fewer in-migrants to Cedral, only 1 percent had return migration to some other place. Unfortunately, in the absence of comparative data it is not possible to say that Monterrey or Cedral has a high, average, or low incidence of return migration within the context of Mexico, Latin America, developing countries, or, for that matter, developed countries. It is indisputable that return migration is a significant phenomenon, for it affects a substantial part of the adult male population of both a rapidly growing metropolis and a stagnant agricultural center.

Who are the men engaging in this form of migration? To answer this question, we will first focus on the Monterrey sample. In Table 6-6 we distinguish between three groups of men: (1) natives, those born in the city; (2) natives by adoption, those born outside Monterrey but who spent their formative years there; and (3) migrants, all the others. Each group is then subclassified between those who had return migration to Monterrey and those who did not, and the distribution in edu-

[12] Caldwell, *African Rural-Urban Migration.*

TABLE 6-6. Education, by Migratory Status and Return Migration to Monterrey (In Percent)

Education	Natives		Natives by Adoption		Migrants	
	Nonreturn	Return	Nonreturn	Return	Nonreturn	Return
None	2	1	9	4	18	17
Incomplete *primaria*	27	22	29	34	42	42
Complete *primaria*	31	21	27	21	19	18
Secundaria and						
preparatoria	27	32	26	27	14	16
University	13	24	8	14	7	7
Total	100	100	99	100	100	100
	(401)	(82)	(172)	(56)	(730)	(168)

cational levels for each of them is presented. Only among the natives are differences in education important, while among natives by adoption they are slight, and among migrants nonexistent. In the first two groups we find a larger percentage with higher education among return migrants. This fact indicates the existence of a group of men who left Monterrey, their home town, either to continue their education elsewhere or for reasons related to occupational careers. Physicians and other professionals, for instance, may go to Mexico City or the United States for advanced training; managers of local enterprises may be sent to a branch in some other city for a period of time. It seems, however, that a good number of return migrants, even among the two categories of natives, do not have high levels of education, and their moves might not be as clearly career oriented. In any case, this type of migration seems to be almost completely absent among migrants to Monterrey.

That return migration to Monterrey tends to have a different meaning for natives and migrants is confirmed by other information. While natives, when leaving Monterrey, tend to go to other large urban places (37 percent went to cities of 100,000 and over), fewer migrants returning to Monterrey went to large cities (19 percent). Possibly more important is the age at which those with return migration reenter Monterrey. For all those who returned after age 15, two-thirds of both natives and natives by adoption are back by age 30. In contrast, only little more than a third of the migrants had returned by this age. Finally, many return migrations among both natives and migrants include a move to the United States (21 percent of all return migrants among natives, 15 percent among migrants). But while the former tend to go for non-agricultural work, the latter go very often to work as farm laborers.

This discussion leads us to the important distinction between types of return migrations, mainly between those that might be labeled "career oriented," and those where the move is more linked to temporary circumstances (availability of job, family relations). The former type is clearly present more often among men of higher status, and therefore we found them among natives more often than among migrants.

What about the reasons for return migration to Cedral? Here there is little "career" migration, because of the general low levels of education and the scarcity of appropriate positions for educated men in Cedral. The distribution in educational levels for those men who had a return migration and those who did not shows almost no difference in Cedral, indicating that those who engage in return migration do not differ greatly from the general population of that place. Only 6 percent of the Cedraleños (more precisely, 6 percent among those presently in Cedral) went out to study. Undoubtedly, many of those who left to study in Monterrey or elsewhere never returned, since their education would be of little use in Cedral. Most return migrants to Cedral left either to take unskilled jobs in the city—work that probably did little to enhance their skills for the return to Cedral—or for agricultural jobs. In both cases, the main reason for leaving is undoubtedly related to the lack of employment in Cedral. But what is the reason for coming back? The responses to the question "Why did you return to Cedral?" are given in Table 6-7. The return migration from other places is dominated by agricultural contract labor, accounting for nearly one-half of the reasons. There are fewer "expulsive" reasons given in the return migration from Monterrey, with family reasons increasing greatly in importance. Although the reasons given do not indicate many positive factors, at least of an economic nature that would account for the return, only about 10 percent of both groups say they are not satisfied to be back in Cedral. Only a trivial 4 percent returned with liquid assets sufficiently large to permit them to start a business or to provide for a comfortable retirement. Evidently, the basis of their satisfaction is of a minimal nature, and to the extent that they find family, community, and climate agreeable they are content. About 60 percent say they live better in Cedral than in other places.

TABLE 6-7. Reasons for Return to Cedral (In Percent)

Reason	Return Migration from Monterrey	Return Migration from Other Places	All Return Migration
Work terminated, no papers	20	47	34
Work became available in Cedral	6	10	8
Family reasons	33	10	21
Did not like, did not adapt	8	10	9
Couldn't get work, earned little	8	0	4
All other reasons	25	23	24
Total	100	100	101
	(49)	(49)	(98)

SOURCE: Cedral survey.

Migration as Process

We have dealt with a number of features of the migratory process in the course of this chapter, and we now need to bring them together and to place them in a somewhat larger context than was possible earlier because of the necessity to follow migration sequences closely and with the necessary descriptive detail.

It has been established that migrants to Monterrey are positively selective in terms of the populations from which they originate. The tests were education and occupation. But we would like to make clear that these two variables do not exhaust the ways in which migrants are likely to be positively selective. For example, the psychological dimension has not been considered. In particular, we have in mind the quality of venturesomeness and the propensity to assume risk. We are confident, even though we have no data to support the assertion, that people vary in this respect even when socioeconomic background is held constant. People differ in their willingness to leave familiar environments and seek out new ones that they have reason to believe will give them greater opportunities. This restlessness and ambition are not to be mistaken with the person's unwillingness to conform to the social norms of village or small-town environments, although this attitude, too, undoubtedly is a factor leading to some out-migration. We believe that migrants to Monterrey disproportionately have the qualities of venturesomeness and a responsiveness to opportunities for economic advancement, when compared to their populations of origin, which are helpful to them in the Monterrey environment.[13]

The various forms of migratory selectivity tend to go together and to reinforce one another. This process can be seen in age as it is related to migration. Most migration occurs at rather early ages. Being young, the migrants are more likely to be single or at least without large numbers of children. Even if they are not well educated or particularly skilled, their chances of landing a job in the city are better than those of older men because physical vitality is the most important requisite for unskilled manual jobs. Finally, the adaptability of individuals to different environments and a willingness to break off ties in the community of origin are related to youth.

The above discussion, unfortunately, gives the impression that migrant selectivity is something almost immutable. In fact, as we earlier demonstrated, there has been a trend in recent decades toward declining positive selectivity. This dynamic feature of selectivity is perhaps the most significant, or at least most unexpected, of our findings, and it was interpreted in the context of "pioneer" versus "mass" migration. An important reason for the decline in positive selectivity is to be found in the idea of a static and diminishing reservoir of potential migrants. That is, a combination of increasing demands put upon the rural reservoir by the continuous high rate of urbanization, and in particular by the rapid growth of Monterrey, with either an absolute decline in the size of the reservoir or at least a decline in its relative rate of growth produces a situation whereby the migratory flow must be supplied from an increasingly representative sample of the origin population.

Our account of the social context of migration has made it quite clear that kinship networks are very important to the great majority of migrants. Indeed, a good part of this chapter was given over to a rather detailed description of the circumstances attending migration that demonstrated just how false is the imagery of the lone and lonely migrant that is often purveyed. It is true that we can say nothing about the mental health of the migrants either prior to their move or after their arrival in Monterrey—this finding would have entailed a project in

---

[13] Robert Van Kemper ("Migration and Adaptation of Tzintzuntzan Peasants in Mexico City," Ph.D. Dissertation, University of California at Berkeley, 1971) found that migrants were more likely to be "innovators" than the nonmigrants. Kemper's findings for the whole process of migration are substantially in accord with the Monterrey results.

itself. We do, however, have other information that leads us to conclude that the migration is not as traumatic as sometimes portrayed.[14] At least some of the conditions named as contributing to personal and social disorganization are not present in the Monterrey case. The kinship networks have been demonstrated to be quite effective in easing the adjustment of migrants to the metropolitan milieu, especially for those who presumably need it most—the *campesinos* coming directly from the country.

Migration, as we have described it for Monterrey, genuinely is a process. Many years of sustained heavy in-migration to Monterrey have generated a system of interpersonal contacts with many other communities. Consider the situation of Cedral. Residential mobility is fundamental to an understanding of the life and institutions of this community. It is a rare adult who either has not migrated himself at some time in his life (only a third of men aged 45 and over have never migrated) or had no brothers who moved out (68 percent of men with brothers had one or more living outside Cedral, with 38 percent in Monterrey). In the year before the survey, three of ten men had made a trip for one reason or another to Monterrey. Cedral, of course, was selected for investigation because of its known high out-migration. While perhaps extreme in this respect, it is not untypical of the situation in many other Mexican communities where residential mobility (including temporary migrations as agricultural labor) has become a way of life.

The result is that migration rightfully should be seen as a continuous activity, nearly always simultaneously involving many people in communities both of origin and of destination. Within this perspective the migratory pattern is quite stable over time; what changes is the people who may occupy different positions at different times. Migrants to Mon-

---

[14] The adjustment of migrants to cities in Latin America is the subject of an expanding literature. Unfortunately, it is often restricted to a particular sector of the population, especially those in squatter settlements. See William P. Mangin, ed., *Peasants in Cities*; and Elizabeth and Anthony Leeds, *A Bibliography of the Sociology of Housing—Settlement Types in Latin America.* A comprehensive review of the political dimension is provided in Wayne Cornelius, Jr., "The Political Sociology of Cityward Migration in Latin America: Toward Empirical Theory," *Latin American Urban Research,* ed. Francine F. Rabinovitz and Felicity M. Trueblood. The situation in the United States is covered by Lyle W. and Magdaline Shannon, "The Assimilation of Migrants to Cities," in *Social Science and the City,* ed. Leo F. Schnore.

terrey rely upon earlier arrivals for help in establishing themselves, and they in turn help subsequent arrivals in settling in. Migration thus begets migration in ways not directly related to economic considerations. Furthermore, return migration doubtless serves an important, if sometimes overlooked, function as a kind of sorting device that removes from Monterrey some of those who are unsuccessful or dissatisfied or both. Just how effective return migration is in this respect is not known, nor do we know if it is more effective at one period than at another.

Our assessment that most migrants react positively to the move to Monterrey is not dependent solely upon their response to the one question asking if they are satisfied with the move. When asked, "Do you consider that your current job is better, the same, or worse than the one your father had at approximately the same age?" 66 percent of all migrants reported their jobs as better than their fathers', a higher figure than for the natives. Another self-appraisal question, "Do you believe your opportunities to live comfortably are greater, the same, or less than those of the majority of people in Mexico?" provides the comparisons shown in Table 6-8. The migrants from Cedral are clearly intermediate between the Cedral and the Monterrey men, although the percent of migrants saying "less" is a good deal closer to the total Monterrey sample than to Cedral men.

If we believe that some sociologists see the migration process through a glass all too darkly, there are other sociologists who see migration more favorably, specifically as a way of expanding the life chances available to men. Although the statement of Blau and Duncan is based upon an investigation of occupational mobility in the United States, it would seem equally appropriate for Mexico and Monterrey: "The com-

TABLE 6-8. Men's Evaluation of Their Living Conditions Relative to Majority of Mexicans, by Regional Background

Regional Background	Percent Saying Greater	Percent Saying Less
Men living in Cedral	6	57
Men originated from Cedral region but living in Monterrey	15	25
Total sample of Monterrey men	27	15

SOURCE: Monterrey actual sample and Cedral survey.

munity in which a man is raised, just as the race or ethnic group into which he is born, defines an ascriptive base that limits his adult occupational chances. Migration, however, partly removes these ascribed restrictions on achievement by enabling a man to take advantage of opportunities not available in his original community . . . selective migration strengthens the operation of universalistic criteria of achievement."[15]

Of course, in this particular chapter we have avoided comment on the occupational achievement of the men in Monterrey. The first stage of occupational histories was discussed in Chapter 5 when it was demonstrated that migrants to the city with comparable work background and experience did not suffer in comparison with the natives, but those coming straight to the city from farm work did have a considerable disadvantage. We shall continue this native-migrant comparison in Chapter 8 when the work years 25–45 will be analyzed.

The most general conclusion that we can derive from the material presented in this chapter is that, for Monterrey at least, the migratory process should be given a more positive evaluation than is often the case. Life in large cities like Monterrey *does* require of in-migrants, particularly those originating in rural areas, many adjustments in work habits and in family and personal life styles. But we maintain that most migrants handle the change rather well. Possibly the adjustment is most difficult for second-generation urbanites, the children of the migrants, for they will not have the experience in other areas, especially depressed rural areas, that leads their parents to have a favorable impression of Monterrey. But this reaction must be speculation, since we did not directly investigate the matter. Rather, we must now turn to another form of adjustment that nearly all our men sooner or later will undergo: marriage and early family formation, the subject of the next chapter.

[15] Peter M. Blau and Otis D. Duncan, *The American Occupational Structure*, p. 275.

7. Marriage and Early Family Formation

Up to this point in our account of the men's life histories, the family has been omnipresent, whether we were discussing the influence of the family of origin upon the educational attainment of the respondents, the family as the context in which many men enter the labor force, or, as in the last chapter, the role of kinship networks in the migration process. In this chapter we will make the family the focus of analysis. The family is the basic unit in any known society, but its importance in Mexico is particularly significant because much of the daily interpersonal contacts are concentrated within familial and kinship contexts.

A first indication of the relative importance of the family context for the Mexican men can be obtained by considering residence arrangements. The majority of single men live with their parents or other relatives, moving to a separate household only when they marry, virtually regardless of the age at which this occurs. The bachelor apartment is not at all common, even in large cities. Only 26 of the 1,640 men in the Monterrey sample lived alone or with nonrelatives. Pressures to leave home seem to be quite weak, excepting when migration takes place, and even in this case most single men end up living with relatives. (Some reasons why this is so will be given below in considering the basic values and family structure in Mexico.) Moreover, most men sooner or later end up married; only 4 percent of men aged 41 or over were single. The marriage, once constituted, does not require the man to make a break with his family of origin, and strong emotional and economic ties often remain between son and parents and son and siblings. The marriages are less subject to breakup from causes other than death than in the United States or Europe. Eighty-two percent of the men aged 41 and over were living with their first wives, and only eighteen men in the actual sample reported themselves divorced or separated and had not married again. Consensual unions are less common within our Monterrey sample than in other parts of Mexico; only little more than 2 percent of the unions were of this nature. The so-called serial monogamy pattern, whereby men engage in a sequence of short-lived unions, does not occur often.[1] Parenthetically, we should mention that one phenomenon sometimes said to be widespread in Mexico, simultaneous multiple stable unions, did not turn up more than a handful of men so engaged. Granted that this is a delicate and difficult area in which to obtain information, considerable probing did not result in more than a few of the men admitting they were currently, or had done so previously, supporting more than one household. Even when it occurs, as in the now famous Sánchez case study by Oscar Lewis,[2] it may be taken as further evidence of the importance of family life for Mexican men.

Family and kinship also are very important because they are closely linked to the men's lives in other areas, mainly the economic one. We already have mentioned this relationship in our treatment of entrance into the labor force, and there are a number of other indicators: (1) over one-third of the men work in enterprises where there is also at least one relative; (2) many firms in Monterrey use the kinship networks to recruit labor, their policies sometimes explicitly favoring applicants who have close relatives in the enterprise; and (3) in Joseph Kahl's surveys in Mexico and Brazil, it was found that a majority of Mexicans agreed with the statement "It is always better to hire a relative instead of a stranger," while this was not the case in Brazil.[3] Outside the work context, it is our impression that much leisure time is spent

---

[1] The serial monogamy pattern is discussed in a different context by Elliot Liebow, *Tally's Corner.*
[2] Oscar Lewis, *The Children of Sánchez: Autobiography of a Mexican Family.*
[3] Joseph Kahl, *The Measurement of Modernism: A Study of Values in Brazil and Mexico,* p. 81.

in family and kinship circles. Television now serves to keep more of the men at home nights and "going out" for the family generally means visits to relatives in the city.

While the central place that family and kinship networks occupy in the lives of Mexicans has been emphasized many times, there are still no really adequate studies devoted exclusively to an analysis of the structure of the Mexican family and its transformation during a period of rapid social change.[4] Most of what we know comes from ethnographic studies of small communities in which one or two chapters are devoted to the family and some "case" studies à la Oscar Lewis of a few working-class families in urban environments.[5] Such essayists as Octavio Paz and Samuel Ramos have provided some insights, and psychologists and psychoanalytically oriented psychiatrists have provided descriptions of the Mexican family, but all have many limitations in terms of structural variation by class and region, and especially in charting changes over time.[6] Kahl's study of values in Mexico appears to lend support to the thesis of the centrality of family life in Mexico, but his interest was not concentrated on this subject. Our study did not make the family the center of attention either, but information was collected about the family life cycle and the men's values regarding family life. In this chapter we will first consider some features of the Mexican family structure and the men's values in this regard. Then, consistent with our concern with events in the life cycle, we shall take up the early stages of family formation, particularly age at first marriage and spacing of first children. Finally, we shall discuss the consequences of some events in the family life cycle as they affect the men's occupational careers.

[4] Various aspects of the Mexican family structure are covered in Oscar Lewis, "Family Dynamics in a Mexican Village," *Marriage and Family Living* 21 (August 1959): 218–226, and "Husbands and Wives in a Mexican Village: A Study of Role Conflict," *American Anthropologist* 51, no. 4 (1949): 602–610; Noel F. McGinn, "Marriage and Family in Middle-Class Mexico," *Journal of Family Living* 28, no. 3 (August 1966): 305–313; and Frank W. and Ruth C. Young, "Differentiation of Family Structure in Rural Mexico," *Journal of Marriage and the Family* 30 (February 1968): 154–161.

[5] Oscar Lewis's best known urban case studies are *Five Families* and *The Children of Sánchez*.

[6] Octavio Paz, *The Labyrinth of Solitude*; Samuel Ramos, *Profile of Man and Culture in Mexico*; and Francisco González Pineda, *El mexicano: Su dinámica psicosocial*.

The Roles of Husbands and Wives and Parents and Children: The Men's Views

The various influences—Spanish, Moorish, and indigenous Indian—that formed the Mexican family as we know it are all in accord in giving the husband and father primacy within the authority structure of the family.[7] The wife clearly is enjoined to subordinate, whenever necessary, her own interests and desires to those of her husband and children. It is her responsibility, in the socialization of the children, to make sure that they demonstrate "respect" for their father. His main responsibility is to provide properly for the sustenance of the family. And as the children grow older, they are expected to contribute, as best they can, to the maintenance of the family, whether by work outside the family or by helping with family economic activities or chores within it.

From an early age, therefore, children are inculcated with a sense of family responsibility and family obligations that take precedence over their own needs and desires. The boys are encouraged to develop these feelings in the economic area, while the girls are supposed to help with the household tasks and the care of the younger children. To a much lesser extent, they also are expected to obligate themselves, whenever requested, to other kin members, particularly grandparents, uncles and aunts, and first cousins. In this way family obligations come to be accepted as "natural," and, thus, an older son will subordinate his own career and life chances by assuming the father role in the case of death of or desertion by the actual father. An older daughter will quit school or never even begin it in order to remain at home to help the mother in bringing up the younger children, or she may have outside employment that enables her to contribute directly to the family finances.

What we have sketched above is the normative description of Mexican family obligations, and wherever there are norms there are violations of them. The question is whether or not Mexicans accept these norms and in general behave in accordance with them. The limited amount of data from the Monterrey survey that we can bring to bear on this point indicates that there is a high degree of consensus with respect to norms connected with authority relations and the role of the wom-

---

[7] The following account is based mainly on Lewis's "Family Dynamics in a Mexican Village" and "Husbands and Wives in a Mexican Village" and, therefore, it is most appropriate for a village environment.

an.[8] Behavioral conformity to these sentiments, however, was not possible to test. It should also be stressed that we are dealing here only with men. Women may not be expected to give as much support to norms that assign them to subordinate positions.

At one point in our questionnaire we asked the men a series of questions tapping family values. In the five pairs of alternatives shown in Table 7-1 they were asked to select the one they were most in agreement with. The order of the questions is the same as in the interview schedule, but the alternatives have been rearranged so that the "traditional" choice is always second. In the matter of birth control, and to a lesser extent with divorce, there is considerable disagreement among the men, even though the position of the Church is well known in its opposition to divorce and nearly all forms of family planning, and the great majority of the men report themselves as Catholics. There is a striking consensus in the area of the authority structure of the family

TABLE 7-1. Family Values of Men

Alternative	Percent
If a husband and wife are not happy, they can divorce each other	33
Marriage is sacred and should never end in divorce	67
If they want to or need to, parents can limit the number of children	50
Parents should never limit the number of children	50
A wife should make her own decisions, even when she disagrees with her husband	10
A good wife is one who always obeys her husband	90
On some occasions, children should be permitted to disagree with parents	16
The most important thing for a child to learn is obedience and respect for the authority of his parents	84
The obligation of a man is only to support his wife and children	9
Aside from supporting his wife and children, a man's obligation is also to help his relatives whenever he can, since they too are part of the family	91

SOURCE: Representative sample.
NOTE: For the alternatives, "no answer" replies were, respectively, 49, 66, 52, 47, and 46.

[8] Very little has been done in the study of the role of women in Mexico. An impressionistic account is in *La vida familiar del mexicano* by María E. Bermudez. Some relevant results from a national survey are given in María del Carmen Elu de Leñero, *¿Hacia dónde va la mujer mexicana?*

and obligations to kin beyond the nuclear family. Obedience to the husband and father and obligation toward the extended family are prevalent, although these elements have little to do with formal Catholic doctrine. This serves to show that possibly much of the "traditionalism" of values regarding family life is not necessarily in consequence of religious beliefs, although they may reinforce it.

We also solicited the men's reactions to the role of the woman in the critical area of work outside the home. A series of three questions were put to them in which they were asked if they believed that it was appropriate for a woman to work (1) before marriage; (2) after marriage, but when there were no children; and (3) after marriage, with children. In each case the men were asked why they said yes or no to such an arrangement. The answers are presented in three categories: (a) approval of work, (b) conditional approval in case of economic necessity, and (3) disapproval (Table 7-2).

The opposite diagonal cells tell the story. While only 9 percent of the men disapprove of a single woman working, just 8 percent approve of a married woman with children working where economic necessity does not require it. When the reasons for their answers are broken down, nearly two-thirds of the men say a single woman can work to meet her own expenses and to help out the family. Only about a quarter said that it was proper that she work in order to learn, to gain experience, because she has the right to, or because she is equal to the man. Of those who said that a married woman without children could work, about 80 percent said that in this way she could help her husband and

TABLE 7-2. Men's Attitudes with Respect to a Woman's Working outside the Home (In Percent)

Situation	Approve	Approve, Economic Necessity	Disapprove	Total[a]
A single woman working	73	18	9	100(1,596)
A married woman without children working	28	18	54	100(1,585)
A married woman with children working	8	22	70	100(1,593)

SOURCE: Representative sample.
[a] Fifty-four, 65, and 57 cases with no information.

family to get established. Of those who disapproved of her working, about half said it was the duty of the husband to support her, and the other half said the place of the woman is in the home. It is the latter reason that dominates the answers of those who say a married woman with children should not work. Some men, disproportionately represented in the lower economic strata, are willing in all three situations to concede that economic necessity may require the entry of the woman into the labor force, but the men's comments indicated that this was not a desirable situation. The designation of woman's role as in the home, even a married woman without children, places the entire burden of support, at least in the critical period before the children are old enough to help out, on the shoulders of the man. Since uneducated and unskilled men are so poorly rewarded in the Mexican marketplace, many have difficulty in fulfilling this responsibility and this failure tends to undermine, in both his eyes and those of his family, his role as father and husband. On the other hand, if the woman's role is exclusively in the home, it follows that there can be no very "good" reasons for her to restrict the number of children: that's her job, isn't it?

The elements of the family structure that we have described—the subordinate position of women, the emphasis on children's obedience, the strength of kinship ties, the attitudes relating to divorce and birth control—all fall within the usual description of a "traditional" family structure of values. However, in contexts where this categorization is used, the association nearly always is with a rural, preindustrial social structure, which in turn is contrasted with the family under conditions of industrialization and urbanization. Obviously, this allocation of "traditional" and "modern" has little relevance for the Monterrey situation. We do not wish here to enter into a discussion of this general point, but only to call attention to the fact that in the case of Mexico rapid urbanization and industrialization seemingly have done very little to undermine the "traditional" pattern. It should be pointed out that the Monterrey men show comparatively few differences in the family areas we have covered according to age or migratory status. Young men tend to favor birth control somewhat more than older men and a slightly smaller proportion of the former emphasizes children's obedience or family allegiance. There are even smaller differences by migratory status. In Table 7-3 the men are divided into six migratory status groups, the main criterion being length of exposure to Monterrey. The

TABLE 7-3. Family Values, by Migratory Status

Item	Short-Exposure Migrants	Medium-Exposure Migrants	Long-Exposure Migrants	Natives by Adoption	First-Generation Natives	Second-Generation Natives
			(Percent selecting "modern" response)			
Divorce	33	33	33	33	34	32
Family limitation	44	47	45	53	53	56
Wife makes decisions	5	8	9	9	15	14
Children may disagree with parents	12	14	9	20	21	19
Family obligations	10	10	8	12	7	6

NOTE: Migratory status is classified as follows: short-exposure migrants: less than 10 years in Monterrey; medium-exposure migrants: 10–19 years in Monterrey; long-exposure migrants: 20 years or more in Monterrey; natives by adoption: born outside Monterrey but community of origin is Monterrey; first-generation natives: neither parent born in Monterrey; second-generation natives: one or both parents born in Monterrey.

variation with respect to family values is strikingly small; the greatest percentage point difference between any of the six groups is twelve. Other than the narrow range, the other distinctive feature in the table is the slight evidence, if any, of a linear relationship between exposure to the Monterrey environment and the various value items, including religion. The significance of this comparison is enhanced if it is understood that occupational, educational, and income differences among the six groups, particularly the extremes of short-exposure migrants and second-generation natives, are quite pronounced.

It is worthwhile noting that Kahl's study of Mexico City and provincial towns, besides coinciding with our picture of family traditionalism, did not find differences between metropolitans (Mexico City), provincials (smaller towns), and migrants to Mexico City. A study by Glen Elder—a secondary analysis of the Almond and Verba survey of Mexico and England, Germany, Italy, and the United States—demonstrates that, when broken down by age, all countries except Mexico show among the younger men a pronounced trend toward more "democratic" rather than "authoritarian" child-rearing practices.[9] Mexico shows only a minor variation between the oldest and youngest men, with the authoritarian model the predominant choice. In these days of the "generation gap" it is indeed surprising that Mexican men in their twenties do not greatly differ in the area of family values from men in their fifties, but this situation is what both our and the Almond and Verba data indicate.

We believe that the evidence we are able to draw out of the Monterrey survey supports our thesis that the Mexican family still is able to inculcate within its members strong feelings of obligation and that the patriarchal pattern, at least as a value system, is still very strong. Doubtless some changes are taking place—more young people are permissive of divorce and birth control, and in these two areas the Cedral men are somewhat more "traditional" than the Monterrey men. However, we are led to the conclusion that the Mexican family structure is not undergoing a major structural transformation, at least in terms of the normative authority structure and the role of the woman, in spite of the changes taking place in other areas. The relative stability and continuity of the Mexican family, we believe, ensure a basic consensus of values that cuts across generational, class, and residential categories. The extent to which these basic values result in similar behavioral patterns is a question we shall examine later in this chapter.

Age at First Marriage

Among the significant events in the male life cycle, first entry into marital union is of special interest. It generally represents a rather profound alteration of the individual's way of life, and it usually marks the first stage of the family life cycle. First entry into marital union often is associated with other key events in the men's lives, mainly because economic self-sufficiency of the couple generally is a requirement for marriage and because it involves the transition from one family context to another. Not everyone marries, but in most contemporary societies about nine of ten men do.[10]

The timing of entry into marital union, significant as it is for the life course of men, is subject to few formal sanctions. The social norm only is that one should marry, but in no way does it specify an exact age for

[9] Glen Elder, "Democratic Parent-Youth Relations in Cross-National Perspective," *Social Science Quarterly* 49, no. 2 (September 1968): 216–228.
[10] See William J. Goode, *World Revolution and Family Patterns.*

entry into marital unions. Not marrying, or marrying either at a very early or a very late age is generally "frowned" upon, but the sanctions that can be applied to the offender are weak. Minimum age-at-marriage laws are set generally at quite early ages and have little impact today upon the pattern of age at first marriage. Of perhaps greater importance in setting the minimum age is the expectation that the couple in most cases will be able to support themselves, and to do this they need to be old enough to obtain those jobs open to adults. An important norm in most modern societies is that mates must choose by themselves. There are indeed criteria and other people that help to guide the selection process, but the emphasis is put upon the individual decision. Therefore, a basic element of indeterminancy as to the age at marriage is introduced, since when one marries depends upon when one "finds" the proper mate.

Variations in age at first marriage in Monterrey are quite large. Our task will be that of explaining these variations, but it is not to be expected that prediction in this area would be very high, first, because of the flexibility of norms regarding age at marriage and the emphasis placed upon individual decision. Second, whether a man marries at age 17, 22, 27, or 32, for example, is a consequence of many factors, some of them due to chance and not identifiable as social factors. Finally, because marriage in itself does not have universal social meaning, different societies and various groups within each society attach different meanings to it. Perhaps one example may serve to illustrate the latter two points.

In Mexico, unlike the United States, university-educated males do not often marry before graduation. Only 7 percent of the Monterrey men who graduated from the university married before age 23. In the United States, it has been argued, increasing affluence and psychological independence of the young explain why so many college students are supported by their families to one extent or another. In Mexico the great majority of students live with their parents, unless there are no universities in the home town and it is necessary to go to another city. Leaving home, getting married, and becoming economically independent all happen together in Mexico, while they are separate events in the United States. For the former, thus, marriage is a symbol of independence, while for the latter men "dependence" on family of orientation, other than economic perhaps, might have been ended some years before. At least independence is often separated from marriage itself.

In Mexico, getting married and not being able to support the family are highly incongruent, although rather commonplace in the United States. This example shows the variety of elements that have to be considered in analyzing age at marriage in one particular group: psychological independence from family of orientation, possibilities of economic self-sufficiency, and the meaning of marriage. To make it a bit more complex, we should add that many American students are supported wholly or in part by their wives until they receive their degree, something that is just about unthinkable in Mexico.

The popular belief that urbanization and industrialization in Western countries brought about an increase in age at marriage is, according to William Goode, quite false.[11] It is also misleading in lending support to the impression that in developing countries age at first marriage occurs much earlier than in industrial countries. In spite of the large proportion of the population born and raised in agrarian communities and the low levels of educational attainment of the adult population, Mexican males do not tend to marry very young. The median age at first marriage for the Monterrey men, for example, is 24.0 years, while the comparable figure for the urban male population of all ages in the United States was 22.3 in 1960.[12] It should be mentioned that the Mexican figure includes men in consensual unions as well as in formal marriages, so there is no possibility of distortion from this source. In Cedral, an agriculturally oriented community, first marriage occurs at an earlier age, the median being 22.5 years.

Education, as may be observed in Table 7-4, bears a positive relationship to male age at first marriage. The higher the educational attainment, the smaller the proportion of men marrying at very early ages. This trend is particularly striking, as we have seen, for university-educated men. However, even at the lowest levels of education, a considerable number of men marry quite late; over one-third with no schooling married at age 25 or later. This delay may seem puzzling, since these men have been in the labor force since their early youth.

A number of reasons can be summoned to account for the not-so-early age at first marriage in Monterrey, particularly among the men with low levels of education. Perhaps family obligations are relevant

[11] Ibid., Chap. 2.
[12] The U.S. data on age at marriage are taken from J. R. Rele, "Trends and Differentials in the American Age at Marriage," *Milbank Memorial Fund Quarterly* 43, no. 2 (April 1965): 219–237.

TABLE 7-4. Distribution of Age at First Marriage, by Educational Attainment (In Percent)

Age at Marriage	None	Incomplete *Primaria*	Complete *Primaria*	Middle	University	All Men
16 or less	5	2	1	0	0	2
17–18	11	7	4	1	1	5
19–20	13	14	13	10	1	12
21–22	17	21	17	15	6	18
23–24	15	13	18	15	16	15
25–26	11	14	13	21	27	15
27–30	14	18	19	23	35	20
31 and over	13	11	14	16	13	13
Total	99	100	99	101	99	100
	(178)	(505)	(318)	(230)	(97)	(1,328)

in that some men do not marry because they are needed in the family of origin to help in the support and education of younger siblings. Then, too, there is often a strong emotional attachment between son and mother, making the severance of the umbilical cord difficult. Neither Mamá nor her son are in any hurry to bring about his departure from home, and he may satisfy the sex urge by recourse to prostitutes without incurring much moral censure.

There is doubtless some truth in the above kinds of explanation, but we prefer to try and explain age at first marriage in other terms; namely, the prospects a man has for getting a stable job that will allow him to assume the responsibilities of marriage and family. Our hypothesis is that the greater the extent to which men have a relatively unambiguous prospect of a "career," in the sense of a stable source of income (even if in relative terms it is at a low level), the greater the likelihood that the marriage of these men will be concentrated within a particular age interval. What this age interval is depends on the time in the life cycle when men with different educational and experience backgrounds find themselves in situations of relative stability. Thus, professionals and technicians will marry at a later age than, say, skilled craftsmen, because one needs fifteen or more years of schooling and the other six to nine years.

We may start (see Table 7-5) by considering men in farm occupations. For these men marriage is closely associated with obtaining land, that is, with economic independence. Thus, we see that those men who got to be independent farmers before age 25 were married by this age in greater proportion than those who were not independent (78 versus 55 percent). In this case economic independence favors early marriage and a concentration of marriages in a rather narrow age range. In the urban occupations, we find that, among those who began their work lives in Monterrey, skilled workers get married in the age interval 21–29 in greater proportion than unskilled workers, while the latter are represented more often in both the very early and the very late categories. Finally, the greatest concentration of marriages in a narrow age range is found among professional and technical personnel, for whom the favored age interval is 25–29.

Independent farmers, skilled workers, and professionals are quite heterogeneous in socioeconomic status, but our argument is that they share in common more clearly defined occupational prospects than do the other groups. The timing of their marriages is related to obtaining land, moving from apprentice to skilled-worker status, or getting a professional degree. An additional confirmation of the relationship between occupational "security" and age at first marriage is provided by the Cedral data. Of those eighty-two men who became land owners before age 35, 66 percent married within the three years before or after the land became theirs.

Knowledge of a man's job prospects does help to predict when he will marry, as does his education, but this prediction is quite imperfect, for the variety of reasons we have already alluded to. There are many exceptions to the association of job security and age at marriage, and the concentration in an age interval is relative.

In the same table we can compare those men who began their work lives in Monterrey with those who came to the city before age 25 and those who arrived after that age. For the equivalent occupational categories we see that the first two migratory groups show similar distributions and that they differ a bit from those presented by the older arrivals. Among the latter we consistently find a larger percentage of men who married at age 20 or earlier, although, as noted, the differences are not very great. Seemingly, for any given occupational category the conditions in Monterrey lead to a later age at marriage. This fact may reflect the higher relative cost of housing in the city and other costs incidental to marriage. It may also mean that a metropolitan area like Monterrey offers a more favorable environment for the man

TABLE 7-5. Distribution of Age at First Marriage, by Place of Residence and Occupation at Age 25 (Ever-Married Men Aged 31 and Over)
(In Percent)

	Monterrey								Elsewhere				
	Began Work Life in Monterrey					Migrated to Monterrey after Beginning Work Life							
	Occupation at Age 25					Occupation at Age 25			Occupation at Age 25				
Age at First Marriage	Unskilled	Skilled	Professional Technical	Other White Collar	Total White Collar	Unskilled	Skilled	White Collar	Farm Laborers	Independent Farmers	Unskilled	Skilled	White Collar
Up to 20	16	12	2	5	4	17	10	0	22	28	23	25	14
21–24	30	32	10	28	22	37	32	28	31	50	25	36	26
25–29	29	41	72	42	52	29	44	39	24	13	36	25	33
30 and over	25	16	16	25	22	16	14	33	22	9	16	14	27
Total	100	101	100	100	100	99	100	100	99	100	100	100	100
	(186)	(135)	(57)	(164)	(221)	(140)	(50)	(36)	(112)	(46)	(128)	(36)	(66)

Place of Residence at Age 25

who doesn't want to get married at an early age than is the case in rural areas.

The Early Stage of Family Formation

Monterrey men marry wives who are considerably younger than they are. Limiting our discussion to men who were 31 and over at the time of the survey, the median difference in ages of spouses is nearly five years. This difference contrasts with the United States, where it is only about two years. (In only 8 percent of the cases does the man marry a woman one year or more older than himself.) Twenty-nine percent married a woman at least seven years younger than themselves. As could be expected, the older the man when he marries, the wider the gap in age: 57 percent of those entering a union at age 30 or over marry a spouse at least seven years younger than themselves. Given the difference in age, many females marry at age 20 or below, so they have maximum exposure to conception during their most fecund years.[13]

The combination of a somewhat late age at marriage of the male, the role of a married woman primarily as mother, and the various other social and religious values favoring parenthood, means that once the union is formed the children are not long in coming. In the minds and in the actual behavior of nearly all Monterrey men, marriage and parenthood are intrinsically the same. The notion that a man and a woman may marry but then defer children for some years is not at all common. As we shall see, delaying parenthood is statistically deviant. It also is deviant in normative terms, for the Catholic heritage, to which the great majority of men and women subscribe, as well as other deep-seated values not necessarily the consequence of religious beliefs, put considerable pressure upon the couple to produce children as soon as possible. These pressures are undoubtedly internalized and linked to concepts of manhood and womanhood rooted in one's physical ability to procreate that are sustained by popular lore. They are also intensified by the direct and indirect comments of both partners' kinship circles and friends. Taken together, these pressures are hard to resist.

[13] On fertility in Monterrey see Alvan O. Zarate, "Differential Fertility in Monterrey, Mexico—Prelude to Transition?" *Milbank Memorial Fund Quarterly* 45, no. 2, pt. 1 (April 1967): 93–108. A comparative perspective is provided by a Mexico City fertility survey in the chapter prepared by Raul Benítez Zenteno, "Fecundidad," in Centro de Estudios Económicos y Demográficos, *Dinámica de la población de México.*

Probably a fair number of men in our sample have practiced some form of birth control at one time in their marital life, although we have no information on this point. But we have good reason to believe that few of the men resort to any form of birth control until the first several children are born. Restricting ourselves to those men age 31 and over who are married, 63 percent had their first child by the end of the first year following that of their marriage. (Unfortunately, the more precise interval of month was not obtained, so the time from marriage to first birth may be up to twenty-four months.) By the end of the second year after that of marriage, 81 percent of the couples have recorded their first birth. The age at first marriage of the male has very little effect on when the child will arrive; those marrying at age 31 or over have only slightly longer intervals than the other age-at-marriage categories. Very probably a number of those couples who have their first child five or more years after marriage have some fertility impairment. Neither age cohort, nor education, nor migratory status has any important effect upon the spacing between marriage and first child.

The second child comes close upon the first one; nearly a third of the couples have it within a year after their first-born, and nearly two-thirds have it within two years. Similarly, the third child comes within two years of the second child in nearly 60 percent of the cases. We may conclude, therefore, that very little birth control is practiced by the couples in the first years of marriage. Perhaps this is one important reason why the men tend to delay marriage in the first place. They anticipate that marriage will be followed quite closely by parenthood, either because they do not want to practice family planning in the initial years or because they have no confidence in their ability to do so, especially if the wife opposes it. This does not mean that at no point in their married life will the couple resort to some form of birth control; most of them will by one means or another. It is only that they do not feel any urgency to do so in the early years of family formation, or until the rather high "ideal" number of children already has been achieved.

The absence of great differences in this area of behavior according to rural-urban background, social strata, or age cohort seems quite congruent with our earlier discussion about the fundamental consensus among the population of Mexico with regard to basic values, however the groups may differ in other respects. Men marry at different ages, as we have seen, but for the large majority, at least, the transition from family of orientation to family of procreation is a crucial point in their lives. It is an abrupt one, for, as we noted, the men generally live with their parents until they marry, and once they are husbands they generally soon become fathers. Thus, they quickly acquire all family responsibilities. They probably can count upon considerable help from their parents and in-laws, for, as we have insisted, ties with kin remain quite strong. But the relationship has changed, since by marrying and becoming fathers they have achieved—perhaps for the first time in their lives—full adulthood and independence.

Marriage, Family Formation, and Occupational Achievement

We wish now to consider the effects of the events we have been analyzing thus far as they influence the men's occupational achievement. A more technical treatment will be provided in Chapter 10, but here we want to advance some results and to comment upon them within the context of the family life cycle.

The timing of marriage may be crucial for the occupational success of a man. Men marrying later may show an advantage over those marrying early in their lives. First, the success-oriented men may delay their entry into marriage more often than the others, so this initial selectivity may help to explain why they later advance farther in the occupational world. Second, the delay in marriage itself may have an effect upon occupational achievement, since freedom from family obligations at an early stage in the occupational life can allow men to take occupational risks that otherwise they would not be inclined to assume. They also would be free to more wholeheartedly devote their time and energies to occupational advancement. There is, however, a contrary hypothesis that some people—and probably most Mexicans—would subscribe to: namely, that early marriage (but not too early) spurs the man on to greater occupational achievement because his family obligations present him with immediate and concrete goals to strive for.

On at least a short-term basis, it turns out, age at first marriage does not seem to have any powerful effect, positive or negative, on occupational achievement. We compared occupational histories for the five years following their marriage of men entering unions at various ages, matching them with men of similar ages who remained single. Those marrying in their teens or very early twenties have on the average substantially lower occupational positions than those who remain single. But whatever the differences at the beginning of the period, their occupational advancement during the five-year period is quite similar. By ages 25 to 27, a time when those with university training tend to get married, it is the men who remain single who have the lower occupational positions than those who marry at these ages, but, once again, following the two groups through the five-year interval does not reveal significant differences. A similar pattern shows up in those men who marry at a later age when compared to those who still remain single. Over a longer time interval, age at first marriage has a somewhat greater effect than for the five-year interval. As we shall see in Chapter 10, when we control for educational level and occupational status of the first job, the men who marry later have on the average a slightly higher occupational status by age 45 than do those who marry younger.

It is not only important to examine the age at which men marry, but it is also necessary to investigate whom they marry. Almost universally, social contacts between males and females, especially those leading to marriage, are restricted to members of the same or contiguous social strata. This restriction results in a pattern whereby most marriages take place within the same social stratum, although the extent to which this concentration prevails varies considerably.[14] In Monterrey, a relatively high association was found between the spouses' fathers' occupations, and an even higher one between the spouses' educational levels. In a cross classification of marriages according to wife's and husband's fathers' occupations, using four broad occupational categories, we found a concentration of marriages within the diagonal cells. There are cases of marriages within cells representing extremes (lower manual and upper nonmanual), but they are very few. Hypergamous marriages, those where the wife married upward, are more frequent than hypogamous marriages, where the husband married upward. The comparison between husband's and wife's education is perhaps more relevant, since spouses' levels of education best indicate the similarities or differences between husband and wife, and also because our information is more reliable in this case. The comparison also shows considerable conformity with the rule of homogamy, and there are more hypergamous than hypogamous marriages. This situation holds especially for wives with primary school completed or secondary education, for they marry in a higher proportion to better-educated husbands than

[14] For a review of studies on homogamy, see Morris Zelditch, Jr., "Family, Marriage, and Kinship," in *Handbook of Modern Sociology*, ed. Robert L. Faris; and Alain Girard, *Le choix du conjoint*.

would be expected by chance. Also, few university-educated men can marry university-educated women, since there are so few of the latter. A summary view of occupational and educational homogamy is possible with two correlation coefficients. That between respondent's father's occupation and his father-in-law's is .49, while that between the education of the respondent and his wife is .66. Given these moderately high coefficients, one could hardly expect that the wives' characteristics could strongly influence the men's occupational careers, since so few marry that much up or down. However, a modest but positive effect was found, as men who marry upward tend to achieve a slightly higher occupational status by age 45 than the others, after controlling for their educational levels and first jobs.

It appears that whom a man marries may be more significant for his occupational achievement than the age at which he marries, but neither has a pronounced effect. How about the number of children he has? As far as we could determine, and our measurement of this factor has been less than ideal, the number of children men have by age 40 has no relation to their occupational achievement by age 45. Seemingly, having many children does not significantly handicap men in their work, nor, for that matter, does it help them. (Or it could be that it helps some and handicaps others, thus canceling each other out.)

In any event, many Monterrey men believe that the number of children they have or will have has little to do with their occupational success. In our survey we solicited their opinion about the relationship between family size and economic progress by asking them to choose one of three alternatives. Over one-half (51 percent) of all respondents say that having many children has nothing to do with one's economic progress. Twenty-nine percent maintained that having more children is beneficial rather than detrimental, as compared with only 18 percent who said that having many children would be detrimental. Interestingly enough, the differences between occupational strata are not to be found in the latter category. Rather, low-status men tend to think that children are beneficial, while upper-status men simply dismiss the idea that they could have any effect on a man's achievement. Perhaps the tendency of low-status men to see large numbers of children positively is a carryover from rural backgrounds, where children are a considerable help, especially in peak work periods, as well as the thought that many children will better ensure that they themselves will be cared for when they become old and can no longer work.

The Basic Continuity of Mexican Family Structure

An important point has emerged from this chapter that we wish to emphasize within the larger context of the book as a whole. Urbanization and industrialization, to judge from our Monterrey results, have done little to seriously disrupt the family as an institution within Mexico. The kinds of social disorganization that many theorists have assumed to be an inevitable part of this transformation are not widespread. What is more, there seems to be a basic continuity of the traditional family pattern. Certainly some features must have changed over time in important ways, and it is most regrettable that neither we nor anyone else (given the unfortunate neglect of the Mexican family as a subject of research) can document these changes, but we believe that at least some basic values and at least some behavioral features are quite persistent. This persistency is the more important because of the relative lack of differentiation by age, social position, and migratory status. This fact suggests that no group is changing at a faster rate or moving in a different direction than the others with respect to family values.

The anthropologist Oscar Lewis, in an article published some years ago entitled "Urbanization without Breakdown," argued that peasants migrating to the large city do not suffer personal disorganization, because they bring their institutions with them, so to speak. We would argue, however, that one need not rely upon the dubious concept of "urban peasants" to explain the situation. If it can be demonstrated that in the realm of fundamental values there is no clear-cut confrontation between rural and urban, because there is no great difference between the two in the first place, then the concept is not needed. More broadly, it can be argued on the value level that there is no confrontation between the social strata, although this lack does not mean that on other levels there is no opposition of interests between classes.

We should like to emphasize once more that our hypothesis of the basic continuity of the Mexican family structure during a time of marked social change has not been tested on the basis of the limited data we have been able to bring to bear on the question. We do maintain, however, that this interpretation best explains our findings in other parts of this study, for example, incorporation into the labor force or migration, and therefore is a plausible hypothesis.

8. Paths of Occupational Mobility

What is the common conception of men and their occupational histories? In the most general sense it is conceived of as a kind of progression—what has been referred to as the "typical lifetime curve" and the "normal career curve."[1] After schooling men begin in jobs requiring little experience, and gradually they move up in the occupational hierarchy. Various means are available to them to make this upward mobility possible, namely, more experience, more skill, more responsibility, more seniority, more capital. Men can use various combinations of the above factors to facilitate their upward mobility. Skill, experience, and seniority are the chief means of advancement in bureaucratic settings, while capital, skill, and responsibility are important for those in self-employed positions. But the "typical lifetime curve" does not continue upward throughout the men's lives. There comes a time when the upward movement stops and the men either remain in the same position, or, with advancing age, they actually may begin a decline, ended only by their complete withdrawal from the labor force.

The above depiction of work histories is supported by aggregate data presented in other sections of this book, for example, in the first table of Chapter 1 and at various points in Chapter 10. The trouble with such a depiction of work-life histories is not that it is wrong, but that it is

[1] Theodore Caplow (*The Sociology of Work*) suggests normal career curves for various occupations.

incomplete and to an extent misleading. While it is true that many men move up the occupational ladder, others remain at virtually the same level for long periods of time, while others move up and down in an "irregular" curve, and a few move only down. The fact is that only a minority of men follow for all, or even a major part, of their work lives the upward career model that is implicit in so many discussions of work histories.

We deliberately have chosen to call this chapter "Paths of Occupational Mobility" to call attention to the variety of ways by which men make their way in the occupational world. Reality is a good deal more untidy than theories of human behavior suggest, and in the work sphere this caution is particularly appropriate. The content of this chapter is diverse in part because our intent is to follow closely what happens to the men, and this is the way their work histories present themselves. The sequence to be followed is to pick up the men where they were left at the end of Chapter 5, when they all had reached age 25. First we shall briefly survey their overall mobility in the twenty years up to age 45. (Of course, we must limit ourselves only to those men who were age 45 and over at the time of the survey.) After this overview of the amount of mobility in the vertical dimension of the occupational hierarchy we shall pause for the first of our extended discussions of particular kinds of occupational mobility: the situational features of the "stable" men (who did not move up or down during this critical period of their work lives) that might help explain their immobility. The next section is something of a diversion, for it takes up again a problem first considered in Chapter 5: the relation of migratory status, stage in the life cycle when migration takes place, and occupational mobility. Because of the centrality of the relationship of migration to occupational mobility in this book, we want to look at what happened to the men between ages 26 and 45, just as earlier we examined the interval up to age 25. The third section of Chapter 8 takes up those men who have experienced upward occupational mobility within the context of career lines. Next self-employment is scrutinized as a path of occupational mobility, up and down. Finally, the last section of the chapter takes up the men who have had downward mobility at some time during their lives.

There are several ways in which the approach adopted in this chapter differs from most analyses of occupational mobility. In the first place, only a minor part of the chapter is devoted to the measurement of

vertical mobility. Furthermore, this measurement is made not by comparing occupational positions in two moments in the life cycle, ages
25 and 45, but by taking into account the entire succession of positions
held during the twenty years. The vertical dimension of occupational
status is present in all our sections, but our concern most often is not
the amount of movement as such. Second, we do not limit ourselves
only to the age span 24–45 and to men who have reached their forty-
fifth birthday if the course of our argument and the data require or
permit the introduction of other age groups. And except for the first
section, we will not attempt to account for the experience of all men in
our sample; a few will not show up on any of our paths of mobility.
Third, the discussion of the various paths of mobility does not involve
mutually exclusive categories of men. The same man, as some of our
case histories will show, can turn up as career and as self-employed,
depending upon what period of his life we examine.

Why do we impose these various conditions on our analyses? Because
we want to concentrate on specific paths of occupational mobility and
we need to provide each one with a sufficiently detailed and concrete
account of what happens to the men who take these paths. (It is for
this reason that we will make liberal use of actual case histories.) Our
primary concern in this chapter, let us repeat, is not—as is so often done
—to divide our men into different groups and then to label them as
"Downward Movers" or "Career Men," but to try to make sense out of
particular sequences of "moves." It is often unwarranted to pigeonhole
a man on the basis of his work situation at some particular time, or at a
few points in time.[2] The majority of men who had downward moves

[2] Studies of intragenerational vertical mobility taking just a few points in time
include Arnold C. Anderson, "Lifetime Inter-Occupational Mobility Patterns in
Sweden," *Acta Sociologica* 1 (1955): 168–202; David V. Glass, *Social Mobility in
Britain*; Vojin Milic, "General Trends in Social Mobility in Yugoslavia," *Acta Sociologica* 9 (1965): 116–136; Gladys L. Palmer, *Labor Mobility in Six Cities*; Leonard Broom and F. Lancaster Jones, "Career Mobility in Three Societies: Australia,
Italy, and the United States," *American Sociological Review* 34, no. 5 (October
1969): 650–658; and Seymour M. Lipset and Reinhard Bendix, *Social Mobility in
Industrial Society*. In the Spanish edition of the last book, Gino Germani's appendix, "Movilidad social en la Argentina," presents data on Buenos Aires. In several of
the above studies the occupational classification is a very simplified one (such as
farm, manual, and nonmanual), and thus significant types of vertical mobility, such
as mobility within the manual category, are lost. In Lipset and Bendix's analysis of
their Oakland data, they take into account the whole occupational experience rather
than discrete points in time, but without introducing age and sequences of occupa-

also had upward and horizontal moves at other times in their work lives. We are free to admit that our approach makes for some conceptual and analytical untidiness, but we hope that these faults are compensated for by a more faithful approximation to reality.

Vertical Mobility

In Chapter 5 we found that the first ten years of the men's work lives were ones of considerable shifting about and the exploration of various job possibilities. There was also considerable upward occupational mobility during the period from first job to that held at age 25. Since many men entered the labor force in unskilled positions (over half of those who began in Monterrey), the upward mobility in part is a consequence of their low beginnings.

At this point we can extend the period of analysis from age 25 through age 45. All occupations held in this twenty-year period by the men age 45 and over at the time of the survey were classified in the four occupational levels first introduced in Chapter 5: lower manual (unskilled workers), upper manual (skilled and semiskilled workers), lower nonmanual, and upper nonmanual. Any movement crossing from one of these four categories to another constitutes a vertical move. Accordingly, we find that, of the 623 men, 58 percent were stable, 28 percent had upward mobility, and 14 percent had downward or irregular mobility during the twenty-year interval. It should be made clear that these figures are not obtained simply by taking the occupation at age 25 and comparing it with the occupation at age 45. Rather, we take into consideration the entire period. We could not have an "irregular" category if we compared only two points in time, and these men all would have been allocated to one of the other categories. Thus, when we say that 58 percent of the men were stable, this means that at no time in the twenty-year period did they cross a boundary between levels. The 28 percent who experienced upward mobility may have crossed more than one boundary, but always in an upward direction, and the same holds for those who were downwardly mobile.

Several other points need to be made about this distribution. The

tions. Kaare Svalastoga's *Prestige, Class, and Mobility* is perhaps the study where age and stage in the life cycle are introduced in the most explicit and systematic way. He reports, for instance, that 37 percent of his sample above age 50 did not experience any vertical mobility as compared to 58 percent between ages 25 and 45 in Monterrey.

amount of mobility measured is of course a function of the number of categories. We restricted ourselves to four categories because of practical and theoretical reasons—the former in order that cell frequencies in cross tabulations not become too small, and the latter because we wanted a move across a category boundary to be genuinely significant in affecting the work situation and the life style of the men. The fact that nearly six of every ten men are "stable" does not mean that they experienced no change whatsoever in their work lives. Some experienced nonvertical mobility in the change from worker to self-employed status. Others changed their workplace or took another occupation of the same occupational level. Each of the four categories is sufficiently "wide" to allow some up-and-down movement within the category. Finally, we know from Chapter 5 that many men moved upward between ages 15 and 25, so a "stable" classification during the following twenty years does not mean that they never have experienced any mobility.

Still, even with all the above caveats in mind, the fact that six of every ten of our men did not cross a category boundary during a twenty-year period is unexpected, especially when contrasted with the model of the "normal career curve" alluded to earlier. Because of the proportional importance of this group, the rest of this section will deal only with the stable men, leaving for later sections consideration of upward and downward mobility. Information that can help us analyze the stable men is provided in Table 8-1. These stable men did not experience anything resembling a "normal career curve," at least for the period here considered. However, as the second column indicates, a substantial proportion (28 percent) of the men had some upward

TABLE 8-1. Mobility Characteristics of "Stable" Men (In Percent)

Occupational Level	Distribution of Stable Men by Occupational Level	Percent in Each Level Who Experienced Upward Mobility within the 15–25 Age Interval	Percent in Each Level Who Remained in the Same Job for the Entire Period (25–45)
Lower manual	58	0	18
Upper manual	20	89	56
Lower nonmanual	7	68	47
Upper nonmanual	15	39	23
Total (360)	100	28	29

mobility within the 15–25 age interval, and the proportions in the upper-manual and lower-nonmanual categories are quite high. The overall
figure is substantially lower because by definition those in the numerically preponderant category, lower manual, could have no earlier upward movement. It is clear that many men in the other three categories
have a very early peak in their occupational histories. This group includes white-collar positions, often thought to conform most closely to
the model of career upward mobility.

We have already suggested that stability does not imply that the
same job is held throughout the twenty-year period. The third column
of Table 8-1 makes this perfectly clear, for only 29 percent of the stable
men remained in the same job throughout the period. In short, there is
much horizontal movement, especially for men in the lowest occupational level.

Combining information about previous upward mobility with information about job stability, we can make some inferences and comparisons between the various occupational levels. Thus, upper-manual
men (mainly skilled workers) show the highest rate of early upward
mobility (89 percent) and the highest rate of job stability (56 percent) in the middle work-life period. Typically, then, the man enters
the labor force in an unskilled position, moves upward to a skilled
position within a few years (as was discussed in detail in Chapter 5),
and then remains there for a long time. A similar pattern, although to a
lesser extent, holds true for men in the lower-nonmanual category.

Upper-nonmanual men, in contrast, tend to enter the labor force
directly within this category, especially professionals who do not experience the upward mobility that characterizes men in managerial
positions. Once in the highest occupational level, the stable men tend
to move from one job to another quite freely, and sometimes they add
second and third jobs to the original one. One example of this pattern
is the case of a man who started working as a typist in court while he
was studying in law school. When he graduated at age 24, he became
an independent attorney. After some years, at age 31, he became a
judge. At age 37 he entered the municipal bureaucracy as a secretary
to the mayor and an attorney for the municipality. At age 43 he went
back to private practice, keeping at the same time his jobs in the
municipality. After three years he gave up his municipality job and
became a judge again, keeping his private practice. Lawyers, as Weber
pointed out years ago, have skills that are transferable among govern-

ment, industry, and private practice employment. Among physicians it is very common to add part-time positions in public and private health organizations until some end up occupying simultaneously as many as five or six positions (e.g., private practice, Seguro Social appointment, private hospital staff, teaching at the university). University professors frequently have more than one job, since their university salaries are not sufficient to support them. There also are the cases of men who have already established themselves in the managerial ranks by age 25 and who will remain there throughout their work lives, even though they may advance to higher and higher levels, either within the same enterprise or by moving to a similar or higher position in another firm.

We are left with the very large group of men in unskilled positions who remain in them for practically their entire lives. Other than their numerical significance, the men in this group are of interest because they are the "losers," those who did not make it in the occupational world. Most have not experienced downward mobility, simply because they were unable to move out of the lowest category. It isn't that the men make no changes; indeed, only 18 percent held the same job from age 25 to age 45, the lowest percentage of the four occupational categories. Are these changes simply erratic movements from one job or occupation to another, or is there any pattern of job changes? Table 8-2 shows the percent of men holding various unskilled occupations by five-year intervals, from age 15 to age 45. This aggregate information reveals for us some regularities in terms of occupational changes associated with the life cycle. We know that the life cycle of many men in Monterrey—as well as in many cities in developing nations—is marked by a change from farm to nonfarm employment. This change usually accompanies the geographical move from the countryside or small towns to the city. Thus, the percent of unskilled men in farm labor decreases from 52 at age 15 (when many men lived outside Monterrey) to 16 at age 45, when most of the farm-origin men have moved to the city. Similarly, the percent of miners also declines, for this is another occupation that must be abandoned in all but a few cases when moving to the city. Compensating for these declines, such nonfarm occupations as construction workers, unskilled production workers, janitors and watchmen, and street vendors increase in importance with advancing age.

Given the numerical importance of men who started their work lives as farm laborers, let us look more closely at their paths of mobility

TABLE 8-2. Men Aged 45 and Over Who Were Unskilled throughout Age
Interval 15 to 45, by Occupation and Age (In Percent)

Occupation	15	20	25	Age 30	35	40	45
Construction workers	4	9	8	9	12	14	20
Unskilled production workers	8	11	12	14	15	14	17
Stevedores	7	6	8	11	8	10	8
Janitors and watchmen	0	0	1	1	5	6	8
Street vendors	4	3	5	7	5	8	8
Other unskilled service workers	9	7	6	5	7	8	7
Farm laborers	52	48	46	39	36	27	16
Miners	7	8	7	5	5	4	2
Other	4	6	6	7	6	8	11
Not working	5	2	0	1	0	1	2
Total (213)	100	100	99	99	99	100	99

when moving to nonfarm occupations. The move to nonfarm occupations keeps them within the lower manual category throughout their entire work lives. The age at which farm men abandon agriculture influences the type of unskilled job they get. The basic change is an increasing concentration of these men with advancing age in construction labor. Of all men moving from farm to nonfarm occupations between ages 15 and 25, 12 percent went into construction work. The proportion increases to 38 percent between ages 25 and 35 and to 48 percent between ages 35 and 45. It should be noted that this increasing concentration in construction work is true not only for this group of stable men, but also for other farm workers who after moving to unskilled occupations experienced some vertical mobility between ages 25 and 45 and thus are not included in the group dealt with here.

The increasing concentration of farm workers in construction labor and the corresponding decreasing variety of destination occupations can be taken as an indication of the increasing handicap that farm men experience with the process of aging. (This point will be dealt with in the next section of the chapter by an analysis of the effect of migration on occupational mobility.) Construction labor is one of the most unstable and low-paying unskilled jobs a man can get. It is also, however, one of the occupations that permits a smoother transition from the kind of labor performed in farm work. In any small town there is some construction going on, and the technology used in both city and town is a very simple one, being basically labor intensive. Thus, construction work is highly visible to farm workers. Furthermore, the conditions of work are similar to farming: the work is performed outdoors and generally in loose groupings rather than as isolated individuals.

The frequent horizontal movements among the unskilled workers affect more men than just those of farm background. Generally, the movement is from jobs that require physical strength, or that offer advancement opportunities, to occupations that are of a less demanding nature, but that are also dead-end occupations. These shifts occur continuously, for there is no one period in the life cycle when they are more likely. Thus, 43 percent of the men changed occupations in the period from age 15 to age 25, 40 percent between ages 25 and 35, and 47 percent between ages 35 and 45.

There is a great variation in the degree of stability of different men. To cite a case of extreme stability, one man arrived in Monterrey at age 13 and began work as a stevedore in a wholesale vegetable market. He was still in the same position at the time of the survey when he was 55 years old. But he had never been a stable employee of any single firm. Daily he is at the market when the trucks arrive and he offers his services to those who will hire him. His marginal status is accented by the fact that for his first twenty years in Monterrey this man did not have a place to live, so he would spend the nights in the market.

An opposite case of extreme job instability is provided by another man. He began work at age 15, when he was living in Saltillo, as a delivery boy in a meat market. He remained in this job for four years and then moved up in the same store to waiting on customers for another three years. From age 22 to age 29 he traveled all around Mexico, with no fixed place of residence, staying and working for just a few months in many places. He naturally had very unstable and variable employment, with all the jobs being unskilled. At various times he was a farm laborer, a construction worker, a street vendor, and a stevedore, as well as holding any other job he could get. At age 30 he went back to Saltillo. He married and lived in that city for four years, but his occupational life was still very unstable, as he took the same kind of jobs mentioned above. He came to Monterrey at age 34 and kept up the same way of life, changing jobs continuously, with periods of unemployment, until age 52, at which time he became a full-time street vendor.

Most cases, of course, fall somewhere between these extremes, with the men having three or four occupational changes during their work lives. For instance, we have a man who was born in a place near Monterrey. He began work at age 10 (while at the same time remaining in school up to the third grade) in a stone quarry. At 14 he moved to San Pedro, within the metropolitan area of Monterrey, and worked as a farm laborer in a vegetable truck farm. At age 21 he entered a flour mill, where he remained for 14 years, first as a janitor and then as a bag packer. When he was 35 he changed to a factory making auto batteries, employed as a watchman, a position he still occupied fourteen years later at the time of the survey.

Migration and Vertical Mobility

As was seen in Chapter 5, migratory status is an important factor affecting occupational mobility in the early years of work experience. In this section we will take up the effect of migratory status on vertical mobility in later years of the work life, from age 25 to age 45.[3] This subject is especially important in a city like Monterrey, where such a large proportion of the population spent many years of their work lives outside the city. Among the men 45 and over in 1965, 41 percent started their work lives in Monterrey (these men will be called here "natives"), and 59 percent got to the city after they had started work.

How do these two groups compare in terms of their occupational mobility between ages 25 and 45? Of the 257 natives, 54 percent were classified as stable, 29 percent as upward, and 17 percent as downward or irregular. The corresponding figures for the 366 migrants were 61, 27, and 12 percent. There is no great difference in the distribution, with the migrants somewhat more represented in the stable category. It might seem odd that migrants would be more stable, since it is obvious that when a man changes his place of residence he must also change his job. But a change of job does not imply a basic change in status as represented by a move across the boundaries between occupational levels. Actually the contrary seems to be the case, for the probability that a change of job at the time of migration will involve upward mobility is lower than when the job shift occurs without any change of residence. And as will be seen in the section on downward mobility, this

---

[3] The effects of migration on mobility in the United States are discussed in Lipset and Bendix, *Social Mobility in Industrial Society,* and in Peter Blau and Otis D. Duncan, *The American Occupational Structure.* Neither takes age at migration into account.

is a moment in life when a downward move is quite likely. When a man enters the labor force in a new community he seldom (unless the migration is a career one) at the beginning can meet the requirements for better jobs (such as union membership), and he has not yet developed the network of social contacts that can help him in searching for a better position.

But it is unwise, as Chapter 6 demonstrated, to think of migrants as a homogeneous group. They come from different kinds of communities, and they have different experiences before arrival in the city. For our purposes here, however, the most important differences are those associated with the work experience of the men before coming to the city, namely, whether they started work in farm or nonfarm occupations. Of the 173 farm-background migrants, 69 percent were classified as stable; 21 percent, upward; and 10 percent, downward or irregular. Corresponding figures for the 193 nonfarm-background migrants were 53, 33, and 14 percent. A higher percent of farm-background migrants show a stable occupational history. The nonfarm migrants, on the other hand, show rates of mobility similar to the men who started work in Monterrey.

Calling a man a migrant leaves unanswered a number of questions, in particular the time in his life cycle when the migration to Monterrey took place. The importance of this factor for occupational attainment has already been noted in Chapter 5. The migrants in our sample are quite heterogeneous in this respect. Included are men who had all their work experience in Monterrey because they arrived before age 25, and men who arrived in Monterrey after age 45 and therefore were without any work experience in the city during the age interval 25–45. The latter lived mostly in rural areas and small towns, where the opportunities for occupational advancement were minimal. Thus, we may expect that for both farm and nonfarm migrants the age at which they arrived in the city will make a considerable difference in their occupational attainment. Those men arriving in Monterrey at an older age will show lower occupational mobility than the men arriving at a younger age. The lack of achievement of the men arriving late in their life cycles could then be taken as an indication of the differences in objective opportunities between Monterrey and the poor areas from which most migrants are recruited.

Table 8-3 presents information about occupational mobility by age at arrival. For both farm- and nonfarm-background men the proportion experiencing upward mobility decreases with age at arrival (excepting farm-background migrants arriving between ages 26 and 35). For those classified as stable, the figure rises from 50 to 84 percent by age at arrival for farm migrants, and from 40 to 73 percent for nonfarm migrants.

These differences support the interpretation advanced above that the older migrants lived longer in communities offering fewer occupational opportunities. Furthermore, when they finally do arrive in the city their age is a considerable handicap. An older man, be he migrant or native, has much reduced opportunities of moving up in the occupational structure if his position is a low one. Finally, the men who delay migration to Monterrey, for whatever reason, until they are in their forties, probably are negatively selective. The more capable and motivated men tend to leave for the large city in their late teens or early twenties. Actually, some of the men who make the move rather late in life may not have made the decision on their own, but were urged into it by their grown-up children or relatives. Then, too, some late migrants do not make the move with any expectation of improving greatly their own work situation. Rather, they come to Monterrey because they believe the opportunities for their children are much better.

Looking again at Table 8-3, a puzzling feature appears. The migrants who come to Monterrey at an early age, before 26, whether from a farm or a nonfarm background, show higher mobility rates than do the natives. The contrast is especially marked when comparing natives with the nonfarm migrants arriving up to age 25. Of the natives, 54 percent are stable, while only 40 percent of the migrants are stable. But both groups spent the years 25–45 in Monterrey and both have had all their previous occupational experience outside agriculture. This situation suggests that they should be quite comparable in terms of their background and in terms of the objective conditions under which they lived and worked. Why, then, this difference in mobility?

The first answer that comes to mind is that the two groups may have different starting points. That is, the natives have a better occupational attainment at age 25 and, since they start from a higher level, stability has a different meaning for them. Stability is quite different for a physician as compared to an unskilled laborer. In other words, there may be a "floor-and-ceiling" effect. The natives will not move up to the same degree as the migrants, because they already were in the higher positions, and the migrants will not be as likely to move down, since they

TABLE 8-3. Mobility between Ages 25 and 45, by Migratory Status, Farm-Nonfarm Background, and Age at Arrival in Monterrey (In Percent)

Mobility Pattern	Natives	Nonfarm-Background Migrants					Farm-Background Migrants				
				Age at Arrival					Age at Arrival		
		Total	Up to 25	26–35	36–45	46+	Total	Up to 25	26–35	36–45	46+
Stable	54	53	40	58	57	73	69	50	57	78	84
Upward	29	33	46	28	26	19	21	22	36	17	9
Downward and irregular	17	14	13	15	17	9	10	28	7	5	7
Total	100 (257)	100 (193)	99 (67)	101 (57)	100 (47)	101 (22)	100 (173)	100 (28)	100 (44)	100 (59)	100 (42)

TABLE 8-4. Mobility of Men between Ages 25 and 45 Who Were Lower Manual at Age 25, by Migratory Status, Farm-Nonfarm Background, and Age at Arrival in Monterrey (In Percent)

Mobility Pattern	Natives	Nonfarm-Background Migrants					Farm-Background Migrants				
				Age at Arrival					Age at Arrival		
		Total	Up to 25	26–35	36–45	46+	Total	Up to 25	26–35	36–45	46+
Stable	50	50	32	55	57	72	70	45	56	80	85
Upward	40	41	56	39	39	14	23	28	38	19	11
Downward and irregular	11	9	12	6	4	14	7	27	7	2	5
Total	101 (113)	100 (104)	100 (34)	100 (33)	100 (23)	100 (14)	100 (158)	100 (22)	101 (43)	101 (54)	101 (39)

are overrepresented in the lowest stratum. The occupational distribution of the two groups at age 25 indicates that to some degree this may be the case. Of the 259 natives, 44 percent were in the lower-manual category, 30 percent in upper manual, 15 percent in lower nonmanual, and 12 percent in upper nonmanual. Percentages of 67 nonfarm migrants up to age 25 in these categories were 51, 24, 19, and 6, respectively. To find out whether this difference in the starting distribution accounts for the difference in mobility, we must control for the distribution at the beginning of the twenty-year period. We do so by taking the numerically most important group (lower-manual workers) at age 25. (The other occupational levels have too few cases to permit any reliable conclusions.) When this is done the differences in mobility between natives and nonfarm migrants arriving up to age 25 stand out even more than before, as shown in Table 8-4. While 40 percent of the lower-manual natives had upward mobility, 56 percent of the migrants moved up. For the other age-at-arrival categories discussed above, the pattern of differences described for the whole sample is maintained only when lower-manual workers arriving by age 25 are considered.

The matter to be explained, therefore, is why the early migrants fare so well in comparison with the natives. It should be remembered that we are discussing men 45 and over at the time of survey, who had lived in the city for at least twenty years. Many of them entered the Monterrey labor force during or prior to the industrial boom that the city experienced during World War II. These migrant men were able to take advantage of the opportunities that the growing economy offered, and many were able to do so to a larger extent than the natives. The reasons for this success are several.

Migration by its very nature has an unsettling effect. It forces some break in routine and it makes men more aware and more sensitive to various alternatives. The migrant must find a place for himself in the occupational structure of the new community and in so doing he may put himself into new situations that would not have occurred to him or even been possible in his old community. In contrast the native may not have to face up to the challenges implicit in changing communities as well as jobs. He may take the line of least resistance and allow the inertia of familiar surroundings and associates to keep him in the same job. The native who has an unskilled "traditional" occupation, perhaps the same one his father has occupied, may unconsciously resign himself to it and not even look for other jobs that could better his position.

Migrants in general will be more prone to keep an eye open for a better position. They do not have the handicap of being embedded in a work, neighborhood, or family context that can discourage change.

The features we have described that provide the migrant an advantage over the native are not restricted to the time following the arrival of the migrant in the city. Among the natives, upward mobility is highly concentrated in the first ten years of the age interval we have been considering: four of five upward moves from lower-manual work were made between ages 25 and 35. For the early-arrival migrants, about half of the moves were made in each of the ten-year intervals, indicating that the migrants still experienced upward mobility at ages when there was little mobility among the natives, and years after arriving in the city.

The group of migrants we are considering are positively selective of the populations from which they originated in terms of education and occupation, as documented in Chapter 6. To these objective criteria we may add the probable selectivity of these "pioneer" migrants in the subjective dimension. The man who is willing to break with his settled and customary life and to look for new opportunities in the large city must differ in motivations and expectations from those who remain behind. On the other hand, the natives who were still unskilled workers at age 25 are on the average an undermotivated group. The more ambitious, unskilled workers probably had largely moved out of the lower-manual positions before age 25, leaving behind the less motivated and perhaps less skilled men. This outward move, incidentally, also would help account for the low mobility of natives between ages 25 and 45.

It may be argued that our interpretation of the differences between natives and migrants at different ages is based on specific historical circumstances affecting the degree of migrant selectivity and the economic growth of the city. If this were the case, the pattern of variations in mobility would be different in the younger cohorts. The problem, of course, is that we do not have comparable work-life spans for the younger cohorts, those men who had not yet reached age 45. We therefore will concentrate on the ten-year period, ages 25 to 35, and compare the achievement of the oldest cohort, the men we have discussed until now, with the men who were aged 35 to 44 at the time of the survey. The two cohorts are presented in Table 8-5.

In general, the pattern that was described for the older cohort (men 45 and over) is also manifest for the younger cohort, that is, the relative

TABLE 8-5. Mobility between Ages 25 and 35, by Birth Cohort, Migratory Status, Farm-Non-farm Background, and Age at Arrival in Monterrey (In Percent)

	Men Born before 1920 (45+ in 1965)							
	Natives	Nonfarm-Background Migrants Age at Arrival			Farm-Background Migrants Age at Arrival			
Mobility Pattern	Total	Up to 25	26–35	36+	Total	Up to 25	26–35	36+
Stable	66	72	66	67	81	83	64	75	92
Upward	26	20	28	23	9	13	25	23	6
Downward and irregular	8	9	6	11	10	4	11	2	2
Total	100	101	100	101	100	100	100	100	100
	(257)	(194)	(67)	(57)	(70)	(172)	(28)	(44)	(100)

	Men Born between 1921 and 1930 (35–44 in 1965)							
	Natives	Nonfarm-Background Migrants Age at Arrival			Farm-Background Migrants Age at Arrival			
Mobility Pattern	Total	Up to 25	26–35	36+	Total	Up to 25	26–35	36+
Stable	71	66	61	66	82	85	82	83	95
Upward	22	25	30	26	6	10	12	9	5
Downward and irregular	7	9	8	9	12	5	5	9	0
Total	100	100	99	101	100	100	99	101	100
	(193)	(111)	(60)	(34)	(17)	(94)	(40)	(35)	(19)

advantage of the nonfarm migrants who arrive in Monterrey at an early age over the natives (except that, in this ten-year period, the advantage in the oldest cohort does not show up) and the handicap of the migrants who come at an older age. The one important difference between the two cohorts is found among the farm-background migrants. Their handicap seems to be growing, whatever the age at which they migrate to the city. The explanation requires us to consider the characteristics of the migrants of this background and the opportunities provided them in the city. In Chapter 6 we remarked on the change from "pioneer" to "mass" migration, such that more recent arrivals were less selective, particularly in educational attainment, of the populations from which they originated. In addition the changes in the Mexican educational system over the last several decades have favored urban places, so that rural-origin migrants (and most farm men have a rural origin) have dropped behind in relative terms. In Monterrey the situation also has changed, as education becomes increasingly important as the determinant of occupational positions (as will be shown in Chapter 10). Each time there are more formalized entry requirements for the better jobs that offer more stability and greater advancement opportunities. Given these conditions, the farm-background men, *even those arriving at a young age,* find it more difficult to move out of the lower-manual category, even into the semiskilled and skilled jobs. The need for educational credentials closes doors that work experience formerly would have left open.

Careers

Probably the feature of occupational histories that has most caught the attention of sociologists, even though it properly applies only to a fraction of all cases, is that of careers. Some occupations are part of functionally related and hierarchically ordered sets of jobs, linked in such a way that performance of one of them is a requisite for entry into the next highest one. Interest in occupations showing such characteristics and the organizations in which they are most likely to exist has a long tradition in sociology. It stems from Weber's characterization of bureaucracy and the position of the official within the bureaucracy. "He [the official] moves from the lower, less important and lower paid, to the higher positions. The average official naturally desires a mechanical fixing of the conditions of promotion. He wants these conditions fixed in terms of 'seniority,' or possibly according to grades achieved in a developed system of expert examinations."[4] Thus the existence of career lines involves, first, a functional link between various occupations and, second, clear and explicit criteria for promotion from one position to the next one.

Bureaucratic settings provide the ideal conditions for career lines to develop. That is, careers exist more often in large and bureaucratized

[4] The quote of Weber's is from H. H. Gerth and C. Wright Mills, *From Max Weber: Essays in Sociology,* p. 203. More recently, Wilensky has used a similar restricted definition in his "Orderly Careers and Social Participation," *American Sociological Review* 26, no. 4 (1961): 521–539. See also his "Work, Careers, and Social Integration," *International Social Science Journal* 12, no. 4 (1960): 543–560, and "Measures and Effects of Mobility," in *Social Structure and Mobility in Economic Development,* ed. Neil J. Smelser and Seymour M. Lipset.

organizations than in smaller and less formalized ones. Among large organizations, the military and civil services are good examples of highly formalized career environments. Of course, in no organization do the ideal and explicitly formulated norms operate exclusively. Unstated rules and conditions and informal criteria have a considerable impact on the way career lines operate in various organizations, and many studies have focused on the nonformal factors affecting advancement.[5]

For our purposes, it is important to differentiate between occupational moves that follow a career line, with being in a career setting, that is, holding a job that could lead to an orderly and predictable occupational advancement. Many occupations in many organizations ideally could be part of a career line, but we do not have adequate information to decide whether this is actually the case. What we do have is a record of occupational changes, and by inference we can establish, with a high degree of reliability, when an occupational change was part of a career line. In effect, we will be dealing with *accomplished* career moves. There undoubtedly are many men who were at one time or another in a career setting, but who did not experience a career sequence, either because they did not stay long enough to fulfill the requirements, or because the advancement opportunities, although existent, were very small. In this section we will not consider these cases. The concept of career setting will be limited to men holding jobs that were *actually* part of a career sequence. The scope of our analysis is restricted in that we will deal only with nonfarm occupations, and professional men will be omitted because of the different advancement criteria that govern their occupational lives. It should also be mentioned here that career moves may exist that do not involve cutting across the occupational levels used in previous sections of this chapter, such as the upward moves within managerial occupations, all of which are classified as upper nonmanual.

Traditionally, the concept of career has been applied to white-collar occupations in bureaucratic settings, but it is equally applicable to other settings. Career lines are possible for blue-collar workers, as in promotions from unskilled to skilled positions within the same line of work and from skilled to supervisory positions. Careers can also exist for self-employed workers. Orderly and predictable movements within self-employed positions are the progressive enlargement of the size of the

[5] See William H. Whyte, Jr., *The Organization Man*; Morris Janowitz, *The Professional Soldier: A Social and Political Portrait*; and Oswald Hall, "The Stages in a Medical Career," *American Journal of Sociology* 53 (1948): 327–336.

enterprise, the hiring of personnel, and the increasing administrative tasks performed, so that the self-employed craftsman or store owner gradually is converted into a manager. Thus we have three types of careers and career settings: white-collar, blue-collar, and self-employment.

Among the men who were 45 years or older at the time of our study, 25 percent had experienced some career move during their work lives. Of these, 19 percent were in white-collar settings, 73 percent in blue-collar contexts, and 8 percent in self-employed positions. These proportions are practically identical for the next youngest age cohort, which is made up of men who were between ages 35 and 44 at the time of the survey. It might be assumed that, by the time this younger cohort reaches the ages of men in the 45-and-older cohort, it will have a higher proportion of men with some career movements. But, as we shall see below, the increase of men with career moves will probably be very small because few career moves occur after age 35. In the rest of this section we shall deal only with white-collar and blue-collar careers, leaving the self-employed men to be discussed in the next section of this chapter.

White-collar careers are the easiest to visualize and to understand. An almost "ideal" case is that of the general manager of an important bank in Monterrey. He was born in 1910 in Mexico City. At that time his father was a chemist in charge of a large pharmacy. A few years later he opened a laboratory of his own. The son finished *primaria* and *secundaria*. He then helped out, as an unpaid family helper, in his father's laboratory, cleaning and arranging the test tubes. After two years in this job, he stopped to go back to school. He studied for two years in a commercial school, but he dropped out before getting his degree. He then entered the enterprise where his career was to unfold— a bank, where he began as an office boy. The next year, at age 19, he started his climb up the bureaucratic ladder, first as a typist, then as a secretary, until he moved to the accounting department as an assistant accountant. His promotions in that department included becoming assistant head of the department with thirty employees under his supervision (at age 33), and nine years later he became head of the deposit department. (He married at age 42 and had five children in the next nine years.) At age 45 he was transferred from Mexico City to Monterrey. This was in 1955, a time when many Mexico City firms were in the process of extending their operations to other parts of Mexico. He was made assistant manager of the Monterrey branch of the bank. Finally, at age 54, he became manager of the bank, with some 135 employees under his direction. Several times during his ascent he took special training courses within the company.

This man, of course, is exceptional in his career line, for few men have such long-term commitments to the same enterprise (35 years), and few men are able to move such a long distance up the bureaucratic ladder. Far more common is the case of a man who enters a company as an office worker, rises to the position of department head, and then leaves the company for some other job. And many of the men who end up in the top positions begin their careers within the managerial ranks.

An early age at entry into a career setting and a relatively long-term commitment to the enterprise are common features for career men. Sixty percent of the white-collar career men (aged 45 and over) entered their career settings before age 25, while only 10 percent entered after age 35. Furthermore, half of the men remained in their career settings for more than twenty years. In addition, there are a few who in 1965 had ten to nineteen years of career history but who will probably remain for a longer period.

White-collar occupations in general, and in particular those where the opportunities for advancement are formalized and predictable, often have clear entry requirements, especially in terms of formal education. Since we know that educational levels steadily have been increasing in Monterrey, we should expect that the educational levels of the career men will increase as we compare the older with the younger birth cohorts. In general, white-collar careers seem to attract men with intermediate levels of education (remember that we are excluding professionals). About seven out of every ten men in both cohorts (over 45 years, and 35 to 44 years) had completed *secundaria* or *preparatoria* (the two-year stage beyond *secundaria*). Actually, most men with intermediate levels of education went to a commerce school, either in place of or after finishing *secundaria*. There are no university graduates in the older cohort and only a few in the younger one. At the other end, although men with less than nine years of schooling (incomplete *secundaria*) could enter white-collar career lines in the older cohort (30 percent do so), these low levels of education do not show up in the younger cohort, indicating an increasing formalization of educational requirements for white-collar careers.

In Monterrey, a highly industrial city with a large proportion of the labor force in manual occupations, blue-collar careers are extremely important. The conditions for promotions and career lines are clearly set forth in the many large enterprises, both local and national in scope. The nationalized industries of Mexico (electricity, railroads, oil) provide perhaps the most elaborate system of rules of promotion: the *escalafón* (rank, or echelon) system. "*Escalafón* of positions is a list of positions whose duties are related or are similar, ordered in accord with the amount of salary of these positions and grouped in such a way that the workers can occupy them in a progressive fashion as positions become vacant" (collective work contract of Compañía de Luz y Fuerza, 1964). Under such a system each worker knows exactly where he stands in terms of promotions, since all are based on positions in the *escalafón*, the complete listing of which is periodically published in several of the largest national enterprises. Large private companies, especially those with labor unions that are national and independent rather than company unions, also have a similar system of *escalafones* and unambiguous rules for promotion. For instance, the *contrato colectivo* for workers of the largest steel plant in Monterrey specifies that "the vacancies that are opened will be filled with personnel of the same speciality and whose position or category is immediately inferior to the open position, taking into account the worker's seniority within the category . . . all workers have a right to ascend within their speciality, up to the highest category, by means of seniority and competence." Competence is generally established by exams and a trial period in the new position, after which the worker's ability in the job is evaluated. He can appeal the decision if it is not favorable to his promotion.

Not as many men as might be expected follow this type of career line for long periods of their lives, for many change enterprises quite often, and thus they cannot benefit from the seniority accumulated in each of them. Even when they do stay for long periods in one enterprise, their chances for promotion must depend upon the availability of vacant positions—and no *escalafón* system can guarantee when these positions will open up. Moreover, there are many horizontal moves within plants. These movements from one department or job to another reduce in effect the rank of the worker in the *escalafón* system because he must establish his seniority within the department and not within the plant.

Perhaps the closest approximation to an ideal case of a blue-collar career is that of a man who worked in the Fundidora steel mill. He entered the plant when he was 18. Prior to that time he had been a helper in a grocery store (both as an unpaid family worker in his father's store and as a wage earner) after finishing *primaria* at age 13. His first job at the Fundidora was as an auxiliary worker in the Departamento de Estructuras. He remained in that department for all of the twenty-three years he was at the Fundidora. He began at the lowest level, helping in assembling chimneys and machines, and moved up to assembling bridges and buildings. His gradual and orderly ascent went through the entire hierarchical system. He started as third-category helper, moved to second and first and then to *aspirante a oficial de montaje*, followed by *oficial* (skilled workman) third category (with two assistants) and *oficial de primera*, where he was engaged in "tasks of greatest responsibility in the work of construction." He remained in this position for eight years, and then he left the Fundidora. Undoubtedly, he had achieved an elite position for a manual worker, with all the benefits of prestige, stability and employment, well-established seniority, and an extremely high income by blue-collar standards, not only because of his rank and the fringe benefits of the Fundidora, but also because his job provided him with much overtime at double pay. There was no higher position to which he could have ascended within the hierarchy of manual labor. He could have switched to a supervisory position, but the lot of a foreman in Mexico is no happier than it is in the United States and other countries, and the pay is little more. The man chose instead to leave the plant and take up a second career in the ranks of the self-employed as a store owner. We will see how successful he was in this endeavor in the section on self-employment.

As frequently mentioned in the literature, manual workers have a ceiling on their mobility opportunities.[6] There is no chance of moving to white-collar positions, except to a supervisory position, a job that involves them in so many tensions and difficulties that many men prefer not to be promoted to such positions. We do have some cases of men who moved to supervisory positions, but we could not find a single case where a supervisory position served as a bridge to further advancement within the white-collar world. For example, one man entered a large glass factory at age 22, after holding various jobs (helper in a grocery store, helper and then welder in an appliance factory). He began as a helper to a mechanic in the maintenance department. He then gradually

[6] Eli Chinoy (*Automobile Workers and the American Dream*) discusses the ceiling for upward mobility of blue-collar workers in large plants.

moved through the hierarchy, becoming a second-category mechanic, then a first-level one. At age 35 he was promoted to a supervisory position in the same department. He stayed there for seven years and finally, at age 42, left the plant to open his own grocery store.

Although the examples we have presented are all from large enterprises, career lines also exist in smaller enterprises, even where there is no labor union or collective contract. These careers are less predictable and less subject to formal criteria, and the worker may be less aware of his position in the promotion order. Since there is no labor union contract and work relationships are more personal, there is less need for the detailed occupational titles and minute gradations between positions that characterize the large enterprises. In the smaller firms there is probably less division of labor, so the career lines have fewer steps, and there are not so many distinctions between various specialties. Printers, bakery workers, construction workers, and those in repair shops of various kinds are some of the occupations more prevalent in small enterprises where career lines exist.

As was true of white-collar careers, most blue-collar workers enter their career settings at a young age. In the older age cohort, two-thirds of the men who experienced career-oriented moves entered the enterprise before age 25. In the 35–44 age cohort the figure is 71 percent. The blue-collar men also stayed quite a long time in the enterprise, but here there is an intercohort difference. The younger cohort shows a higher proportion of men who stayed just a few years in their career settings before moving to another line of work. While 18 percent of the older cohort stayed for ten years or less, 52 percent of the younger cohort did so. This would indicate more job changes within the younger cohort (as discussed also in Chapter 5). What is not expected is that this increasing shifting around and changing of jobs and enterprises should also affect the men who are in a career setting, since these men should have fewer reasons to move about and should be more satisfied with their jobs.

Since large enterprises provide a more clear-cut setting for career lines, we should expect that more men will experience career-oriented promotions in large than in small enterprises. Forty-two percent of career moves among the older cohort took place in enterprises employing more than five hundred workers, while 9 percent took place in enterprises employing five workers or less. In order to know whether large enterprises offer more opportunities for career moves, we have to control for the total blue-collar employment by size of enterprise. This is done in Table 8-6, which shows that, from age 25 on, a higher proportion of men in large enterprises are in career settings. This finding suggests that if the process of bureaucratization continues and there is an increase in the proportion of the labor force employed in large enterprises, as well as governmental agencies, there will also be an increase in the proportion of the labor force working in career environments and experiencing predictable and orderly occupational moves.

Self-Employment

Self-employment occupies a special place in the area of social stratification and mobility. Its relevance is based mainly on two considerations. First, self-employment is an important goal for many men both in industrial and in industrializing societies, for it signifies independence, which is highly valued. Self-employed men are often evaluated as holding better positions than employees, even when there is little difference in income and level of living. Second, a number of sociologists have claimed that self-employment offers the main avenue of upward mobility for manual workers.[7] Of course, not *any* self-employed position means upward mobility for all manual workers.

This discussion brings us to an important point regarding self-employment. It is not a homogeneous category, easy to analyze in its totality. Some differentiation in terms of the hierarchical dimension of social stratification is necessary, since there are self-employed men at

TABLE 8-6. Percent of Blue-Collar Workers Aged 45 and Over Following Career Lines, by Size of Enterprise and Age

Age	Size of Enterprise						
	2–5	6–20	21–50	51–200	201–500	501+	Unknown
15	3	6	13	0	0	8	5
25	13	33	16	17	16	37	13
35	8	26	23	26	22	38	19
45	7	14	27	14	21	38	7

NOTE: The percentages are calculated as follows: number of blue-collar workers in each size category at each age who are in career settings, over the total number of blue-collar workers in each age and size category, times 100.

7 Ibid.; and Lipset and Bendix, *Social Mobility in Industrial Society.*

all levels. Most street vendors are self-employed, and at the other end
of the scale so are many professionals and entrepreneurs (if we consider employers as part of the self-employed). The former are self-
employed not so much by choice as by default, for they cannot get
better work. Furthermore, at the extreme ends of the stratification system, it is often difficult to decide who is and who is not self-employed.
Are salaried managers of large enterprises who own much of the stock
self-employed? Are the porters in railroad and bus stations, where they
must be licensed to operate but whose only income comes from tips, to
be considered workers or self-employed? At the extremes, however, it
probably does not make too much difference whether or not the men
are self-employed. Top managers enjoy a considerable amount of
power and discretion whether or not they own the enterprise. Porters
and street vendors, whether self-employed or workers, must share the
realities of underemployment, instability of employment, and lack of
choice in work.

Consequently, self-employment as an area of research is of most interest at the middle levels of the stratification hierarchy. The intermediate self-employed men are those who own and operate small shops,
stores, taxis, or trucks and who have some capital investment, but not
a large one. It is such positions to which manual workers can and do
aspire to move. Subjectively and ideologically, the change may be important, even if it does not always mean a change in level of living, and
even if the likelihood of failure is very large. It is these intermediate
self-employed categories that we shall be occupied with in this section.

Becoming self-employed involves a large risk, especially for those
men who had stable and secure jobs. Income is uncertain, in particular
during the first perilous years of the business. Often the men lack the
financial and administrative skills needed for successful operation of
the enterprise. Most men are aware of the fact that many small shops
and stores close soon after opening. Some men therefore proceed with
much care when they decide to become self-employed. The worker in
the Fundidora who was described in the section on careers, for instance,
was extremely cautious when he decided to enter the ranks of the self-
employed, after twenty years in the plant. His timing was almost per-
fect. For five years he had been in the highest position he could expect
to attain, so no more mobility could be anticipated within the plant. His
youngest son was three years old, and now his wife would be more free

of household concerns and could help him in the store. He had saved a considerable amount of money during his years in the steel plant. In any event, when he first opened a small shoe store he did not give up his job in the factory until he was sure of the success of his business venture. He moonlighted in his store for three years, his wife tending it when he was not present. During the first year of operation the store lost money, and in the second year it broke even. At the end of the third year it turned a profit, so he decided to leave the factory and devote his full time to the store. Gradually he added to the line of goods offered, selling men's clothing in addition to shoes. The next year he hired a salesman, and by the time of the survey—after fifteen years in operation—he had three employees, plus his wife and his oldest son as unpaid family workers, and the store was still growing and expanding its line.

This case exemplifies some of the conditions necessary to become self-employed and to be successful in the venture, and we can now state them in a more systematic way. First, the man must accumulate some capital and have access to credit. This is no easy matter when he has a manual job and must provide for a large family, so it generally takes years to accumulate enough capital. There must be sufficient funds not only to set up the business but also to keep it going during the first months or years while it runs at a deficit. The amount of money needed is not necessarily very large. It may be the cash to buy a used car and the license needed to become a taxi owner, funds to stock food in sufficient supply and variety to begin store operations in the front room of the home (and this approach implies a large enough house so the front room can be spared), or enough money to buy some tools and set up as a mechanic in the back yard (provided there is one). All these kinds of capital requirements are modest enough, but the capital is not easy to come by for the working classes of Monterrey or elsewhere in Mexico. Besides, those men who best could afford to save money and become self-employed—workers in large industries who are well paid and have plant savings plans and medical and other emergency coverage—are among those least interested in such a risky venture, for they have more to lose.

Second, especially in the case of commercial ventures, success of the operation will be influenced by the contribution of family members who receive no direct pay. The wife and older children can help significantly. Since in most cases these family members would not otherwise be employed outside the household, their contribution to family finances is a "net" one.

Third, a man should have the necessary social contacts in various key positions who will be of help in getting licenses, complying with various governmental regulations, obtaining credit from wholesalers or banks, building a clientele, and so forth. Everywhere, and the more so in Mexico, informal contacts are the key to successfully getting by these necessary steps.

How important numerically are the self-employed we are dealing with in this section? Is there any evidence of a decline in their importance as the process of industrialization proceeds? Table 8-7 presents the percent of men in selected occupations who were self-employed at various ages, by birth cohorts. In relative terms, self-employment is much more important in commerce than in the other occupations. At least half of the retail salesmen at any age in any birth cohort were self-employed, while this situation is never true for more than one-third

TABLE 8-7. Percent Men Self-employed in Selected Occupations, by Age and Birth Cohort

Occupation and Birth Cohort	Age					
	25	30	35	40	45	50
Semiskilled and skilled workers						
1905–1914	7	9	11	15	14	14
1915–1924	4	9	13	11		
1925–1934	13	11				
Vehicle operators						
1905–1914	12	25	21	28	19	33
1915–1924	10	27	33	33		
1925–1934	20	18				
Retail salesmen						
1905–1914	50	60	86	95	90	100
1915–1924	69	92	82	67		
1925–1934	55	70				
Self-employed in above occupations as a percent of the total nonfarm labor force						
1905–1914	4	6	7	11	10	11
1915–1924	4	7	8	7		
1925–1934	6	6				

of vehicle operators or more than 15 percent of operatives and crafts-men. Differences in the economic organization of commerce, transportation, and manufacturing enterprises account for these varying proportions. Manufacturing enterprises can gain most in terms of productivity by an increase in the size of the plant and by economies of scale. Furthermore, as was mentioned in Chapter 2, manufacturing enterprises in Monterrey are more modern and more capital intensive than are commercial or transportation enterprises.

In all parts of Table 8-7 there are no clear patterns of intercohort variation. It is usually maintained that the process of industrialization and the increasing scale of economic activity in a country will bring about a decline in the proportion of self-employed.[8] Our data indicate no such trend for the positions under discussion here. In spite of the increasing concentration of manufacturing in large enterprises that is taking place in Monterrey, there is still room for self-employed positions. Some of the self-employed positions are in the more traditional sectors (the ones with the lowest productivity), but others owe their existence to the process of industrialization itself. Automotive, television, radio, and other electrical appliance repair shops come into being only when the level of living rises sufficiently for large numbers of people to buy these consumption items. The number of these kinds of establishments undoubtedly will grow with increasing levels of industrialization. Arthur Stinchcombe has shown that although these enterprises are a product of modern industry they are organizationally similar to the traditional crafts, and they are well suited for self-employment.[9]

Table 8-7 also allows us to introduce the question of the relationship between self-employment and the life cycle. Is self-employment more common among older men as a kind of alternative to retirement? Are the older men the only ones who can accumulate enough capital and who can count upon the help of their older children? Or is self-employment a "young" adventure, when the competition of seniority (in the case of workers in large plants) is not too great and the desire for new experience is more pronounced? By looking at the rows of Table 8-7, we can see that the percent of self-employed men increases with age.

[8] Wilbert E. Moore, "Changes in Occupational Structure," in *Social Structure and Mobility in Economic Development*, ed. Neil J. Smelser and Seymour M. Lipset.

[9] Arthur L. Stinchcombe, "Social Structure and Organizations," in *Handbook of Organizations*, ed. James G. March.

This trend can be explored further if we take only the men who were 45 years and over in 1965 and follow their occupational histories. Four percent of these men were self-employed at age 25 and 13 percent at age 45. This percentage would seem to demonstrate without doubt that there is an increasing probability of becoming self-employed with increasing age.

But this is actually not the case. If we look at the probabilities of *becoming* self-employed rather than *being* self-employed, the picture we get is quite different. Again restricting ourselves to men aged 45 and over in 1965, the number who entered self-employment in various age intervals is as shown in Table 8-8. There is no increase in the probability of becoming self-employed with increasing age. The increase in the proportion of men occupying self-employed positions can be explained, not by variations in the rate of entry into the positions, but by the probability of remaining self-employed, and its variation by age.

Since self-employment is a goal for many people, we can assume that most men (remember, we are not considering the lowest level of self-employment) would like to remain in such positions as long as possible. Many obstacles present themselves in opposition to such desires. Thus, being able simply to remain in self-employment is a first indication of success. Using as a measure of degree of success the proportion of men who survive for more than ten years in self-employment, it is the men who entered at younger ages who have the higher probability of success. While two-thirds of men entering self-employment before age 25 remain so for more than ten years, the proportion gradually declines until it reaches 43 percent of the men who entered between ages 41 and 45 (and were over 50 at the time of the survey). In summary, the increasing proportion of self-employed men by age is explained by a constant rate of entry and a decreasing probability of remaining there for a long time.

TABLE 8-8. Men Entering Self-Employment in Various Age Intervals

Age Interval	Number	Percent of Cohort
Before 25	32	5
26–30	24	4
31–35	17	3
36–40	22	4
41–45	19	3

Not only do the young men entering self-employment tend to remain longer than the older ones, but they also show considerably better chances of getting ahead in a career sense. The typical self-employed career can be illustrated by the case of a man who became self-employed at age 18, after finishing commercial school and helping his family in a grocery store for several years. He started by repairing radios, gradually enlarging his enterprise by hiring workers until he finally gave up doing repair work himself, adding some radio manufacturing to the repair service. He ended up by assuming the full managerial and administrative tasks of operating an enterprise of about fifteen employees.

While almost a third of the men who entered before age 25 experienced career advancement within self-employment—gradually becoming managers as they enlarged their enterprises—almost none of the men becoming self-employed after age 25 experienced career advancements. In this—the advantage of youth—they resemble the other types of career men described in the previous section of this chapter.

The analysis of self-employed positions can serve to clear up two more issues, both of them linked to the arguments made by various authors. Is it true that self-employment is an important channel of upward mobility for manual workers? Second, what happens to the unsuccessful self-employed? The risks of this position repeatedly have been emphasized. What is the fate of the men who lose out?

Beginning with the first question, among the men 45 and over, more than half of the moves to self-employment (57 percent) involved an upward move. In the majority of cases it was an unskilled manual worker becoming either a grocery store owner, an independent craftsman, or a driver-owner of a vehicle. In about three of every ten cases, the move was a horizontal one, mostly representing operatives and craftsmen moving from a worker to a self-employed position. These cases often mean the continuation of the same kind of skilled work as before, for instance, a bus driver who buys a used car and becomes an independent taxi driver, or a highly skilled mechanic in a large light-bulb factory who leaves to become an "independent contractor" as a master mechanic repairing heating systems and building machinery, sometimes working alone and sometimes hiring workers. Eleven percent of the moves were downward. Probably in these cases the value placed on independence was extremely great, and undoubtedly the men hoped to rise eventually in occupational status within the self-employed world.

We already have considered one such man—the supervisor who opened a small grocery store—and we will examine more cases in the next section on downward mobility.

Turning to the second question posed above, it is quite clear that leaving self-employment most of the time involves a decline in status. Fifty-four percent of the men who left self-employed positions entered an occupation at a lower level. Examples of such moves are the grocery store owner who became an unskilled worker, or the taxi owner who became a policeman (a low-status occupation in Mexico). Usually the men leave self-employment not by choice or because a better opportunity shows up. Most often the move results from failure to keep the operation going. This failure may happen after one to two years, or it may occur following many years of experience and even success. In the latter case, it may take place when the scope of the enterprise is broadened, because the man is unable to cope with the demands of a new set of responsibilities. In the remaining cases, the move out of self-employment is either horizontal (29 percent) or upward (17 percent). Movement out of self-employment thus is an appropriate lead into the next section of this chapter, that dealing with downward mobility.

Downward Mobility

In comparison with the attention devoted to upward mobility, the discussion in the sociological literature of downward mobility has been relatively meager.[10] Possibly more enlightenment of this phenomenon has been provided by novelists, but their imaginations have been kindled by the great falls in social rank, the "Buddenbrooks" pattern, and of course they have been concerned with the personal and idiosyncratic features of downward mobility.

The objective of this section is quite different. To repeat once more, we are not concerned with tracing the experience of men who have fallen, whether a great or a short distance, during the course of their lifetimes. We are concerned with analyzing downward *moves* as such and with asking whether there are consistent and repetitive patterns

---

[10] The emphasis of most studies has been on intergenerational mobility and its political and ideological consequences. See Joseph Lopreato and Janet Saltzman Chafetz, "The Political Orientation of Skidders: A Middle-Range Theory," *American Sociological Review* 35 (June 1970): 440–451; and Harold L. Wilensky and H. Edwards, "The Skidder: Ideological Adjustment of the Downward Mobile Workers," *American Sociological Review* 24 (April 1959): 215–231.

associated with such moves. In other words, under what circumstances is a downward move likely? In line with the rest of this chapter, and the book in general, we will deal mainly with factors related to the previous experience of the men in the areas of work and migration. The treatment necessarily will be at an exploratory level, in light of the paucity of studies on this subject.

Downward moves are not rare events in the lives of our men. One-fourth of those aged 45 and over in 1965 had experienced such a move during their work lives, and of these men one in four had had two or more downward moves. As in previous sections of this chapter, we use the four-level scale of occupations, and this rather broad calibration means that most downward moves involve significant shifts in occupational status. Of all downward moves, 60 percent originated in a manual position and 40 percent in a nonmanual position. Given the overall distribution of such positions at the time of the survey and throughout the time period covered by the work histories of the men, it would appear that there is a greater probability of a downward move from a nonmanual position than from a manual one, but this supposition neglects to take into account the fact that men in the lowest occupational level—unskilled manual—cannot fall into a lower category.

What are the events in a man's life history that can help us locate and explain a downward move? In the previous section dealing with self-employment, we mentioned a situation where downward mobility is likely to occur, namely, when men leave a self-employment position. Of all downward moves, 19 percent took place under these circumstances. As we have seen, the moves usually reflect the man's failure to make a go of it as a self-employed person, rather than a voluntary move on his part. But there is another type of downward move related to self-employment, where men in nonmanual positions *enter* self-employed positions (7 percent of all downward moves). Cases of this nature are the school teacher who after many years as a teacher and school principal leaves to open a very small grocery store, the man occupying a managerial position in a bank in a large city who moves to Monterrey and opens a very small jewelry store, or the sales agent for an important commercial concern who at age 43 decides to leave that job and open a small cantina. Perhaps the most significant fact about these men is that they are downwardly mobile by choice, and the great majority believe that in a short time they will advance rapidly within their new self-employed positions. They know that the first years are hard and risky, but they are willing to make the downward move in the hope of later success. But the odds are against them, and, in fact, few will succeed in greatly enlarging the scope of their businesses.

Other than these cases where downward mobility is linked to changes from and to self-employment, what other patterns can be detected? We can begin to explore this area with the general idea that downward mobility is more likely to take place during unstable periods in a man's life. Several indicators of instability can be used, dealing with different aspects of the lives of the men.

In a previous section of this chapter it was argued that migration has a disruptive effect on the men's lives, especially in their occupational experience. We can expect that downward mobility will occur more often at the time of change in residence. (Here we are interested only in the immediate effect of migration, which may be quite different if looked at from a longer time perspective.) Such a pattern is readily understandable, for, when a man moves from one place to another, he may not have the job qualifications, the social contacts, or the information needed to get a good occupational position. Formal requirements for a job may be quite different in a small town or a rural area when compared to a large city. Thus we have the case of a man who was the head of the post office in a small town who did not even meet the qualifications of postal employee in the Monterrey system. Self-employed men find that the capital they bring with them to the city is not sufficient to set up an operation similar to the one they had before. Skilled operatives may find that they do not have the required skills, or a union card, or any of the other various formal requirements needed to enter large firms at a skilled level. The more rare case where migration out of Monterrey is linked to downward mobility is illustrated by that of a man who was a skilled printer in Monterrey, but gave up his job to spend three years in the United States working as a laborer in a meat-packing plant. When he returned to Monterrey he resumed his skilled position as a printer. In general, one of every four cases of downward moves took place the same year as the change in place of residence, confirming our expectation that migration is a time when downward mobility is likely to occur. This proportion is considerably higher than the proportion of horizontal or upward moves taking place at the same time as the migration.

Besides migration, we can look at instability in the occupational sphere itself. Downward moves will be more likely in periods of the lives of men when they are constantly changing jobs, when they do not have a stable and long-term commitment to a job, an employer, or even a particular line of work. To explore this area we devised a measure of unstable periods in the work life. They are defined as those periods when a man does not stay in a job for more than three years (plus the first three years in a stable job after having such unstable jobs). Of all men 45 and over, 63 percent had such unstable periods at least once in their lifetime. In order to compare the men who experienced downward mobility with those who did not experience it, we must make some alterations in the latter group. All men who were unskilled workers in the lowest occupational level throughout their work lives were eliminated, since no downward move could take place. Also eliminated were those men who had only one job during their entire work lives and therefore did not move in any direction.

The contrast between the two groups is quite striking: 84 percent of the men who experienced downward mobility had unstable work periods, as contrasted to 57 percent who did not have downward moves. Moreover, among the men who had unstable work periods in the two groups, there is a clear difference in the time spent in unstable positions (Table 8-9). There is no question that the downwardly mobile men have more unstable work histories than the rest of the sample. Of course, the downward move tends to occur during the unstable periods. Thus, 70 percent of the downward moves took place during unstable periods.

Not only do the downward moves tend to occur in periods of instability, but also the moves tend to occur from jobs held for a short time. Thirty-five percent of the moves took place after only one or two years on the job, and an additional 35 percent occurred after three to five years. The latter is a period considerably shorter than the average num-

TABLE 8-9. Downward Mobility for Men with Unstable Work Periods (In Percent)

Years in Unstable Jobs	Had Downward Move	Did Not Have Downward Move
Up to 5	14	36
6–10	32	48
11 or more	54	16
Total	100	100
	(127)	(158)

ber of years the men stayed in any position and much shorter than the average length of stay of career men or self-employed men. If we think of downward mobility as an indication of failure of job performance, we can easily see why it happens after a short job tenure. Generally, if a man is not able to perform in a given work position, his employer, or he himself, will recognize this inability relatively soon. We can infer, therefore, that when downward mobility occurs after a short tenure in a given job, it will generally indicate failure to perform adequately the duties of the job. Downward moves taking place after many years in the job are often due to other reasons, as in the voluntary move down already mentioned, or because of labor market conditions, or as a concomitant of the aging process of the worker.

Up to now we have not introduced the relationship between downward mobility and stages in the life cycle. Is the downward move more likely to come at the beginning or at the end of the work cycle? In Chapter 5 it was demonstrated that the early years in the labor force are relatively unstable, with much "shopping around" and shifts of jobs. Does this mean that we should expect more downward mobility at these early ages? In order to answer this question we must explore in detail the periods in the life cycle when unstable work is more likely, so as to be able to relate the incidence of downward moves with these unstable periods.

As mentioned, the first years of work experience are the ones when it is more likely that men will change jobs frequently. They haven't much experience in a specific area of work and their seniority is low; the family responsibilities that would keep them in one position so as to assure continuity of income are light. Thus, they can explore various alternatives before settling into one line of work or one job. Taking again the 285 men 45 and over who had some unstable period in their lives, we see that most of them had instability at early ages, and that the incidence of instability declines quite drastically at older ages: 71 percent had instability at age 15–25, 37 percent at 26–35, 28 percent at 36–45, and 12 percent at 46 and over. The percentages add up to more than 100 because many men had unstable periods at various times in their life cycles. A few even spent their entire work lives in unstable jobs.

If, as has been claimed, work instability is a factor affecting the probability of downward mobility, then we should also expect that downward mobility will be more likely at the younger ages. But this is not the case. Downward mobility is less likely to occur at very early stages in the life cycle up to age 20. But after that age there are no differences in the incidence by age interval (Table 8-10).

How can we reconcile the findings that instability is related to downward mobility and that instability is more likely to occur at early ages with the facts presented above, namely, that the incidence of downward mobility does not vary with age? Job instability has different meanings and consequences at various stages in the life cycle. In the first years of work experience, instability reflects the fact that the men are shopping around, exploring various job alternatives and opportunities, before settling down to one major line of work. This shopping around is mostly from one unskilled manual job to another. At this early stage there is little difference in the incidence of instability between the men who experienced downward mobility and the ones who did not. But more importantly, little downward mobility is associated with instability. Of all men who experienced unstable job periods between ages 15 and 25, only 18 percent experienced downward mobility during these unstable periods.

At later ages instability reflects the fact that the men were unable or unwilling to settle for one line of work or one enterprise. Unstable work periods are more common among the men who experienced downward mobility, and the downward moves increasingly take place in these unstable periods. Thirty-nine percent of the men who experienced unstable job periods between ages 26 and 35, 38 percent of those experi-

TABLE 8-10. Men with Downward Mobility, by Age at Which It Occurred

Age Interval	Number Experiencing Downward Mobility	Percent of all Downward Moves
15–20	13	6
21–25	34	17
26–30	34	17
31–35	33	16
36–40	31	15
41–45	34	17
46 and over[a]	25	12
Total	204	100

[a] This is an open-ended period; some men are just 45, others are 60 years old at the time of the survey.

encing instability between ages 36 and 45, and 51 percent of the ones having unstable periods after age 45 show downward moves during these periods.

For some men, almost their entire lifetime has been one of seemingly aimless shifting from one job to another, and in the course of such shifts upward and downward movements follow each other in random fashion. For instance, one man was born and grew up in a rural area, where he went to *primaria* and commerce schools. At age 16, after finishing commerce school, he started work as a helper in a small grocery store. He stayed in this job for four years and then changed to a very large mining company, employed as a clerk. After three years he moved to a town where he worked as a gas station attendant (a downward move). After two years he went back to his rural community of origin and became a salesman in a grocery store for two years. Then he became a car mechanic in a garage for one year. At age 28 he became a farm laborer, helping his relatives in the family plot for four years (his second downward move). Next he became a truck driver for a large farm, and after three years he moved on to a medium-size city, still working as a truck driver but now employed by a large iron-and-steel firm. After two years in this position, he became a driver of an interurban bus for a year. At age 38 he came to Monterrey and began working in a chemical plant as a warehouse clerk. After three years he changed to a car factory, working as a mechanic (the third downward move). Just a year later he moved to another factory, this one making appliances, still working as a mechanic. Again after a year, he left to become a manager of an office building. Finally, after three years, at age 46 he became head of a branch office in a construction concern, where he was at the time of the survey in 1965.

This man's story, an extreme case of instability, contrasts sharply with the group of men (16 percent) who were not unstable but who experienced downward mobility. It is almost impossible, at least within the context of this chapter, to find any pattern or explanation for this kind of downward mobility. All we know is that this type of downward mobility tends to occur somewhat more frequently at relatively older ages, in connection with entering or leaving a self-employed position, or after leaving a career setting. There is the case of the man who arrived in Monterrey at age 42 after spending his whole work life to that point as a miner. He opened a small grocery store, but after six years of self-employment he was forced to close it and become a watchman in a lumber yard in the city. Another instance of a downward move after a stable history is that of a man who worked all his life in a factory, first as a helper and then moving up to become a welder. After more than twenty years he left to become a night watchman in a store. These and similar histories probably are the ones where more room is left for the play of chance and idiosyncratic factors as determinants of the downward move.

Occupational Mobility and the Fluidity of the Occupational Structure

As already remarked, most mobility studies are concerned only with forms of vertical mobility, and then generally by means of a comparison of occupational position at two points in time. In our case, we found that six of every ten men were "stable" throughout the twenty-year interval, ages 25–44. The problem is to interpret this result. We can hardly say whether it is high or low or whether, as is often described, it is a more or less "rigid" occupational structure, unless we can compare it with other findings. In our case, international comparisons are extremely difficult. Our time interval, ages 25–44, is not a common one, and the fact that we did not restrict ourselves to just two points in time, but took into account any changes *within* the time interval, makes it impossible to compare exactly our results with other studies. One could easily have increased greatly the amount of mobility by increasing the number of occupational strata and by considering the change from farm to urban employment as vertical mobility, instead of assigning, as we did, nearly all cases to the stable category.

But apart from the conditions that affect the magnitude and therefore the interpretation of mobility rates, the purpose of this chapter has been to emphasize specific forms and paths of occupational mobility in addition to the vertical dimension. We have shown that most men experience changes that affect their conditions of work but that do not necessarily affect their vertical mobility. In this context three forms of horizontal mobility can be considered: (1) farm to nonfarm employment via migration, (2) change of place of employment, and (3) self-employment.

Migration, for most men in the 25–44 age interval, does not lead, immediately at least, to vertical mobility, but change of residence does introduce many significant changes of a nonvertical nature, such as acquainting themselves with a complex labor market, learning to work with different time schedules, and even accommodating themselves to a pronounced separation in home and workplace.

There are also frequent changes of firm or place of employment that don't show up as vertical mobility but that can be of considerable significance for the man and his own appraisal of his situation. In the first section of this chapter we were able to show that the amount of "place" stability (the percent of men who remained in the same job for the twenty-year period) was lowest at both ends of the occupational scale. We suggest that both the upper-nonmanual and lower-manual categories have more transferability of skills that facilitate movement from one job to another. Professionals, for example, often change positions, moving into managerial and governmental posts. At the other end, it is the lack of specialization that permits men in lower-manual work to shift from one unskilled job to another.

The consequences of nonvertical mobility cannot be spelled out here in any detail, but one example can be presented. It can be argued that the satisfaction with job and life position that a substantial proportion of men in the lowest occupational strata report for themselves is related to forms of nonvertical mobility. Since the men have a variety of changes open to them—place of residence and place of work—they need not find themselves in the position of being trapped in one work situation or subject to the despotic control of one employer. This situation can be contrasted with the form of debt slavery that characterized relations between the *peón* and the *hacendado* in rural Mexico before the revolution.

It is possible, however, to attribute too much significance to this kind of mobility. After all, many men in the lowest stratum do not change jobs of their own volition; they are fired or let go, often because of the limited duration of the work itself. Most men gladly would trade the "freedom" to move about for the "entrapment" of a stable job offering a decent wage. But the point is that such work opportunities are seldom open to these men.

At the beginning of this chapter we mentioned that the most widely held view of a work life is the "normal career curve." By now, after dealing with the various aspects of occupational paths of mobility, we can evaluate the accuracy of such an image. It is clearly based on aggregate data collected in isolated points in time. By using complete work histories we have been able to examine facets of mobility—irregular movements and downward mobility, for example—that would not have been possible with data limited to isolated points in time. Indeed there is no possibility of even discussing career moves unless complete occupational sequences are available. The richness and the variety of concrete histories of the men indicate that the image of "normal career curve" does not apply to even a significant minority. There are more job changes, ups and downs, horizontal movement, and stability itself than is implied by such a model.

9. Older Men's Biographical Profiles and Sons' Prospects

Ideally, we would want at this point in the description of the chief events in the men's life cycles to be able to reconstruct their complete biographical profiles as a way of summing up. But to do this would require that the men be old enough to have lived through the greater part of their work lives, and of course this is not the case for the substantial majority of the men. Nor can we conveniently regard our birth-cohort distributions as accurate previews of things to come; that is, we cannot assume that the younger cohorts will closely resemble the older cohorts when they reach their age. In previous chapters we have indicated similarities as well as differences between the older and younger cohorts in Monterrey. Given the dynamic nature of the Mexican economy and society, there is little reason to believe that successive cohorts will automatically demonstrate exactly the same patterns as indicated by our 1965 age distribution.

The upshot of this discussion is that we must confine our review of the completed life cycle to the older men in our sample, those aged 45 to 60 at the time of the survey. These men, who already have completed or will soon be completing their occupational, migratory, and family-formation histories, provide us with sufficient information about their lives so that we can construct reasonably complete life-history profiles.

Unlike Chapters 5 and 8, where we looked forward by taking the men at a given age and then observing what happened to them over the next ten or twenty years, our perspective in this chapter will be one of looking backward at the life histories of the older men from the vantage point of their terminal positions, something we cannot do for any other birth cohort. In one section of the chapter, however, our attention will be directed toward the future. The older men are nearing the close of their work lives, but their sons are in the early stages of theirs, or about to begin. In taking up the third generation we can observe the continuity between generations.

We have mentioned that Mexican birth cohorts have their own historical context. It is particularly important to remember that the men to be considered were born between 1905 and 1920. They grew up in a society in the throes of revolution and its aftermath, a period of almost universal uncertainty and considerable structural transformation. In a number of questionnaires the interviewers recorded unsolicited remarks that reflect the effects of the revolution upon the men's everyday lives: "During these years I was attending school whenever it was open, but quite often it had to close because the teacher was absent, or the town was invaded by revolutionary forces, so that I barely learned how to read and write." "I never knew my father, who went to fight in the revolution when I was a child. We never knew if and when or where he died." Most of the men at that time were living in small villages and rural areas, those most affected by the upheaval, and many families moved to the city looking for protection. Then, when most of the men were in the first stages of their work lives, the economy that had been recovering very slowly from the destruction of the revolution was badly hit by the Great Depression, with consequent unemployment in urban areas and a slowdown of the economy in general. But after the Depression, just before and during World War II, rapid industrialization opened up many occupational opportunities in the country.

It may appear questionable that we have chosen so wide an age interval, 45 to 60, to include men who have largely completed the most important events of their life cycles. An age of 45 hardly seems appropriate as the lower limit for such a classification. But such a reaction stems from a perspective on the work-life cycle and the life span that is prevalent in industrialized societies. A distinctive feature of developing societies is the fact that many, if by no means all, men grow old at an early age. This is partly due to the relative domination of young people in developing societies. (In Mexico more than one-half the population is under the age of 18.) But it is also a matter of self-definition. Men in their forties and early fifties refer to themselves as old. Why should this be?

The accelerated aging process has both physical and social dimensions. Many men, especially those originating in farm areas, have had many years of hard and sometimes dangerous labor that has worn them down physically. Only a few have had adequate health care through their lives. Perhaps more important, socially they age rapidly because, as we have pointed out on numerous occasions, uneducated and poorly skilled men are particularly vulnerable in a society as rapidly changing as Mexico's is at the present time. With little to offer employers except brute strength, even by their late thirties they are unable to compete for unskilled jobs with the increasingly large cohorts of young men. While only a few of the older men have withdrawn completely from the labor force, the phasing-out process is evident in their movement into the more marginal of marginal jobs, such as street vending. Such jobs are a way of keeping occupied, but they generally are inadequate to provide the sole support of a family. By the time a man reaches his forties, however, it is probable that he has children in their late adolescence who can contribute to the family finances, and sometimes his wife also enters or reenters the labor force. But these arrangements do not enhance his status as a family provider, and they serve only to reinforce the other factors already enumerated that make for the pattern of growing old at an early age.

Not all men, of course, face such a grim prospect. The histories of the fortunate minority are in sharp contrast to those just described. Men who somehow were able to go beyond *primaria* in their education, or were able to secure employment in the larger industrial enterprises, were in an excellent position to take advantage of the boom years that began in the early 1940's. Being a minority, they have been able to profit by the scarce supply of trained personnel. Today we find some of them in command of strategic positions in industrial, governmental, and educational institutions. The challenge they face of the new generations, who are educationally better prepared, is evident, but seniority is a powerful force in all societies. Possibly the difference between extremes that we find among the men aged 45–60 is greater than will be the case for any of the younger age cohorts, but of course we shall not know for sure until several decades have passed.

TABLE 9-1. Measures of Income and Perceived Status, by Occupational Position in 1965, Men Aged 45–50

| | Occupational Position in 1965 | | | | | | | | | |
| | Lower Manual | | Upper Manual | | | Nonmanual | | | | |
	In Small Firm	In Large Firm	In Small Firm	In Large Firm	Self-employed	Lower White Collar	Small Entrepreneur	Middle White Collar	Manager, Entrepreneur	Professional
Income: Annual income in 1965 in Mexican pesos ('000)										
Median	7.5	9.9	10.0	14.8	16.2	18.8	26.5	36.3	—[a]	—[a]
First quartile	5.4	8.4	8.4	11.4	9.4	13.9	13.5	22.5	—[a]	—[a]
Third quartile	8.5	11.8	11.9	20.8	21.8	30.4	40.5	55.5	—[a]	—[a]
Percent of total income	7	6	2	10	7	5	5	12	29	17
Perceived economic status										
Believes to be better than the majority (%)	14	24	18	25	35	34	29	59	50	67
Believes life has treated him well (%)	41	49	47	57	55	69	75	75	92	100
Percentage distribution	24 (151)	14 (90)	6 (37)	17 (104)	12 (74)	6 (35)	4 (24)	7 (45)	7 (42)	3 (22)

[a] Not calculated: over 50 percent placed in the upper, open-ended interval (over 120,000 pesos a year).

The Older Men in 1965: Occupational Strata and Levels of Living

We begin by analyzing the present positions of the men in the occupational structure, and in the next section we will move to an analysis of the patterns of recruitment into their present positions. The reader is referred to Table 9-1, where the men aged 45 to 60 are classified according to their occupational status in 1965 (or last occupation in the few cases when the men are already retired). The classification used here consists of the same four occupational levels used in previous chapters. In this case, however, we have subdivided each one in order to arrive at more homogeneous categories to use in exploring the differences in the patterns discussed in this chapter. Manual workers, both lower and upper, are divided according to the size of the firm they work in. In Chapter 2, when describing the structure of the labor force in Monterrey, we remarked on the differences of employment in large as compared to small organizations, the former on the whole being technologically modern and providing higher pay, more fringe benefits, and greater stability. Unfortunately, this extremely important dimension (that, as will be argued here and in Chapter 11, may even overshadow differences in skill levels) could not be used systematically up to now in our analysis, due to the unreliability of the life-history information on size of the firm. For this chapter, we consider small firms to be those with twenty workers (employees) or less, and large firms those with more than twenty workers. In the case of the upper-manual workers, a further differentiation is introduced—we separate the self-employed. But such a distinction cannot be introduced among the lower-manual workers, because of the blurredness of the distinction between self-employed and employee in cases of very unstable employment (see discussion in Chapter 8). Among the lower-manual workers, self-employed are included among the workers in small firms.

For the nonmanual workers, the distinction presented in the table points to the two basic career lines, bureaucratic and entrepreneurial. We distinguish among the lower-nonmanual between white-collar workers and small entrepreneurs. We also separate a category of middle-white-collar and technical workers. Due to the small numbers and the blurredness of the distinction, we combine the top managers and entrepreneurs (although they will be compared among themselves later in the discussion). Finally, we keep separate the professionals, a very distinct and rather homogeneous group in Monterrey.

In Table 9-1 the ten categories are arranged in terms of income, showing the existence of a hierarchy. Thus, median annual income earned by the men as well as the first and third quartiles are given for each occupational category. The lowest status is that of unskilled workers employed in small enterprises, and it includes almost one-fourth of the sample of the older men. The median income for this group is slightly below the minimum legal wage in Monterrey at the time of the survey. Actually their income is overestimated. Annual income is calculated on the basis of weekly or monthly income, but we know that many of these men do not work the year around.

Unskilled workers in larger enterprises enjoy somewhat higher wages —less than one-fourth of them are below the minimum legal wage standard—and typically they have greater job stability. Actually, in terms of income this group is very similar to that of skilled workers in small enterprises. Its overall situation may even be better, since these men have on the average greater fringe benefits derived from being employed in larger industries. These three groups taken together—unskilled workers in small and large enterprises and skilled workers in small enterprises—form a numerically important and economically depressed group. They comprise 45 percent of the population of this age category, whose occupations provide low income, unsatisfactory in both relative and absolute terms. In two-thirds of the cases earnings from other members of the family—mostly older sons and daughters—help to lift somewhat the family income, although not a great deal, since there are many mouths to feed. Furthermore, economic help from the children implies that many youngsters are not attending school regularly but are working and contributing at least part of their income to the support of the family. This position jeopardizes their chances for the future.

The other two upper-manual groups—skilled workers in larger enterprises and self-employed craftsmen and shop owners—enjoy considerably higher levels of living. The interquartile range is much greater than for the lower three groups, and a good number of these men earn twice or more the minimum legal wage, which by no means indicates any kind of affluence, but simply an above-subsistence level of consumption. The lowest of the nonmanual groups—composed of men employed in supervisory positions and such control operations as stock clerks in warehouses and routine clerical jobs (labeled "lower white-collar" in the table)—is only moderately better off than the upper-

238 The Life Histories

manual groups. However, among them we find a considerably greater heterogeneity in earnings, indicated by a relatively high figure for the third quartile. The top two manual groups and the lower-nonmanual one represent one-third of the sample, having what might be called "middle-income" levels, enough to raise their levels of living above poverty but providing very limited purchasing power.

Small entrepreneurs, owners of enterprises employing a few workers and carrying out mainly administrative duties, as well as middle-white-collar workers (sales agents, departmental heads, technicians), are at a considerable distance, in terms of median income, from the manual groups. But the really big jump takes place only at the top of the scale. Managers and entrepreneurs, on the one hand, and professionals, on the other, are the truly elite groups. For these two groups we have not calculated median income; more than half of the respondents in each of these two categories reported an income falling into the upper, open-ended bracket of 120,000 pesos (9,600 dollars) a year or more. Probably quite a few of them earned considerably more than reported, but in most cases it would have been difficult and impractical to try to ascertain their exact income. We are referring only to income attributable to work, although for entrepreneurs this is sometimes difficult to determine. Total income is in most cases considerably higher.

A rough measure of income distribution was calculated, considering only the income the men derived from their occupations (see Table 9-1, fourth row). For the top category, that of 120,000 and over, we have conservatively estimated an annual income of 150,000. Among the lower-income groups we have not taken into account possible unemployment during the year. Even with an underestimation of the income of the upper groups and an overestimation of that of the lower groups, our calculations indicate that the men in the two top occupational categories, who represent slightly over 10 percent of the sample, receive 46 percent of the income. These figures are consistent with those reported by Puente Leyva in his study of income distribution in Monterrey, even though his group was not restricted by age as is ours. Also, he used total family rather than individual income and made certain adjustments for the income value of social services.[1] Whatever the qualifications that would be introduced to make comparable our findings and his, we be-

[1] Jesús Puente Leyva, *Distribución del ingreso en un área urbana: El caso de Monterrey, México.*

lieve that it is fair to say that, in rough terms, the top 10 percent in Monterrey receive about 50 percent of all income, while the bottom 40 percent of the population receive less than 15 percent. To state what is perfectly obvious: income distribution in Monterrey is very unequal.

The lower panel of Table 9-1 allows us to examine how the men themselves perceive their position, mainly but not exclusively in terms of levels of living. Their answers to two questions are introduced at this point. First, we asked the men how they compared their levels of living with those of the majority of the people of Mexico. Those who report themselves better off than the majority are given in Table 9-1. There is a wide range, from 14 to 67 percent, and the groups generally move progressively from low to high status. Note that the percent perceiving their position as better than the majority is higher among lower-manual workers in large firms than among workers in small firms, either unskilled or skilled. Evidently, they appraise their position in a broad context, stressing their higher pay and security, rather than appraising it strictly on occupational grounds.

The second question asks "How has life treated you?" and given in the table is the percent answering "well." The substantially higher percent for all categories is typical of the response this kind of question elicits, but there is a fairly regular progression from a low of 41 percent for the unskilled to 100 percent among the professionals. The most important break, it may be noted, comes between manual and nonmanual.

The foregoing analysis of the composition of this cohort in terms of occupational strata, their typical earnings, and their perceptions does not indicate a clear-cut division into two classes, the rich and the poor. A dichotomous stratification, or class system, at least in a pure form that lacks gradations and makes a sharp distinction between a wealthy minority and an impoverished mass, does not obtain among the older men in Monterrey. However, there *are* many men, perhaps one-half of the total, whose levels of living are not greatly above traditional subsistence levels. There are also some variations within this large mass of men, perhaps the main determinant being stability of employment rather than wages. And there *is* a wide gap between them and the top 10 percent, whose earnings typically are fifteen to twenty times greater than those of the bottom groups. What makes the difference, and it is an important one, between the situation we have described and a truly two-class system is the existence of intermediate occupational groups.

Who are these men, placed between poverty and outright privilege?

Although our classification, like any other one, is to some extent arbitrary, there are five intermediate categories ranging from skilled workers in large enterprises to middle-white-collar employees. The former constitute what might be called an "elite" within the working class: men with some skill and employed in (generally speaking) modern enterprise. Not only are their incomes above subsistence, but also they are largely unionized, have fringe benefits, and have labor contracts that protect their rights. (Of course, our definition of "large" enterprise is quite broad, and not-so-modern industries are included here too.) Lower-white-collar men have similar conditions. Stability of employment and other benefits as well as a somewhat higher salary allow them to stay out of the impoverished mass. Two self-employed groups also are included in these intermediate ranks, the distinction being made on the basis of three interrelated criteria: capital invested, labor employed, and nature of tasks. Having little capital, generally not employing wage workers, and doing mainly manual tasks, the lower group actually is hardly distinguishable from skilled workers (except for the psychologically important difference in independence). Finally, the middle-white-collar men bridge this world with that of managers and professionals.

The process of industrialization, as it has created jobs at the middle levels of the industrial hierarchy (skilled workers, supervisors) and as it has generally increased levels of income making for increased business for small enterprises (although at the same time they give place to large enterprises that challenge their economic feasibility), is the main reason for the existence of these intermediate groups. Certainly, this relationship is so when contrasted with the more dichotomized situation in Mexico before industrialization started.

But in Monterrey, at least among the older men, industrialization has not resulted in a numerical predominance of intermediate strata, nor has it seriously reduced the gap between the extremes of wealth and poverty. This is largely a matter for speculation, since we do not have reliable information about the past and we cannot predict with any accuracy how future conditions will affect the younger cohorts when they become older. It seems clear, however, that the numerical weakness of the intermediate groups and the large gap between extremes among the older Monterrey men, in spite of rapid and continued industrialization, are to be explained by the path of industrialization followed by Mexico (as well as other Latin American countries). Characteristic of this path, as discussed in Chapter 1, is the combination of a large supply of unskilled workers (growing through in-migration), a slow rate of labor absorption in the technologically modern sector, and a weakness of governmental policies that could result in income redistribution in favor of low-income groups. It is likely that when the younger cohorts reach maturity they will present a different picture, since they have had greater educational opportunities and have started their work lives with fewer of them in the lower, unskilled positions. Whether these younger cohorts will show a larger proportion in the intermediate categories and a smaller gap between extremes greatly depends on the decline in rates of migration from rural areas (predicted in our discussion in Chapter 6) and a change in governmental policies that affect the process of industrialization and the distribution of its benefits, a change in the direction stated often in 1970 preelectoral campaigns but not yet implemented.

The Older Men in 1965: Patterns of Recruitment

Each of the major occupational categories discussed in the previous section is relatively homogeneous, comprised of men who are involved in similar economic activities and whose earnings and other rewards tend to cluster within a rather narrow range. However, this situation does not imply that their origins are homogeneous. Actually, a search for an answer to the question Where do they come from? may add a new perspective to an analysis of the composition of each stratum. This is what we intend to do in this section.

Studies of occupational mobility, mainly those searching for patterns of mobility between fathers and sons, but also those that study intragenerational mobility, distinguish between *inflow* and *outflow* analysis.[2] The first type consists of an analysis of the origins or patterns of recruitment into a given class or occupational status. The latter refers to the study of the varying destinations of men originating in the same stratum. The questions posed are different, although interrelated, and the answers of course vary. Outflow analysis is particularly suited to measure rates of mobility on a comparative basis, as S. M. Miller has pointed out. Its advantage is based on the fact that the size of the different strata of origin is controlled for. An inflow analysis, on the other hand, gives a picture of the divergent origins of groups of men in each stratum at one

[2] For the distinction between inflow and outflow analysis of mobility tables, see S. M. Miller, "Comparative Social Mobility: A Trend Report and Bibliography," *Current Sociology* 9, no. 1 (1960): 8–39.

242   *The Life Histories*

point in time, thus providing a means of understanding the relative heterogeneity of any stratum—and thus being able to explain better variations in attitude and behavior.[3] The positions that men hold at a given time have a strong influence upon behavior, but the way they got to these positions is equally relevant.

Usually, analysis of intragenerational mobility proceeds by classifying men by their occupations at a given time (the time of the survey) and then looking at previous positions held. We know, however, that people differ greatly in their occupational stability, and that taking a position at one point implies mixing men who have been in it for a long time with other men who are "accidentally" in it and may soon leave. By not taking into consideration variations in stability, analysts tend to reify occupational categories and talk about the origins of "the workers" or "the managers" as if the men encountered in these positions at the time of the survey were the only "workers" or "managers" (that is, failure to consider that other men may have been in these positions before or may move to them in the future), and as if these men are in these positions to stay.[4]

Occupational positions acquire their meaning in the context of a work history and in relation to previous positions held and future expected ones. Being a skilled worker or a clerk at the beginning of one's work history or at the end of it certainly makes a difference. Clerical positions are, for young men, entry occupations from which they expect to move up, while for older men they may constitute the culmination of a blue-collar career. Unless age is introduced systematically in the analysis, the meaning of any given position is too heterogeneous to allow drawing significant conclusions.

These two assumptions—stability of positions and age-related meaning of a given position—which are so often overlooked in mobility anal-

[3] Inflow analysis, or studies of recruitment into occupations, is more common for the elite occupations (mainly, entrepreneurs). See, for instance, Lloyd Warner and James C. Abegglen, *Occupational Mobility in American Business and Industry*; and Seymour M. Lipset and Reinhard Bendix, *Social Mobility in Industrial Society*, Chap. 9. A survey of Latin American data is found in Fernando H. Cardoso, "Entrepreneurial Elites in Latin America," in *Elites in Latin America*, ed. Seymour M. Lipset and Aldo Solari.

[4] This is done, for instance, by Lipset and Bendix in their Oakland study, and by Miller and Form. See Lipset and Bendix, *Social Mobility in Industrial Society*, Chap. 6; and Delbert C. Miller and William H. Form, "Measuring Patterns of Occupational Security," *Sociometry* 10 (1947): 362–375.

yses, are met when we analyze the patterns of recruitment among the older men in Monterrey. These men have completed the main events that we have focused upon in this book. Their occupational, migratory, and family statuses in most cases will not change, except for retirement and death. In occupational terms, job changes do take place after age 45, but few involve status mobility. Many men, mainly at the bottom of the hierarchy, have very unstable jobs, but their statuses are stable, since they circulate in jobs of similar pay and prestige. As for residence, few men over 45 migrate; only a handful of men arrive in the city after that age, and the Cedral survey indicates that few men go back there after age 45. Thus, the composition of this group is bound to be quite stable, with few in-migrants being added and few out-migrants being subtracted. Finally, although these men can expect to live many more years and although they will be confronted with important changes in their families, the two events upon which we have focused our analysis of family formation (marriage and procreation) are for all practical purposes in the past. Not only are the men's positions stable, but also one is tempted to call them "final."

Our approach to the study of patterns of recruitment will be broad, since we do not restrict it to occupational origins, but include also residential and educational origins. Our objective is to trace the profiles of the men's biographies, starting with homogeneous groups in the present, the men who share similar "final" destinations. We will look first at the residential origins of the men. In Table 9-2 we present the proportion of men whose communities of origin and of residence at ages 25 and 35 were respectively Monterrey and rural places. In all occupational categories there is a high proportion of migrants, ranging from about one-half to almost 80 percent. It is clear that lower occupational status in 1965 is associated with a greater proportion of migrants and, among them, with a greater proportion of men brought up in rural communities. Groups higher in the hierarchy show an early arrival in the city or an early move out of rural areas. Only among the lower-manual groups is there a significant number of men still living in rural areas at age 35. In other words, a rural origin is not necessarily associated with low adult status, but a rural place of residence during adulthood (ages 25 and 35) is encountered only among men who find a place at the bottom of the hierarchy when they finally get to the city. This pattern is consistent with the findings reported in Chapter 8, namely, the occupational handicap of late arrivals to the city.

TABLE 9-2. Residential Origins and Education, by Occupational Position in 1965, Men Aged 45–60 (In Percent)

	Lower Manual		Upper Manual			Nonmanual				
	In Small Firm	In Large Firm	In Small Firm	In Large Firm	Self-employed	Lower White Collar	Small Entrepreneur	Middle White Collar	Manager, Entrepreneur	Profes-sional
Residence										
Percent in Monterrey										
Community of origin	21	40	46	30	38	43	29	51	48	55
Age 25	34	52	73	63	55	71	67	76	67	59
Age 35	50	67	81	81	70	83	79	76	83	82
Percent in rural localities										
Community of origin	46	47	27	37	41	31	38	18	17	5
Age 25	37	34	14	14	22	6	21	9	7	5
Age 35	29	19	3	5	15	9	13	0	0	5
Education										
None	42	33	19	15	4	0	0	0	0	0
Incomplete *primaria*	45	45	59	46	48	34	38	11	2	0
Complete *primaria*	11	17	14	27	38	40	50	18	10	0
Middle	3	5	9	13	11	20	13	69	69	0
University	0	0	0	0	0	6	0	2	19	100
Total	101 (151)	100 (91)	101 (37)	101 (105)	101 (74)	100 (35)	101 (24)	100 (45)	100 (42)	100 (22)

Some comparisons between specific groups are of interest here, since the relationship between migratory status and position in 1965 is not linear. Lower-manual workers in large industry, as compared to those in small industry, show a greater proportion of men raised in Monterrey or arriving there rather early in life. However, a comparable difference does not show up among the upper-manual groups. The proportion of rural migrants and late arrivals is higher among self-employed upper manuals and small entrepreneurs than among skilled and lower-white-collar workers. This difference shows that a rural origin is not necessarily a handicap if it allows the accumulation of some capital that can be transferred to the city. Among professionals we find a significant number of men who were not in Monterrey at age 25, a greater proportion than among any other nonmanual group. But migration for these men has a different meaning than for others. Many professionals come from other cities and are attracted to Monterrey rather late in their lives, but their experience before coming to Monterrey does not differ from that of professionals already living there. Others, born in Monterrey, leave the city for some time, only to return to it at a later date. When they were students in professional schools, the National University in Mexico City was the logical place to be rather than the local university in Monterrey. Only recently do we find a majority of professionals in the city being trained here. Thus, as we had an opportunity to discuss in Chapter 6, many professionals engage in return migration to Monterrey.

The relationship between occupational status and educational attainment is more clear and linear than that with residential origins. As we move upward in the scale we find a decreasing proportion of men who have not completed *primaria*, and the differences are of considerable magnitude. Lower-manual workers in large industries have the same percentage as upper-manual workers in small industry. Among the upper-manual categories we find a gradation in terms of education following that of median income. This trend might seem a bit surprising, since it could have been predicted that the self-employed would have lower levels of education than the skilled workers in large firms. Formal training is a requirement for employment in large industry but not for self-employment. Seemingly, for the older men entrance into large industry was not yet very restricted, but it's possible that the history of the younger cohorts will show a pronounced difference in education between those in large industries and the self-employed, in favor of the former.

Two of the five nonmanual groups still have a significant proportion of men with low levels of education: lower-white-collar men and small entrepreneurs. Most of the former, as we will see, have had a manual work history. They achieved their nonmanual statuses late in their lives by moving up from the blue-collar ranks. Thus, it is not surprising that many of them have little formal education. Increasingly, some of the positions included in this category are changing in nature and are being filled by younger men with a secondary education and limited or no blue-collar experience. But these younger, more educated men were scarce until recently, thus allowing for the mobility into the nonmanual ranks of older, experienced men. Small entrepreneurs, on the other hand, do not differ greatly from self-employed skilled workers in education, as was also the case with their residential origins. Actually, the men we call small entrepreneurs are the successful self-employed men, who were able to expand their operations, to increase their capital investment, and to hire wage workers. Their success need not be linked to higher formal training, but rather to other factors not analyzed here. We are faced with two categories showing similar patterns of recruitment. The men have similar origins, but are presently located in different strata.

We can now move on to discuss the occupational experience of our men. In this part, we will concentrate on a comparison between occupational positions held at ages 15, 25, 35 and at the time of the survey. This analysis, based on a comparison between isolated points in time, differs from what was done in Chapters 5 and 8, where the focus was on sequences of occupations and occupational moves. Much may have happened in the years between the moments considered here. Practically all manual workers started their work lives in low-status occupations, either as unskilled nonfarm or farm (see Table 9-3). There is, however, an important difference between lower- and upper-manual groups in the occupational distribution at age 15: while among the former about half had farm occupations, only one-fourth did so among the latter. Moreover, the decline in the proportion of men employed in farm jobs is rather slow among presently unskilled workers: by age 35 over one-third of unskilled workers in small industry and one-fourth of unskilled workers in large industry were still in agriculture. A majority among the skilled workers started in unskilled nonfarm occupations, moving later on to skilled ones. More than 60 percent were already skilled workers by age 35.

TABLE 9-3. Occupational Origins of Manual Workers at Three Ages, by Occupational Position in 1965, Men Aged 45–60 (In Percent)

	Occupational Position in 1965														
	Lower Manual						Upper Manual								
	In Small Firm at Age			In Large Firm at Age			In Small Firm at Age			In Large Firm at Age			Self-employed at Age		
Occupational Position	15a	25	35	15a	25	35	15a	25	35	15a	25	35	15a	25	35
Farm	51	40	36	46	37	25	24	8	5	27	16	6	26	23	8
Lower manual	48	51	57	53	53	61	75	43	22	64	47	34	65	27	19
Upper manual	1	7	7	1	8	10	0	49	70	8	33	59	7	47	64
Nonmanual	0	1	1	0	1	4	0	0	3	1	4	1	3	3	9
Total	100	99	101	100	99	100	99	100	100	100	100	100	101	100	100
	(151)			(91)			(37)			(105)			(74)		

a Occupation at age 15 or, if not in labor force, first occupation.

Very few differences are observed in the patterns of occupational recruitment between the two groups of unskilled workers, with only a
somewhat higher percentage beginning and staying in farm jobs among
those who ended up as unskilled workers in small enterprises. A minority within the two unskilled groups experienced downward mobility,
that is, had skilled or nonmanual occupations earlier in their work lives.
Eight percent of those in small industry and 14 percent in large industry experienced downward mobility between age 35 and the present.

The differences between the three groups of skilled workers are
somewhat puzzling. In the first place, we find a greater proportion of
men with farm occupations at age 25 among self-employed and large-
industry skilled workers than among those employed in small industry,
a pattern for which we have no clear explanation. In the second place,
comparing skilled workers in small and large industry, we find that
among the former a larger percentage achieved skilled status at ages
25 and 35. This finding might seem unexpected, since one could argue
that men in large firms, who tend to follow career lines and have a long-
term commitment to a plant, should have moved up earlier than the
men with more unstable and erratic work lives who end up in small
firms. However, the typical skilled worker in large firms, among the
older men, spent more time in the unskilled ranks, but probably within
a large firm, than the typical skilled worker in small firms, who moved
up earlier in the hierarchy but probably by remaining in similar types
of small enterprises. In other words, there is relatively little mobility
between small and large firms. Probably the barrier between industries
is as strong as the barrier between skill lines. Finally, very few skilled
men had experienced downward mobility (from nonmanual ranks),
while the large majority of them have moved up, when one compares
their occupations at age 15, or even age 25, with their present ones.

The data regarding occupational mobility of nonmanual workers are
presented in Table 9-4. Almost none of these men, in any occupational
category, have had farm experience, and the few who did left such
work at young ages. We find three predominant types among nonmanual men. First, the men in low-white-collar occupations (mainly supervisory and control tasks) and owners of small shops (small entrepreneurs)
largely began their work lives in low-status nonfarm occupations.
Sixty-nine percent of the lower-white-collar workers and 75 percent of the small entrepreneurs had unskilled jobs at age 15. Moreover,
they tended to move up within the manual ranks, starting as unskilled

TABLE 9-4. Occupational Origins of Nonmanual Workers, by Occupational Position in 1965, Men Aged 45–60 (In Percent)

	Lower White Collar			Small Entrepreneur			Middle White Collar			Manager, Entrepreneur			Professional		
	at Age			at Age			at Age			at Age			at Age		
Occupational Origin	15a	25	35	15a	25	35	15a	25	35	15a	25	35	15a	25	35
Farm	9	6	0	13	4	0	4	4	0	2	2	0	0	0	0
Lower manual	69	43	14	75	29	13	40	7	0	31	0	2	5	0	0
Upper manual	3	23	29	4	34	38	11	8	4	9	7	0	5	0	0
Lower white collar	11	17	40	8	17	4	33	38	27	33	29	7	14	9	0
Small entrepreneurs	0	3	9	0	13	33	0	2	7	0	7	10	0	0	0
Middle white collar	3	9	6	0	4	13	11	36	56	5	29	31	9	9	0
Manager, entrepreneur	0	0	3	0	0	0	0	4	7	2	19	48	0	0	0
Professional	0	0	0	0	0	0	0	0	0	0	7	2	5	82	100
Not in labor force	6	0	0	0	0	0	0	0	0	17	0	0	63	0	0
Total	101	101 (35)	101	100	101 (24)	101	99	99 (45)	101	99	100 (42)	100	101	100 (22)	100

a Occupation at age 15 or, if not in labor force, first occupation.

workers, changing by ages 25 and 35 to skilled positions, with many of them arriving at nonmanual jobs rather late in their lives: at age 35 only a modest percentage of them are to be found in their "final" positions (40 percent among lower-white-collar workers and 33 percent among small entrepreneurs had the same occupational position at age 35 and at present). Few men became lower-white-collar workers or small entrepreneurs by starting in nonmanual occupations. Thus, the men in the lower ranks of the nonmanual occupations are characterized, first, by high rates of upward mobility into their present positions and, second, by a comparatively high rate of mobility rather late in their work lives.

The second type—sales agents, technicians, and other middle-white-collar men, as well as managers and entrepreneurs—also includes a substantial number of men who started as manual workers (51 and 40 percent for the two categories included). But, unlike those in the lower-nonmanual occupations, few remained there for a long period of time, and almost none were to be found there by age 25. These men did not move from unskilled manual positions into skilled ones and from there to nonmanual jobs, but rather jumped into nonmanual occupations relatively soon. The men with manual origins had such jobs predominantly as trial ones, and in many cases part-time occupations, held when they were young and are not indicative of their later positions. There is considerable mobility late in life (after age 35) but less than in the lower-nonmanual occupations: 56 percent of middle-white-collar men and 48 percent of managers had the same job at age 35 as at the present. A good number of the rest were probably in career settings that led to their present positions: middle-white-collar workers as lower-white-collar workers (27 percent), and managers and entrepreneurs as middle-white-collar workers (31 percent) and small entrepreneurs (10 percent).

Finally, professionals differ from all others because the great majority of them are recruited directly into professions; that is, they started their work lives in professional jobs. Most professionals remain out of the labor force until comparatively late in their lives, but by age 25 eight of every ten already are professionals.

A contrast between managers and entrepreneurs, on the one hand, and professionals, on the other, is of interest, since they have similar levels of income and are much higher than the rest of the population.

In strictly economic as well as social terms they belong in the same class. However, their histories are rather divergent. For one thing, professionals do not really have occupational histories in a strict sense, since they entered the labor force quite late and from the beginning had mostly professional occupations. Of course, considerable job mobility *within* the professions can have taken place. Typical moves include picking up more prestigious or better-paying jobs, enlarging the scope of their activities, or simply taking on more jobs. Many professionals in 1965 had several different "jobs" they had accumulated over time. On the other hand, most managers and entrepreneurs do have an occupational history showing a clear advancement over time. There are only a few entrepreneurs who inherited big enterprises and who were the top decision makers in them during their entire work lives. A second clear difference between professionals and managers is that all of the former had university education, while only 17 percent of the managers and entrepreneurs got that far. Most of the latter, 52 percent, had only secondary, commercial, or preparatory education. Thus, while professionals remained in school until their early twenties, managers of that age were already in the labor force.

These contrasts indicate two alternative paths leading to top positions in the occupational structure—one via educational attainment, the other within the occupational sphere. Of course these paths are not mutually exclusive, since managers and entrepreneurs have, relatively speaking, high levels of educational attainment that allowed them to climb more rapidly or more successfully the occupational ladder than, say, lower-white-collar men or small entrepreneurs. Probably, among the younger cohorts in Monterrey, as educational levels increase, bureaucratic careers will demand higher initial levels of formal education, and managers will have university degrees, as do the professionals.

One might be tempted to attach the label of "self-made man" to many managers and entrepreneurs who started as manual or lower-nonmanual workers. Actually, many of them come from relatively high family origins, and this beginning helped them in climbing to their present positions. In any case, this climbing assumes different forms. Two basic types, that of "managers" and that of "entrepreneurs," can be distinguished, although we have placed these men together due to their small numbers. The first type is represented by men working their way up within bureaucratic settings leading to high managerial positions, as in the case of the bank manager described in Chapter 8, who climbed from office boy to be the top official of the Monterrey branch of a bank. The entrepreneurial route is best exemplified by men who expand an enterprise they own, often jointly with other members of their families. One man, for instance, reported that his father owned a small store that he and his brothers continued and expanded rapidly. In 1965 the enterprise was the largest chain of supermarkets in Monterrey, and it is still owned by the respondent and his brothers. An unusual number of privately owned enterprises in Monterrey, excepting foreign companies, are controlled by family groups—whatever the legal form of control.

Although there are some professionals who have climbed considerably in relation to their fathers, they constitute a clear minority. This situation is explained by the fact that, when these men went to professional school several decades ago, the secondary and university systems were truly "elitist" in composition. Less than 1 percent of the adult male population until recently had attended a university in Mexico. Professionals in general tend to come from higher backgrounds than managers and entrepreneurs, at least among the older men we are considering. Their small numbers, however, do not allow us to state this difference in more precise terms. As we indicated above, the educational gap between professionals and managers will tend to decrease with wider access to education and with higher educational requirements for managerial jobs. Also, greater access to the universities will probably mean that the professionals will become a more heterogeneous group in terms of social origins and that a professional degree will not be any longer a sufficient condition for an elite status.

The Older Men's Offspring: Completed Family Size

Up to now we have been dealing with the different occupational positions of the older men and the patterns of recruitment into them. The various groups differ considerably in their occupations and income in 1965 and in their residential, educational, and occupational histories leading to their present positions. After exploring all these differences, we can now shift our focus of attention and ask how these diverse experiences manifest themselves in the area of family behavior. We will deal with fertility in this section and with the expectations and achievements of the sons in the next.

Much has been written about patterns of differential fertility according to occupational status, rural-urban origin, education, and so forth.[5] In Chapter 7 we had occasion to comment upon some aspects of family structure in Monterrey, pointing out that most couples have children almost immediately after marriage and that few of them appear to practice any form of birth control during the first few years of marriage. What about their subsequent behavior? Are there any differences in fertility after years of diverse experiences in the labor force and in residential histories? Although the older men in our sample have not completed their reproductive period, technically speaking, for all practical purposes we may consider the number of children they have had up to the time of the interview as completed family size. The children added are few and the overall patterns of differences between groups— a subject that will interest us especially—are not affected in any significant fashion. The average number of children ever born for the men aged 45 to 60, including those few men who never had any children, is 5.7, while the corresponding number at age 45 was 5.2, indicating that only a small number of children were born after that age.

The mean number of children born live as of 1965 as well as the number of children surviving up to that year, for each of the occupational groups we have used in the previous sections of this chapter, are presented in Table 9-5. The average for the whole group, 5.7, is high indeed, whatever the standard of comparison one might use to evaluate it. But the most striking feature of Table 9-5 is the lack of differentials between occupational groups in 1965: only among the top three occupational groups do we find a significantly lower family size. However, the middle-white-collar workers, managers and entrepreneurs, and professionals constitute only 17 percent of the sample of older men. Among the other seven occupational positions, differences are small and do not follow any clear pattern associated with occupational status. The unskilled groups have only slightly greater numbers than the skilled or lower-nonmanual positions.

The three top occupational groups, besides having fewer children born live, share another important characteristic. Few of the men in

---

[5] Carmen Miró and Walter Mertens, "Influences Affecting Fertility in Urban and Rural Latin America," *Milbank Memorial Fund Quarterly* 46, no. 3, pt. 2 (July 1968): 89–117. For Mexico see Centro de Estudios Económicos y Demográficos, *Dinámica de la población de México,* Chap. III.

these groups have experienced the death of children, as is evidenced by the number of children alive in 1965 being very close to the number of children born. In contrast, the other groups, and mainly the manual workers, show high rates of mortality, having lost on the average about one child. This is a crude but impressive demonstration of the high rate of mortality predominant in Mexico until recently, even in relatively more developed regions, as well as a clear demonstration of socioeconomic differences in mortality rates.[6] The result of these differences is to balance out to some extent those produced by differential fertility, since a group placed high in the hierarchy, like managers and entrepreneurs, has at the end only .4 fewer living children than unskilled workers in small industry. It is possible that among the younger cohorts completed fertility will be somewhat lower, but mortality also will be lower, and thus the final number of children alive at a similar age will not differ greatly from that shown by men currently 45 to 60 years of age.

Father's Expectations and Son's Educational Achievement

The succession of generations provides a basis for temporal continuity in the lives of men. Even when our men are at the end of their work lives, they undoubtedly have an orientation toward the future, basically centered in their children's lives. The relationship between generations has a double significance in this context. First, the achievements of children influence their fathers' perceptions and evaluations of their own positions. Thus, for instance, the extent to which the poorer men are satisfied with their present condition in Monterrey or the extent to which they perceive their migration from a rural community to the city as positive are largely colored by how they perceive their children's opportunities, mainly in regard to education. Second, the parents' position influences the level of achievement of their offspring. In Chapter 4 we explored the influence of the family of origin on the level of education of the respondents. Here we can expand and deepen that discussion, because we asked the men information about their children, mainly their educational and occupational status, that can be correlated with the men's positions and histories. Analytical depth can be achieved, thanks to the study conducted by Mir, who supplemented the Monte-

---

[6] For an analysis of trends in mortality rates in Mexico see Centro de Estudios Económicos y Demográficos, *Dinámica de la población de México*, Chap. III.

TABLE 9-5. Children Born Live to Men by Age 45 and in 1965, Children Surviving in 1965, by Occupational Position, Men Aged 45–60

Mean Number of Children	Lower Manual		Occupational Position in 1965 — Upper Manual			Nonmanual				
	In Small Firm	In Large Firm	In Small Firm	In Large Firm	Self-employed	Lower White Collar	Small Entrepreneur	Middle White Collar	Manager, Entrepreneur	Professional
Born live by 1965	5.9	5.9	5.5	5.6	5.4	5.0	5.5	3.8	4.4	3.6
Living in 1965	4.6	4.9	4.4	5.1	4.9	4.3	4.8	3.5	4.2	3.6

TABLE 9-6. Oldest Son's Present Position and Education, by Occupational Positions of the Father in 1965 (In Percent)

	Lower Manual		Occupational Position in 1965 — Upper Manual			Nonmanual				
	In Small Firm	In Large Firm	In Small Firm	In Large Firm	Self-employed	Lower White Collar	Small Entrepreneur	Middle White Collar	Manager, Entrepreneur	Professional
Position of oldest son										
Works	81	82	88	68	64	61	63	62	47	13
Studies	7	5	8	17	22	35	16	28	50	80
Both	3	8	0	10	5	4	11	3	0	0
Other	9	5	4	5	9	0	11	7	3	7
Total	100 (97)	100 (58)	100 (23)	100 (70)	100 (59)	100 (23)	101 (19)	100 (30)	100 (30)	100 (15)
Highest education										
Less than *primaria* completed	47	28	17	11	10	4	5	7	0	7
Primaria completed	29	28	39	23	25	4	11	13	0	0
Post-*primaria*	23	44	43	65	64	92	84	80	100	92
Total	99 (97)	100 (58)	99 (23)	99 (70)	99 (59)	100 (23)	100 (19)	100 (30)	100 (30)	99 (15)

rrey survey by interviewing twenty upwardly mobile and twenty non-mobile sons of working-class men originally selected in the Monterrey sample.[7] Mir's study focused on the impact of family, school, and neighborhood on the socialization process and, mainly, the internalization of high educational expectations among the youngsters. In this section we will review some of his findings so as to provide a broader picture of the older men's expectations and the relationship between their present position and their children's achievements.

Two-thirds of the men aged 45 to 60 have one or more sons aged 15 and over, an age at which we are already able to establish with some approximation what their adult status will be. Restricting ourselves to the oldest sons, we found that about two-thirds of them are already out of school and in the labor force. However, this is the first stage at which differences according to the father's status are evident. The data presented in Table 9-6 indicate clearly that the higher the men's occupational status, the larger the proportion of sons still in school. Among lower-manual men, for instance, four of five sons already are in the labor force, while only some 5 percent are still in school. Almost the reverse situation characterizes sons of professionals, who, by and large, are still in school after age 15. The three lower groups have similar distributions, and they differ considerably from the five intermediate categories. The main differences in the proportion of sons in the labor force are consistent with the differentiation we made in terms of income: the three bottom groups vs. the five intermediate ones.

More interesting than the present activities of the son—since differences in age of the sons could affect the proportion that is still studying —is their educational achievement. The second panel of the table presents the highest level of education attained by the oldest son, also classified by occupation of the father. Since many of the sons still are in school, we do not have "completed education" for them. However, all those in school are presently pursuing post-*primaria* studies, so the percentage in the highest category, post-*primaria* education, will not change. The differences again are extreme, ranging from less than one-fourth of sons with post-*primaria* education among unskilled workers in small firms to 100 percent for sons of managers and entrepreneurs. Although the numbers involved are relatively small, some differences

[7] Adolfo Mir-Araujo, "Movilidad social, educación y grupos de referencia en Monterrey, México: Un estudio sociológico," M.A. Thesis, University of Texas, 1966.

between groups are relevant. Almost half of the sons of unskilled workers in small firms did not complete *primaria*. This figure contrasts sharply with the percent in the other bottom occupational groups and is probably the result of the larger number in this group of rural migrants
arriving late in the city. The little education their sons received was
probably attained in rural areas prior to their migration to the city. In
the other manual categories, about half of the sons attained post-*primaria* education. This is quite an accomplishment, especially if we consider that only a very small minority of the men (ranging from 5 to 13
percent) have gone beyond *primaria*. Undoubtedly much educational
mobility is taking place between our manual respondents and their sons.
To some extent, this educational mobility will be necessary simply to
maintain the father's status, since educational requirements for the
occupational positions the men now hold will be considerably higher
for their children. A post-*primaria* education will no longer guarantee
a nonmanual job.

The largest differences in post-*primaria* education occur between the
sons of men in the three lowest categories and the skilled workers in
large firms and the self-employed, and between the latter and the nonmanual categories. In both cases, the groups that have provided better
education for their children have had occupational histories with considerable upward mobility, and their sons' better education reflects
more their present positions than their origins. This situation is especially marked for the two lower-nonmanual categories. Both the lower-
white-collar workers and the small entrepreneurs have had largely
manual occupational histories, and very few of them (20 and 13 percent) have had post-*primaria* education. Yet, practically all their children have gone beyond *primaria*. The fact that these two categories do
not differ from the other nonmanual ones is misleading. The differences
in their sons' education will undoubtedly show up at higher levels
(middle vs. university education), a difference that, as explained above,
cannot be presented here.

The impressive differences in educational attainment of the sons according to the respondents' occupation show, once more, the inequality
in educational opportunities and the large influence of parents' economic status on educational attainment. This subject, discussed in Chapter 4 in relation to the educational attainment of the respondents and
their parents' characteristics, will be taken up again in the next chapter,
where we will evaluate statistically the influence of parental status

upon sons' education in two pairs of generations—respondents and their parents, and respondents and their sons. Within a given economic stratum, there are variations in educational attainment of the sons. These variations partially reflect the effects of other variables, namely the men's perceptions of the value of education for their children and their expectations as to what kind of life their children will live in comparison to their own.[8] We now turn to analyze these issues.

Most of the older men, whatever their present status, believe their children will be able to live better than they do. The answers to a very general question, "Do you think your oldest son could have a much better life than your present one, somewhat better, about the same, or worse?" indicate this optimism very clearly. Less than 15 percent of the older men thought their sons would live about the same or worse than they did, with only slight variations according to their present status. The most optimistic men seem to be those in the middle: upper manual and lower nonmanual. Only among managers and professionals do many believe that their sons will live "about the same" as they did, reflecting their awareness that they already are at the top and that there isn't much above them for their offspring to aspire to.

When asked the reason for their optimism, or why their sons will be able to have a better life than the one the respondents are now living, over 60 percent indicated that education or training is the key, with the second most common answer being the progress of society in general. Since there is so much educational upward mobility, with the great majority of the sons achieving a better education than their parents, it is evident that there is some basis for their optimism. The men need not necessarily be aware, however, that, when the levels of education increase, the educational requirements increase as well, and therefore the relative value of, say, a *primaria* school certificate actually decreases.

Education is the item most frequently chosen by the respondents among the qualities or characteristics a young man should have in order to get ahead in life. Furthermore, most men agree that in order to move up a youngster must study a great deal and that dropping out of school in order to start working early, even if it is to help the family, is bad strategy. But one might very well question the value of these and similar questions used in sample surveys, since almost everyone replies

[8] For parental expectations of children's education and their link to mobility aspirations, see Melvin M. Tumin and Arnold S. Feldman, *Social Class and Social Change in Puerto Rico.*

affirmatively when asked about the importance of education. The very word has an aura of magic, and nobody is against education anymore than they are against motherhood or good health.

The problem, then, is not primarily one of finding out the men's perception of the value of education in general terms, or even the place it occupies in the men's scale of values. What we need to know is *how much* education the men believe is desirable and reasonable for their children to attain, and the kind and amount of sacrifices they are willing to make in order for their children to attain these goals.

Mir's intensive study of twenty mobile and twenty nonmobile sons of working-class men in Monterrey is relevant in this respect. The word *education* has a very different meaning for the father of the nonmobile boy than for the father of the mobile one. Both would say that education is important but the mobility-oriented father has higher expectations and tries to create the conditions for these expectations to be "natural" for his son. He has instilled in his son not only the mobility aspirations but also the idea that school work is for his own benefit, a means that will allow the son a better life as an adult. School is not perceived as an imposed obligation. For the nonmobile son, "education means learning to read and write, and at most finishing *primaria*. Finishing *primaria* appears to be more important as a requirement than as a body of knowledge to be applied to the performance of an occupation ... The non-mobile boy, however, has learned that his principal obligation is not to miss school, and he knows that this is the principal demand of his father."[9] In other words, there is a great difference in the goal (how much education), the perception of the functional value of education, and the specific meaning of the requirement "to go to school" made by the parents of mobile and nonmobile sons.

That upward educational mobility of sons was preceded by high parental expectations is confirmed by the fact that in most cases the majority of siblings of the boys examined followed the same pattern—either they were upwardly mobile or nonmobile. Furthermore, Mir demonstrates that the difference in family environment between the two types is pervasive. The boy's life is marked by such a strong continuity "that it is impossible to fix a point at which one could say that their careers took a decisive turn."[10] Based on their responses, the up-

9 Mir, *Movilidad social*, p. 121.
10 Ibid., p. 115.

wardly mobile seem always to have taken it for granted, as did their parents, that they would follow a prolonged educational training and end up in nonmanual occupations. They also took for granted that their parents would want to make financial sacrifices for their education. This attitude is in contrast to the usual situation of working-class homes, where it is assumed that the children, whenever they are old enough, will help their parents, even at the risk of jeopardizing their own work careers.

The question then becomes: How was such an environment made possible in a working-class home? Where did the parents pick up the "right" ways to stimulate their sons to academic achievement? There seems to be no completely satisfactory explanation, but one factor seems relevant: in nearly all cases of upwardly mobile sons, the father in one way or another had established relationships with persons of considerably higher socioeconomic status, and doubtless this association provided a source of mobility orientations to be passed on to his sons.

In summary, Mir's study shows that, beyond the direct effect of parents on their children's educational chances through their economic support (particularly for education beyond *primaria*), the parents create an environment that stresses certain values and expectations.[11] These expectations are then translated into specific, although often rather subtle, forms of behavior that either foster or inhibit their children's orientation toward formal education. Families within a given socioeconomic stratum vary in these values and expectations, and in some cases they can even overcome economic handicaps in order to fulfill their expectations placed in their offspring.

Evaluations across Time: Generations, Cohorts, and Life Cycles

Looking back at our analysis of the older men in Monterrey within the context of Part Two of this book, the reader will notice that in our linking of societal transformation (economic development) to changes in the men's lives we have made repeated use of the concepts of "generation," "cohort," and "life cycle." In Chapter 4, we began with an analysis of the influence of one generation upon the next, trying to determine the form and degree to which parents influence their sons' (i.e., re-

[11] These results are similar to the ones reported in Joseph A. Kahl's "Educational and Occupational Aspirations of 'Common Man' Boys," *Harvard Educational Review* 23 (1953): 186–203.

spondents') educational achievement. Since then we have concentrated pretty much upon cohorts and the life cycle, asking what happens as a group of men born at approximately the same time experiences the process of aging, physically and socially. Migratory moves, occupational changes, family formation—all were presented wherever possible within the context of the life cycle. Then to interpret change we often compared various birth cohorts, since their known placement in time provided an indication of the relationship between a changing social environment and the lives of the men. Finally, in this chapter, while taking the oldest of the Monterrey cohorts, we were able to go back to a generational framework by taking up the third generation, made up of the older men's sons.

Perhaps the greatest utility of the generational framework lies in the fact that, when men are asked to appraise their position in life, they not only do so in terms of what has happened to themselves in the course of their lives, but they also compare their lives with those of their parents and with their expectations for their children. In other words, men can and do make judgments concerning how well they have done in comparison with other men in their age cohort, but only rarely do they make comparative judgments of the past or the future within a cohort framework. Psychologically, generations count for more than do cohorts, since it is one's father rather than older men in general and one's son rather than all young men that provide the basic frame of reference.

To understand the basis of men's appraisal of their lives, therefore, it is useful to provide a comparison of where the respondents, their fathers, and their older sons stand with respect to one, but a most important, status attribute: education. The distribution by educational level of all men in the sample who have one or more sons aged 15 or over, as well as their fathers' and sons' levels is presented in Table 9-7.

The differences are so striking that they require very little comment. Note only that, while there is an important jump in educational attainment from the father's to the respondent's generation, there is an even greater one between the respondent's and his son's. In the large majority of the cases, this difference meant intergenerational educational mobility, both between fathers and respondents and between respondents and their sons. Typically, the respondents had functionally illiterate fathers who did not finish *primaria*, while almost one-half of the respondents' sons had gone beyond completed *primaria*.

TABLE 9-7. Educational Attainments of Three Generations

Educational Level	Respondents' Fathers	Respondents	Respondents' Sons
None	31	19	3
Primaria incomplete	43	45	23
Primaria complete	19	21	24
Middle and higher levels	8	15	49
Total	101	100	99
	(520)	(520)	(1,052)

NOTE: Respondents were men with one or more sons 15 and over (90 percent of whom are 45 to 60 years of age in 1965).

It is little wonder, therefore, that, even when one considers the rather large proportion of older men with low occupational status, the highly unequal income distribution in Monterrey, which means that many men are in continual financial difficulties, and the unequal access to middle and higher educational facilities that their sons must face—even after taking these factors into account—a substantial proportion of the older men express a rather optimistic appraisal of their lives. They reflect, from an individual standpoint, the changes that have taken place in Mexico since the revolution.

PART THREE
A BROADER PERSPECTIVE

10. The Process of Stratification

We have now completed the analysis of the men's lives, starting with the early stages of family background and educational attainment, moving through their entry into the labor force, their occupational histories and migratory experiences, the process of family formation, and ending with a consideration of the last stages of their life cycles and the first stage of their sons'. We now want to examine this whole sequence of events once more in a somewhat more rigorous statistical fashion, focusing our attention on one aspect, albeit a very important one, of the men's lives: their placement in the stratified or hierarchical order of society.

Social stratification refers to the arrangement of positions occupied by persons of a society in such a way that members of one stratum enjoy similar advantages and disadvantages in the distribution of goods, services, and other scarce items. Typically they have better access to the distributive process than the members of lower strata, but lesser access than those occupying a higher stratum. In other words, a stratification approach looks for the sources and forms of inequalities associated with the positions or statuses occupied by people in the society.

Seldom, if ever, are people fixed to given positions in the stratification system. But there is some continuity, and large leaps either up or down the hierarchy are more the exception than the rule. We can study the occupancy of stratified positions as a process taking place in time, whereby a temporal sequence is established and the events in this sequence are linked in a causal way. Thus, the circumstances of birth affect to some degree—and to what degree is something we will want to know—the life chances of the men, including the statuses they will occupy later in their lives. The status attained at one stage in a man's life affects his subsequent life chances and statuses. This sequence can be extended to include the man's offspring, thus showing the continuity of stratified inequality through generations.

This approach to the study of the temporal and causal sequence of occupancy of stratified positions is based on the concept of the process of stratification.[1] The hierarchical, or invidious, classification of people in society is considered from a temporal perspective: how does inequality at prior points in men's lives affect inequality at later stages in their development? Here, as in most areas of social stratification, we will find that the family as the unit of analysis has an advantage over the individual: unequal chances in the men's lifetimes are linked to the position of their families of orientation at birth and as they grew up.[2] Later, the great majority of them will form their own families, and in turn what they have achieved will influence the life chances of their offspring. Thus, it will not be enough to take into account the hierarchical dimension only in the men's life cycles. We will consider the positions of three generations: the men's parents, the men themselves, and their male offspring.[3]

It is clear that the process of stratification refers to a continuous series of events. However, some arbitrary points in time can be selected for analysis, so that a causal sequence from one to the other can be estab-

[1] The notion of the process of stratification, closely related to but different from the older one of social mobility, is suggested by Peter M. Blau and Otis D. Duncan (*The American Occupational Structure*, p. 163). Their work is the most sophisticated national study of the determinants of occupational achievement. A somewhat outdated but excellent bibliography of studies of social mobility is found in S. M. Miller, "Comparative Social Mobility: A Trend Report and Bibliography," *Current Sociology* 9, no. 1 (1960): 8–39.

[2] The family as the logical unit for the study of social stratification and mobility has long been emphasized, mainly by functionalist sociologists. See for instance Kurt B. Mayer and Walter Buckley, *Class and Society*.

[3] Most studies of intergenerational mobility take only two generations. Other attempts at measuring three-generational processes are Robert W. Hodge, "Occupational Mobility as a Probability Process," *Demography* 3, no. 1 (1966): 19–34; N. V. Sovani and K. Pradhan, "Occupational Mobility in Poona between Three Generations," *Indian Economic Review* 2, no. 4 (August 1955): 23–36; and David V. Glass, ed., *Social Mobility in Britain*.

lished. At each of these points some dimensions or positions in the stratification system are more relevant than others. What are the points in time, which dimensions are to be taken, and what are the means by which we can evaluate the forms and degrees of influence from one stage to another? All these questions must be addressed.

We will begin with the conditions at birth, that is, the placement of the family of orientation in the stratification system. Three variables will be used to measure different dimensions of socioeconomic status of the family of orientation: father's education and occupation, and mother's education. As explained in Chapter 4, the high intercorrelation between these variables should not obscure the fact that they are different theoretically. Size of community of origin, birth cohort, number of siblings, and age at father's death are not involved in the stratification process, but, nevertheless, they may affect the man's level of attainment (mainly educational), so they will be introduced in the analysis. The next stage, for which we want to measure the effects of the family of orientation and other variables, is completed education. Of course, this point occurs at very different ages for the Monterrey men, since some stay in school until their mid-twenties, while others drop out at age 7 or 8, or never attend.

From educational attainment we will move to the occupational histories of the men. First, we will take the status of the first job and determine the effects of previous events upon it. Then the men's occupational status will be measured every ten years. Given their differences in age, the Monterrey men vary considerably in the length of their work lives. Thus, last occupation, the one taken in most analyses of social mobility, is quite misleading, since it has quite different meanings for men who have just entered the labor force as compared to those who are close to retirement. Taking ten-year intervals will allow us to consider all the men at similar stages in their life cycles. This approach means, of course, that for the younger cohorts fewer observations will be available.

As first occupation we will take that one the man held after completing his education, or the one he held at age 15 if he left school before that age. Actually, by age 15 about 70 percent of the men were out of school and in the labor force. Then we will take occupations at ages 25, 35, 45, and 55. For the youngest cohort, men aged 21 to 30 in 1965, last occupation will replace occupation at age 25 if they are not that old. For the oldest cohort, last occupation replaces that at age 55 if the man is not as yet 55. This procedure enables us to have two statuses for the youngest cohort, first occupation and that at age 25, and three, four, or five statuses for the succeeding cohorts. In each case, the effects of all the previous statuses will be measured.

Finally, from the occupational histories of the men we will move to their sons' educational attainment, although this last step in the analysis will have to be limited to those men who have older sons, which limits us to the older men in our sample. For the sons the process of stratification can be measured over the span of three generations, thus providing us with a unique opportunity for the examination of the process of stratification over long periods of time.

We can conceptualize the process of stratification, as described in this section, with the use of a causal model where the relations are asymmetrical and the effects additive. That is, the model is causal because we are explicitly indicating that previous events "cause" or affect later ones. It is asymmetrical because there is a one-way temporal and causal relation: educational attainment of the men is supposed to influence their occupational chances but not vice versa. (At least this relationship is true for Monterrey, where few men go back to school after entering the labor force.) Finally, we assume that the effects of a set of variables upon a subsequent one in the men's lives are additive. This assumption was tested with some rigor in one case—analyzing the determinants of educational attainment—and was found to be a tenable one.

Path analysis is a statistical technique especially useful for causal models involving additive, asymmetric, and linear relationships. The technique was developed several decades ago in the field of genetics, and recently it has received much attention from sociologists. Because technical discussions can be found in the recent literature,[4] we will describe here only some of the basic characteristics of the technique and its assumptions.

In path analysis we are interested in evaluating the relationships among a set of variables measurable on interval scales where causal

---

[4] The sociological uses and technical details of path analysis are discussed by Otis D. Duncan, "Path Analysis: Sociological Examples," *American Journal of Sociology* 72, no. 1 (July 1966): 1–16; and Kenneth C. Land, "The Principles of Path Analysis," in *Sociological Methodology*, ed. Edgar F. Borgatta.

direction is unequivocal. One or more variables are considered as exogenous to the system; that is, they are not determined or explained by any other variables in the system. In a three-generational analysis of the process of stratification, for instance, the variables that measure socioeconomic status of the first generation are exogenous variables, while all the others are endogenous. Respondent's education is conceived as being determined by antecedent variables, including a residual one that serves to indicate the effects of all unmeasured variables and the nonlinear effects of those measured, while education operates also as a determinant of subsequent statuses, as for example, the first job.

Path coefficients, or the direct effects of one variable upon another, generally are estimated by standardized regression coefficients, or beta weights. Exogenous variables might be related, and, since their causal direction is not analyzed, these relationships are estimated with zero-order correlation coefficients. Although a diagrammatic representation of the system is not essential, it is of value in representing the causal ordering assumed in the analysis. In such diagrams, straight one-headed arrows indicate direct effects of one variable on another one, while curved lines with two-headed arrows indicate intercorrelations where no specific causal direction is assumed. The quantities entered are path and correlation coefficients, respectively.

The starting assumptions of path analysis (asymmetry, additivity, and linearity) can be safely taken in our case. Since we will be dealing with a clear temporal sequence, the relations are asymmetric. Interactive effects, if detected, could be included by the use of dummy variables. However, explorations indicated that, for example, the determinants of educational attainment operate in an additive fashion. Finally, deviations from linearity should not interfere very much with our analysis, since the worst that could happen is that nonlinear effects would not be measured. A detailed analysis of a number of relationships indicated only slight deviations from linearity.

All variables in the model must be measured on interval scales, although some of them can be introduced as dichotomies. Occupational status will be measured by a five-point scale, constructed on the basis of information on occupational title, description of duties involved, and positions of authority and of ownership. The scale was a revised version of one used in a comparative study of stratification and mobility in four Latin American cities.[5] Educational attainment was not measured by the number of years of school completed but was transformed into a five-point scale, so that deviations from a normal distribution are not so great.

Even with these scales some deviations from normality exist, mainly in the form of positively skewed distributions. Bivariate and multivariate relations are not normal, either. Since some skewness is present in the variables and the residuals are not normally distributed, the data, as is so often the case in sociological research, do not strictly meet the assumptions of the statistical techniques used—in this case, path analysis. Therefore, due caution is advised in evaluating the conclusions arrived at by the use of these techniques.

Our strategy of analysis will be to follow the temporal sequence of events and at the end to reconstruct the main elements of the model to describe the process of stratification over the three generations. As was the case in previous chapters, the more we move ahead in the men's lives, the smaller the number we can include in the analysis because fewer men qualify by reason of age. For this reason, and also to investigate possible differences in the process of stratification, we will separate the sample into four birth cohorts.

Determinants of Educational Attainment

Educational attainment, as we have seen in Chapter 4, plays a key role in the process of stratification, serving as an intervening variable between parents' and sons' socioeconomic statuses.[6] Education is the first status attained by the men, but we know that there are varying proportions of achievement versus ascription present in educational attainment. Our first task, therefore, will be to explore how much educational attainment depends upon the socioeconomic status of the family of orientation, how much on other variables measured in our study but operating independently of socioeconomic status, and how much on

[5] The occupational scale used is reported in detail by us in a previous publication, *Movilidad social, migración, y fecundidad en Monterrey metropolitano*. For this analysis the seven original categories were collapsed into five to reduce positive skewness. On the consequences of assigning numerical values to the categories, see Sanford Labovitz, "The Assignment of Numbers to Rank Order Categories," *American Sociological Review* 35, no. 3 (June 1970): 515–524.

[6] References on other studies of determinants of education are found in the notes for Chapter 4, and those on studies of occupational mobility in the notes for Chapters 5 and 8.

other unmeasured variables (intelligence, good luck, and any others the reader might wish to add). Of course, intelligence or other unmeasured variables may play an intervening role in the process, since the parents' socioeconomic status can influence the son's I.Q. and both of them are determinants of educational attainment.

We can begin by considering the zero-order correlation coefficients between education and a set of antecedent variables for our entire sample, as presented in Table 10-1. The coefficients fall into three categories. First are the correlations between education and measures of socioeconomic origin; the three of them are moderately high (around .55) and positive. Second, the two measures related to the community in which the men spent their childhood and to the birth cohort show positive but lower correlations with education (around .30). Third, the other variables—number of siblings and age at father's death—are uncorrelated with educational attainment.

Considering first the groups of variables related to the family of orientation, it is clear that, although the three coefficients are moderately high, they cannot be taken independently, since father's education and occupation and mother's education are undoubtedly interrelated. However, we may conceive of them as they affect the respondent's education as shown in Figure 10-1. The diagram indicates that no causal ordering is assumed between the three measures of socioeconomic status of the family of orientation. Each of them has independent effects on educational attainment, although they are highly intercorrelated. However, we preferred to leave the three measures in the causal model because their predictive power is greater than that of any combination of two variables. That is, $R^2x \cdot abc = .45$, while the multiple correlation coefficients squared for the best combination of two variables (father's

TABLE 10-1. Zero-Order Correlation Coefficients for Analysis
of Process of Stratification

haracteristics	A	B	C	D	E	F	G	H	X
espondent's education (X)	.58	.54	.57	.38	.35	.25	−.06	.10	
espondent's first occupation (Y₁)	.47	.48	.46	.33	.31	.18	−.06	.11	.68

ey: A. Father's education
  B. Father's occupation
  C. Mother's education
  D. Size class of community of origin

  E. Region of community of origin
  F. Birth cohort
  G. Number of siblings
  H. Age of respondent at father's death

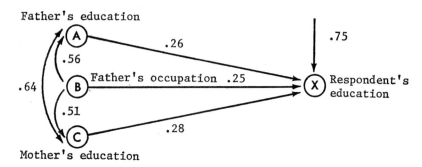

Figure 10-1. Path Coefficients in Determinants of Respondent's Education

occupation and mother's education) is .41. Incidentally, it should be noted that the residual path coefficient shows the effects of the other unmeasured variables, and we have included it to comply with the assumption of complete determination. Technically, it can be demonstrated to be equal to the coefficient of alienation (square root of $1\text{-}R^2$).

As we saw in Table 10-1, three other variables are correlated with education. Size class and region of the community of origin are highly intercorrelated in such a way that when we control for the effects of one of them the other has almost no influence on education. Thus, we have chosen to use only size class of the community of origin, which has a slightly higher correlation with education (.38) than region (.35). Birth cohort is also correlated with education (.25). However, both community of origin and birth cohort theoretically have a different meaning than socioeconomic origin, since they cannot be considered as part of the process of stratification. Although related to socioeconomic origin, community of origin and birth cohort influence education after controlling for the former. This influence can be shown by analyzing the increase in the R^2 when we add size of the community ($R^2 = .47$) and both this variable and birth cohort ($R^2 = .50$). In other words, we can explain a greater proportion of the variance in education by using these two additional variables.

In our scheme, birth cohort is better conceived as a means of classifying men in such a way as to trace changes in time in the determinants of educational attainment. For this reason, we present four different diagrams in Figure 10-2, one for each cohort, and include size of the

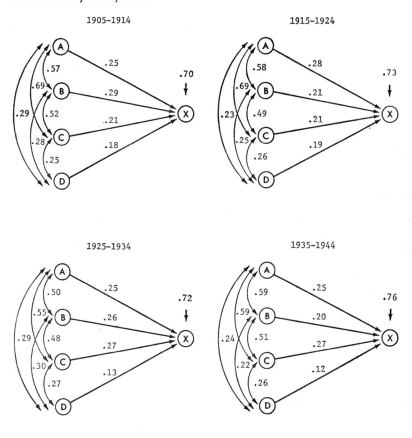

1905-1914   1915-1924

1925-1934   1935-1944

Note: Key as in Table 10-1.

Figure 10-2. Path Coefficients in Determinants of Educational Attainment, by Age Cohort

community of origin as a fourth determinant of education, together with father's education and occupation and mother's education.

Comparing the four diagrams, an interesting difference shows up in the value of the residual path: it is smaller for the oldest cohort and greater for the youngest one, while the two intermediate cohorts fall in between. This difference indicates a decline in the effects of socioeconomic origin and community on educational attainment. (The proportion of the variance explained drops from 51 to 42 percent.) This decline is brought about by a decrease in the direct path from father's occupation to respondent's education, while the path from father's education remains rather constant, and that from mother's education tends to increase. There is also a slight decline in the path from size of the community. However, we can dismiss the latter, since it probably simply reflects the increasing homogeneity of the population in this regard. A large majority of the younger men were raised in Monterrey, while among the older ones both rural and city origins are well represented. A decreasing variation in this factor is responsible for its lesser effect in the young cohort, while there is no such increasing homogeneity among the three other variables.

In interpreting these results one should be aware of the problem of multicollinearity. When the independent variables are highly correlated, as is the case with the three indicators of socioeconomic origin, the estimates of the path coefficients (beta weights) are bound to be quite unstable.[7] The decline in importance of father's occupation, a variable that—as explained in Chapter 4—best reflects the economic resources available for the family of orientation, is consistent with the hypothesis of decreasing importance of economic differentials in the determination of educational opportunities. The expansion of a public system of free education leads us to expect this decrease. When economic differences count for less, as is true in the younger cohorts, other family factors related to the motivational environment surrounding the youngsters can operate to a greater extent. Our hypothesis is that mother's education better reflects that factor and explains its increasing influence upon educational attainment of the son.

Determinants of Status of First Job

The reader is referred to the first table presented in this book, 1-1, where the average scores of occupational status for the four birth cohorts are shown at different times in their life cycles. For all cohorts the process of aging is associated with an overall movement upward in

---

[7] The problem of multicollinearity in evaluating causal structures is discussed extensively in the econometrics literature. See, for instance, J. Johnston, *Econometric Methods*; and Raymond Boudon, "A New Look at Correlation Analysis," in *Methodology in Social Research*, ed. Hubert M. Blalock and Ann B. Blalock.

the occupational scale. This movement, of course, is observed for the sample of men as a whole, but it is accomplished by a variety of moves for individual men; some move up and others move down but most move only the distance of one or two categories.

We will first consider the effects of socioeconomic status of family of orientation, size class of community of origin, and completed education on the occupational status of first job for the whole sample (excluding the seventeen men who never have worked). In Table 10-1 the zero-order correlation coefficients were presented. By far the highest association is that between educational attainment and first job. The zero-order correlations between the measures of socioeconomic status of origin and first job are quite high, although lower than that for education. Size class of community of origin and birth cohort have smaller but still significant correlations with first job.

The question we now want to pose is whether previous events that influenced the men's educational attainment have "delayed" effects on the occupational status of first job (that is, effects that go beyond those explained by education as an intervening factor), or whether they have only an indirect effect through educational attainment. The set of standardized regression coefficients and multiple correlation coefficients presented in Table 10-2 is useful in evaluating these two alternative

TABLE 10-2. Determinants of First Occupation: Standardized Regression Coefficients and Multiple Correlation Coefficients, by Birth Cohort

| Group | Standardized Regression Coefficient of First Occupation on: | | | | | |
	Community of Origin	Education of Mother	Education of Father	Occupation of Father	Education of Respondent	R^2
Total sample	−.01	.04	.05	.13	.56	.48
				.16	.59	.48
Cohort 1905–1914	.06	.03	.01	.14	.59	.46
				.14	.58	.44
Cohort 1915–1924	.01	.03	.06	.13	.53	.43
				.16	.56	.43
Cohort 1925–1934	.03	.05	.10	.08	.58	.52
				.12	.64	.51
Cohort 1935–1944	−.02	.10	.05	.19	.48	.49
				.24	.54	.48

models. It will be noted that for the total sample and for each of the cohorts the regression coefficients of first job on father's and mother's education and size of community of origin are negligible. Some variation exists among the cohorts, but in none of them do any of these variables attain practical significance. Moreover, it is clear that adding them doesn't help in increasing the proportion of the variance in first job explained by education and father's occupation. Even the latter makes only a very modest contribution above and beyond that of education. In summary, it can be safely assumed that the effects of socioeconomic status of origin and of community on the status of first job are mainly indirect, via educational attainment, with the partial exception of father's occupational status, which can be left in the model as having both indirect and very modest direct effects on first job. The path diagram can be drawn for the entire sample as shown in Figure 10-3.

There are no important differences between the four cohorts regarding the pattern of influences upon status of first occupation. There is an increase in the coefficient of determination (R^2) comparing the two older and the two younger ones, which indicates that education and father's occupation have greater influence among the latter. This is not a consistent trend and it should not be stressed. In all cases the most outstanding result is the overall importance of education and the little effect of socioeconomic origin upon first occupation.

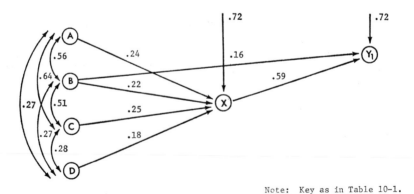

Note: Key as in Table 10-1.

Figure 10-3. Path Coefficients in Determinants of Respondent's First Job

Determination of Entire Work-Life Occupational Achievement

We now shift to an analysis of the patterns of work-life occupational achievement, taking the four birth cohorts. Probably the most interesting pattern is that of the oldest group of men, because we have their nearly complete occupational life cycle to consider, while for the younger age groups this kind of analysis is not possible. However, there are sections of the work histories that are comparable for two or more cohorts, so we can check to what extent the process is repeated in different age cohorts and whether interesting trends show up.

In the four path diagrams presented in Figure 10-4 we have indicated as exogenous variables only respondent's education and father's occupation. This decision is based on the preceding analysis showing that all other variables affect occupational achievement only in an indirect way. Even father's occupation could be omitted in many cases, as is demonstrated by the small path coefficients leading from it to respondent's occupational status at various stages of the life cycle. The relationship between father's occupation and respondent's education is left unanalyzed to simplify the presentation.

Our strategy of analysis will be to center upon the older cohort, while making reference to the other cohorts whenever it is warranted. Consider first the residual paths for occupational status at various ages. These paths decrease in value as the men advance in their work lives, indicating that the later the stage in a man's occupational history the more accurately we can predict his occupational status. For the last one, near the end of the men's work lives, the occupational status of their jobs ten years earlier, educational attainment, and father's occupational status explain three-fourths of the variance in present occupational status.

The decline in the residual path coefficients throughout the men's work lives is not gradual. The most important drop generally appears at age 35, while between ages 15 and 25 there is no great difference in prediction. After age 35 the value of the residual path keeps decreasing but not so sharply, as can be observed among the two oldest cohorts.

The path diagrams provide us with an interpretation of how the occupational status of the men at a given point in their work lives is influenced by previous statuses. Thus we can decompose the total effect into a series of direct and indirect effects of father's occupational status,

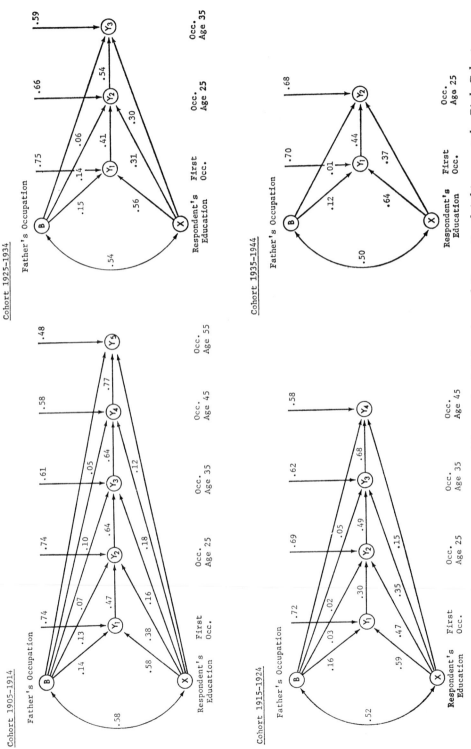

Figure 10.4. Path Diagrams: Father's Occupation and Respondent's Education and Occupational Achievement, by Birth Cohort

respondent's education, and previous occupational statuses. Father's occupational status has rather negligible direct effects on respondent's occupational achievement. That is, controlling for variables that intervene in the process of causation between father's and respondent's occupational statuses, the former has almost no effect upon the latter. The main intervening variable is educational attainment. This variable, as we have seen, has a powerful effect upon status of first job in all four cohorts. At further points in the men's histories education still is an important determinant of occupational achievement. At age 25, for example, the main direct effect on occupational status comes from status of first job, but there is also a significant direct effect of educational attainment. At this point, then, education is important in two senses: an indirect effect because it has previously influenced first job (a variable that considerably affects status at age 25) and a direct effect —one that takes place above and beyond that explained by the association of education with first job. The latter effect, however, tends to disappear after age 35, a point from which education becomes less responsible for occupational achievement (except for the fact that it had affected earlier occupational statuses).

The effect of occupational status at one point in time on the occupational status the men hold ten years later is quite important from the very beginnings of the men's work histories. However, the values of the paths from one occupational status to the next keep increasing during the men's work lifetime, the main breaking point being at age 25. In the two older cohorts we see a sharp increase in the path from age 25 to age 35, and further increases can be observed later. In other words, the prediction of a man's occupational status based on the one he held ten years before increases as the man gets older. Of course, this prediction takes into account only the vertical dimension of occupations, and it is only this dimension that we can explain better when men get older. The probability of changing jobs within the same status levels might be as high for men in their forties and fifties as it was among men in their twenties and thirties.

We are now in a position to attempt a general explanation of the results shown in the path diagrams for the four cohorts. Some work-life trends can be interpreted quite easily. As men mature and advance in their work lives, their occupational statuses become more determined by previous events. Progressively, the main thing we need to know in order to predict a man's occupational status is the one he occupied ten years before. This result is entirely to be expected, since we know that vertical mobility decreases as men get older and that it is clearly reflected in the greater predictive value of previous occupations at later stages in the men's work histories.

The first twenty years of the occupational histories of the Monterrey men merit special attention. Here again we find our results consistent with those arrived at by a different analysis of the same information as presented in Chapter 5. These twenty years can be characterized as a period of relatively high vertical mobility. First jobs do indeed count for the kinds of jobs men will take by age 25 and the latter are also good predictors of future statuses by age 35. However, occupational experience or position during this period is less indicative of future achievement than is the case during the next twenty-year period of the men's work lives, between ages 35 and 55. Also, during these first twenty years formal education persists as an important criterion for status occupancy. The delayed or direct effects of education upon occupational status are important throughout this period. Most men, as we have seen in Table 1-1, and as was subsequently discussed in Chapter 5, begin their work lives in relatively low status jobs. From there the direction of mobility consistently is upward (for those who move). In part, of course, the men could move up because they began in so low a status. Some men with relatively high family background and education may begin their work histories in low-status jobs because of lack of experience and seniority, while other men with inferior backgrounds and education may take advantage of their physical ability to achieve occupational positions that are high in relation to their background. By age 25 the men seem to be in a transitory situation, one in which the influence of social background as well as previous occupational status is minimized in relative terms, although they are quite important in absolute terms.

After age 25, and as a more stable position is sought, the influence of social background variables, mainly education, increases in importance. The "easy" opportunities for mobility by this time largely have been exhausted. The effects of previous occupational statuses are not great, since they were to some extent trial jobs, as we have seen in Chapter 5. At about age 35 a more stable situation is attained and the tendency to remain in the same position increases sharply after that time.

*"Career Contingencies" and Their Effect
upon Occupational Attainment*

During the lifetime of the men events other than those related to their occupational experience can affect their placement in the stratification system, excepting family background and education. We have in mind those events subsumed under migration and family formation of the respondent. Duncan has chosen to call these kinds of variables "career contingencies" that are apart from the temporal causal sequence but related to the process of stratification.[8] The problem in dealing with them is that these events are contingent in the sense that not all men marry, have children, or migrate, and the location of any one of the events in the life cycle is not fixed in the way that we can assume education is intermediate between family background and occupational history.

These events cannot be ignored despite the difficulty in temporally ordering them. Age at first marriage, social background of the wife, number of children and their spacing (variables dealt with in Chapter 7) can affect a man's occupational status. Also, these variables are related to previous events, since men of higher status of origin tend to marry somewhat later, to marry women of statuses similar to their own, and to have a somewhat smaller number of children than the rest of the men. Migration, mainly when it involves an important change in the opportunity structure (as when the move is from an economically stagnant community to Monterrey), can also affect the men's occupational achievements, as we have seen in Chapter 8.

For some subsamples of the population we can ask fruitful questions as to the effects of these events. Thus, among ever-married men, how does age at first marriage influence their achievements? Does marrying upward or downward have any effect? Does the cost involved in having more children affect in any way the men's careers? And among those who ever migrated to Monterrey, how does the age at which they came to the city affect their subsequent occupational achievements? To answer these questions we will limit ourselves to the men who were age 45 or older when interviewed, since only among them can we see the

[8] The concept of career contingency is discussed in Otis D. Duncan, David L. Featherman, and Beverly Duncan, *Socioeconomic Background and Occupational Achievement: Extensions of a Basic Model*, Chap. 9.

possible effects of these events. Furthermore, only ever-married men will be taken for the first three questions and only migrants for the last one. As a matter of fact, the effects of community at an earlier point in the men's lifetimes have already been analyzed earlier in this chapter when we showed the relation between size class of community of origin and educational attainment.

For the four issues a simple causal model has been developed. Educational attainment and status of first job are taken as exogenous variables, occupational status at age 45 is considered the dependent variable, and the four variables described above are taken one at a time as intervening variables. The four path diagrams presented in Figure 10-5 serve to help us evaluate the effects of these contingencies upon the men's occupational achievement.

The linear effects of education and first job upon age at first marriage are positive but low. We emphasize that only linear effects are measured, since in this case we know that the relationships are perfectly linear. Age at first marriage has a negligible effect on occupational achievement, indicating that those men who married later, other things being equal, did not achieve on the average higher statuses than those who married younger. Wife's education is strongly determined by husband's education. Of course, in this case the link is one of selection rather than causation of educational levels of the woman. In any case, the wife's education has a positive effect upon the man's occupational achievement. Number of children, on the other hand, is negatively affected by the man's status (indicating differential fertility), but has no detectable effect upon the man's later achievements.

Migratory status at age 25 is influenced by previous statuses (mainly education), indicating that there is some selectivity involved: younger migrants tend to have higher educational levels than older migrants. Above and beyond this, migratory status itself has an effect upon occupational status by age 45. This result, of course, is entirely consistent with the discussion about age at arrival in Monterrey and occupational achievement in Chapter 8.

The Third Generation

We have arrived at the last stage in our analysis of the process of stratification, namely, the third generation. Two basic questions can be answered in this section. First, we can measure the effects of respondent's family of orientation's status (that is, the grandparents' status) on

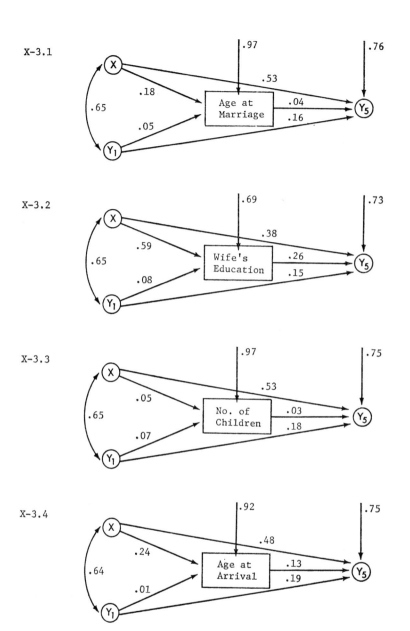

Note: Diagrams X-3.1, X-3.2, and X-3.3 are for married men 45 years of age and older. Diagram X-3.4 is for men 45 years of age and older whose communities of origin are not Monterrey (age at arrival is a dichotomy: arrived at age 25 or earlier is "1," arrived later is "0").

Figure 10-5. Career Contingencies: Effects of Age at Marriage, Wife's Education, Number of Children at Age 45, and Age of Arrival in Monterrey on Occupational Achievement

the respondent's son's status (that is, grandson), and show how this effect takes place. Both the magnitude of the effect and the way it occurs are relevant. Contrary to common assumptions held by social scientists, the few empirical studies focusing on three-generational social mobility have indicated that very little inheritance of status is present for this long period of time and that any such influence is wholly indirect; that is, it is achieved through the grandparents' influence upon the parents' generation.[9] Second, we can compare two pairs of generations, grandparents with respondents and respondents with sons, making it possible to determine if the influence of one generation upon the next is greater or smaller in the older than in the younger pair.

The analysis in this section must be limited to those men who have sons fifteen years or older. Among these sons almost one-third are still out of the labor force studying or otherwise not employed. Thus, we could not possibly take occupational status as an indicator of the sons' positions in the stratification system. Educational attainment will be used in its place. However, since nearly one-third of the sons are still in school, the measure we must take is not completed education. Our solution has been to consider as the dependent variable a dichotomy of sons' education: those who have completed six years of schooling or less (up through completed *primaria*) and those who have seven or more years of schooling. All the sons who were in school have at least seven years of schooling, so the fact that they still have not completed their education does not affect their placement in the dichotomy.

A more difficult technical problem is that our sample is a sample of men, and not of their sons. We take all sons aged 15 and over, but in so doing a number of our respondents are represented more than once while many others, those without sons aged 15 and over, are excluded. It should be evident that we do not have a representative sample of young males. But this does not mean the father-son comparisons are impossible, and given some caution they permit us to make some important, although provisional, conclusions regarding the process of stratification over three generations. Comparisons between the respondents' sons and the younger cohort of respondents (aged 21 to 30) can be used to indicate the accuracy of our measures of effects, since these two groups belong largely to the same universe, although the group of sons, of course, is somewhat younger.

[9] See Hodge, "Occupational Mobility as a Probability Process."

The zero-order correlation coefficients presented in Table 10-3 can serve as a first indication of the effects of grandparents' and parents' statuses upon grandsons' education. Also presented in the same table are comparable correlations for the respondents and for the sample of young respondents (aged 21 to 30). The correlation coefficients between parents' statuses and education are lower in the sample of sons than in that of respondents, while those corresponding to the younger respondents fall in between. Grandparents' statuses are also moderately correlated with grandsons' education, while number of siblings has a weak but negative zero-order correlation with education.

Considering the joint effects and independent contributions of these variables, through the multiple correlation and regressions presented in Table 10-4, we can conclude that the effects of grandparents' characteristics are almost nil when we control for parents' characteristics. That

TABLE 10-3. Determinants of Education among Sons, Respondents, and Youngest Cohort: Zero-Order Correlation Coefficients

Characteristics	Son's Education	Respondent's Education (whole sample)	Respondent's Education (age 21–30)
Grandfather's education	.40	n.a.	n.a.
Grandfather's occupation	.38	n.a.	n.a.
Grandmother's education	.38	n.a.	n.a.
Father's education	.50	.58	.55
Father's occupation	.42	.54	.51
Mother's education	.51	.57	.55
Number of siblings	−.13	−.06	−.14

TABLE 10-4. Multiple Correlation and Regression Analyses of Son's Education

| | Standardized Regression Coefficients Son's Education on: | | | | |
Father's Education	Father's Occupation	Mother's Education	Grandfather's Occupation	Number of Siblings	R^2
.29		.33			.31
	.19	.35			.30
.22	.15	.30			.33
.19	.14	.28	.09		.33
.19	.14	.28	.09	−.02	.33

is, any effect they might have upon grandsons' education is indirect.
The effect of number of siblings disappears when parents' socioeconomic status is controlled for. Finally, as was the case among the respondents, we find that father's education and occupation as well as
mother's education have independent effects upon son's education.
Thus, our diagrammatic interpretation of the causal chain takes the
form shown in Figure 10-6.

It should be noted that the residual path is considerably larger than
that found in a similar diagram for the respondents, indicating that the
effects of family of orientation upon educational attainment were greater among the respondents than among their sons. Moreover, the paths
are quite comparable in magnitude to those we estimated for the
younger cohort of respondents aged 21 to 30: in both cases the residual
path is approximately .80, and the ordering of the other paths is similar
(mother's education having a greater effect than father's occupation
and education). These results, therefore, are congruent with our conclusions stated before: first, the decrease in the general impact of family background upon educational achievement, and, second, a decrease
brought about mainly by a smaller effect of father's occupation as an
indicator of the family's economic status. However, a third expected
result, the emergence of number of siblings as a modest but significant
factor negatively associated with educational attainment, did not
materialize.

In order to provide a sort of summary of the discussion of the process
of stratification during the three-generation period, we will expand the
diagram to the left, explaining the correlations between exogenous
variables in the previous path diagram so as to give an account of the

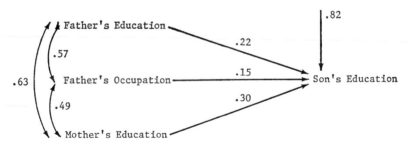

Figure 10-6. Path Coefficients in Determinants of Education of Respondent's Son

entire causal chain that leads to grandsons' education. The paths for this diagram, presented in Figure 10-7, are estimated using the sample of respondents' sons, so some differences in the specific estimates with those calculated for the sample of respondents are to be expected.

Although at first glance the path diagram may appear quite complicated, there is nothing here that has not been presented previously in this chapter. On the contrary, some simplifications have been introduced to make the important points show up more clearly. Thus, references to community of origin and migration status have been omitted and the occupational history of the respondents has been abbreviated in such a way that only one point in time (age 35) is considered. We feel justified in doing this because the diagram is intended to show the process of stratification from the point of view of its end result—son's educational attainment.

We begin the analysis with a set of intercorrelated variables, those of the respondent's family of orientation and his wife's father's occupation. The former have moderately high effects upon respondent's education, while the latter affects wife's education. Of course, wife's education is determined to a lesser degree than her husband's education, simply because we introduce one determinant for the former and three for the latter. (The residual paths indicate, it will be recalled, the degree of determination—the greater the residual path the smaller the effects of the measured variables upon the dependent variable.)

The residuals of the respondent's and his wife's education are intercorrelated, which indicates the existence of educational homogamy above and beyond the homogamy due to socioeconomic origins of the spouses. That is, socioeconomic origins present a first limitation on the choice of mates, probably by limiting heterosexual contacts between males and females of different social strata. Within this limitation a further selection is carried out according to education of the possible mates. As a consequence, the spouses' levels of education are more correlated than what would be expected only on the basis of the correlation between their socioeconomic origins. This factor finds expression in the causal diagram by the correlation between residuals.

At the next stage in the causal diagram we find that the occupational status of the respondent is influenced mainly by his level of education. His father's occupational status exerts both a direct and an indirect influence. There is also a causal link going from wife's education to respondent's occupational status. That is, although the wife's education

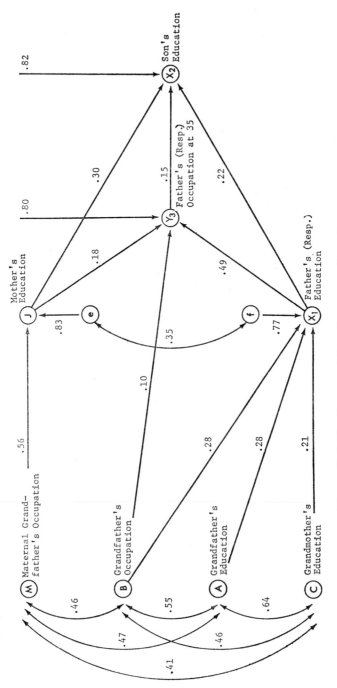

Figure 10-7. The Process of Stratification in Three Generations

is highly correlated with the respondent's education, it makes a net contribution to her husband's occupational achievement: the higher the wife's education, the higher the status achieved by the husband.

From here on the diagram repeats the information presented in the previous path diagram, so we need not repeat our observations. But it should be noted that now we have a causal interpretation of the inter-correlations between respondent's education and occupation and wife's education. Also, the diagram indicates that the first generation's influence upon the third is entirely mediated by the second, or the respondent's, generation. A word should be said again about the possible comparison between the effects of the first generation upon the second and those of the second upon the third. We observe that educational attainment of the respondent is influenced more by family background than is the case of his son. Also, the composition of these effects changes, with a smaller value for father's occupation in the determination of son's education.

Comparisons with Other Studies

The process of stratification over three generations can be broken down into three components: first, from socioeconomic origins to educational achievement of the men; second, from educational levels to occupational status in adulthood; and third, from socioeconomic status of the adult man to educational attainment of the son. Thus, the third stage repeats the first one. Considered in this way the rigidity or flexibility of the process depends basically upon the links between origins and education and between education and occupational status. The more unequal the educational opportunities and the more relevant educational criteria are for occupational achievement, the greater the status inheritance.

The flexibility of the system, or how much status inheritance characterizes this sample of Mexican men, is difficult to say unless one's criteria are made explicit. The more relevant criterion, from our point of view, is a comparative one—the system in Monterrey, Mexico, is "more" or "less" flexible than that found in other situations rather than the system being judged rigid or flexible by some absolute standard. At this point problems arise. In spite of the fact that social stratification and social mobility have drawn more attention and produced more international empirical studies than almost any other subject in the field of sociology, satisfactory comparisons are difficult to make.[10] Recent attempts to bring together the results from a large number of studies have been justly criticized because inadequate attention was given to the great variations in research designs. There is actually little uniformity in setting up the studies—some are national and others are city or regional samples, some take all adult men while others are age and group restricted, and the definition of occupational status and the time in the man's work life taken are all subject to considerable variation. Only recently have investigators begun to use correlation and regression techniques to deal with social mobility data in the fashion presented in this chapter, and as far as we know there is no study where the process of stratification has been followed for three generations in the way we have done. In any event, the great bulk of studies are for the industrialized societies, and there are few reported for countries with a level of development similar to Mexico's. Despite all such restrictions and keeping in mind the very real hazards in comparing our results with other studies conducted differently, we believe the advantages of such comparisons outweigh the disadvantages.

We have seen that most of the correlation coefficients between socio-economic origin, education, and occupational achievement are quite high for Monterrey. Let us now see how "high" they are when compared with those obtained in other studies. The most often reported finding is the correlation coefficient between occupational status of the father (acknowledging the differences deriving from variation in which occupation of the father is selected) and last occupation of the son. Of course, "last occupation" has a different meaning for older men than for younger men, but it is the occupation most often used in the literature.

Blau and Duncan reported a correlation coefficient of .41 between father's and son's occupation for their U.S. sample of men aged 25 to 64, with no regular pattern of variations between cohorts.[11] Using a

---

[10] The best known studies on these topics conducted in other Latin American societies include that by Bertram Hutchinson et al., *Mobilidade e trabalho: Um estudo na cidade de São Paulo*; Melvin M. Tumin and Arnold S. Feldman, *Social Class and Social Change in Puerto Rico*; and a four-city study that has been reported partially in a number of publications, most of which are listed in Sugiyama Iutaka, "Social Stratification Research in Latin America," *Latin American Research Review* 1, no. 1 (Fall 1965): 7–34.

[11] Blau and O. D. Duncan, *The American Occupational Structure*, p. 169.

Chicago sample of men with nonfarm background, Duncan and Hodge found a coefficient of .30.[12] While lower than the one reported for the entire United States, this is to be expected, since the Chicago sample is much more homogeneous. In a secondary analysis of the Indianapolis data, Duncan found a correlation coefficient of .37.[13] Svalastoga obtained a figure of .49 for the oldest and .41 for the youngest men in his national Danish sample.[14]

The above results, obtained with a variety of samples, indicate correlation coefficients between father's and son's last occupation considerably smaller than the .49 obtained for all Monterrey men. Since this correlation is a gross measure of status inheritance, a provisional conclusion of the above comparisons is that inheritance of position in Monterrey is greater than in the other cases, all representing industrialized countries. Variations in sampling and measurement procedures are unlikely to eliminate these differences.

It should be stressed that these results were obtained after much of the positive skewness present in the original distributions was eliminated by grouping extreme categories. Otherwise, the correlation coefficient would be even larger in Monterrey. The results reported recently by Kahl, however, support the impression of higher inheritance in Mexico. He conducted a study of men in Mexico City and some provincial towns, and, while it was not focused on social stratification, it provides relevant information. Kahl obtained a zero-order correlation between father's and son's occupations of .50 for his entire sample, with only slight differences according to locality.[15] Kahl's figure is similar to that obtained in Monterrey, although he eliminated the extremes of university-trained professionals at the top and underemployed workers at the bottom—sectors where there is more succession of position than in the middle—so his correlation tends to underestimate the amount of status inheritance.

[12] Otis D. Duncan and Robert W. Hodge, "Education and Occupational Mobility: A Regression Analysis," *American Journal of Sociology* 68, no. 5 (May 1963): 635.

[13] Otis D. Duncan, "Methodological Issues in the Analysis of Social Mobility," in *Social Structure and Mobility in Economic Development*, ed. Neil J. Smelser and Seymour M. Lipset, p. 66.

[14] Kaare Svalastoga, *Prestige, Class, and Mobility*, p. 77.

[15] Joseph A. Kahl, *The Measurement of Modernism: A Study of Values in Brazil and Mexico*, p. 159.

The comparison of the Monterrey path analysis with that obtained by Blau and Duncan has the advantage that the statistical techniques and many of the procedures are similar. Their sample is a national one in contrast to the Monterrey "city" one, but it still is worthwhile to compare the path diagrams of the two studies. Blau and Duncan's basic model and the replication of that model with the Monterrey data are reproduced in Figure 10-8. Since they did not measure education of the mother, this variable is excluded, and for purposes of comparability we must assume that "last" occupation has the same meaning for all men in the sample. The overall evaluation of the two models presented in Figure 10-8 indicates that, while the form of the diagram is similar, the specific values of the paths are quite different. These two points will be considered separately. In both the U.S. and the Monterrey samples education of the father and occupation of the father have about the same influence on educational attainment of the son. In both cases, there is no direct influence from father's education to son's first occupation, reflecting the fact that any influence of the former on the latter can be assumed to be indirect. Thus, only father's occupation and son's educational attainment have direct effects upon first occupation, as well as last occupation. The paths leading from occupation of the father to respondent's first and last occupations in both Monterrey and the United States are smaller than the paths leading from educational attainment. In other words, most but not all of the effect of father's occupation on son's occupation (first or last) is indirect, by means of its previous influence on son's educational attainment. Educational attainment has the largest gross and net effects on occupational achievement in both the U.S. and the Monterrey samples.

Having seen the similarities in form, the reader should also recognize that the specific values of the path coefficients differ considerably. In four of seven possible comparisons, the paths are larger for the Monterrey sample, and two of the three residual paths are smaller, indicating higher multiple correlation coefficients. This finding should come as no surprise, since the zero-order correlation coefficients are also larger in Monterrey than in the United States. It is not worthwhile to try to account for all the differences in magnitude of the path coefficients, but one does deserve discussion—the strikingly larger one in the Monterrey sample leading from educational attainment to first job. This finding is quite unexpected, since one would have predicted that in the more industrialized countries the educational requirements for any occupation are more strict and, therefore, a reverse pattern would be more plausible. The difference between the Monterrey and the U.S. samples may be partially due to measurement error and differences in procedures. Blau and Duncan might have underestimated the correlation between education and first job because of their problem in estab-

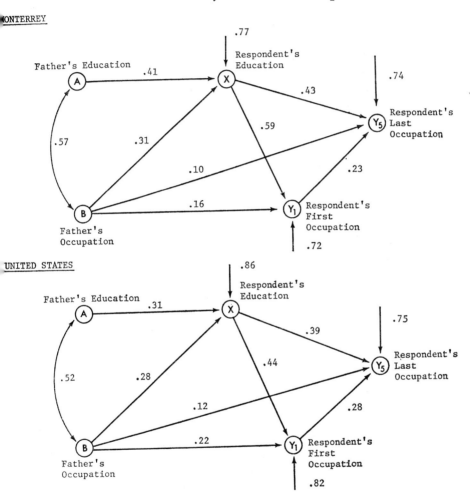

Figure 10-8. Path Diagrams: Father's Occupation and Education, Respondent's Education and Occupational Achievement, Monterrey and the United States

lishing the correct temporal sequence between the two variables. In about 20 percent of their cases first occupation actually precedes educational attainment, while this problem is not present in the Monterrey study.

If we accept that the difference is a real one, that in Monterrey (or urban Mexico in general) the effect of education on occupational status is greater than in the United States (and maybe other industrial countries as well), how can we explain it? Incidentally, a similar result—that is, high correlation between education and occupation—was also reported for São Paulo,[16] another case of rapid industrialization in a developing country. We believe that the causal mechanism involved lies in the combination of a technological setup that requires, at least in the modern sector of the economy, more skilled workers, technicians, and the like than unskilled workers, with the kinds of skills not being very different from those prevalent today in industrialized countries, while the rapid rate of growth of labor supply allows enterprises to place relatively high educational requirements even if some bottlenecks appear.

When at the same time we find a high correlation between education and occupational status and a high correlation between socioeconomic origin and education, we conclude that industrialization has not really brought about a radically more flexible stratification system until now. It has probably been reshaped, with education becoming the key link in the process of stratification, but without seriously upsetting its substance, because of the inequality in educational opportunities. Of course, we do not know this for sure, because there is no comparable study that was carried out several decades ago. In another aspect of the stratification system—the inequality in income distribution, where some information is available—it seems that industrialization also has not seriously affected preexisting inequalities.

In conclusion, we believe that status inheritance in Monterrey is higher than in the industrialized countries that have been reviewed in this section. The Kahl findings for Mexico City and smaller provincial cities are consistent with ours, after allowing for differences in study design, and lead us to believe that in this regard Monterrey is not atypical within urban Mexico. As important, perhaps, is the implication of our three-generation analysis, for which unfortunately we were not able

[16] See the discussion in ibid., Appendix B.

to bring to bear even loosely comparable studies. The trend manifested in the three-generation study is clearly toward a greater equality of educational opportunities. If this is really the case—and we have to be somewhat more skeptical about the results obtained with the sample of sons because of the methodological difficulties involved—it would imply an important alteration of the stratification system.

Summary

It is useful to summarize the main conclusions arrived at in this chapter. We have covered many points, so the main findings may get lost among the many technical details and methodological caveats. Moreover, since findings for the entire sample as well as intercohort differences were dealt with and since we concluded with a comparison with findings obtained by other studies, we run the risk of confusing the basic issues. The major conclusions are as follows:

1. The main determinants of educational achievement are indicators of socioeconomic status of the family of orientation. Father's education and occupation and mother's education all have affected respondent's education. The three have similar weights for the sample as a whole, and their high intercorrelation does not inhibit their showing effects upon education that are independent of each other. Forty-five percent of the variance in respondent's education is explained by socioeconomic origin.

2. Size class of the community of origin and age cohort also are important for educational attainment. Younger men and those brought up in urban areas, other things being equal, achieved higher average levels of education. The impacts of the community and of age, however, are considerably smaller than that of the family.

3. The men began their occupational histories in low-status jobs, and the process of aging is associated with a movement upward in the occupational scale. The bulk of this advance, observed for the sample of men as a whole, takes place between first job and occupation at age 35.

4. Occupational status of first job is mainly a function of education, while the family of orientation is relevant mainly in an indirect form, through the effect it has upon education. Only father's occupation has a modest effect upon first job beyond that explained by its association with respondent's education.

5. Considering the men's jobs every ten years, it is observed that the effect of occupational status at one point in time is quite important,

from the very beginnings of work histories, for occupational achievement ten years later. At each subsequent point in the work life, previous occupation has a greater effect upon present occupational status. Vertical mobility decreases as men grow older, the period between ages 15 and 25 being of relatively high mobility, with the chances of vertical movement decreasing rapidly afterward.

6. Education, the most relevant criterion for occupational status of first job, has a double effect upon subsequent positions. It is important because it affects the men's previous occupations, but it also affects their present ones in a direct form, above and beyond that effect explained by previous occupational achievement. However, this situation is true only up to age 35. After that age the effect of previous occupational status is so overwhelming that education has only the first kind of effect just mentioned, an indirect one through previous occupational achievement.

7. Events related to family formation and migration, which we call career contingencies, have some importance for the men's adult occupational status. Age at first marriage and number of children did not alter the men's chances of moving up or down, but their wives' education did. Getting married to a better-educated woman is associated with a movement upward in the occupational scale. Also, the migrants who arrive in Monterrey before age 25 have better chances of moving up than those arriving later.

8. The men's sons' education, like their own, is strongly affected by socioeconomic status of the family of orientation (in this case, the respondent's occupation and education and his wife's education). However, some differences are observed when comparing the set of influences upon the respondent's and his son's education. First of all, the overall effect of family of orientation is somewhat smaller for the son, his educational achievement being less restricted by status of origin than was that of his father. Second, this difference is largely a consequence of the weaker effect of father's occupational status (an indication of the family's economic well-being) upon son's education.

9. The comparison between respondents and sons in the previous paragraph reinforces the results of a comparison between the four age cohorts of respondents. Younger respondents, when compared with the older ones, show their education to be less affected by family of origin, mainly by father's occupational status.

10. While the association between status of origin and education de-

creased in time, as suggested by comparing cohorts and fathers and sons, the effect of education upon occupational achievement has not. It might actually have increased, but here our results are more inconclusive because the difference is observed only between the very oldest cohorts (51–60) and the rest of the men.

11. The Monterrey Mobility Pattern: Consequences and Prospects

One of the major tasks of this book has been to approach the process of economic development from the standpoint of the men whose lives are affected by this societal transformation. We characterize this as a microsociological approach, and Part Two of the book elaborates the life-cycle perspective, whereby features of the men's lives bearing on their placement in the social structure are considered in chronological order, starting with family background and ending with the third generation. Chapter 10 summarizes this experience within the framework of the process of stratification.

It would be possible to stop at this point, but we believe it appropriate to consider our findings from a different perspective, one that will take us closer to the macrolevel of analysis. We want to move from a consideration of the men to the structures in which they are found and in particular to the structural consequences of the patterns of geographic and social mobility. We shall take the findings that are presented in Chapters 4 through 10 and put a different set of questions to them. Let us at this point warn the reader that the shift from micro- to macrolevel is not to be made in any formal manner, there not being a clear set of rules to be followed in moving from one level to the other.

What we want to do here can be subsumed under two broad themes, both stemming from the literature on social change and economic development as it originated in the analysis of the emergence of industrial society. The first theme involves addressing the phenomenon of social conflict, specifically class conflict, often associated with the process of industrialization. To do so we must move from an analysis of social strata and men's location and mobility between them to an analysis of social classes. In the next section of the chapter we will be concerned mainly with this issue. Our question will be What are the conditions in the Monterrey milieu that do or do not lead to the formation of clearly defined classes and the development of class conflict? The second theme is social disorganization. In the sociological literature rapid social change traditionally has been linked to social disorganization—including the breakdown of social relations and institutions and the weakening of norms that regulate behavior in social groups. We want to explore the extent to which some of the changes predicted in the course of industrialization actually show up. More broadly, the question is What are the institutional arrangements and mechanisms in the central areas of community, work, family, and values that resist or facilitate the strain toward social disorganization? A subject of central interest in the book is linked to the two themes mentioned, namely, the effect of migration upon both communities of origin (Cedral) and communities of destination (Monterrey). In relation to the first theme, the question is Does heavy net in- or out-migration serve to increase or weaken group conflict, especially that of a class origin? In relation to the second, we want to explore the role of migration and its relation to social disorganization.

Finally, the chapter will end with a consideration of the future of Monterrey. Will the mechanisms that have worked during this period of rapid change continue to work over the coming two or three decades as they have in the past? Which aspects are most likely to change and which are likely to remain the same?

Industrialization and Monterrey's Class Structure

In the previous chapters we were concerned with the system of stratification, especially with the movements of men within the system and the factors that facilitate or inhibit that movement. Here we will shift from a stratification to a class framework of analysis. These frameworks are closely linked, so much so that many sociologists don't bother to make a distinction between them and use the terms interchangeably. In so doing, much confusion has been introduced that largely could have been avoided through the clear and consistent separation of the two concepts. Ralf Dahrendorf's distinction is appropriate: "By stratum I shall understand a category of persons who occupy a similar position on a hierarchical scale of certain situational characteristics such as income, prestige, style of life. 'Stratum' is a descriptive category. By contrast, the concept of class is an analytical category which has meaning only in the context of a theory of class. 'Classes' are interest groupings emerging from certain structural conditions which operate as such and effect structure changes."[1]

In our study we have used occupation to place the men within the stratification system, but otherwise our understanding of the difference between a system of stratification and the class structure is in accord with Dahrendorf. Our investigation made the stratification system the central concern, and there are few if any questions in the interview schedule that deal directly with class. Therefore, ours will be an interpretation of the class structure of Monterrey and Cedral, rather than an analysis of survey data bearing directly on the subject.

In considering the relationship of the class structure of Monterrey as it has developed in response to industrialization, there are two models that could serve as guides. The first is that of Marx, who provided an analysis and a prediction of the development of the class structure in capitalist countries, basing his interpretation on the nineteenth-century European, especially English, experience. His prediction was that in the course of industrialization there would inevitably develop a greater polarization of the class structure. The breakdown of the old agrarian order and of traditional urban crafts would cast large numbers of workers into the manufacturing sector, and in the process old differences would be erased in the creation of an industrial proletariat. The working class would become more and more homogeneous as their interests and life experience tended to coincide, and their opposition to the capitalist bourgeoisie would crystallize. As the situation of the proletariat inevitably worsened, there would be an increase in class consciousness and class conflict.

The second model of the development of class relations has emerged as a response to the history of industrialization in Western Europe and the United States and as a critique of the Marxist prediction of increasing class polarization. Among those who have contributed to this model

[1] Ralf Dahrendorf, *Class and Conflict in Industrial Society*, p. ix. See also Rodolfo Stavenhagen, *Las clases sociales en las sociedades agrarias*, Chap. 2.

are Dahrendorf, and his analysis of changes since Marx, and S. M. Lipset's various writings, particularly those dealing with status politics.[2] Both men are concerned with the role of the new middle classes. In addition, there is a growing literature on the "embourgeoisment" of the working class, also dealt with by both authors, and criticized by others, such as John H. Goldthorpe and associates.[3]

This "postindustrial" model points to the real increases in levels of living and working conditions of workers, and its advocates put special emphasis on the relatively more rapid growth of the new middle class. The latter is the product of technological innovations in industry, the growth of services of all kinds, and the general economic affluence generated by the tremendous and unforeseen productivity of the economy. The increase in technical personnel also is manifest in the upper levels of the working class. The class pyramid, seen by Marx as becoming increasingly broad based, is described in the second model as diamond shaped.[4] The changes in working- and middle-class composition, together with universal suffrage and other forms of political participation, have served to prevent polarization and to reduce class conflict.

The foregoing depiction of the two models is highly schematic. They were introduced not for the purpose of critical evaluation, but because, under the "new industrialization" conditions previously described, neither model is adequate to characterize the class situation as it has developed in Mexico and other industrializing countries. Pablo González Casanova, a Mexican sociologist, has argued that in Mexico the most important class cleavage occurs *within* the working class. This situation, he says, makes it difficult if not impossible to expect the kind of class consciousness and the political activity predicted for this class by Marxist theory.[5] In the case of Monterrey the economic boom and the tech-

---

[2] Dahrendorf, *Class and Conflict in Industrial Society*; and Seymour M. Lipset, *Political Man*. Also see Gerhard Lenski, *Power and Privilege*, Chaps. 10–12.

[3] John H. Goldthorpe, et al., *The Affluent Worker: Political Attitudes and Behavior*, and *The Affluent Worker in the Class Structure*. Another good review of this issue can be found in T. B. Bottomore, *Classes in Modern Society*.

[4] Associated with this perspective is Wilensky's concept of the "middle mass." See Harold L. Wilensky, "Work, Careers, and Social Integration," *International Social Science Journal* 12, no. 4 (1960): 543–560.

[5] Pablo González Casanova, *Democracy in Mexico*, and his "Dynamics of the Class Structure," in *Comparative Perspectives on Social Stratification*, ed. Joseph A. Kahl. The changes in the Mexican class structure since the revolution are outlined

nologically advanced nature of the economy might lend support to the postindustrial model, but the dominance of heavy industry and the highly unequal distribution of income are often associated with class conflict. Therefore, let us put forth the salient features of the class structure of Monterrey to show its divergences from both the Marxian and the postindustrial models.

There is little difficulty in identifying the upper class and the power elite of Monterrey. The core is made up of a small number of family capitalists with which are affiliated their business associates and some professionals. The top industry and financial firms are linked by family ties or mutual interest, enabling them to function effectively as a bloc. This business elite is clearly differentiated from the political elite, but in the case of Monterrey, which is probably not typical of Mexico, the local PRI (Party of the Institutional Revolution) leaders serve as intermediaries between the business elite and the federal government, without much independent power of their own.

Probably some authors would describe the top group of Monterrey as an industrial bourgeoisie rather than an upper class, for it is true that the Monterrey elite little resembles the traditional "oligarchy," based on land, that is to be found in many other parts of Latin America. Claudio Véliz has noted that the industrial bourgeoisie in Latin America is weak and dependent upon the landed oligarchy.[6] However appropriate it may be for other parts of Latin America, this interpretation is not applicable to the Monterrey situation. The Monterrey elite is not weak, and it is not dependent upon a landed oligarchy, because the latter doesn't exist in Mexico; the revolution eliminated the *hacendados* as a cohesive political force. To this extent the revolution was, as Rodolfo Stavenhagen and others have suggested, a bourgeois revolution, if not in its origins at least in its consequences.[7]

Since the business elite of Monterrey is firmly in control of the city, and since its members are quite vocal in support of the ideology of "free enterprise" capitalism (which puts them occasionally at odds with the national government but never to the point of rebellion or of jeopardizing their business interests), and since the degree of income con-

---

by Claudio Stern and Joseph A. Kahl in "Stratification since the Revolution," in *Comparative Perspectives on Stratification*, ed. Joseph A. Kahl.

[6] Claudio Véliz, in the Introduction to *Obstacles to Change in Latin America*.

[7] Rodolfo Stavenhagen, "Aspectos sociales de la estructura agraria en México," in *Neolatifundismo y explotación*.

ntration is heavily in their favor and their great wealth is no secret, it might be anticipated that the upper class would be the object of much hostility on the part of the working class. This does not seem to be the case, for in our casual experience in the Monterrey environment we have been struck by the relative lack of hostile comments directed toward the economic elite. That it has not become the target of great hostility can at least partially be accounted for by several reasons.

In part as a way of resisting independent union influence, most family capitalists in Monterrey have adopted paternalistic policies. These policies so far have found favor with the workers, not only because they materially enhance their economic positions but also because most working-class Mexicans are not far removed from rural environments, where a *patrón* relationship is common and accepted. The workers prefer the "personal" relationship with their employer, who can be depended upon to sponsor and protect them. The members of the economic elite continually maintain that they are working for the future of Monterrey and a bigger and better city. They seem to have been able to persuade the majority of *regiomontanos* that there is no conflict between the elite's goals for the city and their private gain. As mentioned in Chapter 2, the *regiomontanos* take genuine pride in their widespread reputation as being hard workers, and this ethos is not limited to one class, although it seems strongest among the middle and upper classes. The ascetic character of the industrial elite, characteristic of the old generation but deteriorating among their sons, is still part of the mystique of Monterrey's capitalism. At least up until the mid-sixties, the big industrial families were able to show their concern in keeping control over their businesses in two ways. They have kept their independence by refusing to sell out to multinational corporations and by not delegating any important decision-making power to hired managers.

The Monterrey middle class can be described in two words: small and emergent. It represents somewhat more than one-fifth of the population of Monterrey. In Chapter 2 we noted some of the reasons for the small size (lack of commercial development and restricted public bureaucracy) that would not, for example, apply to Mexico City. Even though the proportion of the middle class is small relative to, say, U.S. standards, it has experienced relatively rapid growth over the past decades. It also has experienced change in composition. The "old," or independent, occupational groups—small entrepreneurs, merchants, "traditional" professionals—are now joined by the "new" occupational groups deriving from the trend toward greater bureaucratization—the technicians and white-collar functionaries in both native and foreign large firms, in the government, and in specialized services.

The Monterrey middle class, therefore, is of a heterogeneous nature. It is also heterogeneous in its social origins. As was mentioned in Chapter 9 for the older men, the middle class is largely of working-class origin. It is relatively weak and lacking in cohesion and is generally apolitical. Dependent to one degree or another upon the business elite, the middle class has followed the lead of the latter. The middle class has flourished in the last generation, and it accepts the work and community ethic of the upper class. The process of industrialization has opened up new positions and the middle, not the lower class, has been the chief beneficiary of the virtually free public higher education.[8] Consequently, most members of the middle class, especially those who take as reference their working-class origins, have reason to be relatively contented with their lot.

It is the working class, representing as it does the great bulk of the population of Monterrey, that is the key to understanding class relations in that city. The majority of its members are wage earners, while a minority are self-employed. Among wage earners we find a considerable differentiation, mainly along two interrelated lines: skill and type of enterprise. Workers in the largest industrial enterprises of Monterrey, both privately and publically owned, enjoy considerably higher wages, job stability, fringe benefits, and other advantages than workers in more traditional, generally much smaller, plants, or those employed in commerce or services. In part, they receive these benefits because these workers are organized into stronger unions. Both kinds of organizations contain a range of skill levels, but there is a larger proportion of skilled workers in the larger establishments because of their greater utilization of modern technology. The differences in remuneration within the working class are very great. Just to provide some indication of the

---

[8] There is much disagreement and discussion on the emergence and development of middle classes in Latin America. See John J. Johnson, *Political Change in Latin America: The Emergence of the Middle Sectors*; Luis Ratinoff, "The New Urban Groups: The Middle Classes," in *Elites in Latin America*, ed. Seymour M. Lipset and Aldo Solari; Jorge Graciarena, *Poder y clases sociales en el desarrollo de América Latina*, especially Chap. 5; and Glaucio A. D. Soares, "Economic Development and Class Structure," in *Class, Status, and Power*, ed. Reinhard Bendix and S. M. Miller.

range, a skilled worker in the nationalized electric company or in the Fundidora steel plant can earn four to five times the pay of a construction laborer, and, if we take into account the days actually worked and the housing, health, and educational benefits accruing to the former, the difference becomes even greater. Among self-employed men who do not employ wage labor and who are classified in manual positions, there are also important differences. They range from petty street vendors or roving car washers to the men who operate their own taxi cabs, run a grocery store with the help of unpaid family labor, or are highly skilled artisans.

The heterogeneity of working-class positions can be traced to the sharp distinctions between economic sectors in Monterrey. As presented in Chapters 1 and 2, one important characteristic of the new pattern of industrialization encountered in Mexico and other developing countries is the emergence of technologically modern industries, whose organizational structure does not differ greatly from that found in the most advanced countries. This economic sector, the most dynamic in terms of growth of product, does not automatically absorb or eliminate other sectors that are technologically less advanced and whose roots are in the preindustrial economy. In Mexico the foremost representative of the latter is agriculture, where traditional technology still is used by the majority of production units. But even in the cities we find many activities that belong in this classification. Customarily, such units are called "traditional" in contrast to the "modern" sector of the economy. The expectation that the latter would slowly but inevitably absorb the former in the process of economic development has not been fulfilled. Even in such a dynamic center as Monterrey there has been in the last boom decades a relatively slow increase in the proportion of the male labor force employed in the modern sector. Of course, there has been a large increase in the proportion of the "product" of Monterrey generated by modern enterprises, but not an equivalent increase in the labor force they employ.

The relationship between growth in output and growth of the labor force in the traditional and modern sectors touches upon one of the fundamental problems confronting developing countries of today. Because of the dramatic upsurge in population growth that began a generation or so ago, large numbers of men are now entering the labor force, and their absorption has created many difficulties. The reason for this has already been suggested: the most dynamic sector has relatively the least need for manpower because of its capital-intensive organization. Those men without education or skills have no recourse but to try to find employment in the traditional sector, whether or not the "demand" for their labor is there.

The division of the working class of Monterrey into two categories, one of which has derived considerable benefit from the process of industrialization while the other has benefited very little, has greatly handicapped the development of strong class consciousness within the working class as a whole. This is the main distinction drawn by González Casanova in his discussion of cleavages within the working class. Also, much of the theorizing about marginality in Latin America refers to this difference in labor market participation.[9] Those in the integrated sector occupy privileged positions and they are well aware of it. They know that the men in the marginal sector would like very much to have the pay and job security they enjoy. Therefore, far from demonstrating solidarity with their working-class brothers and joining with them to raise the overall level of the working class, men in the integrated sector generally back fully exclusionist policies of both the unions and the employers that would reduce job competition.

There are additional features of the class structure of Monterrey that minimize class solidarity and class consciousness in the working class. The line dividing the upper ranks of the working class and the lower middle class is quite blurred in Monterrey, probably more so than in most Latin American cities. As noted, many of those in the middle class are of working-class origins and many (especially the older men) have themselves crossed the boundary within their own working lives. In Monterrey, possibly in contrast to other places in Latin America, there is relatively little deprecation of manual labor, and this makes for a more egalitarian tone to interpersonal class contacts. It is prestigeful to be employed in one of the large modern firms, but to be employed as a skilled worker does little to decrease one's status. Many workers earn more than those in the middle class. This situation is not uncommon elsewhere, but what is not so common is to find working-class labor so highly esteemed.

The detailed description of paths of occupational mobility provided in Chapter 8 and the analysis of the work profiles of the older men in

---

[9] See González Casanova, "Dynamics of the Class Structure," and the literature on marginality mentioned in Chap. 1, n. 31.

Chapter 9 made it clear that there is much mobility cutting across the integrated-marginal line. For example, it was noted in Chapter 9 that many workers in large modern enterprises have reached these positions from farm origins. Part of the horizontal mobility discussed in Chapter 8 cuts across this line. Until recently, at least, entrance into the integrated sector and the ranks of the skilled workers has not been seriously restricted, except for the relatively small growth of these positions. But the rather fluid situation that characterized Monterrey is changing as "credentials" (education, union membership) are becoming ever more important. The consequences of such changes for the integrated and marginal sectors will be discussed in the section on the future of Monterrey. What all this discussion implies is that, although at any given time a large number of men (40 percent of the working class according to our estimate) are marginal, few are trapped for life—or for generations as some authors have suggested—in the ranks of the marginals. Thus, only a minority of men, either in their experience or in their expectations, have reason to believe that they always will be "marginal"—a term, incidentally, that almost no *regiomontano* would apply to himself or to his work.

The class structure of Monterrey is rendered fluid and permeable in a way that goes beyond the direct work experience and class placement of the men. The family and kinship ties that are so important for all classes often bring together into the kinship circles members who differ considerably in their placement in the class structure. Most working-class men have relatives who have crossed class lines, from marginal to integrated or from working to middle class. Kinship ties are such that a move up or down does not mean a severing of contacts. The upwardly mobile men are not expected to pull their immediate kin up with them, but they are expected to maintain social contacts and to help out if possible.

Finally, there is the political arena, where conflict could be expected to reveal itself. So far, at least, there has been little eruption of class conflict within the political system. The upper and middle classes have little reason to be very dissatisfied with their lot. The working class is clearly divided and not likely to join in any concerted action. The integrated sector is organized into unions, but, as in Mexico as a whole, the autonomy of unions is quite restricted. The leaders have either been coopted by the PRI nationally or, in the case of the company unions, by the managers. The large marginal population of Monterrey is not organized, partly because the nature of their work—street vending, construction, low-status service jobs—makes it difficult to organize, except sporadically, as when street vendors unite to petition (unsuccessfully) the city government to allow them to hawk their wares in the central business district. But even if there is no occupational basis for organizing, might not there be other bases for concerted effort, such as the residential and ethnic bases for political action that are to be found in the Peruvian (Lima) situation?[10] For reasons that are not clear, there has been relatively little illegal land seizure in Monterrey, and so this action has not served to unite people, and there is little ethnic differentiation in Monterrey. Perhaps the key to explaining why the marginals have so little say in the political process is the fact that in a one-party system their massive vote carries less weight than when a number of competing political parties exist. No outsider has tried to organize or mobilize these people in order to get votes, because the ballot box in Mexico is not now a place where important decisions are made. Thus the socioeconomically marginal population is truly marginal in the role it plays in the political process.

The Consequences of Migration on the Community and the Individual Level

Policy makers are not in agreement when it comes to evaluating the effects or consequences of internal migration, particularly rural-urban migration, in the developing countries. Some see it as a means of speeding up economic development, while others believe its consequences are largely undesirable. The latter are likely to mention the difficulty of incorporating the migrants into the labor force and the forms of social and personal disorganization that result from the migration process. In this section we want to examine the effect of internal migration on Cedral as a community of origin and on Monterrey as a community of destination, beginning with the latter at the community and the individual levels.[11]

---

[10] William P. Mangin, "The Role of Regional Associations in the Adaptation of Rural Migrants to Cities in Peru," *Sociologus* 9, no. 1 (1955): 23–35; and John C. Turner, "Barriers and Channels for Housing Development in Modernizing Countries," *Journal of American Institute of Planners* 33 (May 1967): 167–181.

[11] Unfortunately, there are few field studies of the effects of migration for communities of both origin and destination, except where international migrations are

The basic question to be addressed for Monterrey is Under what conditions is migratory status a basis for political organization and political conflict? Conflict is more likely to be encountered if the following six conditions are present: (1) if migrants are homogeneous in socioeconomic status, that is, if they are almost entirely from the lower status; (2) if migrants, once in the city, find it extremely difficult to be upwardly mobile in the occupational structure; (3) if migrants are culturally and ethnically diverse when compared with the natives so that a "we" and a "they" designation develops; (4) if migrants are residentially segregated in the city so that they have little contact with other groups; (5) if there is no possibility of return migration to community of origin for those who for one reason or another do not adjust well to life in the city; and (6) if the migrants are mobilized by one or more political parties who are strong and active in the political process.

In Monterrey none of the above six conditions hold for migrants. The heterogeneity of migrants coming to Monterrey has been emphasized repeatedly, and migrants are to be found in all parts of the socioeconomic hierarchy. The career man sent from Mexico City to head an important branch of the national concern is as much a migrant as the middle-aged arrival who has been a subsistence farmer all his life. As far as occupational mobility is concerned, we have been able to demonstrate in Chapters 5 and 8 that the relative opportunities for advancement are not necessarily lower for migrants as compared to natives. An examination of intergenerational mobility rates (respondents compared to their fathers) shows no important differences between migrants and natives. In addition, the intragenerational mobility rates for the two groups show conclusively that the key to migratory success is age. Provided that migrants to Monterrey arrive at an early age, their handicap in comparison with natives is nil. Those migrants who arrive before age 26, in fact, do better. In northeastern Mexico, in contrast to southern Mexico, there are very few cultural or ethnic distinctions to be made within the population; they all share the same mestizo "national" Mexican culture. And whatever their background before arrival, natives and migrants are not residentially segregated from one another to any important degree. Nor do the patterns of residential mobility after arrival in Monterrey show any important differences be-

---

involved, so our comments about the effects of migration on Cedral and Monterrey cannot be contrasted with empirical studies in other settings.

tween natives and migrants. As far as can be determined from both the Monterrey and the Cedral data, return migration is quite sizable, and it does serve the safety-valve function of providing an "out" for those who are dissatisfied with conditions in Monterrey. Finally, the Mexican political system is not conducive to the mobilization of the migrants as a group, for much the same reasons that were set forth to account for the minor political importance of the marginal sector of the Monterrey population.

Taken together, the six points we have enumerated help to explain why geographic mobility, far from exacerbating group and class conflict in Monterrey, has dampened it. Perhaps in this context we can understand Orlando Fals Borda when, in considering the revolutionary potential of Latin America in general, he speaks of the "ideological sterility of rural-urban migration."[12]

We now turn our attention to Cedral to elaborate the consequences of migration, in this case very substantial net out-migration, for the development of group and political conflict. It should not be taken for granted that Cedral, or places similar to it, is noted for social tranquility. Such communities are very poor and have shared little in the economic boom of the last thirty years, while at the same time the levels of aspiration of their inhabitants have been raised by increasing contact with the outside world brought about largely by external forces, particularly the national government. Our thesis is that migration is an important mechanism that serves to weaken the group and class conflict that would otherwise be engendered by the combination of a stagnant economy and a very high rate of natural increase of the population.

In Cedral, the class structure of Cedral town must be considered separately from that of the rural part of the *municipio*, for the former is considerably more complex. Cedral town, as described in Chapter 3, has commercial agriculture based upon well irrigation and carried out in relatively small holdings. There is also a relatively important non-agricultural sector made up of small commercial and service enterprises. These productive units determine the main class relations and cleavages, and, in order to appreciate the role of migration, it will be necessary first to describe the class structure in some detail. The two crucial relationships connected with the town's economy are between

---

[12] Orlando Fals Borda, *Las revoluciones inconclusas de América Latina*, p. 42.

creditor and debtor and between employer and employed. The creditors are nearly all store owners and relatively large agriculturalists.
Since the creditor has the most scarce goods in the community, he
makes a good profit and exercises substantial control over the economic
activities of the debtor. But this control is limited. The debtor does not
assume obligations of a political or a family nature, as was often the
case in the *hacendado-peón* relationship. In Cedral no one person has
a monopoly of capital. Therefore, the borrower has a certain flexibility,
for he can apply to several places.

The second important relationship in the town is the employer-em-
ployed one, which is mainly between agriculturalist and day laborer,
since there are no large nonagricultural enterprises providing a manage-
ment-labor relationship. Nearly all the commercial agriculturalists employ wage labor, but for only a few months of the year and nearly
always in the form of day contracts, which produces a very restricted
relationship between employers and those employed. The agriculturalists often do not have a level of living much higher than the men they
employ. Consequently, the social distance between employer and employed is small.

In the two relations we have described for the town, the mechanisms
of the market determine the relative advantages of the groups, but they
do not permit a consolidation of class interests. None of them create
obligations of a more permanent and personally diffuse kind, as can be
found in other rural property systems, such as the hacienda or the plantation.[13] The groups formed by the two poles of the relation (debtors
and creditors, laborers and agriculturalists) are not clearly fixed. Day
laborers can become property owners with a certain ease; the problem
is that land ownership does not guarantee a better level of living or any
very significant change in class position. The fact that many of the
Cedraleños may occupy several of these positions simultaneously or
alternatively demonstrates the fluidity and the lack of crystallization of
the class structure.

It might be otherwise were it not for the role that geographic mobility plays in Cedral. Anyone who examines only the census figures for
Cedral town over the past fifty years and its slow growth during this

---

[13] For an analysis of different types of rural class systems, see Arthur L. Stinchcombe, "Agricultural Enterprise and Rural Class Relations," *American Journal of
Sociology* 67, no. 2 (September 1961): 165–176.

period might be tempted to conclude that it is a sleepy, remote, and demographically stagnant community. In actuality, the amount of movement in and out of Cedral is astonishingly large, as are the personal links with the outside world. A large number of Cedraleños have permanently migrated, and they include representatives of all the groups we have described. Of those respondents interviewed in town, 55 percent have had at least one migration of six months or more, and many of the men have been seasonal migrants to other parts of Mexico and to the United States. Of all men who have living brothers, 70 percent had one or more brothers who were born in Cedral but were living elsewhere (mainly Monterrey, the border cities, and the United States). Of those who had sons over age 15, 60 percent had at least one son living outside the Cedral region.

These various forms of geographical mobility introduce a great deal of fluidity into the social structure. They are vital for a community like Cedral, where the capacity of the local economy to absorb ever-increasing numbers of young men (the product of one of the highest rates of natural increase in Mexico) into productive jobs is low. Thus, migration, in its various forms, serves the important function of maintaining the status quo.[14] Since local resources and opportunities are inadequate to support the population, many men who do not wish to leave the community permanently take the options of seasonal and return migration as a means of maintaining themselves and their families in Cedral. Out-migration is facilitated because Cedral is a culturally homogeneous community, and those who migrate do not encounter cultural or ethnic barriers in the places to which they go. In terms of the class relations earlier described, migration offers several "outs" to the subordinate groups. Debtors can pay off their debts with a good crop, or by working several months of the year outside Cedral in the cotton or tomato harvests, or by working as construction laborers in the city. Laborers are not "bound" to any one employer within the town; they are free to seek work elsewhere, either permanently or temporarily.

The situation outside Cedral town is somewhat different, but the role of seasonal and permanent migration is similar. In subsistence farming

---

[14] Gino Germani discusses briefly the "stabilizing mechanism" provided by mass internal migration and compares it with a similar one shared by mass overseas emigration for the European countries. See his "Stages of Modernization in Latin America," *Studies in Comparative International Development* 8 (1969–1970): 155–174.

the men and their families work on their own, having little contact with the outside economy. The situation is different when they work as *ixtleros*, collecting and processing plants to sell the hard fiber. Ixtle is the main source of cash for many of them, and the market where they sell it is controlled directly or indirectly by the government. Since most *ixtleros* and subsistence farmers are *ejidatarios*, the key relationship is between the communities and the government, and not class relations within the communities, there being little differentiation on this basis. Potentially, this is a much more explosive situation than that prevailing in the town, aggravated as it is by the extreme poverty of the *ejidatarios*. But seasonal work in Cedral town or in other agricultural regions as well as permanent out-migration serve as safety valves. In comparison with the town dwellers, the *ejidatarios* have a higher proportion of temporary migrations, mainly as seasonal laborers in Mexican areas of commercial agriculture, or as braceros (when that program existed) and wetbacks to the United States. There is less migration to the cities than from the town, and when it occurs it is generally for shorter periods of time. The possibility of migrating, in whatever form, offers an escape valve when conditions become extremely difficult for the *ejidatarios*, and it functions regularly to offset population growth and permanent poverty.

Our arguments support the hypothesis that migration weakens expressions of group and class conflict in communities both of origin and of destination. This hypothesis is reinforced when considering the migratory experience at the individual level. In previous chapters we had the opportunity to discuss the family context of migration and the actual opportunities encountered by migrants when arriving in the city. But, for an analysis of the conflict potential of the migratory experience, the subjective evaluations of the men are equally important.

The relationship between age at migration to the city and possibility of moving up occupationally is well understood by our respondents, both in Monterrey and in Cedral. The great majority of those interviewed in Monterrey, 71 percent of the natives and 77 percent of the migrants, were in accord with the statement that, to progress, the best thing a young man living in a village could do would be to migrate to a city like Monterrey. The Cedral respondents not only are in agreement with this statement, but they also know that the young have much better chances than the old. More than 90 percent of the respondents agreed with the statement that a young man would do well to go to the city, whereas only 31 percent were of the same opinion for an older man.

Apart from the actual position of the migrants in the structure of Monterrey is their perceived position, that is, their subjective evaluations of their social position. This judgment may be at variance with what actually is happening to them, because a subjective judgment about one's position is always a comparative judgment, and it will vary according to which group a man compares himself with. For example, a man may have advanced a considerable distance up the occupational ladder, but, if he believes that his friends and neighbors have done better, he is likely to be dissatisfied with his lot. In contrast, a migrant to Monterrey, even though he has not been able to find a good job and his living situation is poor by Monterrey standards, may evaluate himself as doing well, because his basis of comparison is his relatives and friends in his community of origin who live close to the margin of subsistence. In the terminology of sociology, what we have been discussing are "reference groups." A migrant's evaluation of his social position also has a temporal dimension, for it is dependent not only upon his present circumstances and those with whom he has some contact. Generationally he compares his situation with that of his father and of his sons when they will reach maturity. These generational evaluations color and affect the man's evaluation of his current situation and prospects, and they can be separated only analytically.

The evaluation of one's position is always done in comparative terms: it depends on the reference groups used. We asked our migrants to Monterrey to compare their current work with the work their fathers had at approximately the same age (if the father had died before this age, the comparison was with the father's last employment). Over two-thirds (68 percent) of the migrants believe their work is better than their fathers', with only a bit over a fifth (22 percent) saying it is worse. This favorable comparison with the prior generation can be attributed to several reasons. First, many migrants do occupy higher occupational positions and so have moved up in comparison with their fathers. Second, many of the migrants originate in rural areas, and their father's work was in agriculture, often subsistence farming. Many men believe that city work is superior because it is less physically demanding, less dirty, and less subject to the calamities of nature, even though the city job is at a low skill level. Third, the Mexican population as a whole has experienced a relative bettering of their economic position, at least those in metropolitan environments, and even those who have not directly shared in the advance may be influenced by the incessant trumpeting in the mass media of Mexico's economic "miracle," to the extent that they themselves believe they have benefited.

But these explanations still do nothing to dispel the doubt that many migrants say they are better off than their fathers simply in order to provide an optimistic report for the interviewer; after all, who cares to admit to others that in his work he has been a relative failure? The possible bias introduced by painting a falsely rosy picture of one's situation can be looked at from the perspective of the migrant's evaluation of his situation in comparison with that of his brothers (or the majority of his brothers). If the men do bias their reports toward the rosy side, then we should expect this to show up in the comparison with their brothers, such that the men will, on the average, report themselves as better off. If, however, they make realistic appraisals, then there is little reason to believe that they would be either much better or much worse off than their brothers. Upon examination, the results support the latter hypothesis. Among men who are native to Monterrey, 32 percent reported themselves as better off, 33 percent the same, and 32 percent as worse off than their brothers. Among the migrants, however, the respective figures were 41, 30, and 27 percent. Does this mean that the migrants were more roseate in their self-appraisals? Not necessarily. Many migrants have brothers still living in rural areas, so the objective differences would justify the more favorable appraisals. The comparison with their brothers leads us to conclude that the respondents do not falsify to any great extent their evaluation of their positions relative to their fathers'. It should also be mentioned that when the Monterrey men are cross-classified by their actual intragenerational mobility with their self-evaluation of their situation, there is a linear relationship between amount of mobility and satisfaction with one's situation.

The men's optimism really soars when they are asked about the occupational expectations they hold for their sons. Of the natives who have sons, 65 percent aspire university training for them and 61 percent a career as a professional or a top executive. Four-fifths of the native fathers expect their sons to hold nonmanual positions. The migrants' expectations for their sons are lower but still reflect great optimism. Forty-nine percent of the migrants who have sons aspire university training for them and 44 percent a professional or a top executive career. Two-thirds of the migrant fathers expect their sons to hold non-

manual positions. These high aspirations are also reflected in their view
of the life chances for their sons. When those men who have sons were
asked the question "Do you think that your oldest son can live much
better than you live now, somewhat better, relatively the same, or
worse?" natives and migrants gave virtually the same answers. Twenty-
eight percent said "much better," 60 percent "better," 10 percent "the
same," and a mere 1 percent "worse." The 88 percent who believed
their oldest son would do better than themselves were asked the reasons for their optimism. Two-thirds of them (64 percent) mentioned
increased education or superior preparation for occupational life, while
11 percent believed that the general progress of Mexican society and
its economic development would provide better circumstances for their
sons.

It would be easy to dismiss the men's aspirations for their sons as no
more than wishful thinking. The actual educational and occupational
attainment of the first sons certainly does not match these lofty aspirations, and it is manifestly impossible for either the educational or the
occupational system to absorb so large a proportion of the third generation in such elevated positions. But these unrealistic aspirations have
another significance that should not be forgotten. The majority of our
men consider the stratification system of Monterrey to be a very "open"
one that will allow for the sons' ascent, even if the fathers remain low
in the system. And there is widespread agreement that education is the
principal mechanism that will enable the sons to do better. The superior education they foresee for their sons should be translated into superior jobs. Now the fathers have every reason to believe that the sons
will occupy higher positions than their fathers, since the sons on the
average have a better education. The question really becomes one of
asking how much longer the pattern of generational optimism we have
just described can continue, a matter to be taken up in the last section
of this chapter.

We have tried to show that the migrant's successful incorporation
into the structure of Monterrey is dependent, among other things, upon
his age at arrival and his subjective perception of his situation. A third
feature, which was also mentioned earlier in a structural context, is return migration, which psychologically is quite important to the migrant
in Monterrey. There is always the possibility of going back home, for
the door is always open, so to speak. Actually a fair number do so.
Mostly, they return within a few years after arriving in Monterrey, and

this return migration serves to separate out of the population of Monterrey those who are most discontented. In communities like Cedral, the high rate of net out-migration makes it likely that return migrants will not have great difficulty finding housing of a kind and a small plot to farm in a subsistence manner. And if they return, kinship obligations will serve them in good stead in getting settled once again. We were much impressed, in conversations in Cedral, by the casualness with which most decisions to return were taken. The community of origin plays a most important role in the life of a migrant who ends up on the lower rungs of the stratification ladder. Depending upon his disposition, which may fluctuate, he may feel he is better off in Monterrey precisely because he compares himself not with other workers in Monterrey but with his relatives and friends who may be eking out a living as subsistence farmers, or he may be pessimistic about present and prospective conditions in Monterrey and so "home" becomes a way out of his problems, whether he actually returns or not. With either frame of mind he is less likely to be concerned with doing something about his situation, particularly in developing strong class consciousness and participation in various forms of political protest.

Stability amid Change

We have seen that migration, contrary to what is generally believed, may operate as a stabilizing factor in communities both of origin and of destination. Now we want to take up another common assumption, namely, that the processes of industrialization and urbanization are sources of personal and social disorganization. It is often argued that these processes introduce rapid and profound changes into men's lives, especially those who are migrants, and that a series of undesirable consequences follows these changes: maladjustments in work roles, disintegration of family groups, breakdown of normative patterns. Personal disorganization, anomic behavior, and social unrest are seen as the end results of the industrialization and urbanization processes.[15]

Mexico, as will be recalled from our discussion in Chapter 1, is one of the countries showing rapid change within the course of the last decades, as revealed by such indicators as percent urban, life expectancy, and proportion illiterate. Monterrey, as one of the most dynamic

[15] For a perspective that emphasizes the disruptive effect, see DESAL, *Marginalidad en América Latina: Un ensayo de diagnóstico.*

growth centers of the country, has been fully involved in this transformation. Our investigation, it is true, was not designed to test directly
the amount of personal and social disorganization engendered by this
change. Yet it is our impression, based on the totality of the findings of
this investigation, that the Monterrey men have lived through this period of rapid change without displaying many of the disruptive symp-
toms predicted by "classical" theory. We will try to explain how stability amid change is possible by examining in turn key institutional
areas—work, community, family, and values—to show how each serves
to make the transition a relatively smooth one.

Work is central in a man's life. It determines to a considerable degree
his level of living, his pattern of behavior, his attitudes, and his political
stance. Different work contexts, therefore, should have ramifications beyond the workplace itself. The work circumstances of the Monterrey
men have been quite diverse, particularly because of the rural background of many of them. In the work histories of our men are experiences as varied as herding goats on the rock hills of southern Nuevo
León, gathering ixtle fibers in arid northern San Luis Potosí, driving a
large tractor in a sugar-beet field in Colorado, U.S.A., operating an automatic milling machine in a Monterrey steel mill, or running an IBM
counter-sorter. The literature dealing with the human problems of industrialization is full of analyses of the difficulties of commitment and
performance in modern industrial establishments when compared to
traditional farming or handicrafts.[16] The extent to which these problems are present, however, will depend upon a variety of factors, the
most important of which is the nature of the organization of work in
industrial firms. When work is physically demanding or dangerous,
when it requires constant attention and responsibility in the handling of
complex and expensive machinery, and when it precludes or interferes
with socializing among workers, those men who have had little exposure to such a work context will experience considerable strain.

There are two complementary arguments we want to introduce to
explain why, for the great majority of Monterrey men, the process of

[16] Wilbert E. Moore and Arnold S. Feldman, eds., *Labor Commitment and Social
Change in Developing Areas.* Studies of the adjustment of rural migrants to indus-
trial work include Juarez Rubens Brandão Lopes, "Aspects of the Adjustment of
Rural Migrants to Urban-Industrial Conditions in São Paulo, Brazil" in *Urbaniza-
tion in Latin America,* ed. Philip M. Hauser; and Guillermo Briones and José Mejía
Valera, *El obrero industrial.*

industrialization has not resulted in important stresses and strains associated with work performance. Most of the technologically advanced industries do not impose physically demanding and hazardous work conditions, as was frequently the case with nineteenth-century industrialization. Indeed, men with agricultural backgrounds believe that almost all jobs to be found in Monterrey are less wearing physically and are cleaner than farm work. Also, the likelihood of local particularistic adjustments to the formal demands of industrial organization is great. For example, Manning Nash's study of a small Indian community in Guatemala showed quite clearly that the textile mill (granted that it was not technologically advanced) did not impose serious ruptures in the life patterns of the male and female workers, whose only previous experience had been on the family farm or as plantation laborers.[17] There being no Indian culture of consequence in northeastern Mexico, the problem of adjustment would not be as dramatic as in the Guatemalan case.

The second argument is the key to understanding the relatively smooth adjustments to the process of industrialization. Many writers have made the profound error of assuming that as a rule the same man will be asked to perform within his lifetime widely different work tasks. To return to one of the examples cited earlier, the goat herder will be asked to operate the automated machinery in the steel mill. Actually, such a change would be quite exceptional, and it would be almost impossible for a mature man. It is possible within the lifetime of one man, but this situation would require that he be a goat herder as a boy. Then he would migrate at an early age to Monterrey, where, if he is fortunate, he might eventually work up to the status of a skilled machine operator. But for the great majority of older migrants to the city, the work they are able to find is not very different from the kind of work done in their communities of origin. Construction, petty commerce, watchmen's or similar service jobs—this kind of work does not thrust them into wholly new occupational worlds. The example of the construction industry has been cited many times, for most of the older, uneducated, and inexperienced migrants to Monterrey at one time or another are employed as construction laborers. This work is carried out in much the same way in urban and rural environments, and its conditions are similar to those of farm work—physical labor, outdoor situa-

[17] Manning Nash, *Machine Age Maya*.

tions, and relative flexibility of scheduling tasks. Thus, it turns out that the migrants from rural areas, who presumably face the greatest challenges in adapting to changes in work environments, only rarely are called upon to do so. It isn't that peasants reject work in modern industrial surroundings; they simply have very little chance of getting it, because of their lack of qualifications. As a result, it is mainly the sons of peasants who become industrial workers in large modern plants. The one exception to this rule is the peasant who comes to the city as a boy or a very young man. But even this route is less and less open because of the increasing importance of credentials, particularly school certificates, as automatic prerequisites to occupying almost all positions, no matter what the skill level, in modern industrial firms.

Basically, there are two mechanisms that permit the transformation of the occupational structure: changes in the kind of jobs held by successive cohorts entering the labor force, and changes during the work-life cycles of men. One of the principal findings of the Monterrey study has been that the basic mechanism for the transformation of the occupational structure, even in a society as rapidly changing as Mexico's, is provided by a succession of age cohorts, each of which enters the labor force at higher occupational levels on the average than the previous ones. The reasons for this progression are the successively higher level of educational attainment by the cohorts and the tendency of new industries to recruit their new workers from among younger men. In Monterrey, therefore, change is effected by the entry of young, better-educated cohorts in the labor force, rather than by drastic changes in the work experience of individual men. This is not to say that there is not considerable work mobility among the Monterrey men, but it seldom involves great shifts in the work environment. Nor is Monterrey unusual in this respect. Duncan, after analyzing the changes in the occupational structure of the United States, arrived at the conclusion, "the changes at the aggregate level are in general consistent with changes among cohorts; this suggests that the succession of cohorts is the fundamental mechanism of change in the occupational structure."[18] And E. P. Thompson, in his fascinating history of the working class in England, reports that "when we follow in detail the history of particular industries and we analyze how new specialties emerged and the old ones de-

---

[18] Otis D. Duncan, "Occupational Trends and Patterns of Net Mobility in the United States," *Demography* 3, no. 1 (1966): 15.

clined, it is easy to forget that in almost all cases the old specialties and the new ones were in the hands of different persons."[19]

Work is connected with community, and here, too, there has been a distorted image of the amount of adaptation required of a migrant coming to a large metropolitan area. Stereotypes that idealize the integration of the rural community of origin, on the one hand, while characterizing the city as cold and lacking in interpersonal contacts, on the other hand, were challenged in Chapter 6, where it was shown that the great majority of migrants, especially those of farm background, were much involved in kinship networks upon their arrival in Monterrey. The degree of impersonality in social relations is not always a consequence of size of community. In any event, it is the neighborhood rather than the entire city that represents for nearly all Monterrey families the meaningful unit for social interaction, and within this context there often is not a great deal of difference in interpersonal exchanges than would be found in a village. In a fast-growing city like Monterrey most of the people who make up the neighborhoods within the city either come directly from villages or have parents who have done so, so there is a continuity between the rural and urban institutions. This continuity is also revealed in the organization of the family and in the basic value system, to which we now turn our attention.

Of all institutions, it is probably the family that has been most important in easing adjustment to the metropolitan industrial setting and making it smoother than it otherwise might be. In Chapter 6 we spelled out in some detail how deeply the kinship network was involved in the process of migration. Only a small fraction of migrants experienced the journey to and settlement in Monterrey without contacts and various forms of assistance from relatives or close friends. Doubtless the family in Mexico is changing as is everything else, but our impression—and it has to be just that because we did not make the family the object of our investigation and there is little research in Mexico on this key institution—is that it is in no way suffering a "breakdown" or a decline. We are impressed not only by the evident stability of the family as an institution, but also by its relative uniformity in rural and urban environments and across the lines of social strata. The degree of family cohesion, the extent of kinship interaction, fundamental values—these

---

[19] E. P. Thompson, *The Making of the English Working Class: 1780–1830*, p. 247.

characteristics do not vary widely between such disparate communities as Cedral and Monterrey, between migrants and natives in the latter place, between rich and poor, or between generations.

The enormous importance of the family for the people of Mexico perhaps is best appreciated when it is under greatest strain. The famous children of Sánchez[20] were part of a "malfunctioning" family system, but, no matter how great their conflicts with their father and with each other, none of them could bring themselves to separate from the rest of the family. Family ties have great affective significance for the members, and family obligations cannot be lightly disregarded. We do not know how much a man's occupational mobility or that of his nuclear family is affected by the concentration of social contacts with kin groups and by the exercise of family obligations to the extended kin circle—in general, a family-oriented existence. In some cases it may deflect attention from economic goals and may even constitute an economic drain, and it may discourage the assumption of risks. But even if this is true, perhaps the benefits accruing to the men and their families in terms of an easier adjustment to a changing environment might, in their eyes as well as those of the observer, balance out the negative effects. Since only a few men ever can ascend very far up the status ladder, in any event, family and kin ties are a "solace" not to be deprecated.

The last factor that eases the transition is the basic value system. One of the often implicit and sometimes explicit assumptions of the social scientists who work within a theoretical framework of dichotomies —folk-urban, traditional-modern—is the propensity to construct opposing and mutually exclusive value systems. Nothing that we have encountered in the course of this investigation lends support to the position that there are two distinct cultural and normative systems—the rural and the urban—that demand complete and exclusive allegiance from every one of their members. If this were true, then migrants to Monterrey originating in rural areas would be forced to abandon whole sets of normative expectations or face considerable conflict in their new environment. The challenge would be, of course, greatest for older migrants. But few migrants ever experienced such a dilemma, for it exists only in the minds of some writers. We have repeatedly stressed the ba-

---

[20] The reference here is to *The Children of Sánchez: Autobiography of a Mexican Family*, by Oscar Lewis.

sic continuity between rural and urban areas, at least in northeastern Mexico. In a place like Cedral the natives have no fears of going to urban places as migrants, for the basic cultural features of urban areas are of mestizo Mexico. Then, too, the "metropolitan" character of Monterrey is quite recent: only two generations ago the city was a rather provincial town.

The question really is Who socializes whom? for true urbanites are far outnumbered; only one of seven of our respondents in Monterrey goes back as far as two generations. Under such conditions it would be difficult for a purely "urban" culture to be widely diffused. Mexico City, with a greater flow of migrants from Indian communities, on the one hand, and a much richer urban tradition, on the other hand, may present greater contrasts and conflicts of values. But Oscar Lewis's observations about the urban poor of Mexico City emphasize the basic continuity between urban and rural values, although he would go further than we would in his designation of migrants from rural areas as "urban peasants."[21] Our position is that newcomers are able to take on city attitudes and behaviors because they are seldom required to reject or abandon their rural heritage; the urban experience is simply "layered" over it.

The Future of Monterrey Men

The men of Monterrey and the city itself have experienced a relatively smooth transition in the process of industrialization up to now. It is fair to ask, however, whether the reasons we have set forth to account for this relatively smooth transition will continue to be as effective in the future as they have been in the past. More specifically, what are the prospects for the Monterrey men over an intermediate period, say twenty years from the date of the survey, 1965?

To approach this question we will have to consider what will happen in the larger Mexican society and in Monterrey during the interval to 1985. The difficulty here is that many aspects of society are unpredictable. There is no way to predict a successful social revolution, and even in a more limited area, such as income distribution, it is hard to guess whether the trend of increasing income concentration that characterized Mexico over the last few decades will continue or whether there

[21] Oscar Lewis, "Further Observations on the Folk-Urban Continuum and Urbanization with Special Reference to Mexico City," in *The Study of Urbanization,* ed. Philip M. Hauser and Leo F. Schnore.

will be some basic reorientation in response to the mounting pressures toward income redistribution. For the sake of simplicity of discussion we will therefore assume that the basic sociopolitical structure of Mexico will not change. Within this general framework we will consider only those structural changes that are more likely to affect the prospects of the men.

Here the use of a replacement model is helpful. Thinking in terms of the four age cohorts frequently used in this study (21–30, 31–40, 41–50, and 51–60), by 1985 the two older cohorts largely will have exited from the labor force and most of the men will be dead. The two younger cohorts will then be aged 41–50 and 51–60, respectively, and the men who in 1985 will occupy the youngest age cohort categories, 21–30 and 31–40, will be completely new to the overall group, although all will have been born in 1965. In terms of these three groupings, "older," "younger," and "new" men, only the last two need be considered, since the "older" men largely will be out of the labor force.

We can start by looking at the composition of the two groups. In both the younger and the new groups there will be changes due to mortality and migration. The effects of the former are negligible, since mortality is very low for the age span here considered. Regarding migration, there is some evidence that the strikingly rapid increase in Monterrey's population during recent decades (sufficient to double the population every eleven years) will not continue. The results of the 1970 census provide a figure of 1.15 million for metropolitan Monterrey. This is a 65 percent increase over 1960, which is certainly rapid growth, but still noticeably inferior to the 90 percent gain recorded for each of the two preceding decades. Natural increase may have declined somewhat during the 1960–1970 decade, but most of the decline in the rate of growth is due to a lower rate of net migration to Monterrey. This decline at least partially is a consequence of the dwindling pool of potential migrants within the region of the country from which Monterrey has drawn most of its migrants. The combined rural populations of the states of Nuevo León, San Luis Potosí, and Coahuila grew by only 18 percent between 1960 and 1970. Whereas in the last several decades migration accounted for roughly one-half of Monterrey's total growth, in the 1965–1985 interval it may be no more than one-third.

This declining rate of in-migration to the city means that in 1985 the proportion of migrants in the younger group will be lower than the figure for the older group in 1965. The latter was made up of 75 percent migrants (defined by community of origin) in 1965, while the younger group had 54 percent. Although this 54 percent will grow, it will not reach 75 percent. Thus, the addition of 10 to 15 percent of migrants to the younger group will not alter drastically the composition of the group. We can expect that the striking intercohort differences that show up in 1965 in terms of education and positions in the first years of the work life will diminish. That is, when comparing the older men in 1965 and the younger in 1985, the latter will still show higher levels than the former, but the differences will be smaller than when looking at both groups in the present. We can base this prediction on the fact that migrants still will be predominantly from rural areas, the lack of selectivity of migrants will continue (especially if we think of migrants that come to the city at relatively older ages), and, if out-migration will have some effect, it will probably affect mostly the higher strata who will engage in career moves to Mexico City.

The situation is more problematic for the new men. Although all these men were alive in 1965, we don't have any information about them. If our predictions about migratory streams to the city hold up, this group should have a lower proportion of migrants by the time they reach ages 21–40 in 1985 than the comparable group in 1965. Less than half of them will be migrants, and it is likely that in this group the fact of whether or not they were raised in the city definitely will show up as *the* big factor determining their fate. Differences between natives and migrants in terms of education should be very great, given trends of increasing rural-urban and regional differences in educational attainment in Mexico. We can estimate the educational levels of some of the natives of this group by the data on the "third generation," the sons of our older respondents. (This is not an accurate estimate, since some of our sons are older than age 21, there may be a good number of young men in the city who don't have a father living in Monterrey, and we only took sons aged 15 or older, thus excluding the younger men in the new group.) Fourteen percent of the sons of respondents had some university experience, a figure that will grow as the even younger natives and early arrivals to the city continue to benefit from the increasing availability of higher education. Although the migrants who will be added to this new group probably will have higher levels of education than the migrants in the earlier cohorts (given the general increase in

the educational levels of the Mexican population), the difference between natives and migrants will keep widening throughout the intermediate future.

In summary, given the trends in population growth of the city and
in rural-urban and regional differences in Mexico, we can expect that
each new cohort will have a somewhat smaller proportion of migrants
when they reach maturity, while at the same time the differences between natives and migrants in terms of education will become larger.

The occupational prospects of the younger and new groups will depend largely on the changes in the Mexican economy. The economic
prospects for the country as a whole fundamentally reduce to the question of whether Mexico can maintain, or even improve upon, the rate
of economic growth of recent decades. Recently, Mexican economists
have considered the matter, and their opinions seem to be that it is
possible for Mexico to continue the growth of the GNP at an average
rate of 6 percent per annum, *provided* certain adjustments are made to
meet changed conditions. Víctor Urquidi, for example, believes an annual rate of growth of 8 percent is possible if a series of necessary conditions (i.e., agricultural development, rate of investment, improvement
of educational system) is met and if certain restrictions on the development of the economy are overcome, specifically, growth of external
demand, distribution of income, and the nature of the planning process
and public administration.[22] Without minimizing the difficulties posed
in making such adjustments and assuming no drastically unfavorable
changes in the world economy, it can be assumed, given the record of
considerable flexibility of the Mexican economy in the past, that the
past rate of growth will be maintained.

Within the national context, Monterrey's prospects are favorable for
several reasons. Like the country, the city has the momentum of several
decades of rapid sustained growth. Because Monterrey has been in the
forefront of Mexico's industrialization, she is in the position to take
advantage of her experience in large-scale production, using modern
techniques. For example, the government has been most anxious to
increase the share that manufactured products are of all exports, and
to do so it is offering various inducements to manufacturers to sell
abroad. As a result of past efforts to create external markets for her
manufactured products, Monterrey is in an excellent competitive posi-

---

[22] Víctor Urquidi, "La economía y la población," in *El Perfil de México en 1980.*

tion to take advantage of this orientation. Monterrey's main competitor within Mexico, Mexico City, soon may become subject to various restraints on her growth, for the capital's great size (8.5 million in 1970) and the resulting congestion and pollution have made visible to all the need to formulate governmental policies that can to some degree control the growth of the Mexican leviathan. Monterrey, being much smaller, is unlikely to be subject to similar restrictions.

Even though Monterrey's overall economic prospects are favorable over the intermediate term (in the long run, dependence upon heavy industry may become a handicap), this does not imply that the problems of absorption of manpower into the labor force will be eliminated. As in the past, it is the modern sector that will be favorably affected, and the trend toward capital-intensive operations will continue. Whether or not the proportion of "marginal" employment of the labor force will be lesser or greater in 1985 than it was in 1965 is an arguable point, but what is not at issue is the fact that at both dates a significant proportion of men will hold jobs providing them with a precarious and an inadequate income, jobs that exclude them from participation in the most dynamic sectors of the economy. As in 1965, marginal employment will be more prevalent among older men. Furthermore, within each new cohort, the concentration of marginal employment among migrants should be higher.

Increasing reliance on complex technology and greater bureaucratization will have two related consequences: first, an increasing emphasis on improving the educational levels of the population, and, second, a heavy emphasis on education in the placement of men at all levels of the occupational structure. Even more so than was the case for the men in 1965, throughout the period to 1985 education will perform two distinct functions. The first is the acquisition of skills that permit men to perform the tasks required in a modern complex society. The second is as a device to screen applicants for work positions, requiring "credentials" for the occupancy of even relatively low skill positions. In the larger, better-paying organizations generally there are more applicants than openings, so educational requirements provide an easy and defensible mode of excluding applicants. All that is needed is to make completion of *primaria* or *secundaria* or some higher level a prerequisite for the job—whether such educational attainment actually is needed to do the work is an independent question. Those who cannot produce their certificates are eliminated at one stroke.

As a consequence of the trends we are positing, the occupational prospects of the younger and the new groups will differ. The younger group will probably show little change in patterns of mobility from those described in Chapter 8. Among those with some post-*primaria* education we will find an increasing number following career patterns in bureaucratic settings. At the same time many small entrepreneurs will lose their gambles for survival and success. On the other hand, the prospects for the less-educated men—still a numerically important group in this cohort—will become worse. Those with industrial experience, living now in Monterrey, will not move up much occupationally but will benefit from net income gains obtained partially as a consequence of increasing union strength. But those who do not have such experience, including the migrants to be added to the cohort who originate from rural areas, will be as bad off as their counterparts are today (which may well mean relatively worse).

The prospects for the new cohort are more difficult to predict. At least, it seems obvious that a larger number of them, at all levels, will begin their work histories in bureaucratic settings and will experience mobility under more formalized norms than those observed in Chapter 8. Of course, as has been the case with all cohorts, this new group will enter the labor force at a relatively higher level than did the previous one. The trend for the concentration of upward mobility in the youthful years should also continue, since bureaucratization of industry may favor job security but it will hardly favor mobility after a given age and status have been attained. This is especially true for the blue-collar ranks. Mobility into supervisory and nonmanual statuses will be, as always, difficult within large industry, and prospects as independent workers—although they may always seem attractive—objectively will be increasingly more difficult.

As important as the objective conditions attained by these two cohorts in 1985 and their prospects of occupational mobility will be their self-evaluation of the positions they have attained in society. In discussing this, we will distinguish four broad strata: the elite, the middle class, the skilled workers, and the "marginal" groups.

It seems safe to predict that members of the elite will lose some ground, relatively speaking. If there is any trend toward a more equal distribution of income, it will affect them, although in absolute terms their incomes will continue to rise. We assume continued economic growth, based primarily on a capitalist model, so as a class the economic elite will be in no great danger. Yet, along with some decline in the current very high returns to capital and perhaps a more strict enforcement of tax laws, the political dominance of this group, particularly at the level of local and state politics, increasingly will be challenged.[23] As a result, a sense of decreasing control over the situation and a general malaise will certainly affect the elite. Doubtless some among this group, especially the younger men, will be able to adjust to the new situation by redefining their roles, but for others, especially the older men, it will be more difficult.

For the middle classes, with the exception of a decrease in opportunities as independent entrepreneurs, this type of economic growth will be most favorable. Education will increase in importance, as the meritocratic features of society crystallize, and education has always been the standard of the middle class. Only if the increase of educational "output" in relation to growth of middle-class occupational opportunities occurs will this group be negatively affected. Our impression is that such will not be the case by 1985. The output of the educational system at the middle and higher levels is not growing that fast, and continued economic growth with characteristics specified above will guarantee an acceptable expansion of demand for technical, managerial, and professional positions—mainly in large industry.

The situation for organized skilled labor is quite similar. Here the key difference may take place through a change in the political integration of unions in national and local government. Until now, governmental influence in labor has been great but also helpful in economic terms for workers. As compared with company unions, national "independent" (PRI linked) unions have been more effective in obtaining benefits for the workers. The questions are whether company unions will increasingly become independent and whether national unions will more and more try to free themselves from governmental tutelage. If both things happen, labor will become more militant. Or rather, labor must become more militant in order for these two things to happen. This change will occur only if, in subjective terms, the mass of industrial organized workers becomes dissatisfied with the current leadership. Although objectively, as shown by trends in income redistribution and growth of real wages, this sector has benefited to some extent by the

[23] At the time of this writing (1971), one of the main issues stirring the Mexican political scene is tax reform. The discussion is centered around the degree to which a progressive tax system will be enforced.

process of industrialization during recent decades, it is possible that this will not be "enough" in the next two decades. The key feature of this complex situation will be the link between unions and government at a national level. If the government becomes less sensitive to the rank-and-file economic demands—either by becoming more procapital, on the one hand, or more pro-"marginal" groups, on the other—the greater the probability that the union leadership will not be able to keep a lid on rank-and-file discontent. Since governmental policies ultimately are so dependent upon a single person—the president—we believe that any prediction in this area is even riskier than others.

Probably the group most affected by differences between 1965 and 1985 in the relationship between objective situation and self-evaluation will be the marginal one. Even if its numbers do not increase in relative terms and, at least in a metropolitan center like Monterrey, relative income does not go down, members of this group increasingly will become more dissatisfied. Earlier in this chapter we drew upon reference-group theory to help account for the surprisingly large proportion of low-status men who reported their life situation in positive terms. But the complex of factors we used to interpret their responses will be less effective in 1985. First of all, the proportion of men who can make favorable comparisons with their fathers, relatives and friends will be lower, because proportionally fewer will be of subsistence-agriculture origins. Second, the anticipated increase in "credentialism" at all levels should dampen optimism about the openness of the system. And, finally, many men will be less sanguine that their children can attain a much higher occupational status than theirs via the educational route.

In addition, the effectiveness of the marginal group in influencing the political power structure should increase with greater urban experience and the growth of mass communications, all leading to a greater capacity for organization and a greater disposition to use it. In one form or another, we anticipate a greater activism among the once nearly quiescent marginal groups. It seems clear to us that, for virtually all the groups we have reviewed, what made for acceptance of authority and a smooth transition in the past will be much less effective in the future. Thus, we arrive at the somewhat paradoxical conclusion that the very success of Monterrey's development over the past several decades, far from ensuring a continuation of the "formula" that has worked so well in the past, has created the conditions for a rise in discontent and an increase in group and class conflict.[24] Just how these discontents will be expressed will depend largely upon the famous flexibility of the Mexican political system. If it is able to coopt, absorb, and integrate the new forces, while at the same time not lose the old sources of support (evidently the problem confronting President Echevarría at this writing), then most probably a strong and violent reaction will be avoided. If, on the other hand, the system moves in the direction of greater rigidity, then some form of violent reaction can be expected.

[24] Overt and, sometimes, violent conflict has not been absent from the Mexican (and Monterrey) scene during the last few years. As in many other regions of the world, the universities have been focuses of confrontation with the government. The 1968 events, culminating in the Tlaltelolco massacre, are well known. At the time of this writing (1971), Monterrey has been the new focus of student rebellion. The confrontation was centered upon the issue of university autonomy versus university control by the key economic and political groups in Monterrey, but it widened to include a debate on major economic policies at the national level. The movement initiated in Nuevo León assumed national scope and was met with harsh repression, culminating with the attack of student demonstrators in Mexico City by paramilitary groups on June 10, 1971. The Nuevo León state governor, a representative of the powerful economic groups of Monterrey, as well as important national political figures related to the repression, resigned. It is difficult to interpret student rebellions, in Mexico and elsewhere, as an expression of *class* conflict, but undoubtedly students and intellectuals have been in the forefront of confrontation with elitist policies and supporters of the status quo. Organized labor and marginal workers have not backed student rebels to any great extent; indeed the former in many cases backed governmental policies against the students. For significant expressions of the opposition of intellectuals to governmental policies that maintain the inequalitarian and exclusionist traits of Mexican development, see Octavio Paz, *Posdata* (written after the Tlaltelolco affair), and Carlos Fuentes, "La disyuntiva mexicana," in his book of essays, *Tiempo mexicano* (written after the June 10 events).

APPENDIX A

Technical Aspects of the Execution of the Monterrey and the Cedral Surveys

Selection of the Monterrey Sample

The universe was defined as the resident male population, 21–60 years of age, of the metropolitan area of Monterrey. The limitations imposed by this definition are as follows:

1. *Sex.* Several considerations led us to eliminate females from the sample. In the first place, women constitute only a small part of the labor force. In general, a woman's position in Mexican society depends upon that of her husband (in the case of married women) or upon that of her father (in the case of single women). In addition, women's occupational careers are usually interrupted by marriage or childbearing. For these reasons, we can only rarely measure adult female status and mobility in terms of changes in occupation.

2. *Age.* Men 20 years of age or less were excluded because their occupational history is either brief or nonexistent. Those over 60 were excluded for practical reasons. At these ages the difficulties in obtaining reliable information on occupational, migratory, and family history are enormous. It should be noted that these difficulties also exist at younger ages, but they increase with age and are especially significant after age 60.

3. *Geographical location.* In economic, social, and geographic terms, the city of Monterrey extends beyond the political and administrative limits of the *municipio* of Monterrey. The neighboring *municipios* are intimately linked to the life of the central city. We therefore have included in the metropolitan area of Monterrey the *municipios* of Monterrey, Santa Catarina, Garza García, San Nicolás, and Guadalupe. Previous investigations conducted by the Centro de Investigaciones Económicas of the Facultad de Economía of the Universidad de Nuevo León have successfully utilized this same definition, and its continued use was therefore advisable.

4. *Resident population.* A resident was defined as a man who had lived continuously within the metropolitan area for the last six months or a man who considered as his permanent residence a dwelling located within the metropolitan area.

SAMPLING PROCEDURE

The sample was designed to obtain respondents who were representative of the universe as defined above and to provide a sufficient number of cases for the type of analysis planned. In view of the aims of the study, the decision was made to obtain a two-stage stratified cluster sample of approximately 1,800 cases. The sample was designed to overrepresent older men and men from upper socioeconomic areas. A random sample would have meant approximately twice as many men in the 21–40 age category as in the 41–60 age category, but it was important, for purposes of analysis, to have well represented the older men, with their longer occupational and residential histories. The same argument applies to men from higher income areas. Therefore, the steps taken to secure the sample were as follows:

1. From a total of 6,500 blocks comprising the metropolitan area of Monterrey, a simple random sample of 400 was taken.

2. In each one of these 400 blocks, a census of the resident male population between the ages of 21 and 60 was carried out. The enumerators canvassed each block inquiring at all dwelling units how many males within these age limits lived there and noting the age of the individual or individuals in each case. In this manner, the address, number of males, and their ages were obtained for each one of the dwelling units in the 400 blocks. This procedure yielded a total of 11,362 eligible men.

3. In the previous surveys by the Centro de Investigaciones Económicas the city had been divided into forty geographic zones with arbitrary boundaries. The limits of each zone consist generally of principal avenues or natural boundaries. Using data from these surveys, the average per capita family income was calculated for each of these zones. These averages were then used to rank each zone by income, from high to low. In addition, a map of the city showing each of the forty geographic zones was given to several members of the Centro not connected with the present survey, and they were asked to order the zones according to their estimate of the average economic level, from the highest to the lowest. Comparison of the two resulting rankings revealed a high degree of similarity. The zones were then divided into two groups of high- and low-income zones, such that the former included 33 percent of the 11,362 enumerated individuals and the latter included the remaining 67 percent. Using this allocation, the coincidence between the order based upon the calculated incomes and that based upon the judgment of the consultants was total: all the zones falling into one category by means of one ranking procedure also fell into the same category by means of the other procedure.

4. Within each group of zones (high and low income), the enumerated men were divided into two age groups: those between 21 and 40 and those

between 41 and 60. This yielded four groups, or strata. The percentage distribution of the enumerated population by strata is given in Table A-1.

5. A simple random sample of 450 cases was taken within each of the four strata. Our final sample, then, consisted of 1,800 men (an error resulted in an additional three cases so that the actual sample size is 1,803), a sample size judged adequate for our purposes. Among these 1,800 individuals, older persons and those residing in zones of greater income are overrepresented—by a known proportion.

THE REPRESENTATIVE SAMPLE

Summarizing what we have said so far, our sample consisted of 1,803 randomly selected individuals, drawn in a predetermined proportion from each of four age and income strata. In order to make our sample representative of the total population, we have to "inflate" the number of cases in the young-age and low-income categories, so as to bring them into the actual proportion they represented of the project census.

TABLE A-1. Percent Distribution of the Population Enumerated
in Project Census, by Age and Income Zone

Income zone	Age 21–40	41–60	Total
Low income	48.3	18.6	66.9
High income	22.5	10.6	33.1
Total	70.8	29.2	100.0
			(11,362)

SOURCE: Monterrey Mobility Study.

TABLE A-2. Procedure for Inflation of Sample

	Age 21–40		41–60		
	Income Zone				
	Low	High	Low	High	Total
Number of interviews made in each group	422	413	427	378	1640
Percent each group is of project census	48.3	22.5	18.6	10.6	100.0
Inflation factor	4.081	1.943	1.553	1.000	

SOURCE: Monterrey Mobility Study.

In Table A-2 we indicate how the inflation of the sample was carried out. Each inflation factor represents the ratio between the number of cases actually obtained in a given stratum and the number of cases that should be present if the sample was representative. The calculation takes as a base the stratum most overrepresented (41–60 years of age in high-income zones), and then the number necessary to maintain the census proportions is calculated for each of the other three strata. Tables in this book are based upon either the actual sample of the 1,640 cases or the representative sample obtained by multiplying each case by the corresponding factor. Whenever the representative sample is used this is indicated explicitly, but we always give the actual number of cases involved. It should be noted that the major difference between the two samples is in the age distribution, but, whenever age is controlled for, the results based on the two samples do not differ greatly.

COMPARISON OF CENSUS AND SURVEY DATA

In Tables A-3, A-4, and A-5 we compare some of the survey data (age, industry, and years of schooling) based upon the representative sample with data obtained from the Mexican census of population of 1960. Two factors limit the comparability between these two sources of information. First, our definition of the Monterrey Metropolitan Area does not include the rural population within the five municipalities of which it is comprised, whereas the census data are based upon the entire population of these municipalities. The rural population excluded in the survey, however, makes up a very small part of the total population. Second, there is a difference of five years between the times of the census and of the survey, but this should not greatly affect comparisons between the two sets of data.

In Table A-3 are given the age distributions of the two populations. In general, they are quite similar. However, in the census there is a greater percentage of persons between ages 26 and 30, but this is just about balanced out by the greater percentage of the sample in the following age group, 31–35. On the other hand, in the sample there is a greater percentage in the 41–45 group, which is partially offset by a census excess of 2.8 percent at ages 46–50. Thus, there are two instances in which there are relatively more persons in certain age groups in the census than in the sample, and in both cases the differences are counterbalanced by contrary differences in the neighboring age groups. While these differences may be due to sampling error, it should be noted that the two instances in which the census is greater involve age groups containing a year ending in the digit zero (26–30 and 46–50). A very common error in censuses is the tendency to overreport ages ending in multiples of ten, and this is the case in Mexican censuses over a number of years.

In Table A-4 are the distributions of the census and sample populations by

TABLE A-3. Age Distribution of Male Population of Metropolitan Area
of Monterrey, According to Census and Survey (In Percent)

Age	Census (1960)	Survey (1965)
21–25	22.5	22.6
26–30	17.9	15.8
31–35	14.2	16.3
36–40	13.6	13.9
41–45	8.8	10.8
46–50	9.5	6.7
51–55	7.0	7.5
56–60	6.6	6.3
Total	100.1	99.9
	(144,819)	(1,640)

SOURCE: Censo General de Población, 1960. State of Nuevo León. Included in the metropolitan area are the following *municipios*: Monterrey, San Nicolás, Santa Catarina, Guadalupe, and Garza García. The geographical area of the survey is somewhat less than the census because purely rural areas were excluded. The sample is the representative one.

branch of economic activity. The comparison is limited by the fact that the census does not publish this information by age. Therefore, the census distribution refers to economically active men of all ages, whereas the sample refers only to men 21–60 years of age. We have also excluded a comparison of the population engaged in agriculture for two reasons: first, because of the elimination of rural zones from consideration we obtained very few respondents in agriculture. Second, those in agriculture in the census represent a rather large percentage of the economically active population of the metropolitan area of Monterrey (10.6 percent), a fact for which we have no satisfactory explanation. The distributions are quite similar. The important differences are the following:

1. The percentage in manufacturing is 4.4 percent higher in the sample than in the census, and the percentage of the sample in commerce is less than the percentage of the census in this branch of economic activity. The latter difference appears to be due to variations in age composition, for there is a relatively heavy concentration of older men in commerce. If this is also true of men over 60, their exclusion would account for the smaller percentage in commerce found in the sample. A similar situation may account for the differences between census and sample with respect to percent in manufacturing.

2. In the census there is a larger percentage in transportation and communication than in the sample. This difference probably is due to the fact that

TABLE A-4. Major Industry of Male Population According to Census and Survey
(In Percent)

Major Industry	Census (1960) (All males)	Survey (1965) (Males 21–60)
Extractive	1.0	0.7
Manufacturing	43.4	47.8
Construction	10.8	10.0
Commerce and finance	19.0	16.6
Electricity, gas, and water	0.8	2.1
Transportation and communication	8.3	6.9
Public and private services	15.6	15.6
Activities insufficiently specified	1.1	0.3
Total	100.0	100.0
	(167,413)	(1,594)

SOURCE: Censo General de Población, 1960. State of Nuevo León. For the definition of the Monterrey Metropolitan Area, see Table A-3. The sample is the representative one.
NOTE: Agriculture is excluded from both populations.

we were unable to interview some bus drivers and railroad personnel who were selected for the sample but who proved very difficult to locate.

Finally, in Table A-5 we present data on completed years of education for the census male population of 30 years or more and the sample population of 30 to 60 years of age. The differences in age composition and the five-year interval between the census in 1960 and the survey in 1965 may explain, in our opinion, the higher average education of the sample when compared to that of the census. One of the reasons for the lower level of education found in the census is the presence of men over 60, for they have a much lower average level of education than younger men. Furthermore, while changes in educational level do occur rather slowly, during the five years separating the census and the survey a major governmental program (Plan de Once Años) to assist education was begun, and our data may reflect such improvements. This possibility is indicated by the lower percentage of the sample population that has had no education and the increase in the percentage who completed post-*primaria* studies.

On balance, it is our judgment that the sampling procedure, field work, and transformation of the original weighted sample to a representative one have produced results comparable with those obtained in the 1960 census, and therefore we may use the data contained in the representative sample with confidence.

The Questionnaire and Its Execution

The basic data for this investigation were collected by means of a questionnaire. Several pretests of the questionnaire were conducted, and after each one modifications of form and content were made. The last pretest of the questionnaire involved a pilot survey of fifty men—not included in the final sample—selected at random. The questionnaire contained 198 questions, some open-ended, in addition to the life-history section described in Appendix B.

The survey was conducted during the months of July, August, and September of 1965. The team of interviewers was composed of male students of the Facultad de Economía of the Universidad de Nuevo León, some of whom had had previous interviewing experience. The survey was carried out during the students' summer vacation when we could count on their working full time. They were paid by completed interview and the work was completely independent of classroom assignments.

All interviewers received one week of intensive training, which included three interviews as a test of their competence. Once approved, the interview-

TABLE A-5. Completed Years of Schooling of Male Adult Population of Monterrey Metropolitan Area, According to Census and Survey (In Percent)

Years of Schooling	Census (1960)	Survey (1965)
None	18.0	14.5
1–5	42.5	42.4
6	24.4	22.4
7–9[a]	6.8	11.9
10 or more[b]	8.3	8.8
Total	100.0	100.0
	(105,891)	(1,229)

SOURCE: Censo General de Población, 1960. State of Nuevo León. For the definition of the Monterrey Metropolitan Area see Table A-3. The census data correspond to the male population 30 years and over, while the survey population is between 30 and 60 years. The sample is the representative one.

[a] In the survey this category includes all those with a "middle" educational level (*secundaria*, commercial, or technical). It includes those who studied in more than one of these kinds of schools; if a respondent has completed three years of *secundaria* and two of commercial, making a total of eleven years, he is included in this category.

[b] In the survey only those are included who have studied in *preparatoria* or above. Those who have ten or more years but within the "middle" educational level are excluded.

ers were divided into five groups, each group under the direction of a supervisor. The supervisors, more advanced students and those with more survey experience, were put in charge of the distribution, collection, and correction of the questionnaires. The supervisors were in direct contact with the chief of field work, who in turn reported to the directors of the study.

The field work began with forty-five interviewers, but, as the summer passed, the interviewer ranks became depleted for various reasons. Each interviewer was to secure a weekly minimum of seven interviews, or one interview per day, on the average. Completed interviews were revised immediately by a supervisor, who then either approved the interview or returned it to the interviewer for correction. In addition the supervisors revisited 10 percent of the respondents already surveyed by the interviewers in their group in order to ensure that there had been no errors in the selection of the respondent and to verify portions of the data collected. For the latter, an abbreviated questionnaire was used in which some of the questions in the original questionnaire were repeated so that the responses might be compared at the central office. No cases of falsification of information were discovered, and the few instances in which irregularities were encountered were insignificant.

In general, the interviewers encountered a high level of cooperation on the part of the respondents. Nevertheless, difficulties arose. These were most often the result of the fact that the men interviewed were in the most active ages, and nearly all of them were employed. It should be recalled that all information sought was to be obtained from the individual selected for the sample and not from other members of the family (except when the respondent could not remember with precision facts concerning the dates of birth of his children or information concerning his wife or her parents—in which case the information was obtained from the respondent's wife). In twenty-five cases we were unable to follow this procedure, because of illness on the part of the respondent or a similar reason, and in these cases we chose to obtain some basic items of information from a close relative, omitting the questions referring to attitudes and opinions.

Because most respondents worked during the day, usually two or more visits were required before the chosen individual could be interviewed, even though the field work was conducted at unusual hours, and full advantage was taken of evenings and holidays. Generally, it was desirable to conduct the interview in the respondent's home, but some men had to be interviewed at their place of work. The average length of the interview was eighty minutes, but this was subject to wide variation, the principal factor determining such variation being the age of the respondent. The older men required a great deal of time to complete the life history, especially when the man had many children, moves, and job changes.

Other difficulties were the result of the sampling canvass. As previously indicated, the sample was drawn from a census carried out in four hundred blocks of the city. In some cases the census information did not coincide with what the interviewer actually encountered. The interviewer was provided with the precise address and age of the individual whom he was to interview, but in several instances discrepancies required the interviewer to return to the central office for instructions because he could not proceed with the interview.

Errors due to discrepancies in age, changes of residence between the time of the canvass and the survey, and similar reasons made it necessary to replace 150 of the individuals originally selected. This replacement was accomplished by means of the same sampling design, with each individual who could not be interviewed being replaced by one selected at random from the same stratum. The principal reasons for replacing originally selected individuals were the following:

1. The individual originally selected no longer lived at the same address, and either it was impossible to determine his new address or he had left the metropolitan area. In some cases, even though the individual was absent from the city only temporarily, his absence extended beyond the time limits established for the field work. Seventy-six individuals were replaced because of these circumstances. For half of these it was determined that they had left the city temporarily or permanently. For the remaining men, all that was known was that they had changed their address and it was impossible to determine if they had remained in Monterrey.

2. There were age discrepancies between the individual canvassed and the individual selected in the sample. Thirty-seven cases were replaced for this reason, either because the individual's age was five years more or less than that indicated in the canvass or because his age was outside the limits of the universe (i.e., less than 21 or greater than 60). Regarding the latter, some deviation was accepted, and if an individual turned out to be 20, 61, or 62, he was not replaced. In the data presented, individuals of 20 years are put in the 21–25 age category and those of 61 and 62 years are put in the 56–60 group. In total there were twenty-one cases in which the individual's age was 20, 61, or 62.

3. Some men were selected by mistake. There were seventeen who were erroneously identified as residents of Monterrey but who actually were only visiting.

The remaining instances of replacement were due to various reasons: difficulty in locating the address, cases in which the man enumerated in the canvass did not exist or was enumerated erroneously, death of the selected man, and similar reasons.

The principal effect of these replacements was the delay created for the interviewers in their work, because of their having to make one or more visits to a man who later had to be replaced by another.

As was inevitable in this type of investigation, not all the men selected for study could be interviewed. There are always people who are either very difficult to locate or who do not wish to be interviewed (a desire that they are, of course, entirely privileged to have, since involvement with the survey was at all times on a voluntary basis). There are, however, two very important factors that might have influenced the proportion of nonresponse cases. The first concerns the quality of interviewer training, the way in which interviewers were organized, and their attitude toward their work. The second involves the type of people interviewed and the topic of the investigation.

Regarding the first factor, in our opinion the level of performance on the part of the interviewers was quite satisfactory; they were trained intensively, and every attempt was made to arouse their interest in the investigation itself. Moreover, the reader will recall that all the interviewers were students of economics and it is reasonable to suppose that they possessed a professional interest in the study. In addition, they were paid for the work and never were asked to volunteer their labor. They were responsible to a supervisor, the latter's main tasks being to verify all work and to try to resolve any problems encountered by the interviewers. One of these problems involved difficulties in establishing rapport with the interviewee. In all such cases, the supervisor either sent a different interviewer or conducted the interview himself.

Regarding the second factor affecting the nonresponse rate, the male population, especially those in the active ages, is difficult to interview for obvious reasons: many men work long hours, and they have little desire to spend their limited free time answering questions, especially when an average of an hour and twenty minutes was required to complete the questionnaire.

In spite of these difficulties, the total percentage of nonresponses was low, 163 of the total of 1,803 interviews, or 9 percent. This percentage we believe to be quite acceptable, especially in view of the type of population interviewed.

We may classify the nonresponses into two main categories: those who directly refused to be interviewed, and those who could not be interviewed for other reasons, by either the interviewers or the supervisors. In the second category we include those cases in which the interview could not be realized because of the peculiarities of the respondent's occupation, typical examples being bus drivers and railroad personnel—men whose occupations require them to spend long periods away from home. This category also includes several men who, after repeated calls, still could not be found at home. It is likely that some men were not visited a sufficient number of times because of the difficulty in getting to their homes.

A summary of the cases of nonresponse and reasons for them is presented in Table A-6, with 58 percent of them attributable to direct refusal. Also presented in this table is a brief description of the reasons given for refusing to

TABLE A-6. Interviews Not Carried Out, by Principal Reason

Reason	Number	Percent
Refusals		
Distrust, fear[a]	27	17
Lack of interest or time	23	14
Without explanations	19	12
Skepticism	10	6
Other reasons	15	9
Subtotal	94	58
Nonrefusals		
Could not locate interviewee	39	24
The interviewee not found at home, because of work	22	14
Excessive postponement of interviews	4	2
Subtotal	65	40
No information	4	2
Total	163	100

SOURCE: Monterrey Mobility Study.
[a] See the text for an explanation of the categories utilized.

be interviewed. Those refusing for the first reason (lack of confidence or fear) include men who manifested some form of fear of being harmed by their answering questions or who distrusted the motives of the interviewer or representatives of the university. Many were of the opinion that the investigation was being conducted for motives other than those indicated (e.g., for purposes of taxation). Others simply said they considered the survey to be an invasion of privacy. Those men refusing to be interviewed for the second reason included those who said they either had no time or were not interested in being interviewed. Another category of refusals involved individuals who flatly refused to be interviewed, without giving a reason.

Considering those men classified as nonresponses for reasons other than direct refusal, there were thirty-nine cases in which, after repeated call backs, the interviewer was unable to secure an appointment for an interview. Generally, no one was at home when the interviewer called or if there was someone at home no definite time could be established for the interview. In another twenty-two cases the interview could not be carried out, because the man was almost always absent, generally because of reasons connected with his job. In four cases, appointments were made but for a date beyond the limit established for the completion of field work.

We should like now to consider the characteristics of the men who could not be interviewed. In Table A-7 they are classified according to the four strata employed in the sample that, as we have indicated, utilize the criteria of age and average income of zone. The percentage of nonresponse in each stratum clearly shows that most nonresponses occurred among those living in high-income zones of the city and those between 41 and 60 years of age. It appears that distrust or lack of interest are greatest among those of higher economic positions and, especially, among older men.

As we have previously indicated, in each case in which difficulties were encountered, several visits were paid by different interviewers. In all those cases in which an interview could not be obtained after every effort had been made, the interviewer had instructions to collect all possible information that might aid us in establishing the socioeconomic standing of the selected individual or his family. We made a special effort to obtain information on occupation and on those housing characteristics visible from the exterior. With the use of these two items of information (the latter when the former was not available) we classified the nonresponse cases into four categories. The results are presented in Table A-8. Despite the fact that no information was available for thirty-two cases, this table calls to our attention the elevated number of cases in the highest occupational category. In general, these are professionals, managers or directors of private firms, and persons with similar occupations. In those cases in which only characteristics of dwelling were available, many of the nonrespondents appeared to live in relatively sumptuous surroundings (as

TABLE A-7. Percent of Interviews Not Carried Out, by Income Zone and Age

Zone	Age		Total
	21–40	41–60	
Low income	6[a]	6	6
	(29)	(26)	(55)
High income	8	16	12
	(37)	(71)	(108)
Total	7	11	9
	(66)	(97)	(163)

Source: Monterrey Mobility Study.

[a] In each cell, the percentage refers to the proportion of selected interviews that were not carried out; within parentheses is given the absolute number of interviews not carried out.

indicated by one or several of the following indicators: type of construction, size of garden, garage(s), automobile(s), number of servants). In total we have a minimum of forty-seven cases that we may classify with some certainty as being in the upper quintile of the socioeconomic hierarchy.

The Cedral Survey

The 1967 Cedral survey was conceived as a follow-up of the 1965 Monterrey survey, and it was seen as an opportunity to investigate a *municipio* of heavy out-migration, much of it directed toward Monterrey. The resources for the Cedral study, in terms of time and money, were limited, and this limitation affected the size and the nature of the sample.

A sample target of five hundred men aged 15 to 64 was established, with the wider age range than in Monterrey introduced in order to examine the nature of out-migration for ages 15–19 and migratory processes in the early decades of the century for men aged 61–65.

The five hundred men were not to be randomly selected within the *municipio*. Although the population of Cedral town was only about one-half the population in the rural area of the *municipio*, four hundred cases were allocated to it and only one hundred to the rural area. This was done not only because it was much easier to carry out interviews in the compact area of the town, but also because we anticipated much greater variation in the town for most of our variables. (This anticipation turned out to be sound, for there was very limited variation within the rural population.)

In the town the first-stage sampling unit was the household rather than the individuals. A short census was made of two-thirds of the households to establish the presence of males in the 15–64 age range. Only one male was chosen (randomly) within each household, which meant an overrepresentation of heads of households in their 30's and 40's.

In the rural area two different localities were selected. They really are sets of *rancherías*, each *ranchería* made up of a small group of families, and the whole forming an ejido. Because of the dispersion of the population, no sampling instructions were given to the interviewers, other than to obtain fifty interviews of men aged 15–65 from each ejido to fulfill the quota.

The interviewing team was made up of seven interviewers plus the field director. Six of the eight had worked for the Monterrey survey. The team lived in Cedral between July 1 and August 6. Among the problems encountered in executing the survey were the following:

1. There were fewer inhabited houses than the census had led us to believe (530 versus the anticipated 700) and this fact prolonged the early stage of the project.

2. Nearly one of five households had no male aged 15–64. Presumably this lack reflected the men's absence in work outside the community, but the inter-

viewing was conducted during the peak of the summer season when local employment was at its height.

3. Once an appropriate male was selected, it was often hard to get hold of him for an interview. The men, especially the younger ones, spent little time at home. Usually the best opportunity to interview was during the week days after 6:00 P.M., but because many houses had no electricity this meant that two interviewers were needed to conduct an interview, one to hold the battery lamp.

4. Direct refusals were relatively few (16). There were twenty-eight cases that were selected but could not be interviewed, and some of these doubtless avoided contact. Of the direct refusals, most expressed some sort of suspicion and fear. These suspicions and fears were widespread, but they were not strong enough in most cases to provoke a refusal. The men believed the interviewers were "communists" or were sent by the federal government for some dark purpose, such as taking the sons off to war. There were also fears that the interviewers were Protestants or Mormons (a fear reinforced by the fact that two of the interviewers were blond-haired with blue eyes).

5. The only case of organized opposition came from a rightist political organization. The leadership of the group was contacted and the purpose and the nature of the survey explained, but the initial acceptance weakened steadily during the course of the field work. The deep-seated suspicion of outsiders (from Monterrey) never could be overcome.

Field work was terminated on August 5, in spite of the fact that only 312 of the projected 400 interviews had been completed for the town, and 68 of the projected 100 in the rural areas. Interviews were very difficult to obtain in the first two weeks of August because of the yearly fiestas that absorbed most of the free time of the Cedraleños.

TABLE A-8. Interviews Not Carried Out, by Occupation of Men
or Type of Dwelling Inhabited

Occupation	No.	Housing	No.	Total
Workers	17	Shacks and other substandard housing	20	37
Artisans and small independent merchants	10	Modest housing, two or three rooms of brick, etc.	19	29
Office employees, technicians, and similar occupations	11	Housing in good condition, not luxurious	7	18
Managers, professionals, and similar occupations	31	Luxurious housing (garden, garage, servant quarters, etc.)	16	47
		Total		131

SOURCE: Monterrey Mobility Study.

APPENDIX B

The Securing and Processing of the Life Histories

Life-history data were collected as part of a questionnaire administered to all respondents. The questionnaire opened with a series of questions about the respondent's current job. Next followed the schedule for systematically entering life-history data on migration, education, marital status and family formation, health impairment, and work. The format of the life-history schedule (see Table B-1) was the same for each respondent, regardless of his age. The areas of investigation were assigned columns, and each possible year (sixty in all) was provided with a row. The fact that only a very few histories made use of all sixty rows resulted in much unused space, but it also ensured that each year was accounted for, because no open rows were allowed once the activity represented by a column had begun. It also permitted the instant inspection of the characteristics of the respondent for any given year.

The interviewers were given special training in the administration of the life-history part of the questionnaire. Close supervision was required, since the instructions given to the interviewers allowed for a relatively high degree of discretion in the interview situation. For this reason the ratio of supervisors to interviewers was a low 1:6.

The general instructions were to take one area of the life history as a "focus," to follow the sequence of events in this area, and then, for every change in it, to relate the change to the sequences in other areas. The area selected as a point of reference varied according to the stage in the life cycle and also to the respondent's particular history. Generally, after asking year and place of birth, education was taken as the focus and it was related to residence changes. Then the focus was switched to occupation, or marital status and family, and migration continued to be related to them.

There was much variation in procedure from one person to another for two reasons. First, there were objective differences in the life histories themselves. For example, the selection of a focus area was very different for a man of 30 who had remained in school until he reached 24 and who had never migrated, when compared with another man of 60 with only two years of schooling and many changes of residence. Second, the respondent's recall was better in

TABLE B-1. Illustrative Life History.[a]

Year	Age	Migration History					Educational History	Family History	Health	Work History							Year
		Name of Place	State	Size						Name of Occupation	Description of Duties	Position and Dependent Personnel	Enterprise			Income (in pesos)	
				Rural	Town	City							Type of Industry	No. of Persons Employed	Relatives		
1940	10	San Isidro	Coahuila	x			primaria 5th grade			farm worker	helps his father	family help	agriculture	3	yes	none	1940
1941	11	San Isidro	Coahuila	x			primaria 6th grade			farm worker	helps his father	family help	agriculture	3	yes	none	1941
1942	12	Monterrey (colonia Lomas)	Nuevo León			x	commerce 1st grade			NOT	EMPLOYED						1942
1943	13	Monterrey (colonia Lomas)	Nuevo León			x	commerce 2nd grade			NOT	EMPLOYED						1943
1944	14	Monterrey (colonia Lomas)	Nuevo León			x	commerce 3rd grade			NOT	EMPLOYED						1944
1945	15	Mexico City	Distrito Federal			x	not in school			messenger	office boy	employee 0	railroad office	350	no	300 monthly	1945
1946	16	Mexico City	Distrito Federal			x	not in school			messenger	office boy	employee 0	railroad office	350	no	300 monthly	1946
1947	17	Mexico City	Distrito Federal			x	not in school			messenger	office boy	employee 0	railroad office	350	no	300 monthly	1947
1948	18	Monterrey (colonia Regina)	Nuevo León			x	not in school			UNEMPLOYED	FOR EIGHT MONTHS						1948
1949	19	Monterrey (colonia Regina)	Nuevo León			x	not in school	courtship		clerk	types letters	employee 0	mattress factory	50	no	150 weekly	1949
1950	20	Monterrey (colonia Regina)	Nuevo León			x	not in school	courtship		clerk	types letters	employee 0	mattress factory	50	no	150 weekly	1950
1951	21	Monterrey	Nuevo León			x	not in school	marriage		clerk	types letters	employee	mattress	50	no	180 weekly	1951

Year	No.	Residence	State	School mark	School	Family event	Occupation	Role	Employment & no.	Business type	No.	Own business	Income	Year
1952	22	Monterrey (colonia Modelo)	Nuevo León	x	not in school	first child born, male	purchasing agent buys all materials		employee 2	mattress factory	70	no	250 weekly	1952
1953	23	Monterrey (colonia Modelo)	Nuevo León	x	not in school		purchasing agent buys all materials		employee 2	mattress factory	70	no	250 weekly	1953
1954	24	Monterrey (colonia Modelo)	Nuevo León	x	not in school	second child born, female	owner of small factory	manager	employer 5	plastic toy factory	6	yes	800 monthly	1954
1955	25	Monterrey (colonia Modelo)	Nuevo León	•	not in school	third child born, died first month	owner of small factory	manager	employer 5	plastic toy factory	6	yes	800 monthly	1955
1956	26	Monterrey (colonia Modelo)	Nuevo León	x	not in school	fourth child born, male	owner of small factory	manager	employer 5	plastic toy factory	6	yes	800 monthly	1956
1957	27	Monterrey (colonia Modelo)	Nuevo León	x	not in school		owner of small factory	manager	employer 5	plastic toy factory	6	yes	800 monthly	1957
1958	28	Monterrey (colonia Modelo)	Nuevo León	x	not in school	fifth child born, female	owner of small factory	manager	employer 3	plastic toy factory	4	yes	about 1,500 monthly	1958
1959	29	Monterrey (colonia Modelo)	Nuevo León	x	not in school		sales agent	visits stores selling skirts	employee 0	skirts factory	250	no	business losses	1959

SOURCE: Jorge Balán, Harley L. Browning, Elizabeth Jelin, and Lee Litzler, "A Computerized Approach to the Processing and Analysis of Life Histories Obtained in Sample Surveys, *Behavioral Science* 14 (March 1969): 108.

[a] Only twenty years of the respondent's life are presented here. The last year recorded for all respondents was that of the survey, 1965.

one area than in another. Some men more easily remembered changes in terms of their family history, while others preferred to anchor their recall in relation to their work history or to changes in residence.

QUESTIONNAIRE

In order that the reader may have a more concrete idea of the way in which the life-history data were obtained, we present below an abbreviated example of the procedure followed by the interviewer and the sequence of his questions.

Question: How old are you? That is, in what year were you born? (*Reply*)

Q.: Where were you born? Where were your parents living when you were born? (*R*)

Q.: Have you ever gone to school? (*R*)

Q.: When did you begin school? (*R*)

Q.: Were you still living in the same place when you began school? (*R*) [If the respondent had moved, dates and places were obtained. Then he was asked, year by year, if he was a student, what was he studying, and the results—grade promotion, grade repetition, left school—until a complete review of his education had been achieved. For each entry he was asked if he was still living in the same place. If the response was negative, dates and places of moves were obtained.]

Q.: At the time you left school, were you working? (*R*)

Q.: Did you work any time before leaving school? (*R*)

Q.: When did you have your first job? Where were you living at that time? What were you studying then? (*R*)

Q.: What was your occupation; what did you do? (*R*)

Q.: What were your duties in this occupation? (*R*)

Q.: Were you self-employed, worker, employee, or employer? (*R*)

Q.: Were you in charge of other persons and, if so, how many? (*R*)

Q.: In what type of enterprise or business were you employed? What was made or sold? (*R*)

Q.: How many people worked there? (*R*)

Q.: Did you have any relative working in that enterprise or business? (*R*)

Q.: Do you remember approximately how much you earned in this work? (*R*) [If the enterprise was agriculture or a related activity and the respondent was the owner of the land, the amount of land holdings and the type of land use were requested. As the interview progressed, the interviewer continued his inquiry as to any change in occupation, year by year. As each change was reported, questions concerning migration were introduced. At some point in the life history, usually when the respondent was about 25, the following question was asked:]

Q.: Up to this time were you still single or were you married or "united"? (*R*) [If the response was affirmative, the date of the first union and the duration of the courtship were obtained. From then on until the end of the life history the interviewer continued relating occupational changes with births and deaths of children, termination of marital unions, and changes of residence. If the respondent had not already volunteered the information, at various moments of the life history he was asked:]

Q.: During all this time, did you have any illness that hindered your work for any period of time or that was very expensive? What was it? (*R*)

Q.: When did it happen? Where were you living then? What was your job? (*R*)

Q.: Did your wife or children have any serious illness? What was it? (*R*)

Q.: When did it happen? (*R*)

RELIABILITY

Problems of reliability of response are of special significance for the evaluation of life histories. Deliberate falsification is, of course, a problem common to all surveys, and the usual precautions were taken. It should be emphasized that the life history did not attempt to tap sensitive areas of the respondent's life. The items on the schedule pertained only to the behavior of the respondent (i.e., changes in residence, jobs, education) rather than to his attitudes. We believe that deliberate falsification is less of a problem in life histories than in most other survey data. It is clearly easier to fabricate a single item of information than a whole life history. Few respondents have the talent to make up plausible and consistent histories on the spot.

The problem of error deriving from recall is a more serious one, and it is naturally magnified when respondents are asked to remember events that took place many years ago. However, the questions asked the respondent about his early years are the ones he would be most likely to remember, that is, place of birth, number of school years completed, first job. Nonetheless, the unwitting falsification of portions of the life history is an important source of error, resulting from one or more of the following: (1) omission of changes in status, (2) improper ordering of changes in status, and (3) improper dating of changes in status. We attempted to minimize these errors through the following procedures.

1. *Systematic recording.* The format of the life-history schedule was designed to force the interviewer to account for all years for each area of investigation. It also enabled him to tell at a glance the gaps (unaccounted-for years) that needed to be filled in. In many cases this procedure also helped to establish good rapport with the respondent. The completion of the life history became a genuine cooperative enterprise with interviewer and re-

spondent engaged in a continuous dialogue in order to complete the life history.

2. *Facilitation of recall.* The probability that an individual will be able to recall distinct events is much greater if he can do so as part of a continuous sequence instead of being asked to recall some isolated event. We maintain that this procedure is particularly helpful in working with respondents with low levels of education, a characteristic of a large part of the Monterrey sample. Individuals living in societies in which the filling out of forms requiring life-history information is a frequent experience acquire a certain facility in recalling discrete events. This is not the case for many of our respondents, for they live within an "oral" tradition. This does not imply, however, that their memory of past events is necessarily inferior to those with better education. They often have amazingly detailed recall, provided they are given sufficient time for reflection and an opportunity to link together events as part of a sequence.

Recall was enhanced, we believe, by the practice of gathering information not for one major area (such as work) but for several. The necessity to think about several areas of one's life for a given time period strengthened rather than weakened the recall for any one of them. By moving back and forth among the areas the respondent often was able to give a more complete account than otherwise. (The reader may make a test of this assertion himself. He should, for example, try to remember his place of residence for a specific year (1954) or a specific age (29) without taking into account any other feature of his life. It will be quite difficult to do so without also thinking about where he worked at the time, his family situation, and so forth.) The account also was more likely to be accurate because he himself could recognize inconsistencies. Since each area had to be congruent with all others at any one point in time, the likelihood of any one of them getting very much "out of phase" with the others was reduced. In turn, the task of the interviewer was facilitated because he could seek clarification or correction of inconsistencies and omissions during the interview.

3. *Checks on consistency of response.* The questionnaire was designed so that consistency of response could be checked. A number of specific questions covering the same points as the life history were introduced in other parts of the questionnaire. For example, we asked for the last job before migrating to Monterrey, the number and ages of children alive, and so on. During the interview the interviewer was instructed to check the consistency of the two sources each time he reached one of these questions. And his supervisor in turn could check the interviewer's performance in this regard.

In summary, we believe that errors of recall were minimized by the procedures just outlined. The emphasis upon sequence and temporal congruity served to reduce the probability either of forgetting a change in status or of getting it out of sequence. Probably the greatest source of error is that of identifying the specific year of occurrence. But it is unlikely that improper dating would involve more than a few years, for otherwise the incongruity with other areas would become apparent.

Possibly the manner of obtaining the life history led to a greater congruity than may have really existed. The interviewers were instructed to probe whenever inconsistencies appeared, and probably some respondents simply made their histories more congruent to "please" the interviewer. Doubtless there are omissions of change of status. Such omissions may not be as serious as they might appear, however, because it is likely that they represent changes of minor importance in the respondent's life. For example, he may have changed jobs more often than is reported, but the omitted jobs were probably very similar in character.

The analyses of life-history data from the Monterrey study have been reassuring, for nothing has appeared to date that is senseless. Of course, this in itself cannot be considered proof of the reliability of the data. Since satisfactory checks external to the respondent's report are rarely available for life histories, some doubts always will exist about such data. If the procedures outlined above are followed carefully, major distortion of life histories will be minimized.

Coding and Processing of Data

In the Monterrey study it was necessary to develop a technique for the efficient transfer of the life histories from the interview schedules to computer tape. The goal was to conserve as much of the life-history data as possible, while at the same time minimizing the time and the cost involved in the transfer. Because of the innovative character of the life-history procedures, the coding of the life histories was done entirely by Balán and Jelin.

Given the great variation in length and content of life histories from one respondent to another, the usual coding procedures calling for comparable "fields" on coding schedules, cards, and tape were not applicable. The goal was to put complete life histories on computer tape, but to code and punch all the information would have been very time-consuming and costly. Since we had thirty variables (about half with two digits) and a maximum of sixty years, this would have meant approximately 2,700 fields to be coded for each respondent. This procedure would involve many repetitions in coding and punching operations (for example, for a 50-year-old man who had always lived in Monterrey the code representing residence would have to be repeated fifty times) and there would be much unused space, especially for the younger respondents.

We tried to overcome these difficulties by separating the process into two sets of operations. The first was the coding-and-card-punching operation and the second the reconstruction of the complete life history by computer operation. Only *changes* in the content of each of the variables were coded and punched. Each change in the content of a variable was coded in a six-digit block. The first two digits identify the age, the third and fourth identify the variable, and the last two digits refer to the specific content of the variable. There were some variations of this arrangement. Two conceptually separated variables were combined under one identification number whenever both were one-digit variables. For one variable, income, only one digit was used for identification purposes, so as to leave three digits for the content. The coding entries were made on large forms, each having age and variable identification already printed in the cells. Table B-2 presents a small section of the coding form. Since only changes in the variables were coded, many cells remained "incomplete." Even with the streamlining of the coding procedures, it took approximately eighty man-days to complete the coding and revision of the 1,640 life histories.

The information was then transferred from the forms to cards. Only the cells having six digits were punched. In Table B-3 the information coded and punched on cards is presented for ages 10 to 14 of the illustrative life history (Table B-1). Because each life history is different from all others no fixed meaning can be attached to a particular field on the punched cards. (All we know is that columns 7–8, 13–14, and so on always refer to ages; columns 9–10, 15–16, and so on refer to the identification of variables; and columns 11–12, 17–18, and so on refer to specific content of the variables.) The number of cards required for each respondent varied with his age and number of changes recorded for each of the variables. The average number of cards per respondent was 3.4.

The coding and punching of the information was an intermediate step, and it should be evident that no analysis could be carried out directly with the cards. A special program for the transfer of the information to computer tape was necessary, one that would permit the reconstruction of the entire life histories from the "change" data cards. A general Fortran program for this purpose was written by Litzler. This program not only permits the recon-

TABLE B-2. Illustrative Section of Coding Sheet

| Age | Variable Number | | | | |
	01	02	03	04	05
10	1001 10	1002 54	1003	1004 15	1005
11	1101	1102	1103	1104 16	1105
12	1201 50	1202 11	1203 45	1204 31	1205
13	1301	1302	1303	1304 32	1305
14	1401	1402	1403	1404 33	1405

struction of the sequences regarding the coded variables, but also allows for the formation of new index variables and the collapsing of others. It performs the following five basic operations in the reconstruction of the life histories: (1) repeats the code each year until a change in the variable is recorded (e.g., size of the place of residence), (2) cumulates the number of changes in a given variable (e.g., number of places the respondent lived in, recorded cumulatively for each year), (3) collapses the categories of a given variable into fewer categories (e.g., a nine-category industry code derived from the original eighty-five categories coded), (4) creates new, "moving" variables (e.g., the number of dependent children less than 13 years old, year by year), (5) transforms values of a given variable according to instructions (e.g., transformation of the various forms of reported income—daily, weekly, monthly in pesos or dollars—to a standard yearly peso income).

TABLE B-3. Six-Digit Blocks Recording Changes during Ages 10–14 of "Illustrative Life History"

Block	Age	Variable Identification	Variable Content
10 01 10	10	Size of community	Rural
10 20 54	10	Zone of country	Northern Coahuila
10 04 15	10	Education	*Primaria*: grade 5
10 09 04	10	Employment	Works whole year
10 10 51	10	Position	Family helper
10 11 01	10	Type of industry	Agriculture
10 12 12	10	Relatives and number employed	Yes, from 2 to 5
10 14 01	10	Use of mechanical tools	None
10 15 51	10	Occupational grouping	Farm worker
10 49 10	10	Income	None
11 04 16	11	Education	*Primaria*: grade 6
12 01 50	12	Size of community	Monterrey
12 02 11	12	Zone of country	Monterrey
12 03 45	12	*Colonia*	Lomas
12 04 31	12	Education	Commerce: 1 year
12 09 03	12	Employment	Does not work, studie
12 10 99	12	Position	Not applicable
12 11 99	12	Type of industry	Not applicable
12 12 99	12	Relatives and number employed	Not applicable
12 14 99	12	Use of mechanical tools	Not applicable
12 15 99	12	Occupational group	Not applicable
12 49 99	12	Income	Not applicable
13 04 32	13	Education	Commerce: 2 years
14 04 33	14	Education	Commerce: 3 years

APPENDIX C

The Monterrey Mobility Study

Results of the Monterrey and Cedral investigations have appeared in various outlets over the past few years. Unpublished are the following three dissertations and three master's theses, all submitted to The University of Texas at Austin. (The numbers to the left of these and all subsequent citations indicate the chapters in this book that are most closely covered by the material in the citations.)

Dissertations

2, 4, 7, 9, 10   1. Jorge Balán. "The Process of Stratification in an Industrializing Society: The Case of Mexico." 1968.

2, 5, 8, 9   2. Elizabeth Jelin. "Men and Jobs: Lifetime Occupational Changes in Monterrey, Mexico." 1968.

11   3. Richard Rockwell. "Socio-Economic Status, Values, and Socialization: The Case of Monterrey, Mexico." 1970.

Theses

6   4. David Alvirez. "The Consequences of Migration to the United States on Men from Monterrey and Cedral, Mexico." 1970.

9   5. Adolfo Mir-Araujo. "Movilidad social, educación y grupos de referencia en Monterrey, México: Un estudio sociológico." 1966.

6   6. Denton R. Vaughan. "The Spatial Distribution of Initial Residence and Post-Arrival Residential Mobility of Migrants to Monterrey, Mexico." 1970.

The first published results of the Monterrey survey appear in:

7. Jorge Balán, Harley L. Browning, and Elizabeth Jelin, eds. *Movilidad social, migración, y fecundidad en Monterrey metropolitano.* Monterrey: Centro de Investigaciones Económicas, Universidad de Nuevo León, 1967. Chapter 1. Jorge Balán. "Metodología."

Chapter 2. Harley L. Browning and Waltraut Feindt. "Patrones de migración a Monterrey."

Chapter 3. Harley L. Browning and Waltraut Feindt. "Contexto social de la migración a Monterrey."

Chapter 4. Elizabeth Jelin. "Fuerza de trabajo."

Chapter 5. Elizabeth Jelin. "Movilidad intrageneracional."

Chapter 6. Elizabeth Jelin. "Movilidad intergeneracional."

Chapter 7. Jorge Balán. "Educación y movilidad social."

Chapter 8. Alvan O. Zarate y Alejandro Martínez. "Fecundidad diferencial."

Chapter 9. Jorge Balán. "Imagen de la movilidad."

The following articles based on the Monterrey and Cedral data are listed in order of appearance in chapters of the present book:

3, 11   8. Jorge Balán. "Clases sociales en un municipio rural no indígena en México." *Revista Mexicana de Sociología* 32 (September–October 1970): 1227–1250.

3   9. Harley L. Browning and Waltraut Feindt. "Patterns of Migration to Monterrey, Mexico." *International Migration Review* 5 (Fall 1971): 309–324.

3, 6   10. Harley L. Browning and Waltraut Feindt. "Selectivity of Migrants to a Metropolis in a Developing Country." *Demography* 6 (November 1969): 347–357.

3, 6   11. Harley L. Browning and Waltraut Feindt. "Selectividad de migrantes a una metropoli en un país en desarrollo: Estudio de un caso mexicano." *Demografía y Economía* 3 (1969): 186–200.

4   12. Jorge Balán. "Determinantes del nivel educacional: Un analisis multivariado." *Revista Latinoamericana de Sociología* 6 (July 1970): 262–292.

4, 5, 8   13. Jorge Balán. "Are Farmers' Sons Handicapped in the City?" *Rural Sociology* 33 (June 1968): 160–174.

6, 8   14. Jorge Balán and Elizabeth Jelin. "Migración a la ciudad y movilidad social: Un caso Mexicano." *Conferencia Regional Latinoamericano de Población, Actas I.* Mexico City: El Colegio de México, 1972.

6   15. Harley L. Browning and Waltraut Feindt. "Diferencias entre la población nativa y migrante en Monterrey." *Demografía y Economía* 2 (1968): 183–204.

6   16. Harley L. Browning and Waltraut Feindt. "The Social

and Economic Context of Migration to Monterrey, Mexico." In *Latin American Urban Research*, ed. Francine F. Rabinovitz and Felicity M. Trueblood. Vol. 1. Beverley Hills: Sage Publications, 1971.

6   17. Waltraut Feindt and Harley L. Browning. "Return Migration: Its Significance in an Industrial Metropolis and an Agricultural Town in Mexico." *International Migration Review* 6 (Summer 1972): 158–165.

6   18. Kenneth C. Land. "Duration of Residence and Prospective Migration: Further Evidence." *Demography* 6 (May 1969): 133–140.

7, 9   19. Alvan O. Zarate. "Differential Fertility in Monterrey, Mexico—Prelude to Transition?" *Milbank Memorial Fund Quarterly* 45, pt. 1 (April 1967): 93–108.

7, 9   20. Alvan O. Zarate. "A Note on the Reliability of Male Responses to Questions on Fertility." *Demography* 4, no. 2 (1967): 846–849.

8   21. Elizabeth Jelin de Balán. "Trabajadores por cuenta propia y asalariados: ¿Distinción vertical u horizontal?" *Revista Latinoamericana de Sociología* 3 (1967): 388–410.

9, 11 22. Elizabeth Jelin. "Estructura ocupacional, cohortes y ciclo vital." *Conferencia Regional Latinoamericana de Población, Actas II*. Mexico City: El Colegio de México, 1972.

Appendix B   23. Jorge Balán, Harley L. Browning, Elizabeth Jelin, and Lee Litzler. "A Computerized Approach to the Processing and Analysis of Life Histories Obtained in Sample Surveys." *Behavioral Science* 14 (March 1969): 105–120.

Appendix B   24. Jorge Balán, Harley L. Browning, Elizabeth Jelin, and Lee Litzler. "El uso de computadores en el analisis de historias vitales." *Demografía y Economía* 2 (1968): 428–442.

Appendix B   25. Jorge Balán. "Migration Histories: The Monterrey Mobility Study." To be published in the Proceedings of the Conference on Migratory Histories, Washington, D.C., 1970.

A collection of articles related to the Monterrey and Cedral studies is to be found in:

26. Jorge Balán, Harley L. Browning, and Elizabeth Jelin. *Estudios sobre migración, estructura ocupacional y movilidad en México*. Mexico City: Universidad Nacional Autónoma de México. Instituto de Investigaciones Sociales, 1972.

Included are versions of articles numbered above as 11, 12, 13, 14, 15, 16, 17, 18, 21, and 25. New to the volume are the following:

27. David Alvirez. "Efectos de la migración a los Estados Unidos."
28. Denton Vaughan and Waltraut Feindt. "Movilidad residencial dentro de Monterrey."
29. Elizabeth Jelin. "Estructura ocupacional y ciclo vital."
30. Adolfo Mir-Araujo. "Grupos de referencia, movilidad social y vision del mundo."
31. Humberto Muñoz, Orlandina de Oliveira, and Claudio Stern. "Categorias de migrantes y algunas de sus caracteristicas socioeconomicas: Comparacion entre las ciudades de Monterrey y México."

BIBLIOGRAPHY

Adams, Richard N. *The Second Sowing: Power and Secondary Development in Latin America.* San Francisco: Chandler, 1967.

Alemán, Eloisa A. "Investigación socioeconómica directa de los ejidos de San Luis Potosí." M.A. Thesis, Universidad Nacional Autónoma de México, 1966.

Anderson, Arnold C. "Lifetime Inter-Occupational Mobility Patterns in Sweden." *Acta Sociologica* 1 (1955): 168–202.

Arriaga, Eduardo E. "Components of City Growth in Selected Latin American Countries." *Milbank Memorial Fund Quarterly* 46, no. 2, pt. 1 (January 1968): 237–252.

Balán, Jorge, Harley L. Browning, and Elizabeth Jelin. *Movilidad social, migración, y fecundidad en Monterrey metropolitano.* Monterrey: Centro de Investigaciones Económicas, Universidad de Nuevo León, 1967.

Bataillon, Claude. *Las regiones geográficas en México.* Mexico City: Siglo XXI, 1969.

Bauer, P. T., and B. S. Yamey. "Economic Progress and Occupational Distribution." *The Economic Journal* 61 (December 1951): 741–755.

Beijer, G. *Rural Migrants in Urban Settings.* The Hague: Martinus Nijhoff, 1963.

Bendix, Reinhard. *Work and Authority in Industry.* New York: Harper & Row, 1963.

Bermudez, María E. *La vida familiar del mexicano.* Mexico City: Antigua Librería Robredo, 1955.

Bernert, Eleanor H. *America's Children.* New York: John Wiley, 1958.

Beyer, Glenn H., ed. *The Urban Explosion in Latin America.* Ithaca: Cornell University Press, 1967.

Blau, Peter M., and Otis D. Duncan. *The American Occupational Structure.* New York: John Wiley, 1967.

Bottomore, T. B. *Classes in Modern Society.* New York: Pantheon Books, 1966.

Bottomore, T. B., and M. Rubel, eds., *See* Karl Marx.

Boudon, Raymond. "A New Look at Correlation Analysis." In *Methodology in*

Social Research, edited by Hubert M. Blalock and Ann B. Blalock. New York: McGraw-Hill, 1968.

Briones, Guillermo, and José Majía Valera. *El obrero industrial.* Lima: Universidad Nacional Mayor de San Marcos, 1964.

Broom, Leonard, and F. Lancaster Jones. "Career Mobility in Three Societies: Australia, Italy, and the United States." *American Sociological Review* 34, no. 5 (October 1969): 650–658.

Broom, Leonard, and J. H. Smith. "Bridging Occupations." *British Journal of Sociology* 14, no. 4 (December 1963): 321–334.

Browning, Harley L. "Migrant Selectivity and the Growth of Large Cities in Developing Societies." In *Rapid Population Growth,* edited by the National Academy of Sciences. Baltimore: Johns Hopkins University Press, 1971.

———. "Primacy Variation in Latin America during the Twentieth Century." Paper delivered at the XXXIX Congreso Internacional de Americanistas, Lima, Peru, 2–9 August, 1970.

———. "Urbanization in Mexico." Ph.D. Dissertation, University of California at Berkeley, 1962.

Cain, Leonard D., Jr. "Life Course and Social Structure." In *Handbook of Modern Sociology,* edited by Robert L. Faris. Chicago: Rand McNally, 1964.

Caldwell, John D. *African Rural-Urban Migration.* Canberra: Australia National University Press, 1969.

Canales, Isidro Vizcaya. *Los orígenes de la industrialización de Monterrey 1867–1920.* Serie Historia, 9. Monterrey: Instituto Tecnológico y de Estudios Superiores de Monterrey, 1969.

Caplow, Theodore. *The Sociology of Work.* Minneapolis: University of Minnesota Press, 1954.

Cardona Gutierrez, Ramiro. "Migración, urbanización y marginalidad." In *Seminario nacional sobre urbanización y marginalidad.* Bogotá: Asociación Colombiana de Facultades de Medicina, 1968.

Cardoso, Fernando H. "Comētário sobre os conceitos de superpopulação relativa e marginalidade." In *Sôbre teoria e método en sociologia.* São Paulo: Edições Cebrap, 1971.

———. "Entrepreneurial Elites in Latin America." In *Elites in Latin America,* edited by Seymour M. Lipset and Aldo Solari. New York: Oxford University Press, 1967.

Cardoso, Fernando H., and Enzo Faletto. *Dependencia y desarrollo en América Latina.* Mexico City: Siglo XXI, 1969.

Cardoso, Fernando H., and José Luis Reyna. "Industrialization, Occupational Structure, and Social Stratification in Latin America." In *Constructive Change in Latin America,* edited by Cole S. Blasier. Pittsburgh: University of Pittsburgh Press, 1968.

Carlsson, Gosta, and Katarina Carlsson. "Age, Cohorts, and the Generation of Generations." *American Sociological Review* 35, no. 4 (August 1970): 710–718.

Carter, Michael. *Into Work*. Baltimore: Penguin, 1966.

Centro de Estudios Económicos y Demográficos. *Dinámica de la población de México*. Mexico City: El Colegio de México, 1970.

CEPAL. *El cambio social y la política de desarrollo social en América Latina*. New York: United Nations, 1969.

Chaplin, David. *The Peruvian Industrial Labor Force*. Princeton: Princeton University Press, 1967.

Chinoy, Eli. *Automobile Workers and the American Dream*. New York: Random House, 1955.

Clark, Colin. *The Conditions of Economic Progress*. 2nd ed. London: Macmillan, 1951.

Cline, Howard F. *The United States and Mexico*. Rev. ed. New York: Atheneum, 1965.

Coleman, James S., et al. *Equality of Educational Opportunity*. Washington, D.C.: U.S. Department of Health, Education, and Welfare, 1966.

Comisión Nacional de los Salarios Mínimos. *Memoria de los trabajos de 1963*. 4 vols. Mexico City, 1964.

Cornelius, Wayne, Jr. "The Political Sociology of Cityward Migration in Latin America: Toward Empirical Theory." In *Latin American Urban Research*, edited by Francine F. Rabinovitz and Felicity M. Trueblood. Vol. I. Beverly Hills: Sage Publications, 1971.

Cutright, Phillips. "Occupational Inheritance: A Cross-National Analysis." *American Journal of Sociology* 73, no. 4 (January 1968): 400–416.

Dahrendorf, Ralf. *Class and Class Conflict in Industrial Society*. Stanford: Stanford University Press, 1959.

David, Paul T. *Barriers to Youth Employment*. Washington, D.C.: American Council on Education, 1942.

Davis, Kingsley. *Las causas y efectos del fenómeno de primacía urbana con referencia especial a América Latina*. Mexico City: Instituto de Investigaciones Sociales, n.d.

———. "The Urbanization of the Human Population." *Scientific American* 213 (September 1965): 41–53.

———. *World Urbanization 1950–1970*. Volume I. *Basic Data for Cities, Countries, and Regions*. Berkeley: Institute of International Studies, 1969.

De la Peña, Moisés T. *El pueblo y su tierra: Mito y realidad de la reforma agraria en México*. Mexico City: Cuadernos Americanos, 1964.

DESAL (Center for the Economic and Social Development of Latin America). *Marginalidad en América Latina: Un ensayo de diagnóstico*. Santiago de Chile: DESAL—Editorial Herder, 1969.

Dicken, Samuel N. "Monterrey and Northeastern Mexico." *Annals of the Association of American Geographers* 29, no. 2 (June 1939): 127–158.

Di Tella, Torcuato S. "Economía y estructura ocupacional en un país subdesarrollado." *Desarrollo Económico* 1, no. 3 (October–December 1961): 123–153.

———. *Teoría del primer impacto de la industrialización*. Buenos Aires: Instituto de Sociología, 1962.

Donghi, Tulio Halperin. *Historia contemporánea de América Latina*. Madrid: Alianza Editorial, 1969.

Duncan, Beverly. "Education and Social Background." *American Journal of Sociology* 72, no. 4 (January 1967): 363–372.

Duncan, Otis D. "Methodological Issues in the Analysis of Social Mobility." In *Social Structure and Mobility in Economic Development*, edited by Neil J. Smelser and Seymour M. Lipset. Chicago: Aldine, 1966.

———. "Occupational Trends and Patterns of Net Mobility in the United States." *Demography* 3, no. 1 (1966): 1–18.

———. "Path Analysis: Sociological Examples." *American Journal of Sociology* 72, no. 1 (July 1966): 1–16.

Duncan, Otis D., and Robert W. Hodge. "Education and Occupational Mobility: A Regression Analysis." *American Journal of Sociology* 68, no. 5 (May 1963): 629–644.

Duncan, Otis D., David L. Featherman, and Beverly Duncan. *Socioeconomic Background and Occupational Achievement: Extensions of a Basic Model*. Washington, D.C.: U.S. Department of Health, Education, and Welfare, Office of Education, Bureau of Research, 1968.

Durkheim, Émile. *The Division of Labor in Society*. Glencoe: Free Press, 1947.

Eckstein, Shlomo. "Collective Farming in Mexico." In *Agrarian Problems and Peasant Movements in Latin America*, edited by Rodolfo Stavenhagen. New York: Doubleday Anchor Books, 1970.

ECLA (Economic Commission for Latin America). "Changes in Employment Structure in Latin America, 1945–1955." *Economic Bulletin for Latin America* 2, no. 1 (February 1957): 15–42.

———. "Structural Changes in Employment within the Context of Latin America's Economic Development." *Economic Bulletin for Latin America* 10, no. 2 (October 1965): 163–187.

Eisenstadt, S. N. *From Generation to Generation: Age Groups and Social Structure*. New York: Free Press, 1956.

Elder, Glen H. "Democratic Parent-Youth Relations in Cross-National Perspective." *Social Science Quarterly* 49, no. 2 (September 1968): 216–228.

Elizaga, Juan C. "Internal Migration: An Overview." *International Migration Review* 6 (Summer 1972): 121–146.

————. "Internal Migrations in Latin America." In "Components of Population Change in Latin America," edited by Claude V. Kiser. *Milbank Memorial Fund Quarterly* 43, no. 4, pt. 2 (October 1965): 144–161.

————. *Migraciones a las áreas metropolitanas de América Latina.* Santiago de Chile: Centro Latinoamericano de Demografía, 1970.

Elu de Leñero, María del Carmen. *¿Hacia dónde va la mujer mexicana?* Mexico City: Instituto Mexicano de Estudios Sociales, 1969.

Fals Borda, Orlando. *Las revoluciones inconclusas de América Latina.* Mexico City: Siglo XXI, 1968.

Feldman, Arnold H. "Economic Development and Social Mobility." *Economic Development and Cultural Change* 8 (1960): 311–320.

Form, William H., and Delbert C. Miller. "Occupational Career Pattern as a Sociological Instrument." *American Journal of Sociology* 54, no. 4 (1949): 317–329.

Foster, George M. *Tzintzuntzan: Mexican Peasants in a Changing World.* Boston: Little, Brown, 1967.

Frank, Andre. *Capitalism and Underdevelopment in Latin America.* Rev. ed. New York: Monthly Review, 1969.

Friedmann, John, and Tomás Lackington. "Hyperurbanization and National Development in Chile." *Urban Affairs Quarterly* 2, no. 4 (1967): 3–29.

Fuentes, Carlos. "La disyuntiva mexicana," in *Tiempo mexicano.* Mexico City: Joaquín Mortiz, 1971.

Furtado, Celso. *Development and Underdevelopment.* Berkeley: University of California Press, 1965.

————. *Economic Development of Latin America.* Cambridge: Cambridge University Press, 1970.

Gallo Martínez, Víctor. *Estructura económica de la educación mexicana.* Mexico City: Secretaría de Educación Pública, 1959.

Galtung, Johan. *Theory and Methods of Social Research.* New York: Columbia University Press, 1967.

Garza, Virgilio, Jr. "Brief Sketch of the Industrial Development of Monterrey." In *Basic Industries in Texas and Northern Mexico.* Institute of Latin American Studies, IX. Austin: University of Texas Press, 1950.

Germani, Gino. "Grados de desarrollo, tipos de estratificación y movilidad social en América Latina." In *Política y sociedad en una época de transición: De la sociedad transicional a la sociedad de masas.* Buenos Aires: Editorial Paidós, 1962.

————. "Inquiry into the Social Effects of Urbanization in a Working-Class Sector of Buenos Aires." In *Urbanization in Latin America*, edited by Philip M. Hauser. Paris: UNESCO, 1961.

————. "Movilidad social en la Argentina." In *Movilidad social en la sociedad industrial*, edited by Seymour M. Lipset and Reinhard Bendix. Buenos Aires: EUDEBA, 1963.

——. *Política y sociedad en una época de transición*. Buenos Aires: Editorial Paidós, 1962.

——. "Stages of Modernization in Latin America." *Studies in Comparative International Development* 8 (1969–1970): 155–174.

Gerth, H. H., and C. Wright Mills, eds. *From Max Weber: Essays in Sociology*. New York: Oxford University Press, 1958.

Gibbs, Jack P., and Harley L. Browning. "The Division of Labor, Technology, and the Organization of Production in Twelve Countries." *American Sociological Review* 31, no. 1 (February 1966): 81–92.

Girard, Alain. *Le choix du conjoint*. Paris: Presses Universitaires de France, 1964.

Girod, Roger, and Firouz Tofigh. "Family Background and Income, School Career, and Social Mobility of Young Males of Working-Class Origin—A Geneva Survey." *Acta Sociologica* 9 (1965): 94–109.

Glade, William P., Jr. "Revolution and Economic Development: A Mexican Reprise." In *The Political Economy of Mexico*, by William P. Glade, Jr., and Charles W. Anderson. Madison: University of Wisconsin Press, 1968.

Glass, David V. *Social Mobility in Britain*. London: Routledge and Kegan Paul, 1954.

Goldthorpe, John H., David Lockwood, Frank Bechhofer, and Jennifer Platt. *The Affluent Worker in the Class Structure*. Cambridge: Cambridge University Press, 1969.

——. *The Affluent Worker: Political Attitudes and Behavior*. Cambridge: Cambridge University Press, 1968.

González, Luis. *Pueblo en vilo: Microhistoria de San José de Gracia*. Mexico City: Colegio de México, 1969.

González Casanova, Pablo. *Democracy in Mexico*. New York: Oxford University Press, 1970.

——. "Dynamics of the Class Structure." In *Comparative Perspectives on Stratification: Mexico, Great Britain, Japan*, edited by Joseph A. Kahl. Boston: Little, Brown, 1967.

——. "Internal Colonialism and National Development." *Studies in Comparative International Development* 1, no. 4 (1965): 27–37.

González Pineda, Francisco. *El mexicano: Su dinámica psicosocial*. Mexico City: Editorial Pax, 1959.

Goode, William J. *World Revolution and Family Patterns*. New York: Free Press of Glencoe, 1963.

Goodman, Leo A. "On the Statistical Analysis of Mobility Tables." *American Journal of Sociology* 70 (March 1965): 564–585.

Graciarena, Jorge. *Poder y clases sociales en el desarrollo de América Latina.* Buenos Aires: Editorial Paidós, 1967.

Grebler, Leo, Joan W. Moore, and Ralph C. Guzman. *The Mexican-American People.* New York: Free Press, 1970.

Gusfield, Joseph R. "Tradition and Modernity: Misplaced Polarities in the Study of Social Change." *American Journal of Sociology* 72, no. 4 (1967): 351–362.

Hall, Oswald. "The Stages in a Medical Career." *American Journal of Sociology* 53 (1948): 327–336.

Hauser, Philip M., and Leo F. Schnore, eds. *The Study of Urbanization.* New York: John Wiley, 1965.

Hirschman, Albert O. "The Political Economy of Import-Substituting Industrialization in Latin America." *Quarterly Journal of Economics* 82 (February 1968): 2–32.

———. *The Strategy of Economic Development.* New Haven: Yale University Press, 1958.

Hobsbawn, E. J. *Industry and Empire.* London: Weidenfeld and Nicolson, 1968.

———. "La marginalidad social en la historia de la industrialización europea." *Revista Latinoamericana de Sociología* 5, no. 2 (July 1969): 237–248.

Hodge, Robert W. "Occupational Mobility as a Probability Process." *Demography* 3, no. 1 (1966): 19–34.

Hoselitz, Bert F. "The Development of a Labor Market in the Process of Economic Growth." In *Transactions of the Fifth World Congress of Sociology.* Vol II. Louvain: International Sociological Association, 1962.

———. "The Role of Cities in the Economic Growth of Underdeveloped Countries." *Journal of Political Economy* 61 (1953): 195–208.

Hutchinson, Bertram, et al. *Mobilidade e trabalho: Um estudo na cidade de São Paulo.* Rio de Janeiro: Centro de Pesquisas Educacionais, 1960.

Ibarra, David. "Mercados, desarrollo y política económica: Perspectivas de la economía de México." In *El perfil de México en 1980.* Vol. I. Mexico City: Siglo XXI, 1970.

Inkeles, Alex. "Making Men Modern: On the Causes and Consequences of Individual Change in Six Developing Countries." *American Journal of Sociology* 75, no. 2 (September 1969): 208–225.

Iturriaga, José E. *La estructura social y cultural de México.* Mexico City: Fondo de Cultura Económica, 1951.

Iutaka, Sugiyama. "Estratificación social y oportunidades educacionales en tres metrópolis latinoamericanas." *América Latina* 5, no. 4 (October 1962): 53–71.

———. "Social Stratification Research in Latin America." *Latin American Research Review* 1, no. 1 (Fall 1965): 7–34.

Jaffe, A. J. *People, Jobs, and Economic Development*. Glencoe: Free Press, 1959.

Janowitz, Morris. *The Professional Soldier: A Social and Political Portrait*. New York: Free Press of Glencoe, 1960.

Johnson, John J. *Political Change in Latin America: The Emergence of the Middle Sectors*. Stanford: Stanford University Press, 1958.

Johnston, James. *Econometric Methods*. New York: McGraw Hill, 1963.

Kahl, Joseph A. *The American Class Structure*. New York: Reinhart, 1957.

———. "Educational and Occupational Aspirations of 'Common Man' Boys." *Harvard Educational Review* 23 (1953): 186–203.

———. *The Measurement of Modernism: A Study of Values in Brazil and Mexico*. Austin: University of Texas Press, 1968.

———. "Modern Values and Fertility Ideals in Brazil and Mexico." *Journal of Social Issues* 23 (October 1967): 99–114.

Kemper, Robert Van. "Migration and Adaptation of Tzintzuntzan Peasants in Mexico City." Ph.D. Dissertation, University of California at Berkeley, 1971.

Kerr, Clark, John T. Dunlop, Frederick Harbison, and Charles A. Myers. *Industrialism and Industrial Man*. Cambridge: Harvard University Press, 1960.

Korbel, John. "Labor Force Entry and Attachment of Young People." *Journal of the American Statistical Association* 61, no. 313 (1966): 117–127.

Kuznets, Simon. "Introduction: Population Redistribution, Migration, and Economic Growth." In *Population Redistribution and Economic Growth, United States 1870–1950*, edited by Hope T. Eldridge and Dorothy Swaine Thomas. New York: Columbia University Press, 1968.

Labovitz, Sanford. "The Assignment of Numbers to Rank Order Categories." *American Sociological Review* 35, no. 3 (June 1970): 515–524.

Land, Kenneth C. "The Principles of Path Analysis." In *Sociological Methodology*, edited by Edgar F. Borgatta. San Francisco: Jossey-Bass, 1969.

Leeds, Elizabeth, and Anthony Leeds. *A Bibliography of the Sociology of Housing-Settlement Types in Latin America*. Los Angeles: UCLA, Latin American Center, in press.

Lenski, Gerhard. *Power and Privilege*. New York: McGraw Hill, 1966.

Lewis, Oscar. *The Children of Sánchez: Autobiography of a Mexican Family*. New York: Random House, 1961.

———. "Family Dynamics in a Mexican Village." *Marriage and Family Living* 21 (August 1959): 218–226.

———. *Five Families: Mexican Case Studies in the Culture of Poverty*. New York: Basic Books, 1959.

———. "Further Observations on the Folk-Urban Continuum and Urbanization with Special Reference to Mexico City." In *The Study of Urbanization*, edited by Philip M. Hauser and Leo F. Schnore. New York: John Wiley, 1965.

————. "Husbands and Wives in a Mexican Village: A Study of Role Conflict." *American Anthropologist* 51, no. 4 (1949): 602–610.

————. *Life in a Mexican Village: Tepotzlán Restudied.* Urbana: University of Illinois Press, 1963.

————. *Pedro Martínez.* New York: Random House, 1964.

————. "Urbanization without Breakdown." *Scientific Monthly* 75, no. 1 (1952): 31–41.

————. *La Vida: A Puerto Rican Family in the Culture of Poverty—San Juan and New York.* New York: Random House, 1966.

Liebow, Elliot. *Tally's Corner.* Boston: Little, Brown, 1967.

Lipset, Seymour M. *Political Man.* New York: Doubleday, 1960.

Lipset, Seymour M., and Reinhard Bendix. *Social Mobility in Industrial Society.* Berkeley: University of California Press, 1959.

Lipset, Seymour M., and Aldo Solari, eds. *Elites in Latin America.* New York: Oxford University Press, 1967.

Lipset, Seymour M., and Hans L. Zetterberg. "A Theory of Social Mobility." In *Class, Status, and Power,* edited by Seymour M. Lipset and Reinhard Bendix. 2nd ed. New York: Free Press, 1966.

Lopes, Juarez Rubens Brandão. "Aspects of the Adjustment of Rural Migrants to Urban-Industrial Conditions in São Paulo, Brazil." In *Urbanization in Latin America,* edited by Philip M. Hauser. Brussels: UNESCO, 1961.

Lopreato, Joseph, and Janet Saltzman Chafetz. "The Political Orientation of Skidders: A Middle-Range Theory." *American Sociological Review* 35 (June 1970): 440–451.

McGinn, Noel F. "Marriage and Family in Middle-Class Mexico." *Journal of Family Living* 28, no. 3 (August 1966): 305–313.

Macisco, John J., Jr. "Some Directions for Further Research on Internal Migration in Latin America." *International Migration Review* 6 (Summer 1972): 216–223.

Maine, Henry J. S. *Ancient Law.* London: J. Murray, 1861.

Mangin, William P. "Latin American Squatter Settlements: A Problem and a Solution." *Latin American Research Review* 2, no. 3 (Summer 1967): 65–98.

————, ed. *Peasants in Cities.* Boston: Houghton Mifflin, 1970.

————. "The Role of Regional Associations in the Adaptation of Rural Migrants to Cities in Peru." *Sociologus* 9, no. 1 (1955): 23–35.

Marx, Karl. *Selected Writings in Sociology and Social Philosophy,* edited by T. B. Bottomore and M. Rubel. New York: McGraw-Hill, 1964.

Mauro, Frederic. "Le développement économique de Monterrey 1890–1960." *Caravelle,* no. 2 (1964), pp. 35–126.

Mayer, Kurt B., and Walter Buckley. *Class and Society*. New York: Random House, 1970.

Megee, Mary Catherine. *Monterrey, Mexico: Internal Patterns and External Relations*. Chicago: University of Chicago Press, 1958.

Milic, Vojin. "General Trends in Social Mobility in Yugoslavia." *Acta Sociologica* 9 (1965): 116–136.

Miller, Delbert C., and William H. Form. "Measuring Patterns of Occupational Security." *Sociometry* 10 (1947): 362–375.

Miller, S. M. "A Comment: The Future of Social Mobility Studies." *American Journal of Sociology* 77, no. 1 (July 1971): 62–65.

———. "Comparative Social Mobility: A Trend Report and Bibliography." *Current Sociology* 9, no. 1 (1960): 8–39.

Miller, S. M., and Herrington Bryce. "Social Mobility and Economic Growth and Structure." In *Comparative Perspectives on Industrial Society*, edited by William A. Faunce and William H. Form. Boston: Little, Brown, 1969.

Mir-Araujo, Adolfo. "Ecological Inequalities in Educational Attainment in Mexico." Ph.D. Dissertation, University of Texas, 1970.

———. "Movilidad social, educación y grupos de referencia en Monterrey, México: Un estudio sociológico." M.A. Thesis, University of Texas, 1966.

Miró, Carmen, and Walter Mertens. "Influences Affecting Fertility in Urban and Rural Latin America." *Milbank Memorial Fund Quarterly* 46, no. 3, pt. 2 (July 1968): 89–117.

Moore, Barrington, Jr. *Social Origins of Dictatorship and Democracy*. Boston: Beacon Press, 1966.

Moore, Wilbert E. "Aging and the Social System." In *Aging and Social Policy*, edited by John C. McKinney and Frank T. DeVyverx. New York: Appleton-Century-Crofts, 1968.

———. "Changes in Occupational Structures." In *Social Structure and Mobility in Economic Development*, edited by Neil J. Smelser and Seymour M. Lipset. Chicago: Aldine, 1966.

Moore, Wilbert E., and Arnold S. Feldman, eds. *Labor Commitment and Social Change in Developing Areas*. New York: Social Science Research Council, 1960.

Morris, David. *The Emergence of a Labor Force in India*. Berkeley: University of California Press, 1965.

Morse, Richard M. "Internal Migrants and the Urban Ethos in Latin America." Paper delivered at the Seventh World Congress of Sociology, Varna, Bulgaria, September, 1970.

———. "Recent Research on Latin American Urbanization: A Selective Survey with Commentary." *Latin American Research Review* 1, no. 1 (Fall 1965): 35–74.

———. "Trends and Issues in Latin American Research, 1965–1970." *Latin*

American Research Review 6, no. 1 (Spring 1971): 3–52, and 6, no. 2 (Summer 1971): 19–75.

Myers, Charles N. *Education and National Development in Mexico.* Princeton: Princeton University Press, 1965.

Nash, Manning. *Machine Age Maya.* American Anthropological Association Memoir 87. Chicago: University of Chicago Press, 1967.

Navarrette, Ifigenia M. de. "La distribución del ingreso en México: Tendencias y perspectivas." In *El perfil de México en 1980.* Vol. I. Mexico City: Siglo XXI, 1970.

Niemeyer, Eberhardt Victor, Jr. "The Public Career of General Bernardo Reyes." Ph.D. Dissertation, University of Texas, 1958.

Nun, José. "Superpoblación relativa, ejército industrial de reserva y masa marginal." *Revista Latinoamericana de Sociología* 5, no. 2 (July 1969): 178–236.

Palmer, Gladys L. *Labor Mobility in Six Cities.* New York: Social Science Research Council, 1954.

Paz, Octavio. *The Labyrinth of Solitude.* New York: Grove, 1961.

———. *Postdata.* Mexico City: Siglo XXI, 1970.

Petersen, William. *Population.* New York: Macmillan, 1965.

Pinto, Luis A. Costa. *Estructura de clases y cambio social.* Buenos Aires: Editorial Paidós, 1964.

Puente Leyva, Jesús. *Distribución del ingreso en un área urbana: El caso de Monterrey, México.* Mexico City: Siglo XXI, 1969.

———. "Estructura de la ocupación y el nivel del los salarios en el área metropolitana de Monterrey." In *El salario mínimo en Monterrey,* by Centro de Investigaciones Económicas. Monterrey: Centro de Investigaciones Económicas, 1965.

Quijano, Aníbal. *Notas sobre el concepto de marginalidad social.* Santiago de Chile: CEPAL, División de Asuntos Sociales, 1966.

Rabinovitz, Francine F., and Felicity M. Trueblood, eds. *Latin American Urban Research.* Vol. I. Beverly Hills: Sage Publications, 1971.

Ramos, Samuel. *Profile of Man and Culture in Mexico.* Austin: University of Texas Press, 1962.

Ratinoff, Luis. "The New Urban Groups: The Middle Classes." In *Elites in Latin America,* edited by Seymour M. Lipset and Aldo Solari. New York: Oxford University Press, 1967.

Ravenstein, E. G. "The Laws of Migration." *Journal of the Royal Statistical Society* 48, pt. 2 (June 1885): 167–235.

Redfield, R. *The Folk Culture of Yucatan.* Chicago: University of Chicago Press, 1941.

Rehberg, Richard A., and David L. Westby. "Parental Encouragement, Occupation, Education, and Family Size: Artifactual or Independent Determinants of Adolescent Educational Expectations?" *Social Forces* 45 (March 1967): 362–374.

Rele, J. R. "Trends and Differentials in the American Age at Marriage." *Milbank Memorial Fund Quarterly* 43, no. 2 (April 1965): 219–239.

Reynolds, Clark W. *The Mexican Economy: Twentieth-Century Structure and Growth.* New Haven: Yale University Press, 1970.

Roberts, Bryan. *Organizing Strangers: Poor Families in Guatemala City.* Austin: University of Texas Press, 1973.

Roel, Santiago. *Nuevo León: Apuntes históricos.* Monterrey: Imprenta Monterrey, 1961.

Ruíz, Ramón E. *Mexico: The Challenge of Poverty and Illiteracy.* San Marino: Huntington Library, 1963.

Ryder, Norman. "The Cohort as a Concept in the Study of Social Change." *American Sociological Review* 30 (December 1965): 843–861.

Sewell, William H. "Inequality of Opportunity for Higher Education." *American Sociological Review* 36 (October 1971): 793–809.

Sewell, William H., and Vimal P. Shah. "Social Class, Parental Encouragement, and Educational Aspirations." *American Journal of Sociology* 73 (March 1968): 559–572.

Sexton, Patricia C. *Education and Income.* New York: Viking Press, 1961.

Shannon, Lyle W., and Magdaline Shannon. "The Assimilation of Migrants to Cities." In *Social Science and the City,* edited by Leo F. Schnore. New York: Praeger, 1968.

Shryock, Henry. "Survey Statistics on Reasons for Moving." Paper presented at the Meetings of the International Union for the Scientific Study of Population, London, September, 1969.

Simmons, Alan B. *The Emergence of Planning Orientations in a Modernizing Community: Migration, Adaptation, and Family Planning in Highland Colombia.* Cornell University, Latin American Studies Program Dissertation Series, no. 15. Ithaca, 1970.

Simmons, Alan B., and Ramiro Cardona G. "Rural-Urban Migration: Who Comes, Who Stays, Who Returns? The Case of Bogota, Colombia, 1919–1968." *International Migration Review* 6 (Summer 1972): 166–181.

Simpson, Eyler N. *The Ejido: Mexico's Way Out.* Chapel Hill: University of North Carolina Press, 1937.

Singer, Paul I. *Fôrca de trabalho e emprêgo no Brasil: 1920–1969.* São Paulo: Edições Cebrap, 1971.

Smelser, Neil J., and Seymour M. Lipset, eds. "Measures and Effects of Mobility." In *Social Structure and Mobility in Economic Development.* Chicago: Aldine, 1966.

Soares, Glaucio A. D. "Desenvolvimento economico e estructura de classe." *Dados,* no. 6 (1969), pp. 91–128.

————. "Economic Development and Class Structure." In *Class, Status, and Power*, edited by Seymour M. Lipset and Reinhard Bendix. 2nd ed. New York: Free Press, 1966.

————. "The New Industrialization and the Brazilian Political System." In *Latin America: Reform or Revolution?* Edited by James Petras and Maurice Zeitlin. Greenwich, Conn.: Fawcett Publication, 1968.

Solís, Leopoldo. *La realidad económica mexicana: Retrovisión y perspectivas.* Mexico City: Siglo XXI, 1970.

Sonquist, John A., and James N. Morgan. *The Detection of Interaction Effects.* Ann Arbor: University of Michigan Press, 1964.

Sovani, N. V. "The Analysis of Overurbanization." *Economic Development and Cultural Change* 12, no. 2 (1964): 113–122.

Sovani, N. V., and K. Pradhan. "Occupational Mobility in Poona between Three Generations." *Indian Economic Review* 2, no. 4 (August 1955): 23–36.

Spencer, Herbert. *Principles of Sociology.* New York: Appleton, 1897.

Stavenhagen, Rodolfo, ed. *Agrarian Problems and Peasant Movements in Latin America.* New York: Doubleday Anchor Books, 1970.

————. "Aspectos sociales de la estructura agraria en México." In *Neolatifundismo y explotación.* Mexico City: Editorial Nuestro Tiempo, 1968.

————. *Las clases sociales en las sociedades agrarias.* Mexico City: Siglo XXI, 1969.

————. "Classes, Colonialism, and Acculturation." In *Comparative Perspectives on Stratification: Mexico, Great Britain, Japan*, edited by Joseph A. Kahl. Boston: Little, Brown, 1968.

————. "Social Aspects of Agrarian Structure in Mexico." In *Agrarian Problems and Peasant Movements in Latin America.* New York: Doubleday Anchor Books, 1970.

Stern, Claudio. "Un análisis regional de México." *Demografía y Economía* 1 (1967): 92–117.

Stern, Claudio, and Joseph A. Kahl. "Stratification since the Revolution." In *Comparative Perspectives on Stratification: Mexico, Great Britain, Japan*, edited by Joseph A. Kahl. Boston: Little, Brown, 1968.

Stinchcombe, Arthur L. "Agricultural Enterprise and Rural Class Relations." *American Journal of Sociology* 67, no. 2 (September 1961): 165–176.

————. "Social Structure and Organizations." In *Handbook of Organizations*, edited by James G. March. Chicago: Rand McNally, 1965.

Strassman, Paul. *Technological Change and Economic Development: The Manufacturing Experience of Mexico and Puerto Rico.* Ithaca: Cornell University Press, 1968.

Svalastoga, Kaare. *Prestige, Class, and Mobility.* Copenhagen: Gyldendal, 1959.

Thompson, E. P. *The Making of the English Working Class: 1780–1830.* New York: Vintage Books, 1963.

Tönnies, F. *Fundamental Concepts of Sociology.* New York: America Book, 1940.

Treiman, Donald. "Industrialization and Social Stratification." In *Social Stratification,* edited by E. Laumann. New York: Bobbs-Merrill, 1970.

Truett, Dale B. "Productivity Differences in Like Industries in Mexico's Major Areas of Industrial Concentration." Manuscript. Population Research Center, University of Texas at Austin, 1964.

Tumin, Melvin M., and Arnold S. Feldman. *Social Class and Social Change in Puerto Rico.* Princeton: Princeton University Press, 1961.

Turner, John C. "Barriers and Channels for Housing Development in Modernizing Countries." *Journal of American Institute of Planners* 33 (May 1967): 167–181.

Unikel, Luis. "Ensayo sobre una nueva clasificación de población rural y urbana en México." *Demografía y Economía* 2, no. 1 (1968): 1–18.

———. "El proceso de urbanización en México: Distribución y crecimiento de la población urbana." *Demografía y Economía* 2, no. 2 (1968): 139–182.

———. "El proceso de urbanización." In *El perfil de México en 1980.* Vol. II. Mexico City: Siglo XXI, 1970.

United Nations. *Handbook of Population Census Methods.* Volume II. *Economic Characteristics of the Population.* New York: United Nations, 1958.

United Nations, Department of Economic and Social Affairs. *Growth of the World's Urban and Rural Population, 1920–2000.* Population Studies, no. 44. New York: United Nations, 1969.

U.S. Bureau of the Census. "Reasons for Moving: March 1962 to March 1963." In *Current Population Reports.* Series P-20, no. 154. Washington, D.C.: Government Printing Office, 1966.

Urquidi, Víctor L. "La economía y la población." In *El perfil de México en 1980.* Vol. I. Mexico City: Siglo XXI, 1970.

Urquidi, Víctor L., and Adrian Lajous Vargas. *Educación superior, ciencia y tecnología en el desarrollo económico de México.* Mexico City: El Colegio de Mexico, 1967.

Vaughn, Denton R. *Urbanization in Twentieth Century Latin America: A Working Bibliography.* Austin: Institute of Latin American Studies, 1969.

Vekemans, Roger, and Jorge Giusti. "Marginality and Ideology in Latin American Development." *Studies in Comparative International Development* 5, no. 11 (1969–1970): 221–234.

Véliz, Claudio, ed. *Obstacles to Change in Latin America.* London: Oxford University Press, 1965.

Vernon, Raymond. *The Dilemma of Mexico's Development.* Cambridge: Harvard University Press, 1963.

Warner, Lloyd, and James C. Abegglen. *Occupational Mobility in American Business and Industry.* Minneapolis: University of Minnesota Press, 1955.

Weber, Max. *From Max Weber: Essays in Sociology,* edited by H. H. Gerth and C. Wright Mills. New York: Oxford University Press, 1958.

————. *General Economic History,* translated by Frank H. Knight. New York: Collier Books, 1961.

Whetten, Nathan L. *Rural Mexico.* Chicago: University of Chicago Press, 1948.

Whyte, William H., Jr. *The Organization Man.* New York: Simon and Schuster, 1956.

Wilensky, Harold L. "Measures and Effects of Social Mobility." In *Social Structure and Mobility in Economic Development,* edited by Neil J. Smelser and Seymour M. Lipset. Chicago: Aldine, 1966.

————. "Orderly Careers and Social Participation." *American Sociological Review* 26, no. 4 (1961): 521–539.

————. "Work, Careers, and Social Integration." *International Social Science Journal* 12, no. 4 (1960): 543–560.

Wilensky, Harold L., and H. Edwards. "The Skidders: Ideological Adjustment of the Downward Mobile Workers." *American Sociological Review* 24 (April 1959): 215–231.

Yasuda, Saburo. "A Methodological Inquiry into Social Mobility." *American Sociological Review* 29, no. 1 (February 1964): 16–23.

Yates, Paul Lamartine. *El desarrollo regional de México.* Mexico City: Banco de México, 1961.

Young, Frank W., and Ruth C. Young. "Differentiation of Family Structure in Rural Mexico." *Journal of Marriage and the Family* 30 (February 1968): 154–161.

Zarate, Alvan O. "Differential Fertility in Monterrey, Mexico—Prelude to Transition?" *Milbank Memorial Fund Quarterly* 45, no. 2, pt. 1 (April 1967): 93–108.

Zelditch, Morris, Jr. "Family, Marriage, and Kinship." In *Handbook of Modern Sociology,* edited by Robert L. Faris. Chicago: Rand McNally, 1964.

INDEX

Adams, Richard: on industrialization, 14
agriculture: development of, 25; in Monterrey area, 37; in Comarca Lagunera, 70–71; in Cedral, 76; job alternatives in, 121
Altos Hornos steel mill: 70
American Civil War: effect of, on Monterrey development, 38
American Occupational Structure, The: 7
antioqueños: 37
Argentina: industrialization in, 22
aspirations: 315, 316
Automatic Interaction Detector (AID): definition of, 103–104

birth cohort: historical context of, 58–59, 233; and occupational categories, 124; effect of, on educational attainment, 267, 271, 272–274, 295; effect of, on first occupation, 275
birth control: attitudes toward, 176, 187
Blau, Peter M.: on status dimension, 9; on occupational mobility, 170–171; on correlation between father's and son's occupations, 290–292; on correlation between education and first occupation, 293–294
blue-collar workers: ratio of, to white-collar workers in Monterrey, 54; career lines of, 209, 212, 214
bracero program: effect of, on Monterrey, 43–148
Brazil: industrialization in, 22; mentioned, 37

brewery: choice of Monterrey as site of, 49
"Buddenbrooks" pattern: 222
Buenos Aires: social mobility in, 7
bureaucracies: effects of industrialization on, 20; development of, in Monterrey, 52, 54; development of careers in, 208
bureaucratization: of industry, 17; in Latin America, 18; and productivity, 52–53; in Monterrey, 53; consequences of, 327

Cárdenas, Lázaro: economic change during term of, 23; and steel production, 42; mentioned, 59
Cardoso, Fernando H.: on industrialization, 18
career contingencies: definition of, 281, 282; effect of, on occupational status, 296
careers: definition of, 134, 208; effect of personal factors on, 183, 211; traditional conception of, 209; of self-employed workers, 209–210, 214, 236; of blue-collar workers, 209, 212; of white-collar workers, 210–211; bureaucratic, 236
Cedral: contacts of, 75; economy of, 75, 76, 77; effects of migration on, 75, 82, 299, 308, 310, 312–313; agriculture in, 76; differences between town and *municipio*, 76; stratification in, 77, 78, 300, 310–311; nonfarm population of, 78; educational differ-

of states in, 66; education in, 86, 87, 88, 91, 92; characteristics of northern, 135–136; status inheritance in, 291
Mexico City: development of, 36; economy of, 42; income distribution in, 44; as primary city, 46; relationship of, to Monterrey, 46–47, 53; worker productivity in, 48; local market in, 49; production in, 49, 54; migrants in, 66, 67, 71; student demonstrations in, 331 n. 24; mentioned, 41
middle class: in Monterrey, 303–304; effect of industrialization on, 304; prospects of, 329
middle-level schools: description of, 87
migrants: differentiations among, 12; selectivity of, 12, 143–144, 145, 146–147, 167, 282, 325; absorption of, into labor force, 13; origins of, 31, 64–71, 157–159; adaptation of, 32, 154–155, 316–317, 321; volume of, to Monterrey, 58; differences of, from natives, 61, 325; communities of origin of, 62–63, 163; sources of, 80; prior work situations of, 153–154; marital status of, 156; kinship contacts of, 159–160, 161, 162, 168–169; homogeneity of, 202; vertical mobility of, 205; occupational status of, 243, 314–315; political organization of, 309; expectations of, 315–316
migration: in industrializing society, 3, 4, 10, 13; and economic development, 12, 26; reasons for, in Latin America, 17–18; approaches to study of, 30–31; and occupational mobility, 34, 113, 193, 201, 206, 224, 229, 230, 281; in Monterrey, 61; reasons for, 72–73; effect of community of origin on, 142, 219; chronology of, 149, 168, 202; factors influencing decision about, 152; simultaneous, 157, 158; solitary, 157, 158; split, 157, 158; assistance in, 159, 160; return, 164–166; continuous nature of, 169–170; role of kinship contacts in, 172, 321; effect of, on group conflict, 299, 309, 313; func-

tion of, 312; as stabilizing factor, 317; effect of basic value system on, 322
migratory status: effects of, 282
"military and industrial": dichotomy of, 149
Miller, S. M.: measurement of rates of mobility by, 241
minimum legal wage: establishment of, 55; in Monterrey, 55, 57–58, 237
mining: worker productivity in, 48; in San Luis Potosí, 73; in Zacatecas, 73; unskilled labor in, 198
Mir-Araujo, Adolfo: on educational attainment, 90, 254, 259–260
mobility: relation of migration to, 113; of manual workers, 133–134, 213; measurement of, 196; and self-employment, 215
—educational: necessity of, 257; optimistic attitude toward, 258; of sons, 259
—geographic: relationship of, to social mobility, 13, 312; and class conflict, 310
—horizontal: forms of, 229; of upper-nonmanual workers, 230; of lower manual workers, 230; across integrated-marginal line, 307
—intragenerational: analysis of, 241–252, 315; probability of, 260–262; rates of, 309; of Monterrey men, 315
—occupational: in industrializing society, 3, 4, 5; effect of migration on, 3, 26, 34, 139, 193, 201, 206; paths of, 3, 194–195, 229, 306–307; factors contributing to, 4, 198, 202, 208, 322, 328; and economic development, 26; nonvertical aspects of, 33–34, 113; of Monterrey natives, 139; definition of, 193; of self-employed persons, 193; and career lines, 209; analysis of, 241–252
—social: overview of study of, 5–7; relationship of, to industrialization, 7; criticisms of global approach to, 8; complexity of, 9; relationship of, to geographic mobility, 13; measurement

of, 267; structural consequences of, 298
—status: global approach to, 8; component parts of, 9; and economic development, 26; determination of, 278, 279
—vertical: and occupational achievement, 33, 34, 280; career motivation for, 135; of Monterrey natives, 139; factors affecting, 140, 192, 266, 280; measurement of, 193–194; among white-collar workers, 195; of manual workers, 195, 223; relationship of, to first occupation, 195, 328; and nonmanual workers, 197, 223; effect of stability on, 197, 224, 225, 229; effect of migration on, 204, 205, 224, 229–230; explanations of, 223; and self-employment, 223; and social status, 296
Monterrey: industrial development of, 3, 37, 38, 39, 42, 47–48, 49–50, 52, 326–327; industrialization in, 10, 22, 40–41; population growth in, 26, 40, 41, 305, 326; historical development of, 31, 38; selection of, as regional capital, 37; geographic situation of, 37, 38, 333; contact of, with United States, 38, 43; relationship of, to Mexico City, 38, 46–47; exports from, 39, 40, 43; and bracero program, 43; tourism in, 43; distribution of income in, 43, 238, 302–303; labor force in, 47–48, 241; productivity in, 48, 54; bureaucratization in, 52, 53; minimum legal wage in, 55; occupational distribution in, 55, 123; migrants to, 58, 66–67, 71, 75, 80, 137–138, 142, 144, 164, 299, 308, 309, 310, 314, 316, 317, 324; sources of growth, 60, 148; marriage patterns in, 182–186; stratification in, 239, 265–297; status inheritance in, 289–294; stratification process in, compared with U.S.A., 293, 294; class structure of, 300, 302–307; land seizure in, 308; student rebellion in, 331 n. 24; mentioned, 21

Monterrey Metropolitan Area: definition of, 336
Montevideo: social mobility in, 7
Moore, Barrington, Jr.: on modernization, 22
Moore, Wilbert E.: on consequences of industrialization, 18–19
mother: education of, 99–100, 105–106, 109–110, 267, 271–272, 274, 276, 286, 292, 295
multiple linear regression analysis: 103

Nash, Manning: on effects of industrialization on work performance, 319
nationalized industries: rules of promotion in, 212
native by adoption: definition of, 62
Navarrete, Ifigenia de: on concentration of income in Mexico, 25; mentioned, 43
nonmanual workers: occupational mobility of, 223, 248; career lines of, 236
"normal career curve": definition of, 192; importance of, 196; applicability of, 230–231
normal superior: description of, 87
Nuevo Laredo: as source of migrants to Monterrey, 71
Nuevo León: effect of, on Monterrey economy, 38; tax exemptions to industries established in, 39; population growth in, 43, 324; socioeconomic level of, 65; illiteracy in, 91; schools in, 91, 92; student rebellion in, 331 n. 24; mentioned, 64

occupational achievement: in developing society, 29; effect of father's occupational status on, 30, 93, 279; effect of educational attainment on, 32, 279, 296; effect of father's education on, 105; personal factors affecting, 188–189, 190, 277, 280, 282; analysis of, 277–280; mobility in, 280, 295; effect of migration on, 281; of migrants' sons, 316. SEE ALSO first occupation
occupational stability: and the "normal